First Certificate in English Course

Revised Edition

Ona Low

Nelson

Thomas Nelson and Sons Ltd
Nelson House Mayfield Road
Walton-on-Thames Surrey
KT12 5PL UK

51 York Place
Edinburgh
EH1 3JD UK

Thomas Nelson (Hong Kong) Ltd
Toppan Building 10/F
22A Westlands Road
Quarry Bay Hong Kong

First published by Edward Arnold (Publishers) Ltd 1974
Reprinted ten times

Revised edition 1985
Reprinted 1985, 1986, 1987, 1989, 1990
ISBN 071 318 2555

This edition published by Thomas Nelson and Sons Ltd 1991

ISBN 017 556 1028
NPN 9 8 7 6 5 3

Printed in China

Preface to the Revised Edition

With the introduction of the amended 1984 syllabus, *First Certificate in English Course* — formerly *Lower Certificate English Course* and subsequently *First Certificate in English Course for foreign students* — has again been adapted to conform to the new examination requirements. The considerable amount of new material introduced is associated in particular with the new type of Reading Comprehension passage, the Directed Writing exercise, which now forms part of the Use of English paper, and the Structured Communication topics featured in the Interview.

In addition, the book as a whole has been restructured and standardised. The component parts of each section, including the Reading Passages, Composition subjects, Reading Comprehension material and some features of the Interview, have been linked by a theme of common interest, and information has been updated where applicable.

While a considerable amount of practice material for the First Certificate examination is presented, this is essentially a course book for the intermediate student who wishes to extend his or her general command of English. When classes have as many as ten weekly lessons, most of the material can be dealt with in class, but students in groups which meet for not more than 4–5 hours weekly will have to do a good deal of preparation at home with class guidance and checking. A Key is available separately, and the material in *First Certificate in English Course* is presented clearly enough to enable a student working alone to derive considerable benefit from it.

More intensive practice for the examination itself is available in the accompanying publication *First Certificate in English Practice*.

Acknowledgements

The publishers would like to thank the following for permission to include copyright material:

The Office of Fair Trading for an extract from the 'How to put things right' leaflet, p. 205; The Scottish Health Education Group for an extract from 'Forgetfulness and the Elderly', p. 130; The Youth Hostels Association (England and Wales) for part of one of their leaflets, p. 106.

For copyright illustrations: Barnabys Picture Library, pp. 23, 68 & 90; Andrew Besley, pp. 111 & 238; Central Office of Information, Crown Copyright reserved, p. 135; The Mansell Collection Ltd, p. 211; Tish Murtha, p. 187; Steve Richards, pp. 46 & 259; David Richardson, p. 160.

Abbreviations

The following abbreviations are used in *First Certificate in English Course:*

Adj	= adjective	opp.	= opposite
Adv	= adverb	Pl	= plural
C	= countable	Prep	= preposition
Cf.	= compare	Sing	= singular
e.g.	= for example	Unc	= uncountable
N	= noun	V	= verb

An asterisk (*) before a phrase denotes unacceptable English.

Contents

Composition writing

Preparation

Understanding

1 Read the wording of the subject carefully so that you are sure you have understood exactly what you have to write about.
2 Follow any instructions carefully about length (number of words), treatment of the subject (in the form of a letter, a story, a dialogue, an explanation, expression of opinion etc.) and arrangement.

Planning

1 Spend a few minutes thinking about your ideas on the subject. You may want to make a few notes.
2 Make a plan suggesting the subject of each paragraph.

> *Example:* My feelings about taking this examination.
> 1 Why I decided to enter for it.
> 2 My feelings during the past day or two.
> 3 How I feel at this moment.

Writing the composition

1 Keep to the plan you have made.
2 Think in English using the English you know already. Do not translate from your own language.
3 Write in sentences unless for some special reason sentences are not needed.
4 Read each sentence through as you finish it, looking out for careless mistakes.
5 Remember that your teacher or the examiner must be able to read your writing.

On completion, read through the composition slowly, correcting mistakes.

Examination choices

You are asked to write 2 compositions in the First Certificate examination. Read through all the possibilities before choosing the first. You can make your second choice at the same time or later.

Length and timing

You have $1\frac{1}{2}$ hours to write 2 compositions, that is, 45 minutes for each; each composition should be between 120 and 180 words in length.

Suggested timetable:
1 Consideration of ideas and planning (10 minutes)
2 Writing (25−30 minutes)
3 Reading through and correcting (5−10 minutes)

Improving your compositions

Practice

1 Take every opportunity of writing the compositions set and corrected by your teacher. You can also write compositions on your own. Leave these a few weeks before correcting them: by then you should be able to criticise them and make some corrections yourself.

2 Make a note of your teacher's corrections and suggestions and make sure you don't make the same mistakes again.

3 Write down and make use of words and phrases you find in your English coursebook and in English books and magazines you read in your free time.

Using a dictionary

1 Remember that a dictionary is for occasional use when you are writing. Your ideas should be expressed in the English you know already but there may be a single unknown word or phrase you would like to use.

2 Choose a dictionary carefully. It should be fairly detailed with examples of how words and phrases are used.

3 Use your dictionary sensibly. Words of quite different meaning may be spelt the same so check carefully that you have chosen the right form.

4 Always have a dictionary handy when reading English for pleasure. You need not look up every unknown word, just those you think will be useful later or those you will remember easily.

Some conventions of formal written English

1 Spoken abbreviations (such as *I'm, didn't, isn't, can't*) are used in dialogues and informal writing (such as letters to friends) but rarely in business letters, study books, learned articles and other kinds of formal writing.

2 Numbers may appear as figures in dates (*31st March, 1908*), technical and scientific writing and a few other cases but (as in many other languages) are normally written as words unless they are long and complicated ones: *three lessons a week, half an hour, four thousand people.*

3 Abbreviations such as *e.g.* and *etc.* often appear in notes but in formal writing these are usually avoided with the help of other expressions like *including, such as, as for example.*

Spoken English

First Certificate Interview

Besides a passage to be read aloud and identified, the Interview is likely to include a variety of topics as subjects of a conversation between the examiner and one or more candidates. A candidate will probably also be asked for his/her ideas about a photograph.

In addition a candidate could be asked to talk about or answer questions on:
1   a map, timetable, programme, diagram (of a house for example)
2   preferences and criticisms, giving reasons
3   how to deal with a situation in action or speech
4   a specific topic
5   giving instructions (e.g. how to make or do something), directions, advice
6   his or her opinion on a certain subject
or to take part in a discussion.

While the ideas expressed should be sensible ones, the examiner's judgment depends less on the quality of the ideas than on
(a)   how well the candidate has understood what has been said
(b)   his/her ability to express ideas effectively.

Pre-examination practice

Fluency in a language depends to a large extent on:
(a)   how widely the speaker has read, heard and absorbed the language
(b)   how much practice he/she has had in making use of it
(c)   self-confidence which partly depends on ability and practice.

Practical advice

1   Listen as often as possible to
    (a)   English radio programmes (e.g. B.B.C. World Service and English by Radio)
    (b)   English tapes, cassettes, English-spoken films and video
    (c)   your teacher
    (d)   local English-speaking people

2   Speak English
    (a)   in class
    (b)   with friends
    (c)   silently or aloud when alone
    Examples: talking about or repeating a story or dialogue you have heard; talking about a picture; imagining what you might say in a certain situation.
    When you talk about the photograph of a person (for example), examine it for interesting things you can say, including

the person's: height, build, position, facial features, hair, clothes (with comments: e.g. *too big for him*), personality, mood, probable occupation.

One advantage of talking to yourself is that you can take your time in deciding how best to express your ideas.

Speaking English in the classroom and at the Interview

Remember

1 Shyness and silence are luxuries you can't afford. If success depends on speaking, you must speak.

2 Talking carelessly, too quickly and too much is dangerous. You may irritate the other students and you will almost certainly make a lot of unnecessary mistakes.

3 Single word or phrase answers are useless: add ideas or opinions.
   Example: Have you ever visited London?
         No, not yet. But I hope to spend some time there soon.

4 Speak clearly (don't mumble) and slowly enough to avoid mistakes and have time to introduce useful expressions and ideas.

5 Make use of the natural and colloquial English you have learned. Natural and colloquial forms include:
   Short answers: Yes, I do/No, I don't.   I think so.
   Question tags: You will come, won't you.
   Other expressions: Well, . . .   Oh, . . .   Yes, I see.   I'm afraid
                  . . . I wonder if . . .   By the way . . .
   Polite requests: Would you mind . . ., (*etc*).
   Slang may sound unnatural and out of date so is best avoided.

6 If you don't understand what has been said to you, ask for it to be repeated:
   I'm sorry. I didn't quite understand that. Would you mind saying it again.
   If you know very little about the subject, don't hesitate to say so:
   Well, I'm afraid that's something I know very little about.
   I've got the impression that . . . but I haven't any definite opinion.

7 In class, be ready to learn from your teacher's corrections. Keep a notebook handy even in a conversation class: note down things worth remembering and study them again after the lesson.

8 Look as if you are interested in the conversation. There are examination candidates who (probably because of nervousness) give the impression that they consider the exam interview is a waste of time.

9 Almost every exam interviewee is nervous but most of them are successful.

1 Never Trust Appearances

Rush hour in a provincial town is certainly not so busy as in London, but even so there are plenty of people moving about. Long, patient queues wait wearily for buses. Never-ending lines of cars are checked while red traffic lights change to green. Thousands of people are packed tightly in
5 trains, the men's faces buried in their evening papers while women try in vain to knit. In a slow train it may well be an hour's journey to their station.

James Saxon is in his usual comfortable corner, quietly smoking a cigarette. When he is travelling by train at this time, he always reaches the
10 station at ten past five by the station clock, but he never catches the 5.14 train. Instead he travels by the train which leaves at twenty-four minutes past five so as to be sure of getting his corner seat. There are no first-class compartments or reserved seats on this train. He appears to be absorbed in the sports news on the back page of his paper and ignores the hurrying
15 crowds.

Facing him this evening there is a Finnish youth of eighteen, Matti Arpola. This is his first visit to England, though he already knows Geoffrey, the eldest son of the Jackson family, with whom he is going to stay.
20 As there are several people standing, James Saxon is the only person he can see clearly. Matti decides that he is probably a typical Englishman, and he observes James carefully.

'Can he really be typical?' he thinks. 'He has an umbrella, neatly rolled, but no bowler hat; in fact, no hat at all. Of course, he is reading about
25 cricket and he is reserved and not interested in other people. But he is only of average height and his hair is not fair, but as dark as that of an Italian, and curly, with almost no parting. He is not smoking a pipe, and although we foreigners think that a real Englishman ought to have a moustache, he is clean-shaven. His nose is slightly crooked. What a serious face he has!
30 He is frowning a little, but the eyes beneath his worried-looking forehead are sincere and honest. I don't think he is intelligent.

'His clothes are anything but smart. In fact, they are rather old, though well-brushed. Even though he is not wearing a wedding ring, he is probably married, with perhaps three children. His gloves are fur-lined and
35 his trousers well pressed. He keeps far too many things in his pockets, so his suit looks badly out of shape. What dull, old-fashioned leather shoes he is wearing! His briefcase is old too and bulging, so that the zip-fastener does not close properly. There are the initials J.S. on it. Is his name John Smith?
40 'I think he is probably an office clerk or a shop assistant. Does he look like a teacher, though? Anyhow, he lives with a plain wife and five children in a small worker's house with a tiny garden, where he spends his leisure time digging and weeding and mowing the lawn, or painting the tool-shed. But tonight, first he is helping his wife to put the children to bed
45 and then he is taking her to the cinema as this is pay-day. Or is he visiting the local pub? Does he drink whisky (I believe most Englishmen do) or

does he prefer beer? I am sure he very much likes a cup of tea. He seems quite energetic, but his complexion is pale and he is very thin. Does he find it difficult to satisfy the needs of his miserable wife and seven unfortunate
50 children? Poor fellow! I am sorry for him.'

At last, shortly after a quarter past six by Matti's watch, the train reaches Lakewell Junction, and Matti immediately sees Geoffrey waiting for him. They greet each other. At first Matti cannot find his ticket, but it is discovered in his bulging coat pocket. He gives it up to the ticket-
55 collector and the two boys go off to find Geoffrey's father's car. Near it there stands another car, a magnificent Rolls-Royce, and a handsome, uniformed chauffeur is holding the door open while James Saxon steps in.

'Who is that?' Matti asks. 'Why is he getting into that car? Where does he live? He looks like a poorly-paid clerk or a workman.'
60 Geoffrey laughs loudly as if this is a good joke.

'That is Sir James Saxon,' he replies. 'He has a fortune of around two million pounds, and controls forty-two factories in this area alone. He is a bachelor who lives in a fourth-storey luxury flat, so, if he feels like it, he can go off to the Riviera for a month or two. Next week he is flying to
65 Japan on business in his private aeroplane, though people say he very much prefers travelling by train. He is said to have twenty-one suits, but he is always seen in the same old one. By the way, I remember now. His father and mother are both Finns: perhaps that is why he takes no interest in cricket. His real name is Jussi Saksalainen, but he is now a naturalised
70 British subject with an English name. He doesn't look at all Finnish.

'Here's your other case. Put it down a minute while I unlock the car. Do you enjoy gardening? If so, you can help me: digging, weeding and mowing the lawn. And I'm painting the tool-shed tomorrow. You don't know how to play cricket yet, but I'm taking you to a match on Saturday.
75 Can you speak English any better now? You can soon lose that Finnish reserve. Come along! Let's get going! I'm hungry and hot.'

Matti remembers sadly all that his school-teachers say about his over-active and unreliable imagination. Perhaps they are right after all.

Notes on the passage

Vocabulary

1 *provincial* The *provinces* are the part of the country away from London.

2 *plenty of* is used with singular and plural nouns. Here are some similar expressions: Singular forms: *He has a great deal of / a good deal of / very much / a lot of / work to do.* Plural forms: *He has many / a lot of hobbies*: Not: *a good (great) deal of hobbies. Lots of* is used normally only in conversation.

2 *queue* (N and V) Spelling: *queueing.*

3 *bus* Plural: *buses.* Also: *gases.*

3 *wearily* *tired* has no adverb.

3 *check* (V and N) = hold back, stop (possibly temporarily): *check a disease; a check to his plans.* Also = make sure of correctness: *check figures, oil, batteries, a careful check of examination marks.*
cheque (N) = *a traveller's cheque; a cheque book.*

5 *their* Cf. *there.* Which? (a) _____ are (b) _____ shoes (c) over _____ (d) put it _____.

6 *a slow train* *a fast train; an express; a goods train; an excursion train. A through train* travels all the way to a certain place so one need not change.

8 *quietly* Spelling: *a quiet holiday* but *quite finished.*

10 *a clock* (on the wall). Cf. *a (wrist) watch.*

11 *leave* Notice: *leave home early; live at home.*

13 *reserved seats* Not: **sitting places.*

14 the *sports* news or page Not: *sporting.*

14 *ignores* = takes no notice of: *He ignores me when he is angry.*
is ignorant of = does not know: *He is ignorant of his real name.*

16 *a (the) youth* = a boy between about fifteen and twenty-one.
youth (Unc N) = the time when one is young: *Youth is not always the best part of life.*

18 *eldest elder* used only for members of a family: *his eldest son. elder* cannot be followed by *than: He is older than his brother.*

18 the *Jackson family* Not: **the family Jackson.*

24 *no hat at all I have none at all. He is doing nothing at all. at all* makes the negative stronger.

25 *interested* Do not confuse these: *interested spectators,* but *interesting films; an absorbed reader,* but *absorbing books; annoyed parents,* but *annoying disturbances; excited children,* but *exciting games; bored students,* but *boring lessons; amused listeners,* but *amusing jokes.*

26 *fair hair* is more normally used than *blonde hair,* which is possibly coloured or dyed.

28 *we foreigners we students.* Not: **we other students.*

32 *clothes cloth (Unc and C N) clothing* (Unc N) *clothes* (Pl N) (see Pronunciation, page 16)
cloth = either material or a piece of material for a special job: *to buy cloth* (Unc), *a tablecloth, a floorcloth, a dishcloth* (all C).
clothing (Sing), *clothes* (Pl).
These mean the same but the second is more commonly used. A single piece of clothing is *a garment* (C).

33 *well-brushed* The adverb *well* can be used with several past participles to form adjectives. Examples: *well-dressed; well-made; well-spoken* (speaking correctly and pleasantly); *well-preserved* (still in good condition); *well-mannered; well-paid.* Opposites usually start with *badly: badly-made* etc., though *little-known* is normal and *poorly-paid* (1.59) is possible. Notice: *So you passed your examination. Well done!*

34 *fur-lined* An outdoor coat has a *lining* inside it. What is the meaning of this proverb: *Every cloud has a silver lining?*

36 *out of shape* The *shape* of a table, a room, a geometrical figure. *What shape is it?* (Not: **What form?) That cardigan has been washed twenty times and yet it still keeps its shape. It has not gone out of shape.*

41 *a plain woman* (not beautiful); *a plain cake* (not rich); *a plain answer* (with no unnecessary words); *a plain explanation* (clear); *a plain* (flat land).

44 *put the children to bed go to bed* (Not: **to the bed.*)

45 *take* someone or something to another place: *take his wife to the cinema. lead* living things by walking in front: *Officers lead the soldiers when they march through a town. conduct* someone to a place, usually with ceremony: *The Bishop will conduct the Queen round the new church.*

49 *a miserable person* (opp. *cheerful*); *miserable weather.*

53 *at first* suggests a following contradiction: *but . . ., though . . .: English is easy to learn at first but mastery of the language is difficult. first* suggests that other

things follow: *First write your name, then your address and last your date of birth.* *at last* suggests there has been a long wait: *At last the spring has come after a long winter.* *last* suggests a final action: *It should be the teacher who arrives in the classroom last.*

54 *a ticket-collector collects or inspects* railway tickets. He is not a controller and does not control them. An official *examines* your passport when you go through Passport Control. The normal meaning of *control* (1. 62) is 'have power over' or 'keep under discipline'.

56 *handsome* A man is *handsome.* A woman is *beautiful.* A child is *pretty.* *Good-looking*, with much the same meaning, is used to describe either a man or a woman.

65 *aeroplane aerodrome* But: *air*port, *air*man, *Air* Force (Spelling!)

67 *his father and mother* Not: **his father and his mother.*

69 *cricket* and *football* are *games.* We *play* games. 'Hamlet' is a *play.* We *act* in plays. But: *He plays the part of Hamlet.*

75 *Can you speak English?* Not: **Can you English?*

Pronunciation

Special difficulties:
Japan /dʒəpǽn/ but Japanese /dʒæpəniːz/; forehead /fɔ́rɪd/ or /fɔ́rəd/; comfortable /kʌ́mf(ə)təbl/; clerk /klɑːk/; magnificent /mægnífɪsənt/; unreliable /ʌnrɪláɪəbl/; cloth /klɒθ/; clothing /klə́uðɪŋ/; clothes /kləuðz/.

Day: today /tədéɪ/ (stressed) but yesterday /jéstədi/; holiday /hɒ́lədi/; Monday /mʌ́ndi/ and other names of days (all unstressed).

ə (as in *a*go): *a*bsorbed /əbzɔ́ːbd/; m*ou*stache /məstɑ́ːʃ/; leis*ure* /léʒə/; miser*a*ble /mízrəbl/; hands*ome* /hǽnsəm/; bachel*or* /bǽtʃələ/; init*i*als /ɪníʃəlz/.

ɪ (as in *ci*ty): aver*a*ge /ǽv(ə)rɪdʒ/; crook*ed* /krúkɪd/; unfortun*a*te /ʌnfɔ́ːtʃənɪt/; b*u*siness /bíznɪs/.

Silent letter: *k*nit /nɪt/.

Stress: cigar*ette* /sɪɡərét/; energetic /enədʒétɪk/.

Others: worried /wʌ́rɪd/; gloves /ɡlʌvz/; bulging /bʌ́ldʒɪŋ/; discovered /dɪskʌ́vəd/; uniformed /júːnɪfɔːmd/; queue /kjuː/; wearily /wíərɪli/; instead /ɪnstéd/; buried /bérɪd/; height /haɪt/; chauffeur /ʃə́ufə/; area /éərɪə/; Riviera /rɪvɪéərə/; naturalised /nǽtʃərəlaɪzd/.

Grammatical and structural points

(a) *When If* Do not confuse these. Compare: *When I get my pay, I spend it.* *If I get my pay, I spend it.*

(b) *so as to be sure of getting* *so as* followed by an infinitive expresses purpose.

(c) *there are several people standing* (1.20) *standing*, the present participle, shortens and is more normal than 'who are standing'.

(d) *anything but smart* (1.32) means *not at all smart.* In these two cases *but* means *except: You can choose anyone but me. I want to live anywhere but London.*

(e) *look like* (1.40) *feel like* (1.63) *His garden looks like a park. I feel like something the cat has brought in.* Also: *I feel like having a swim. I'll go if I feel like it.*
look as if   feel as if + subject and verb. *He is so strongly built that he looks as if he can lift an elephant, but when he is a bit ill, he says he feels as if he is going to die.*

(f) *greet each other* (1.53) *greet* always has an object. People do not just 'greet'.

(g) *am   is   are* hungry, thirsty, hot, cold, right, wrong, ten (years old).

(h) *trousers,   scissors,   shears,   are* (plural). *A pair of* trousers, scissors, shears *is* (singular).

(i) laughs *as if* (though) this is a good joke. You are walking *as if* you are / were tired.

(j) *not / no   not* makes a verb negative.   *no*, the opposite of 'yes', may also mean 'not any'. Which? (a) It is _____ cold. (b) I have _____ money. (c) There is _____ more left. (d) I do _____ need any more. (e) That is _____ business of yours.

(k) *person   people* The plural form 'persons' is unusual. The word *people* is always followed by a plural verb form: People *are sitting* in cafés.

(l) *Countable and uncountable nouns*
Most nouns are the names of things of which there can be one (singular) or more than one (plural). These are *countable* nouns. Some nouns have only a singular form. These are spoken of as *uncountable*. They cannot be preceded by *a* and they normally have no plural form.
Examples: *Countables*: coin, table, loaf, box, kick. *Uncountables*: money, furniture, bread, shopping, unkindness.
Notice: (i)   Some uncountables may be preceded by *a* when they are defined in some way: *a darkness that made him afraid to go on.*
(ii)   Some nouns may be countable or uncountable according to their meaning: *a light/lights; light and darkness.*
(iii)   *a hair/hairs* = separate ones. *hair of the head* (Unc). *Both his and his wife's hair is white now.*
(iv)   *journey* (C): *A journey from London to Bath.*
travel (Unc): *I enjoy travel. Travel broadens the mind.*
(v)   *news* is singular only: *The news is mainly bad. It is worrying.*

(m) *Verbal constructions*
Deciding the form of the second verb in a sentence group is a difficulty for students as it may take any one of these forms: (a) an *infinitive*; (b) a *gerund* — that is, a noun formed by adding *-ing* to a verb; (c) a *clause*, with subject and verb. There are few rules to help so examples have be be learned as they occur. Here are some examples from the passage:
(i) *Infinitive:*   *try* to knit, *help* to put; he *is said* to be a millionaire; *know how* to play.
(ii) *Gerund:*   *enjoy* gardening; *spend time* painting, but *time is spent* (in) painting.
(iii) *Clause:*   he *decides* that he is an Englishman; he *thinks* he is a clerk.

Prepositions

(a) I enjoy travelling $\frac{by}{in}$ a car/aeroplane, $\frac{by}{on/in}$ a train/bus; go *by* boat, be *on/in* a ship. Do not use *with*: I go to town *with* my dog (but not my car).
(b) read, think, learn, talk *about* something; but: discuss something.
(c) interested *in*/ absorbed *in* a book.

17

(d)   stay *with* a friend.

(e)   sorry *for* a person (feel pity); sorry *about* a thing or event: e.g. *about* your illness.

(f)   *on* the back page.

(g)   a visit *to* England.

(h)   *of* average height.

(i)   *facing* him.

(j)   wait *for* a bus.

(k)   five o'clock *by* the hall clock.

(l)   live *in* a flat *on* the fourth storey.

(m)   sure *of* getting.

(n)   Notice: *near* (not: *near of, near by, near from*): *near* London, *near* the fire station.

Expressions for use in written work	When you write English, you should of course never translate from your own language. One of the best ways of improving your style of writing is to make use of expressions you have found in your reading and which you really understand how to use. After each reading passage in this book, a list of expressions for you to learn and make use of is given.

(a)   Trains/buses/shops can be *packed with* people.

(b)   Women try *in vain* to knit.

(c)   He *is said to be* a millionaire.

(d)   *It may well be* an hour's journey/*There may well be* a thousand victims.

(e)   *absorbed in* the sports news/in doing a crossword puzzle.

(f)   *of average height.*

(g)   *Even though* he is tired, he is still working.

(h)   He *spends his leisure time painting.*

(i)   He *gives up* his ticket to the ticket-collector.

(j)   He *looks like* a poorly-paid clerk.

(k)   *If he feels like it*, he can go to Majorca.

(l)   *By the way*, I remember now.

(m)   Perhaps they are right *after all.*

Spoken English

Shortened verbal forms	Practise each of these by using them in short sentences. *Examples:* I'm hungry. Tom's not at home.

I'm   he's   she's   it's   we're   you're   they're   Tom's   the bread's here's   there's   that's   I've   he's   we've   you've   they've   I can't I mustn't   I mayn't   I'm not   he's not   (he isn't)   we're not   we (aren't)   I haven't   he hasn't   I don't   he doesn't   we don't

Pronunciation	we're /wɪə/; you're /jɔ:/; they're /ðeə/; mustn't /mʌ́sənt/ mayn't /méɪənt/; aren't /ɑ:nt/.

Practice

1   Give the short forms of the following:

(a) He is out.   (b) We have not time.   (c) He does not smoke.
(d) You may not come.   (e) They cannot see.   (f) I do not like it.
(g) Are you not coming?   (h) It is cold.   (i) Has she not got a car?
(j) The dog is not barking.   (k) I have not got a ticket.   (l) That is right.   (m) Here is your briefcase.   (n) Here is my glove.

2 Say something about each of the following, using a shortened verb form. Then repeat the statement, first about one of your friends and then about two (he or she/they).

(a) your age.   (b) a language unknown to you.   (c) the weather now.   (d) how many great-grandparents you have.   (e) the name of the smallest village in Australia.   (f) driving a car when drunk.   (g) how many elephants you have in your home.   (h) your intelligence.   (i) how often you are in prison.

3 Give a short answer (yes/no, subject and verb) to each of these questions:

(a) Can you speak Ancient Egyptian?   (b) May people smoke in non-smoking compartments?   (c) Does James enjoy travelling by train?   (d) Is it snowing now?   (e) Are you ninety?   (f) Have I got bright green hair?   (g) Are there any mice in your room? (h) May we drive past a red traffic light?   (i) Must train passengers have tickets?   (j) Are there people living on the moon?

Got

Got is often used with the verb *have* in spoken English, and what is said seems more natural as a result. It is not often used in written English.
> *I've got a cold. Fred hasn't got a ticket. Have you got a car? Haven't the children got anything to eat? We've got to hurry* (We have to (must) hurry).

Practice

Make sentences with *got* together with these expressions:

(a) (he) a headache?   (b) (we not) any tea.   (c) (the postman not) a bicycle.   (d) (I) to telephone.   (e) (you) give it back?   (f) (I) to do it again?
Practise using these forms whenever possible when you speak.

Forms of address

Sir and *Madam* are used in hotels and some shops when the person's name is unknown. Public servants such as officials and policemen use these forms. A young man speaking to an older man or a boy speaking to his teacher may say 'sir'. A woman teacher should be called by her name: Mrs Lane/Miss Day. Strangers who do not know each other rarely have any special form of address. Somehow they avoid the necessity of using one.

People who are not worried about making a polite impression — assistants in small shops, newspaper sellers, bus conductors — may call a man 'mate' or 'Joe' (or any short Christian name) and a woman of any age 'love', 'duck' or 'dear'.

A boy may be called 'son' or 'lad' and a girl 'dear'. 'Miss' is normally only used when calling a shop assistant or waitress, though children often use this form to a woman teacher or a woman unknown to them.

Travelling by train

Booking Office: Two singles (returns) to Brighton, please. (The passenger says 'first class' if he wants this).
A weekly season ticket to Victoria, please.
May I reserve a seat on the Plymouth train leaving at 8.30 tomorrow morning? Second class, window seat, facing (back to) the engine, if possible, please.

Barrier or Information Office: When does the next train for Waterloo leave, please? Does it stop at Basingstoke? What platform does it leave from? Do I have to change anywhere?

In the train: Is this seat free?
Would you mind helping me to lift my case down, please?
Can I help with your luggage (case)?
Thank you. That's very kind of you. It is rather heavy.

Reading comprehension

Choice of words

In this exercise you must choose the word or phrase which best completes each sentence.

1 Fishing is a hobby which needs a good deal of _____ .
   A money   **B** intelligence   **C** patience   **D** strength

2 No one is so _____ as the person who has no wish to learn.
   A sensible   **B** ignorant   **C** useless   **D** simple

3 He is writing his name _____ and carefully at the top of the paper.
   A seriously   **B** largely   **C** obviously   **D** clearly

4 Normally he is rather _____ but sometimes he talks freely about himself.
   A sociable   **B** reserved   **C** serious   **D** peaceful

5 Although only of _____ intelligence, he speaks four languages fluently.
   A average   **B** middle   **C** minor   **D** slow

6 He sends his _____ wishes for your future happiness.
   A honest   **B** sincere   **C** many   **D** hopeful

7 The three climbers can employ a guide to _____ them on their way up the mountain.
   A guide   **B** conduct   **C** lead   **D** bring

8 He always takes a _____ with him to clean the windscreen of his car.
   A garment   **B** cloth   **C** clothing   **D** stuff

9 In _____ the room resembles the letter L.
   A form   **B** pattern   **C** formation   **D** shape

10 Why are you always so _____ ? You never smile or look cheerful.
   A angry   **B** sorry   **C** unfortunate   **D** miserable

Multiple choice responses

Below are a number of questions or unfinished statements about lines 1-36 of the reading passage on page 13. Read through the section of the passage again, then choose the best answer or ending in each case.

1 People waiting for buses
   A are bad-tempered and miserable.
   B accept the long wait without complaint.
   C know that they must wait a long time.
   D have little hope of getting on the next bus.

2 James Saxon does not catch the 5.14 train because
   A he does not want to hurry.
   B the later train is less crowded.
   C he has not reserved a seat in it.
   D it is a slow train.

3 Why does Matti give all his attention to James Saxon?
   A James Saxon is the first Englishman he has seen.
   B It is difficult to pay attention to anyone else.
   C He has no idea of what an Englishman looks like.
   D He doesn't believe that James Saxon is a typical Englishman.

4 Why is Matti uncertain whether James Saxon is really an Englishman?
   A He looks very quiet.
   B He is reading about cricket.
   C He is not wearing a hat.
   D He is not interested in other people.

5 Which of the following details of his appearance show that James Saxon pays some attention to what he looks like?
   A his shoes.
   B his briefcase.
   C his suit.
   D his trousers.

Composition

Sentences

Write five or six short sentences on one of these subjects. Use very simple English. Some of the expressions in the reading passage may be useful.

(a) Describe what one of your relations or friends looks like.
(b) You are a very rich person with no family. How do you spend your time?
(c) What ideas have you about the typical Englishman — his appearance, clothes, manners, interests and ways of spending his time?
Example: Here is a possible beginning to subject (a):
   My Uncle Jock is forty-four but he looks much younger. He is of average height and has a round face, red hair and green eyes. He likes to wear . . .

Use of English

1 **Fill in each of the numbered blanks with one suitable word.**

Christopher is not married yet: he is still a _____(1). He is interested _____(2) football, which is an exciting _____(3) and enjoys _____(4) to watch a football _____(5). So most winter Saturday afternoons he puts on his old raincoat, which is badly out of _____(6) and _____(7) the house at five past twelve so _____(8) to arrive early. He goes _____(9) bus and gets _____(10) the bus at the football ground. Even _____(11) it may be raining, he finds thousands of _____(12) already waiting in a long _____(13) outside the gates. Sometimes, if it is raining _____(14) hard for him to enjoy himself, he watches another match on television _____(15) of going out. He likes to spend Saturday evening _____(16) about football matches _____ (17) the back page of the newspaper. Some people like to spend the evening _____(18) in noisy pubs but Christopher prefers his comfortable and _____(19) sitting-room. He feels as _____(20) he is a completely happy man until work starts again on Monday morning.

2 **Finish each of the following sentences in such a way that it means exactly the same as the sentence before it.**
Example: This is his first visit to England.
　　　　　He is _____
Answer: He is visiting England for the first time.

1 I think it may rain.
 It looks as _____
2 He is coming because he wants to be sure of meeting you.
 He is coming so _____
3 Walking in the rain gives him pleasure.
 He enjoys _____
4 Most of a child's life is spent in playing.
 A child spends _____
5 The fox was unsuccessful in reaching the grapes.
 The fox tried in _____
6 His briefcase is too full for the zip fastener to close properly.
 His briefcase is so full _____
7 People say that he beats his wife.
 It is _____
8 He appears to be running away from your fierce dog.
 It looks _____

Interview

Talking about a photograph

1 Describe three of the people you can see: their approximate age, their height, build, facial expression (if you can see it), clothing and anything else of interest.
2 Describe the surroundings.
3 What is each person shown in the picture doing?
4 Why do you think the car has been parked on the pavement and what difficulties might this cause?

Topics

Suggest some ways in which this picture resembles and differs from an area of your own town.
What are some of the ways in which older people in a small town spend their free time?
Are you happy living in your own town or village or are you hoping to move elsewhere? Why?

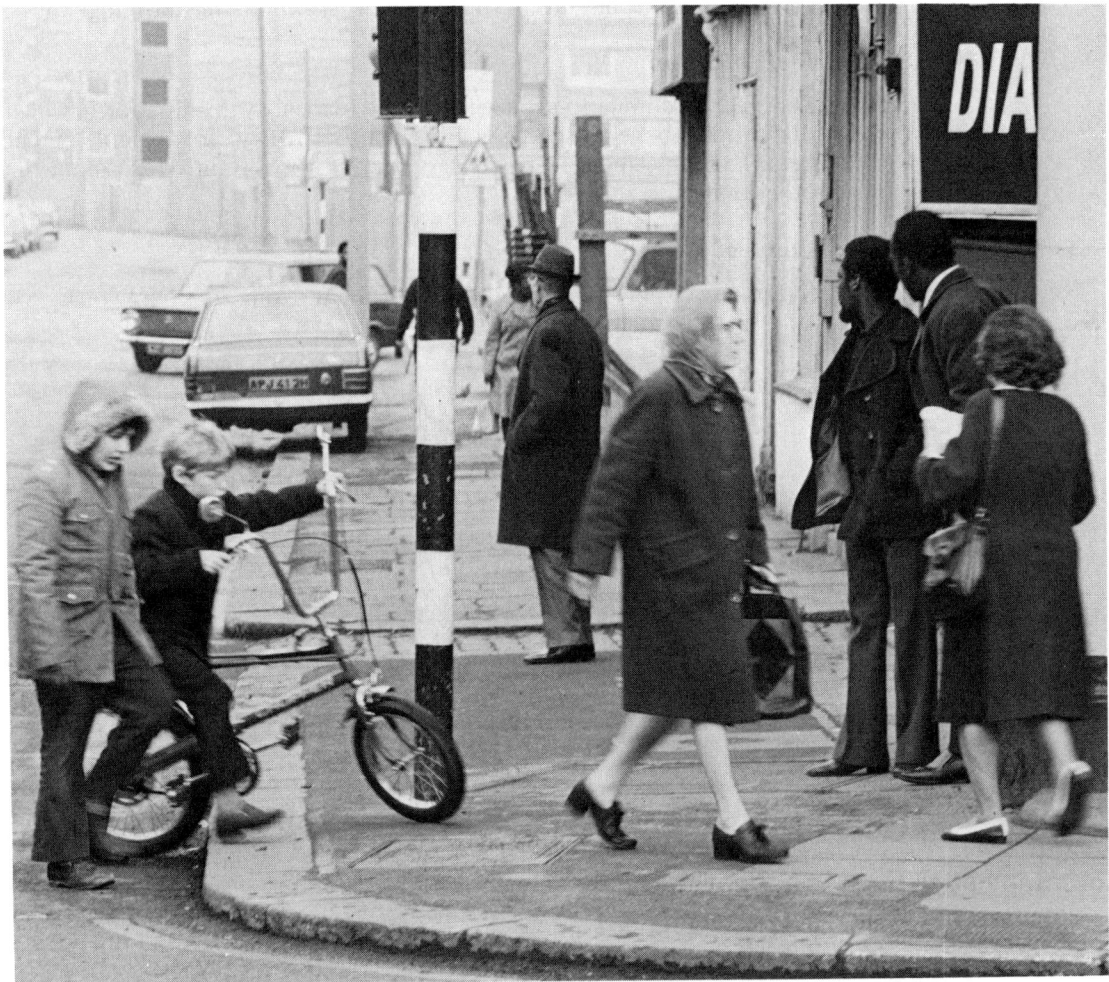

Reading aloud

Look through each of the following passages before reading it aloud. You may find it useful during this preparation to read the passage quietly but in such a way that you can hear your own voice. Start by practising single words, making sure that vowel and consonant sounds are correct. Some advice is given about vowel sounds below the three passages. Further reading advice is given in later sections.

Passages

1   We regret to inform you that the 9.35 train calling at Long Beech, Wood Green, Birch Hill and Seatown has been cancelled. Passengers for these stations are advised to take the 9.53 train to Witting leaving from Platform 4 and change at Marton Junction.

2   Well, I couldn't see the man who stayed inside the car but the one who got out looked a really nasty type. He was wearing a long grey overcoat with the collar turned up to hide his chin, leather gloves and a knitted cap drawn down over his forehead. One pocket was bulging as if he had a gun in it.

3   Now I expect you'd like to have half an hour or so to unpack and perhaps have a wash. Come down as soon as you're ready and Peter will show you the garden. Dinner will be ready in about an hour but I've put some biscuits in your room in case you're feeling hungry now.

Identification

During the examination you will be asked to identify the situation in which each of the above passages might be heard. The first, for example, might be an announcement to passengers waiting for a train. How about the other two?

Vowels

Short vowels in English may be different from those in your own language, so practise:

æ	man cap platform cancelled
e	ready regret /rɪgrét/ expect
ɪ	Witting knitted /nítɪd/ biscuits /bískɪts/
ɒ	got pocket /pɒ́kɪt/ collar
ʊ	put looked couldn't /kʊ́d(ə)nt/
ʌ	gun bulging junction /dʒʌ́nkʃ(ən)/
ə	leather perhaps garden cancelled

Notice the difference between:

ɔ:	walk drawn inform
ɜ:	work earn birch

Unexpected pronunciation: forehead /fɒ́rəd/ or /fɒ́rɪd/

Structured communication

This last section of the Interview may involve various activities. Suggestions about the most likely of these are given in different parts of this book. Here are two possibilities.

Expressing opinions

Give your own ideas about one or more of the following subjects. You can have a minute or two to make notes before you begin and other class members may want to add their own ideas after you finish.

1 Describe the kind of person you think is typical of your own fellow-countrymen or countrywomen.

2 Give three reasons why many people think that smoking is a bad habit.

3 For what reasons do some people take an interest in clothes and others not?

4 How do you enjoy spending your leisure time?

5 Why do some people very much enjoy gardening? What is your opinion?

6 What are some of the things that may help you to guess a stranger's nationality?

Describing people

Group members take it in turn to describe in detail one of the people shown below. The listeners wait till the end of the description and then guess which figure is being referred to.

(a)   (b)   (c)   (d)   (e)   (f)   (g)   (h)   (i)   (j)

General guidance and practice

1 Present Simple and Present Continuous tenses

The Present Simple
I eat   he, she, it eats   we, you, they eat

Use

This tense is used for actions that are *habitual* (that is to say, actions that happen all the time, regularly, several times or never happen).

Many Swiss people speak three languages: French, German and Italian.
A cat likes rabbit.
Students often make mistakes.
He occasionally works in the evening.

The Present Continous
I am sitting   he, she, it is sitting   we, you, they are sitting

Uses

(a)   This tense is used for an action that is happening *now, at this moment*:

I am now learning about tenses.
The birds are singing. Can you hear them?

The action may last for some time continuously, but it extends through now even though nothing may actually be happening at the moment one is speaking.

Your work is improving.
We are all getting older.

The following examples show the difference between the Present Simple and Present Continuous tenses:

She knits beautiful jumpers; just now she is knitting a silk one.
They are drinking coffee, though normally they drink tea.

(b)   The Present Continuous tense also expresses an *arranged future* action:

He is making a speech at the meeting tomorrow.
The train is leaving in five minutes.

(The Present Continuous of the verb 'to go' with an infinitive may also express the future. This is explained on page 193.)

(c)   In conversation the Present Continuous is sometimes used with the adverb 'always' to express a repeated action. The action may be annoying to the speaker. Notice the position of 'always':

That student is always coming in late.
You are always causing trouble.

(d)   Certain verbs are rarely used in the Present Continuous tense (except in a few cases to express the arranged future). A few of these verbs are:

can, may, must, ought
see, hear, smell
seem, appear, matter, mean
think, know, (understand), (remember), (forget), recognise
notice, (wonder), believe, suppose
(like), (love), dislike, (hate), (want)
own, possess, consist

The verbs given in brackets may be found in the Present Continuous form, but are best not used in this way by students.

Notice:
    I *am seeing* him next Monday. (arranged future)
    The flower *smells* sweet but She *is smelling* the flower.
    He *appears* stupid but He *is appearing* in the new film.
    What is he doing? I *think* he *is thinking* hard.

If either the Present Simple or the Present Continuous form can be used, the first is more often used unless the present moment is stressed:
    The river flows into the sea.
    The river is flowing faster after yesterday's rain.

Practice

Use the correct form of either the Present Simple or the Present Continuous tense in each of the following sentences:

(a)   Look! They (laugh) at his story.
(b)   People (laugh) when they are amused.
(c)   The baby (cry). Give him some food.
(d)   Children (cry) when they are frightened.
(e)   That naughty boy (throw) stones. Send him away.
(f)   In winter she (throw) out crumbs for the birds.
(g)   Peaches (ripen) in warm sunny places but not in the shade.
(h)   He (seem) very thoughtful. I (think) he (write) a poem.
(i)   We (buy) a new refrigerator next month.
(j)   Soldiers (salute) their officers.
(k)   He (play always) his trumpet when I (want) to sleep.
(l)   The famous violinist (play) in tonight's concert. He (play) superbly.
(m)   I (lose always) my umbrella! What (happen) to all the umbrellas people (lose)?
(n)   Every day I (work) by the window, so I (see) everyone who (come) to the house. The postman (come) now. He (carry) two letters.
(o)   She (work) as a nurse in a hospital but as she (have) her holiday now, she (stay) at the seaside.

2 Negatives and interrogatives

The Present Simple tense

Negative forms
    I do not understand
    he, she, it does not understand
    we, you, they do not understand
In conversation *do not* usually has the form *don't* and *does not* the form *doesn't*.

Interrogative forms
    do I look?
    does he (she, it) look?
    do we (you, they) look?

Exceptions
In the case of the verbs *have, be, can, may, must, ought, should, need* and *dare,* a simpler form of negative and interrogative is used (though in the cases of the verbs *have, need* and *dare* there are exceptions, which are explained later).

Negative forms
    I am not
    he, she, it is not
    we, you, they are not
    I may not, he ought not, etc.
Cannot is the one case in which the *not* in full is joined to the verb itself.

Interrogative forms
    am I?   are we (you, they)?
    is he (she, it)?
Notice the unusual first person singular form *aren't I?*
    may I?   ought he?   must they?   etc.

The Present Continuous tense

Negative forms

Written	*Spoken*
I am not staying	I'm not staying
he, she, it is not staying	he's, she's, it's not staying
we, you, they are not staying	we, you, they aren't staying, *or*
	we're, you're, they're not staying

Interrogative forms
    am I walking?
    are we, you, they walking?

Questions

When a question begins with *whom, what, why, where, how* etc., the interrogative form of the verb must follow:
    Where are you going?
    What exercise are the students doing?
    Whom do the people want as their President?
    How many workers does that factory employ?
But: Who likes chocolate? (*Who* is the subject of the verb.)

Practice

1   The following sentences are answers to questions. Give each of the questions. (In most cases the form of the answer is suggested by the word or words in the brackets.)

    (a)   I live in England. (Where?)
    (b)   Yes. A dog certainly eats meat.
    (c)   The train arrives at eight o'clock. (When?)
    (d)   There are two boys and three girls in my family. (How many?)
    (e)   No. The committee is not meeting until tomorrow evening.
    (f)   He is crying because he is hungry. (Why? the baby)
    (g)   The students travel by the 36 bus. (What bus?)
    (h)   Yes, the whole exercise must be completed.
    (i)   The journey takes an hour. (How long?)
    (j)   No one knows how birds can find their way. (How?)

2   Using the ideas given below construct *negative* sentences, giving both the full written form and the spoken form in each case. Only the infinitive of the verb is given; the right tense must be supplied.
    (a)   Kangaroos / live / in Europe.
    (b)   The sun / shine / today / and the birds / sing.
    (c)   Why / you / study? Your book / be / open.

(d) You / can / use the lift. It / work.
(e) Housewives / buy / bread / at the butcher's.
(f) Why / people / like / hard work?
(g) People / meet / polar bears / in the streets of Helsinki.
(h) It / be / always foggy in London.
(i) Even English people / can / always spell their language correctly.
(j) All Italians / sing / the whole day.

3 Passives

A tailor *makes* suits
Suits *are made* by a tailor.
In the first of these sentences the tailor, the subject of the verb, does the action of the verb. The verb is in the *active voice*. In the second sentence the action of the verb is done to the subject, which does nothing. The verb is in the *passive voice*.

Only transitive verbs, those that can take an object, can be used passively. It is the *object* of an active form which is usually the *subject* of the passive form, as in the example above.

Here is the passive form of the **Present Simple** tense:
I am carried
he, she, it is carried
we, you, they are carried

and here is the **Present Continuous** tense:
I am being carried
he, she, it is being carried
we, you, they are being carried.

Main uses of the passive

1 To express an action that is performed by a subject that is unknown or of so little importance as to need no mention. Other pronouns and generalised nouns such as 'people' can usually be omitted from the passive forms unless they are specially emphasised.
Active: *They are counting the votes.*
Passive: *The votes are being counted.*
Active: *We are making tea.*
Passive: *Tea is being made.*

2 In apparent contrast, to emphasise the agent:
Penicillin was discovered by Sir Alexander Fleming. The car was being driven by a man of ninety.
When the pronoun subject of the active voice is emphasised, therefore, it still appears in the passive form, preceded by the preposition *by*:
You caused the breakdown. The breakdown was caused by you.
Notice: 'People say' becomes 'It is said'.

To change an active to a passive form

1 Decide the tense of the active form.
2 Form the same tense of the verb 'to be'.
3 Add the past participle of the verb being used.

Example: *A tailor makes suits.* (Present Simple)
New subject: *suits*
Present simple of *be: are*
Past participle of *make: made*
The passive form is therefore: *Suits are made by a tailor.*
The preposition *by* is used before the agent.

Practice

Change the verbs in the following sentences into the passive voice.

(a) An announcer is reading the news.
(b) Horses pull carts.
(c) The Queen is opening that hospital next week.
(d) The Prime Minister is making a speech this evening.
(e) A policeman is using the telephone.
(f) A greengrocer sells potatoes.
(g) Teenagers buy a lot of pop records.
(h) Architects design buildings.
(i) Father is cooking the dinner. Mother is cleaning up the kitchen afterwards.
(j) A group of small boys are feeding the monkeys.

4 Exclamations

Formation

What (a) (adj) noun (subject, verb):
What a surprise! What nonsense! What a silly thing to say! What a donkey you are! What a cold day it is today!

How adjective/adverb (subject, verb):
How strange! How kind of you! How cold it is today!

Practice

Write the exclamation you would make in each of the following circumstances:

(a) Someone suggests a good idea.
(b) You are very tired.
(c) You are admiring a friend's dress.
(d) You are greeting friends on arrival.
(e) The weather is awful.

5 Basic word order

We have seen how the order of subject and verb depends on whether the sentence is a statement or a question. In a simple statement containing a direct object, the words are usually in the following order:

Subject	*Verb*	*Direct Object*	*Adverbial*
The man	is having	a meal	in a restaurant

An adverbial sometimes starts a sentence. In most cases, this is an adverbial of *time*:

Adverbial	*Subject*	*Verb*	*Direct Object*
This morning	the housewife	is doing	her washing

Place adverbials seldom start a sentence:
Not: **In the sky are stars.* But: *There are stars in the sky.*
Not: **In this office work two clerks.* But: *Two clerks work in this office.*

A very common mistake: Remember that 'very much' and other adverbials must not separate the verb from a short direct object unless these words qualify the direct object.
Not: **I enjoy very much the cinema.* But: *I very much enjoy the cinema* or: *I enjoy the cinema very much.*
It is correct to say: *A small bird does not need very much food* because *very much* qualifies the direct object *food*.

It is wrong to say: *He is writing slowly his letter. He is writing his letter slowly* is correct here.

Remember not to change the order of subject and verb after an opening adverbial:
Not: *Then eat we our supper.* But: *Then we eat our supper.*
Not: *Today go I to the dentist's.* But: *Today I am going to the dentist's.*

The subject of the verb in a statement or question must not be left out. It is wrong to say in English: *Is a fine day* or *Is not at home now.*

Practice

Arrange the following groups of words in correctly formed sentences.

(a) her shopping / in a paper bag / is carrying / the woman.
(b) beautifully / the / piano / she plays.
(c) very much / children / enjoy / fairy stories / most.
(d) must / at the top of the paper / you / your name / write.
(e) writes / his homework / neatly / this student.
(f) porridge for breakfast / dislikes / he / very much. (This can be arranged in two ways with two different meanings. What are they?)
(g) from the canal bank / boys / are fishing.
(h) in the new stadium / an international football match / this afternoon / is being played.

6 The apostrophe

This has two different uses:

(a) To show that a letter (or letters) have been left out.
It appears mainly in conversational verb abbreviations: *I've, he's, we're, you'll, isn't, they'd* and so on. Notice the apostrophe in *o'clock* ('of the clock').

(b) To show the possessive case of nouns.
Usually the apostrophe comes before the -s when the possessor is singular and after when the possessor is plural:
  a lady's shoe   ladies' shoes
But when the noun indicating the possessor does not add -s to form the plural, the apostrophe still comes before the -s even in the plural form. This normally affects only a few words:
  men's   policemen's
  women's   children's
  workmen's   people's

The time expressions: *second, minute, hour, day, week, fortnight, month, year, century*, may all be used possessively, according to the rule:
  a second's delay   three weeks' pay
  two months' holiday   five years' imprisonment

Notice the following sentences:
  They are now at the Saunders'.
  I sometimes go into Woolworth's.
The first case refers to the Saunders' house, and the second to Woolworth's shop.

Here is a conversational expression which indicates slight impatience:
  For goodness' sake hurry up!

The possessive pronouns: *hers, its, ours, yours, theirs,* have no apostrophe. Be careful not to confuse *it's* = 'it is' and *its* = 'belonging to it'.

31

It is not impossible for nouns indicating things to be used possessively but it is safer for the intermediate student to use the longer form:
the price of the book   the name of the street.

Practice

Show where apostrophes are needed in the following.

(a) He doesnt know where hes going
(b) the students memory
(c) the students minds
(d) policemens wives
(e) for goodness sake be quiet
(f) five hours sleep
(g) Its a long way
(h) Is this yours?
(i) old peoples homes
(j) We spent the evening at Joans
(k) The book is losing its cover
(l) four oclock
(m) the dolls dress
(n) a brother of Henrys

7 Numbers

(a) Notice the hyphen in all numbers from twenty-one to ninety-nine except the tens.

(b) 185 is written as words or spoken as *one* (or *a*) *hundred and eighty-five*. 364 — *three hundred and sixty-four.*

(c) Dates, such as 1924, are usually written as figures and spoken as *nineteen twenty-four*, though *nineteen hundred and twenty-four* is not wrong. The number itself is spoken in the second way, or as *one thousand nine hundred and twenty-four.*

(d) 532,478 is spoken as *five hundred and thirty-two thousand, four hundred and seventy-eight.*

(e) Notice: *four hundred and ten, three thousand and twenty, five million, six hundred thousand* (no plurals).
But: *hundreds of pounds, thousands of people, millions of insects.*

(f) Notice the spellings: *four, four*teen, but *forty.*

(g) Ordinal numbers are used in dates.
Dates can be written: 1st January, 2nd February, 3rd March, 4th April, 21st May, 22nd June, 23rd July, 31st August.
Otherwise 4th, 5th (fifth), 8th (eighth), 9th (ninth), 11th, 12th etc. At the head of a letter the date is written: 9th February, 1910.
In other written work 'the ninth of February' is usual.

(h) Kings are indicated by ordinal numbers written in Roman figures: *George VI* (George the Sixth).

(i) Fractions are written as *one-half, two-thirds, three-quarters* and so on. Decimals are read aloud as 15·36 — *fifteen point three six.*

Practice

Write the following as words.

44,   175,   832,   2,407,   2,436,000,   500,   the year 1425,
the date 3.9.1930 (on a letter),   Henry VIII, $\frac{4}{5}$,   27·82.

8 Times

Many students are unsure of the correct way of telling the time in English. The British do not always use the twenty-four hour clock. *a.m.* indicates 'before midday', *p.m.* 'after midday'. However one does not say **I go out at twenty past eight a.m.*, but: *I go out at twenty past eight in the morning.*

8.00	eight o'clock
8.15	(a) quarter past eight
8.30	half past eight
8.45	(a) quarter to nine.

The figures in the first column are used mainly in timetables, in the second in everyday speech.

Notice: five past eight   ten past eight   twenty-five to nine   twenty to nine

But: one *minute* past eight   seven *minutes* past eight   eighteen *minutes* to nine, etc.

B.C. is used with years to indicate the time before Christ. A.D. indicates the time after Christ (Latin — Anno Domini).

Practice

Write the following in words as they are used in everyday speech.

9.15 a.m.,   10.30 p.m.,   6.45,   4.25,   3.14 p.m.,   7.43,   11.2, 8.52,   1.18 a.m.

9 First, at first, last, at last

First is used when some kind of list of happenings is suggested or at least the idea is given that another action or other actions are following:
He *first* hangs up his hat and coat and then he is ready to start his morning's work.

At first always suggests that the action it is used with is followed by a completely different action or often the opposite:
He worked hard *at first*, but later he did nothing.

Last suggest that no more actions should happen later:
It should be the teacher who arrives in the classroom *last*.

At last suggests that there has been a long wait before the expected action:
At last the spring has come after a long winter.

Practice

Which of the four expressions should be used in the following?

(a) This term is ending _____
(b) _____ put in a coin and then press the button.
(c) _____ he knew nobody but now he has many friends.
(d) The slowest runner usually comes _____
(e) _____ knock at the door and then go in.
(f) _____ the bus is coming.
(g) Tom, who is always sleepy, is the one who gets up _____

2 Settling Down in England

My husband and I are Danish. As a matter of fact, many of my ancestors were English: I was born in England and was originally of British nationality. My parents were killed in a car crash when I was a baby, so I was brought up in Denmark by my grandmother and educated in Danish
5 schools so that Danish is really my native language.

We arrived in England last February at five o'clock on a Wednesday morning after an appallingly rough crossing. Waves which seemed as high as mountains rocked the boat from side to side. We were both sick on the journey and a fine drizzle met us as we disembarked. To make matters
10 worse, Klaus, my husband, left his camera on the ship; I lost a gold bracelet, (which has never been found to this day) and we nearly forgot to tip the taxi-driver, a surly individual, who grumbled about our luggage and seemed to be in a thoroughly bad temper. Few visitors can have experienced such an unfortunate beginning to their stay, and we certainly felt
15 like going straight home again.

We stayed for a week in a hotel, and were then lucky enough to find a furnished bungalow in the suburbs of London. It is not so convenient as our flat in Copenhagen, but it is less expensive than some we saw advertised. Klaus is studying at the local Technical College and, in addition, he
20 often attends public lectures at the University of London on as many subjects as possible, chiefly to improve his English. He is a qualified engineer who has been employed for several years in a factory. Our two children have joined us, and they are being educated in an English private school. I am working as a part-time nurse in a hospital, and I have so much to do
25 that I have almost no leisure time.

Most of the neighbours are kindly, but not so sociable as people at home. They tend to ask dull questions, such as: 'What is the weather like in Denmark?' or 'What kind of games do you play?' We are occasionally paid some odd compliments. I remember the time when a well-meaning
30 old lady told us, 'You have such delightful manners. I always think of you both as quite English.' I think she meant this as the height of flattery.

We have made a few close friends, who often invite us to their homes. One of them, who is a widower living on the other side of London, even fetches us in his car on Sunday mornings and brings us back in the even-
35 ings. Little Kristina, our small daughter, calls him Uncle Sunday. He speaks Swedish and has an elderly Swedish housekeeper, who has been looking after him for more than twenty years, so we chat for hours in a language that is in some ways similar to our own.

Our children can already speak English more fluently than we can. They
40 obviously feel superior to us, and are always making fun of our mistakes, but spelling causes all of us many headaches.

Notes on the passage

Vocabulary

Title   *settle down* = stay in one place. *a settler* = someone who settles in a new country or place. *settle (up)* a bill = pay it. *settle a matter, an argument* = decide it. *settled* weather (not changeable).

1   *ancestors* = great-great-grandparents etc. *descendants* = great-grandchildren etc. the present *generation* which you belong to.

2   *originally* = earlier, in the beginning. the *origin* of the trouble (beginning or cause). the *origin* of a word (what language or idea it comes from). *original* = first, fresh or new: *the original manuscript, the original plan.* *an original writer or thinker who has original ideas.* *originality* is the quality of being clever and fresh.

2   An Englishman/Englishwoman, a Scot/Scotswoman, a Welshman/Welshwoman and Northern Irishmen/Irishwomen are *of British nationality* (British by birth). Great Britain is the bigger of the two islands; the United Kingdom is Great Britain and Northern Ireland and the British Isles are the two islands.

3   *a car crash*   This could be a *collision* in which two cars *run into* each other.

4   *bring up* children in the home (*upbringing*). *educate* them in school (*education*).

7   *appallingly* should mean completely horrifying and shocking. In conversation it often has only the meaning 'very'. Similar words used with this meaning in conversation are *awfully, terribly, dreadfully, frightfully.*

7   *a rough sea* (opp. *calm*). *a rough surface* (opp. *smooth*). *a rough boy* (opp. *gentle*). *a rough answer* (opp. *exact*).

7   *a sea crossing*   *a level crossing* (where a railway crosses a road); *a pedestrian crossing* for people to cross the road.

7   a mountain is *high*. buildings are *high* or *tall*. a man is *tall* (Not: *long* or *high*).

8   *sick* as a result of over-eating or travel. *ill* = not well. Notice however: *People who are ill visit this spa*. But: *Sick* (Not *ill*) *people visit this spa*. *ill* almost never precedes a noun.

9   *a drizzle, a shower, a downpour, a cloudburst* are all kinds of *rain* (Unc). *to drizzle, to pour* (with rain) are the only verbs.

9   *embark* on a boat   *disembark from* a boat (or: *go ashore*). One can also embark on a new scheme: *The company is embarking on a new production line.*

10   *gold* is the metal: *a gold ring*. *golden* is the colour: *golden hair*.

10   *a bracelet* is worn round the arm; *a necklace* is worn around the neck; *an earring* is worn on the ear; *a brooch* is worn on the clothes.

11   *forget*   Not: *I sometimes forget my book at home*. You can say: I sometimes *forget to bring* my book. Or: I sometimes *leave my book at home*.

13   in a *bad temper*   A person can be only in a good or a bad *temper*. He can however be in a good, bad, cheerful, friendly, contented, optimistic, pessimistic, depressed (etc.) *mood*. (Adj *moody* = of changing moods, often miserable ones.)

15   *go straight home* = go home without stopping to do anything on the way.

16   *lucky* = getting good things by chance: *lucky at cards*. *happy* = contented.

17   *a bungalow*, a house, a flat (a block of flats), a cottage, a farmhouse.

17   the town *centre*, the *suburbs* (Adj. *suburban*), the *outskirts* of a town.

17   *convenient* = well-situated for work, buses and trains. *comfortable* = built and furnished to give ease and pleasure. *Is it convenient for me to come tomorrow?*

18   *expensive* = costing a lot: *an expensive* fur coat. *dear* = costing more than it should: *Eggs are dear just now.*

18 *advertise* (N *advertisement*) = publicise something (make it known) so as to gain something.
announce (N *announcement*) = make something important known to people.

20 *attend* (N *attendance*) = be present at a meeting, class, performance.
assist (N *assistance*) = help. Not: *I assisted in the lecture*, but: *I attended the lecture*. Not: *I assisted in an accident*, but: *I saw (was involved in) an accident*.

20 *A lecture* is given by a lecturer on a certain subject.
Reading (Unc N) *is an enjoyable pastime. Charles Dickens often gave readings* (C N) *from his novels.*
A conference of international eye specialists will take place in Vienna.
The teachers will have *a staff meeting* this afternoon.

21 *improve* (N *improvement*) *improve one's English, writing*, etc. (make it better).
His behaviour/work/standard/manners has/have improved. (got better). *better* as a verb is rarely used. *better oneself* = (get a better position or job). A teacher *corrects* or *marks* written work and pupils *get marks* and *do corrections.*

21 *qualified* (N *qualification*) *for* a job = with the right knowledge to do it.
experienced = knowing the job from having done it for some time.
disqualified from = not allowed to take part (e.g. in sport), usually because of bad conduct or unsuitability.

21 *An engineer* may design and construct.   *A mechanic* repairs and maintains.

22 *A factory* is a place where things are made.   *A fabric* is a material.

26 *sociable* (Adj) = liking to mix with other people.
a society (c) = a club: *a Dramatic Society. society* (Unc) = (a) people living in a community: *a danger to society.* (b) a group of rich people who entertain a lot: *He wanted to be accepted in society.*
a social = an informal party. (Adj) referring to community life: *the social history of England.*
an associate = (a) a friend (b) a title for a member of certain learned societies.
associate with (V) = be or mix with other people.
an association = a club or organised group.

27 *tend to* = happening very often: *Day temperatures tend to be high in this region.*

27 a *dull* question or book (opp. *interesting*).   a *dull boy* (opp. *bright* or *clever*).
a *dull sky* (opp. *bright*).

29 *odd*   strange. But also: *odd numbers*: 1, 3, 5, etc; *even numbers*: 2, 4, 6 etc.

29 *compliments*   The word *flattery* in line 31 is the art of *paying compliments.*

30 *manners* (Pl): *have good or bad manners* (politeness); *table manners.*
manner (Unc) = way: *He is behaving in a strange manner.*

31 *height* = abstract noun from high. Notice also: long, *length*; wide, *width*; broad, breadth; deep, *depth.*

32 *close* friends   *close to* (Prep): *He lives close to the park.* (Pronunciation of both forms: /kləʊs/.)

34 *take* from here to there: *Take your books home after class* (take away).
bring from there to here: *Bring your books to class again tomorrow.*
fetch = go to something and bring it here: *Fetch a doctor quickly!* (But when writing to someone: Shall I *bring* my skis with me?

36 *elderly*   young, middle-aged, elderly, old, aged.
Note: *the Middle Ages*. Adj *medieval.*

36 *a housekeeper* is paid to look after a house for someone.
a caretaker is paid to look after a building — he may have *cleaners* to help.
a housewife is the lady of the house (without wages).

37 *chat* together about unimportant things. *chatter* = talk a great deal.

38 *similar to/dissimilar to* = like/unlike (N *similarity*).

identical to = exactly the same as. *different from.*

40   *superior to* = better than (N *superiority*). But: an *advanced* course/class.

40   *make fun of* someone's mistakes.   *mock* in a cruel way. (N *mockery*). Children *tease* one another.

Pronunciation

Stress changes: ancestors /ǽnsestəz/, ancestral /ænséstrəl/; origin /ɒ́rɪdʒɪn/, original /ərídʒɪnəl/, originate /ərídʒɪneɪt/, originality /ərɪdʒɪnǽlɪti/;   suburbs /sʌ́bɜ:bz/, suburban /səbɜ́:bən/; advertise /ǽdvətaɪz/, advertisement /ədvɜ́:tɪzmənt/; social /sə́ʊʃl/, sociable /sə́ʊʃəbl/, society /səsáɪəti/; associate (V) /əsə́ʊʃieɪt/, (N) /əsə́ʊʃiət/.

ə   (as in *a*go):   husb*a*nd /hʌ́zbənd/;   Febru*a*ry /fébruəri/; *a*ppallingly /əpɔ́:lɪŋli/;   cert*ai*nly /sɜ́:tənli/;   convenient /kənví:nɪənt/; lect*u*res /léktʃəz/;   hospit*a*l /hɒ́spɪtəl/;   neighb*ou*rs /néɪbəz/; simil*ar* /sɪ́mɪlə/;   *o*ccasionally /əkéɪʒənəli/;   obvi*ou*sly /ɒ́bvɪəsli/.

ɪ   (as in c*i*ty):   mount*ai*ns /máʊntɪnz/;   bracel*e*t /bréɪslɪt/; neckl*a*ce /néklɪs/;   lugg*a*ge /lʌ́gɪdʒ/;   college /kɒ́lɪdʒ/.

Others: mean /mi:n/ but meant /ment/;   close (*V*) /kləʊz/, (*Adj., Prep. and Adv.*) /kləʊs/;   rough /rʌf/;   qualified /kwɒ́lɪfaɪd/; headache /hédeɪk/;   brooch /brəʊtʃ/;   thoroughly /θʌ́rəli/; mistakes /mɪstéɪks/.

Grammatical and structural points

(a)   When two pronouns or a noun and a pronoun, one of them in the first person, are connected by a conjunction, the first person pronoun always has the second place: *You and I. The children and I. We* and *they* are seldom used in this way. The sentence: 'The children and we went out' would more probably be written *We went out with the children.*
Notice: the pronoun as object: Father met *John and me* at the station. After a preposition: The farmer was angry *with John and me.*

(b)   *I was born* in London in 1960. Not: **I am born.*

(c)   *a* normally precedes a countable noun after the verb 'to be' (in many languages it does not): I was *a baby.* He is *a qualified engineer,* who is *a widower.*

(d)   He arrived *last February.* It happened *last week.* He arrived *in the last week* of the year. It happened *on the last days* he was here. He is coming *next week.* He came *the following week* (after an incident already referred to).

(e)   *A few visitors came to the hotel even in winter* (some). *Few visitors ever returned* (a very small number).
a little work (some) (with Unc N): He has done *a little homework,* more than he did yesterday. *little* work (not enough): Few of the newcomers had a job as there was *little work* for them in that area.
Notice however: *only a little/only a few*   Not: **only little/only few.*

(f)   *most of the neighbours*   *both the brothers*   Not: **the most/the both of them.*

(g)   he *feels well, ill, tired, cold* etc. No reflexive form (e.g. *himself*) with 'feel'.

(h)   I remember *the time when/the place where* something happened. (In most cases it is normal to say: *I remember when/where.*)

(i) I have *so much/little* to do that life seems rather dull. He has *so many/few* troubles that he has little interest in life.

(j) She works *as a nurse* (this is her job). She works *like a slave* (very hard). Complete the following with *as* or *like:* (a) He eats _____ a horse. (b) _____ a lawyer, he can give legal advice. (c) He practises _____ a doctor. (d) She sings _____ a nightingale. (e) He is serving _____ a soldier.

(k) Uncountable nouns: *luggage: My luggage* is in my car. *It is* heavy. *weather:* We had *beautiful weather. What cold weather!* England has *many different kinds of weather.*

(l) *Verbal constructions*
Infinitive: seem/appear to be; *tend* to ask; he attends lectures *to improve* his English (Purpose); lucky *enough to find* (construction with *enough*).
Gerund: felt like going.
Infinitive or Gerund (with meaning change): *remember/forget to do* something that should be done; *remember/forget doing* something that has been done.
Complete the following with the infinitive or gerund of the verb in brackets: (a) I have forgotten _____ my book (bring). (b) Do you remember _____ to read? (learn). (c) Please remember _____ some bread (buy). (d) I shall never forget _____ the mountains in midwinter (climb).

Prepositions

(a) arrive *in* a place (England, Canterbury) but *at* a point (London Airport, our hotel: *We arrived in Hull at four but didn't arrive at our hotel till an hour later.*

(b) be *at* home, but *go home, leave home. invite someone home* (or *to* one's home.)

(c) We arrived *last* February/*in* February *at* five o'clock *on a* Wednesday (morning). But: *in* the morning, *in* the afternoon, *in* the evening, *at* night. *early in* the morning, *late at* night.

(d) *in:* stay *in* a hotel; *in* the centre and *in* the suburbs (but: *on* the outskirts); employed *in* a factory; fetch us *in* his car; *in* a bad temper; killed/injured *in* a car crash; chat *in* a language that is similar.

(e) *on: on* the journey; lecture (N and V) *on* something; live *on* the other side of London; embark *on* a ship (but: disembark *from*); leave something *on* a ship (*on/in* a bus, train, *in* a car).

(f) *to:* a beginning *to* our stay; superior/inferior *to* (but: better *than*).

(g) *at:* be educated *at* Cornchester School (but: *in* a Grammar School); study *at* University, *at* a Technical College.

(h) *of: of* British nationality; make fun *of*.

(i) *about:* grumble *about*.

Expressions for use in written work

(a) *thorough(ly)* in a *thoroughly* bad temper; make a *thorough* search; clean, wash, examine, check something *thoroughly*.

(b) *feel like* having a cup of tea, going for a walk, changing my job.

(c) we were *lucky enough* to find/make several friends, have good weather.

(d) the *local* school, people, firms, bus service, customs etc.

(e) work *as* a nurse; think of her *as* a friend; say something *as* a joke.

(f) they *tend to* ask; the summers *tend to* be hot; children *tend to* be noisy.

(g) a *native* language; speak a language *fluently*.

(h) it is *in some ways* similar; *in some ways* it is ideal.

(i) *What is* the weather *like? What was* your holiday/the film/the journey *like?*

(j) a *well-meaning* person   a person who means to be kind but is not always successful.

(k) Adverbials: *As a matter of fact* he happens to be my cousin. The boat rocked *from side to side.* I have never found it *to this day. To make matters worse* we lost our way. He is interested *chiefly* in music. You are lazy, untidy and bad-mannered and, *in addition*, you can't even spell your own name properly. He saves as much money *as possible.*

Spoken English

More shortened verbal forms

I/he wasn't   we/you/they weren't   I hadn't   I couldn't   I didn't

Note: The form *hadn't* is normally used only as part of the past perfect tense. The usual past simple question is 'Did you have . . .?' with the short answer form: 'Yes, I did' or 'No, I didn't.'

have to
'Do you have to help?'   'No, I don't.'
'Did you have to help?'   'No, I didn't.'

Practice

1 Give short answers ('Yes' or 'No' followed by subject and verb) to these questions.

(a) Did the couple enjoy their journey?   (b) Were the children with their parents?   (c) Was the sun shining when they arrived?   (d) Could the Romans fly?   (e) Have you ever written a book?   (f) Did I write the first sentence in French?   (g) Has the Queen asked you to Buckingham Palace yet?   (h) Did you have a headache when you woke this morning?   (i) Was the sun shining when the couple arrived in England?   (j) Have you been learning English for more than ten years?

2 Answer each of these questions or suggestions, using at least one shortened verbal form in each case.

(a) Why couldn't the Romans fly?   (b) Why don't you offer me a cigarette?   (c) Why don't you learn Cornish? (an almost-forgotten language of Cornwall)   (d) Suggest one reason why the family were pleased with their flat. ('family' can be thought of as either Singular or Plural)   (e) Why do most people have difficulties in a foreign country?   (f) What two European countries haven't you visited yet?   (g) Why can't pigs fly?   (h) Why don't the family see much of the neighbours?   (i) Why didn't Julius Caesar sail to America?   (j) What kind of weather don't you like?

3 Say at least 15 words about each of these subjects, using a shortened verbal form.

(a) last winter   (b) watching television   (c) yesterday's weather   (d) people's holidays two hundred years ago   (e) children's education long ago   (f) books and people in the Middle Ages.

Expressing similarities: so/neither

Here are two ways of agreeing, the first with affirmative, the second with negative statements.

Affirmative
'I'm afraid of large hairy spiders.'   'So am I.'
'We must hurry.'   'What's the time then? My goodness! So must I.'
'You look really well.'   'So do you.'
'Factory-workers had to work very hard long ago.'   'So did farmers.'

Negative
'I haven't got any free time.'   'Neither (or: nor) have I.'
'Students don't always want to work.'   'Neither do teachers.'
'Primitive people didn't think much.'   'Nor do most modern people.'
'My husband wasn't very pleased with me when I came back from the sales.'   'Neither was mine.'

Practice

Add statements similar to those above to the following remarks. Where an unknown subject must be introduced, this is suggested in brackets.

(a)   I enjoy freshly-fried fish.
(b)   You talk too much.
(c)   We don't like living in this town.
(d)   My teacher is angry with me and (Father).
(e)   I couldn't sleep last night.
(f)   My husband forgot my birthday.
(g)   I didn't pass the exam.
(h)   The porter grumbled about our luggage and (the taxi-driver).
(i)   Motorists have to be careful on the road and (cyclists).
(j)   I must go and visit Aunt Jane in hospital and (you).
(k)   I can ride a bicycle.
(l)   Teachers didn't have to work today and (bank clerks).
(m)   My son had to write home for extra money and (Fred's).

Meeting people

(a)   A formal greeting at a first meeting:
          How do you do?
      Answer: *How do you do?*

      An informal greeting:
          Glad to meet you. I'm Pete. What's your name?
      or: *Hallo, Margaret. I'm Joan. Can I fetch you some coffee?*

      A formal greeting to someone you have already met:
          Good morning/afternoon/evening. How are you?
      Answer: *Very well, thank you. And how are you?*
          Oh, I'm fine, thank you.

      Good night is used when seeing someone for the last time in the day if this is after about 5 p.m.

      If you've been ill, you may be asked:
          Are you feeling better now?
      Answer: *Much better, thank you.*
      or: *Well, not too good yet. Better than I was though.*

(b)   After a journey:
          Have you had a good journey?
      Answer: *Very pleasant, thank you.*

After a sea crossing:
> *Did you have a good crossing?*
> Answer: *No, I'm afraid not. It was really rough and I'm not a good sailor.*

A telephone enquiry about something lost

A Good morning. I want to make an enquiry about something I've lost. Could you put me through to the right department, please.

B Yes, sir. That'll be the Lost Property Department. Just a moment. I'll put you through. (*Pause*) You're through now, sir.

C Lost Property Department. Can I help you?

A I wonder if you have a camera of mine. I left it on the 'Margate Mermaid' when we crossed from Ostend yesterday morning.

C Have you any idea where you left it, sir?

A Probably in the restaurant, though I might have put it down when we were collecting our luggage from the storage space.

C Can you describe the camera?

A It's a Wonderview model in a brown leather case and there's an exposure meter in a case attached.

C Just a minute. *(Pause)* Yes. The camera was handed in to the purser.

A Oh, that's good. What a relief! But how can I get it? I live in Northampton. Look, could you send it to your London office and I'll call for it there at the end of next week?

C Yes, we could do that. There'll be a small charge, of course. Can I have your name and address please? Thank you. I'll see that it's sent off.

A Thank you very much. Goodbye.

Booking a hotel room

Guest: Have you a single room for tonight and tomorrow night with telephone and shower?

Receptionist: We haven't any rooms with a shower free just now, but there's a bathroom available on each floor.

G All right. That'll do. How much is the room for the night?

R Twenty-seven pounds. That includes full English breakfast, of course.

G Yes, I'll take the room.

R Room 108. On the first floor. Here's your key and the lift's just round the corner. The porter will be back in a minute if you need help with your luggage.

G Thank you. And could I arrange to be called at seven tomorrow please?

R Certainly sir.

Reading comprehension

Choice of words

Choose the word or phrase which best completes each sentence below.

1 The mechanic examined the car engine _____ but could find nothing wrong with it.
   A throughout   **B** exactly   **C** thoroughly
   D altogether

2 Angus Graham is the person who can advise you best. _____, he is coming here tomorrow.
   A It is true   **B** Even so   **C** In effect
   D As a matter of fact

3 The flat we have rented is very _____ for the Underground station.
   A suitable   **B** comfortable   **C** convenient   **D** near

4 Are you going to attend Dr Barker's _____ on 'Brain Electronics' tomorrow?
   A conference   **B** lecture   **C** discussion   **D** reading

5 I can't find my umbrella. I must have _____ it on the bus.
   A lost   **B** left   **C** forgotten   **D** mislaid

6 The policeman looked me _____ several times and obviously disliked what he saw.
   A over and over again   **B** up and down
   C from side to side   **D** round and round

7 You must remember to _____ all your belongings out of this classroom today.
   A fetch   **B** take away   **C** bring   **D** take

8 He always studies the _____ in the paper as he wants to find a good second-hand car.
   A reclamations   **B** advertisements   **C** publicity
   D announcements

9 It was a horrible ride through pouring rain. _____ he had a puncture and for the last hour had to push the bicycle.
   A As a matter of fact   **B** Even so
   C To make matters worse   **D** In fact

10 Spanish is the _____ language of most Spaniards.
   A mother   **B** home   **C** native   **D** natural

Multiple choice responses

The following extracts are taken from an information booklet for car ferry passengers travelling between the United Kingdom and Scandinavia.

CAR DECKS
Car drivers are advised to apply the handbrake before leaving their vehicles, to lock all doors and to take with them all belongings that may be needed during the crossing. Car decks will be open for half an hour after departure and for one hour before arrival.

CURRENCY EXCHANGE
We regret that there are no facilities aboard for the exchange of cheques of any kind but most European currencies (notes but not coins) together with Eurocards and various types of international credit cards are accepted for payment in restaurants, shops, cinemas etc. and to carry out other transactions on board.

PASSENGER FACILITIES ON BOARD
The following are a small selection of those available:

PROMENADE DECK: Here you can enjoy a pleasant stroll, go for a jog, or sit or lie back in the sunshine in adaptable reclining seats. We would however advise passengers that decks may be slippery in wet or freezing weather.

VIEWING BRIDGE: This is situated below the Captain's Bridge and offers a view over the bow of the ship. The viewing bridge is reached from the promenade deck via the foremost stairway.

A LA CARTE RESTAURANT: This serves the same breakfast buffet as the main dining-room. Scandinavian and international specialities are available at lunch and dinner times. No reservations required.

DUTY-FREE SHOP: This is a supermarket offering Scandinavian and international goods, foodstuffs, spirits, tobacco goods, sweets etc.

OPENING TIMES: The opening times of the various shops, restaurants and other facilities are shown on the relevant entrance doors as well as on the boards in the main halls on Decks 4 and 5.

Here are a number of questions or unfinished statements about the passage, each with four suggested answers or endings. Choose the one you think fits best in each case. Read the information right through before choosing your answers.

1 According to the information given the promenade deck can be used for
   A exercise and relaxation.
   B taking exercise in all kinds of weather.
   C enjoying the view over the sea.
   D spending the night if no other accommodation is available.

2 The viewing bridge
   A provides a wide view of the decks below.
   B is the highest deck apart from the Captain's bridge.
   C offers a direct view over the sea below.
   D crosses the forward half of the ship.

3 Which of these instructions for car drivers suggests a possible result of bad weather?
   A Drivers are not allowed on the car deck during the crossing.
   B The handbrake must be left on.
   C Car doors must be locked.
   D Everything needed for the journey should be removed.

4 Which of the following people would have difficulty in making use of the shopping and eating facilities provided?
   A An Australian holding an American Express credit card but no European money.
   B A Canadian with only banknotes from his own country.
   C A German with German marks and a Eurocard.
   D A Swede with German and British coins and a credit card.

5 Passengers in the A La Carte restaurant
   A can have the full menu whenever they like.
   B can sit wherever they like when they come in.
   C can order their breakfast from the menu.
   D cannot reserve a place for lunch or dinner.

6 Passengers visiting the duty-free shop.
   A need not pay tax on the things they buy there.
   B pay less for many purchases than they would ashore.
   C can buy there only things to eat and drink.
   D do not have to pay tax on what they buy as they go through Customs.

7 Information about opening times of shops and restaurants is available
   A outside the shop or restaurant.
   B inside the shop or restaurant.
   C elsewhere in the booklet from which these extracts are taken.
   D from the information office.

Composition

Sentences

Write about eight simple sentences on one of these subjects. Use only words and expressions you already know, and even though this probably means you cannot write all the things you want to, write only the things you know how to express in correct English. Make use of the new words and expressions you have already learned in this book whenever you can.

(a) A very unpleasant journey by boat, train or car.
(b) Different ways in which you spend Sunday or some other day you have free every week.

Use of English

1 **The words in capitals at the end of each of the following sentences can be used to form a related word that fits suitably in the blank space. Fill each blank in this way.**
   Example: On our **arrival** we were greeted by an enormous dog.
            ARRIVE

   1 Do you know the _____ of St. Paul's Cathedral?   HIGH
   2 Switzerland is a _____ country.   MOUNTAIN
   3 He is very anxious about the _____ of his passport.   LOSE
   4 The nineteenth-century faith in the power of science is now very _____   QUESTION
   5 George made an unusually _____ remark about his wife's new dress.   COMPLIMENT
   6 A person with an _____ complex can be very disagreeable.   INFERIOR
   7 He has put on his _____ as it is bitterly cold.   COAT
   8 There was loud _____ as the clown fell off the ladder.   LAUGH
   9 We had an _____ day sailing our new boat.   ENJOY
   10 Although he is now middle-aged, he still looks quite _____   YOUTH

2 **The Fosters, a Canadian family from Toronto, have recently settled in England where Martin Foster is starting a new job. A few days after**

their arrival his wife, Annette Foster, describes their experiences so far in a letter to her parents.

The following word groups when extended into complete sentences form part of the letter. Make all the changes and additions necessary to produce grammatical and properly-constructed sentences. Note carefully from the example below some of the types of changes that may have to be made.

Example: We / not enjoy / travel / England / as we / delay / fog / Atlantic Ocean / and / reach / Heathrow / more / two hours late.

Answer: We didn't enjoy travelling to England as we were delayed by fog over the Atlantic Ocean and reached Heathrow more than two hours late.

Dear Mum and Dad,

1 We / arrive / the city / York / Sunday / our long tiring journey.
2 We / find / room / small hotel / quite near / town centre.
3 Martin / must / start work / next day / but I / spend the day look / somewhere / live.
4 I / buy / two newspapers / so as / study / accommodation advertisements / their back pages.
5 We / go / inspect / two flats / same evening / but one / look / a prison cell / and / other / be / far / expensive / us.
6 / you know / Martin / work / lecturer / technical college and / two days / colleague / tell / flat / let / the suburbs.
7 The colleague / take / us / his car / see it.
8 We / decide / rent it as / it / be / much / comfortable and convenient / those we / see / Monday.

3 Some form of Directed Writing usually appears on the Use of English paper. Information of various kinds and in various forms has to be reproduced in prose paragraphs and usually in well-constructed sentences. It may be necessary to select from the given material, to add to it or to express opinions or preferences. The following example provides elementary practice. The first paragraph is completed as an example of what to do.

Write three paragraphs about a real or imaginary journey to England by air. Each paragraph should consist of answers to the following groups of sentences and be expressed in about 50 words. The first sentence of each paragraph is suggested below.

1 When did·you visit England?
   Why did you go?
   Why did you decide to travel by air?
   What time did you leave home?
   What was the weather like?
   How did you get to the airport?
   What time did you get to the airport?

2 How crowded was the airport?
   How long did you have to wait there?
   What did you do while you were waiting?
   What time was the flight announced?
   Whom did you sit next to on the plane?
   What food were you given?
   How did you spend your time while you were travelling?

3   What time did you land at the airport in England?
    Who met you there? Say something about the person/people who
    met you.
    Where did you go to from the airport?
    Where did you spend your first evening and night?
    Describe your feelings after you arrived.

First Paragraph — Example

I visited England last summer when I went to stay with friends. Even
though flying is more expensive than land and sea travel, I went by air
to save time. I left home at midday on a gloriously sunny day. My
father drove me to Frankfurt Airport where we arrived at about one
o'clock.   (*54 words*)

2   As it was a Friday there were not many people at the airport.
3   We landed at Heathrow at half past three and I was met by John
    and Mary who asked about my journey.

Interview

Talking about a photograph

1 Suggest what this man has actually said in an attempt to identify his lost property. (You may get some ideas from the notice in the top right hand corner).

2 How is the assistant able to find out if the property is actually in the office?

3 What kinds of things are most often lost? Suggest why in each case.

Topics

Describe an incident when you lost something important and how you got it back.

What would you do if you found someone's handbag in a telephone box?

Suggest some situations which might cause people to lose things.

Reading aloud

Read through each of the following passages silently before reading it aloud. During the preparation give special practice to the vowel sounds listed in the previous section and also to the diphthongs referred to below. Suggest a situation in which each of the passages is likely to be heard.

Passages

1 I wonder whether anyone has handed in a rather old brown leather briefcase with a zip-fastener on three sides and one of its handles broken. I left it on an armchair in the lounge together with a magazine to keep my place there while I went to have breakfast in the restaurant and when I returned it had disappeared. I can't imagine anyone stealing it but perhaps someone has brought it to you as lost property.

2 So you're from Spain, are you? We spent a most enjoyable holiday there last summer on the Costa Brava. Beautiful weather we had, though the beaches were a bit too crowded. You must find it quite cold here in England, especially now in November. Well, we'll be your nearest neighbours so if there's anything you need to know or have help with, don't hesitate to ask.

3 I'm afraid I can't spare the time to attend Friday's meeting as just now I'm working till late at night in a hospital where I've got a part-time job. May I let you have some of my ideas on paper so that they can be discussed by the committee? I hope I'll be available for next Tuesday's meeting.

Practising diphthongs

Diphthongs are sounds made up of two vowel sounds following each other. In English the second of these vowels is usually shortened. These are the main diphthongs:

- **aɪ** I, I'll, find, quite, time, I'm, ideas /aɪdíəz/
- **aʊ** brown, lounge, crowded
- **eɪ** (open e) case, place, Spain, neighbours, afraid, late, paper, available /əvéɪləbl/
- **ɔɪ** enjoy /ɪndʒɔ́ɪ/
- **əʊ** old, most, cold, November, know, don't, so, hope
- **juː** can also be classified as a diphthong: you, beautiful, Tuesday

Diphthongs with the sound /ə/:

eə   there, chair, spare

ɪə   disappear, ideas

ʊe   sure

Diphthong + /ə/   tired /táɪəd/

Pay special attention to the following words:
fastener /fá:sənə/, magazine /mæɡəzí:n/, breakfast /brékfəst/,
hospital /hɒ́spɪtl/, committee /kəmíti/.

Structured communication

Expressing opinions

1   Do you prefer to travel by aeroplane, train, boat or car? What are the advantages and disadvantages of such a method. (A single student could choose one of the methods to talk about. Each of 2–4 students could be given one of the methods of transport on a piece of paper and asked to talk about it, the other(s) adding ideas or disagreeing in each case.)

2   You have to spend a year in a foreign country. Do you think it is better to have your own flat, to live in a hostel or to stay with a family? What are the advantages and disadvantages of each? (Single student or group work as above.)

3   Give some examples of good manners. (Single student.)

4   Suggest some aspects of English that cause you 'many headaches', suggesting why and what you can do about them. (Some examples might be pronunciation, grammar, the very wide vocabulary, spelling.)

Discussion of accommodation

The following single people or couples are looking for accommodation. Each person or couple chooses the most suitable of the four advertisements for free accommodation below. He or she then (a) explains why he or she thinks that the accommodation is suitable and (b) suggests some requests for additional information he or she might ask for when telephoning to make an appointment to go and see the accommodation.

1   A student starting the second year in a university college after spending the first year in a college hostel.
2   A single middle-aged teacher with a car who has just taken a job locally and enjoys living alone.
3   A couple who are getting married shortly and are both working.
4   A couple with four children of school age. The husband is a well-paid travelling salesman and has his own car. His wife also has a car but has no job outside the home.

When a group of students are involved, each of four students can be identified with one of the above people and, after each has given his or her own ideas, the rest of the group can add ideas of their own.

MODERN DETACHED HOUSE with large garden. Two storeys. Dining-room, sitting-room, 3 bedrooms, bathroom, kitchen. Garage. Station 2 miles (main line service). In picturesque village 10 miles from Brighton and sea. Beautiful area. Tel. 0132 46578. £80 weekly.	**UNFURNISHED MAISONETTE** on new housing estate in beautifully-designed garden suburb. Sitting-room, 2 bedrooms, well-fitted kitchen, bathroom, entrance hall. Garage. Gas central heating. Five-year lease. £50 weekly. Tel. 9876 12345.
FURNISHED FLAT to let in excellent condition. On ground floor of large older house. Small garden available. Long tenancy preferred. Gas fires and water heating. Bus service 10 minutes from house. £40 weekly. Tel. 8029 32435.	**FURNISHED BED-SITTING ROOM** to let with half-board (breakfast and evening meal). Central heating. Near bus route — 30 minutes to town centre. Quiet residential area. £30 weekly. Tel. 413 7225.

General guidance and practice

1 Past Simple, Present Perfect Simple and Present Perfect Continuous tenses: Active

---
Past Simple

I took   I did not take   Did I take?

---

is used to express an action that happened in the past and is finished. Sometimes a definite time in the past is stated:
   He died last year. He arrived a minute ago.

The action may have happened *only once:*
   I took a chocolate from the box.

repeatedly:
   The teacher who usually took us for Geography was Mr Winter.
(If the suggestion that the action no longer takes place is very strong, the form 'used to take' would be used here.)

or *continuously:*
   For several years he worked for the B.B.C.

(The Past Continuous could be used here if the *length* of the time were emphasised: *He was working for the B.B.C. for a very long time.*)

Important: In many languages the Present Perfect is used in cases where only the Past Simple is correct in English. It is important to remember that in cases where a definite past time is stated or understood, the Present Perfect form is wrong in English.

Present Perfect Simple

I have written

General use

Both Present Perfect Simple and Present Perfect Continuous express some kind of connection between a past state or action and the present time. The past state or action may
(1)   have existed or happened during a period of time that includes the

present:

I have written three letters this morning. (It is still morning.)

compare:

I wrote three letters this morning. (It is now afternoon.)

(2) have only just finished, no past time having been mentioned. Adverbs such as *just* or *now* are often used

He has just come in.

compare:

He came in a minute ago.

(3) suggest a future possibility. Adverbs such as yet or ever may suggest this:

The concert hasn't started yet.

Have you ever visited New Zealand?

(4) produce a present result:

I have made some coffee. Would you like a cup?

She has moved to a new flat. (She moved recently and is living there now.)

(5) refer to an understood present statement:

I'm sorry. I've forgotten to bring my book. (I haven't got it.)

compare:

Who has opened the window? (It's cold in here.)

with:

Who opened the window? (Who was it?)

Present Perfect Continuous

I have been writing

The continuous action referred to started in the past but

(1) is still happening

(2) has only just finished.

The length of time taken by the action is emphasised.

Verbs commonly used in this tense are: *live, stay, sleep, visit, work, lie* (flat), *rain, snow, shine.*

How long have you been living in England?

It has been raining all day.

I have been waiting for an hour and a half.

You have been spending far too much money.

Practice

Use the correct form of the Present Simple or Continuous, Past Simple or Present Perfect Simple or Continuous tenses in the following sentences. The adverb in (e) and (g) comes after the auxiliary (or helping) verb.

(a) He (work) at present in an office.

(b) He (start) work last Christmas.

(c) It (be) now time for lunch. I (work) all the morning.

(d) He (open) the window and then I (shut) it. Now it is open again. Who (open) it?

(e) He is still a young man but he (already visit) many countries.

(f) When he was a diplomat, he (visit) many countries.

(g) The children (finish) their dinner an hour ago and their mother (now wash) up.

50

(h)   I am sorry. I (forget) to bring my book to class.
(i)   When I was at college I (speak) four languages but I (forget) all but a very few words.
(j)   Where (hide you) since breakfast?
(k)   He (comb) his hair and now he is ready.
(l)   For the past hour I (try) to work but you (make) too much noise.

2   Past Simple, Present Perfect Simple and Present Perfect Continuous tenses: Passive

Past Simple: Passive	Present Perfect: Passive
I was taken	**I have been taken**

The Passive form of the Present Perfect Continuous is complicated and very seldom used.

The impersonal pronoun *one* is less often used in English than in some other languages. Instead of making it the subject of a transitive verb, English usage often prefers to express the idea in the Passive Voice. *French is spoken here* is the form of the shop-window notice, not *One speaks French here.*

Practice

Rewrite the following sentences in the Passive Voice. Remember that it is the object of the active form which usually becomes the new subject. Use the same tense as the one given.

(a)   They are making new arrangements.
(b)   They keep lost property in a special office.
(c)   People have praised the play highly.
(d)   Our new friends have invited us home.
(e)   Our Member of Parliament made a speech.
(f)   People believe that they are soon introducing important changes.
(There are two verbs here.)

3   Yet, still

The adverb *still* is used in connection with something which started in the past and is continuing now:
They are still repairing damage resulting from the last war.

Yet refers to the future, and is used in connection with things that may happen, but are not in existence at the present time:
They have not started to build the new skyscraper yet.

Yet may also be used with the meaning 'however', 'in spite of that':
He is very independent and yet he is popular.

Yet referring to something that may happen in the future often comes at the end of its clause. It is rarely found in an affirmative statement.

Practice

Use either *yet* or *still* in each of the following sentences:

(a)   He came for breakfast and is _____ here.
(b)   Good gracious! Hasn't he left _____?
(c)   Old traditions are _____ observed in isolated places.
(d)   It is after midnight. Are the Underground trains _____ running?
(e)   I don't believe the baby has gone to sleep _____
(f)   How cold you must have been! You are _____ shivering.
(g)   Aren't you ready _____?

(h) The young birds are _____ in their nest. They have not flown away

(i) She speaks English fluently and _____ she prefers to chatter in French.

4 The definite and indefinite articles

The name given to each of these forms suggests the general use, the one indefinite, possibly unknown, the other definite and known.

(a) The indefinite article is used with a noun introduced for the first time and therefore unknown. The next time the same noun appears, it is usually accompanied by the definite article:

A man I know lives in *an* old twelve-roomed house in *a* village. He has *a* son who occupies *a* modern three-roomed flat in *a* nearby town. *The* son pays more rent for *the* small flat in *the* town than *the* man pays for *the* large old house in *the* village.

(b) The indefinite article suggests that the person or thing it accompanies is one of several; the definite article shows either that the person or thing is the only one of its kind or that a special known case is being referred to.

He is studying at *a* college in Chingfield. (There are several there.)
He is studying at *the* college in Chingfield. (Either there is only one college in Chingfield or we already know which one is being spoken of.)
The house he has bought.
The Queen (of England), *The* National Gallery (of Great Britain), *The* Nile Delta, *The* Isle of Wight, *The* Foreign Secretary.

(c) *Doctor, Captain, Professor* etc. used as a title have no definite article: *Dr Green*. This also applies to such titles as *Uncle* and *Aunt*.

(d) A proper noun qualified by an adjective has no definite article: *Little Susan*.

Practice

Insert the definite or indefinite articles where necessary in the following sentences:

(a) He is _____ member of _____ City Council of Birmingham.
(b) He lives in _____ house at _____ seaside not far from _____ factory where he works.
(c) _____ special announcement was made on _____ radio this morning. I don't know what it was.
(d) _____ Prime Minister made _____ speech to _____ chief representatives of his party.
(e) Yesterday _____ Queen opened _____ hospital, received _____ group of foreign delegates, and visited _____ children's home, all in different places.
(f) _____ Doctor Smith works in _____ hospital in London, near _____ British Museum.
(g) During last night's fog, _____ train was derailed and _____ ship ran aground in _____ Thames estuary.
(h) We have bought _____ new refrigerator; now we must get rid of _____ old one.
(i) Once upon a time, in _____ far-distant country, there lived _____ great king, who had _____ lovely daughter.
(j) It was _____ cold dark evening and _____ warm fire and _____ book seemed _____ best way of passing _____ time.

5 Such a, such, so

(a) *so* is used with an adjective when no noun follows, or with an adverb:

I am *so tired*.
He speaks *so quickly*.

(b) *such a* is used with a singular countable noun, with or without an adjective:

He is *such a liar*.
It is *such a long way*.

(c) *such* is used with uncountable nouns and also plural nouns:

I have never before experienced *such cold weather*.
He told *such stupid lies*.

(d) *so* is used with nouns when these are preceded by 'much' 'little' 'many' or 'few':

so little time   *so many* people

The construction *so (adjective) a (noun)* is also used but less commonly:

It was *so long a story* that we nearly fell asleep.

Notice: *noise* is not uncountable: *such a noise*.

Practice

Use one of the above expressions in each of the following:

_____ many friends; _____ courage; _____ wonderful garden; _____ dull journey; _____ few opportunities; _____ noise; _____impossible events; _____ hard work; _____ little money; _____ unfriendly people.

Remember that these expressions serve to emphasise the quality of a noun, adjective or adverb. It sounds unnatural to say *In our school library are such dictionaries. This should be: *There are dictionaries of this kind (like this) in our school library.*

6 Capital letters

The use of capital letters differs in English from their use in various other languages. It is important to learn carefully these differences.
The following have capital letters:

(a) Days of the week, months of the year and special holidays: Christmas, Easter, Whitsun, August Bank Holiday.

(b) Names denoting nationality and languages and adjectives referring to these: A Spaniard, Spanish.

(c) Names of places including rivers, seas and mountains.
Notice: *a* river   but *the* River Thames
a station but   Victoria Station
a street but   Oxford Street

(d) Names of theatres, cinemas, hotels, restaurants, museums, ships, trains, aeroplanes: The Palace Theatre, The Grand Hotel, The Mayflower, The British Museum, The Blue Train.

(e) The more important words in the title of a book, play, film, chapter, composition: The Way of the World, The Uses of Steel.

Practice

Use capital letters where necessary in the following:

last saturday; in july; a dutch painter; the study of latin; the fortune theatre; the red lion hotel; the golden arrow (a train); the house of commons; guy fawkes day; a little guide to the english hills and mountains; a siamese cat.

7 Prepositions

Practice

Complete the following sentences with suitable prepositions or particles. They are all based on examples from the first two reading passages.

(a) What time did you arrive _____ Edinburgh?

(b) The bus which left the Market Place _____ twenty-six minutes to nine _____ the Town Hall clock had only one passenger.

(c) He was absorbed _____ the crossword puzzle _____ the back page.

(d) The concert started _____ eight o'clock _____ Thursday.

(e) Before the hospital treatment he looked _____ a skeleton, but a month later he said he felt _____ an Olympic champion.

(f) Foreigners are always grumbling _____ the English weather.

(g) He prefers to travel _____ bus because he can wait _____ it _____ the terminus _____ his home.

(h) We are sorry _____ the misunderstanding.

(i) He moves _____ the country very often _____ business, but he has so many friends that he is usually able to stay _____ a family he knows.

(j) His oil paintings are superior _____ his water-colours.

(k) People tend to be sorry _____ him because he is lame, but he is interested _____ so many things and enjoys reading _____ them so much that he is anything _____ unhappy.

(l) He has been _____ such a bad temper all day.

(m) Remember not to give _____ the return half of your railway ticket.

(n) He was only _____ average height but he had unusually broad shoulders.

3 An Irish Wedding

Have you ever been to an Irish wedding? I have just returned from one. It is a quarter to five in the morning; the sun has already climbed above the horizon; the birds are busy celebrating the new day and have eagerly been in search of food. But some of the guests have not yet left. They are still
5 prolonging the night: dancing, singing, gossiping, postponing the unfortunate necessity of undertaking a day's work in the fields after a sleepless night.

Throughout most of her life, Bridget Mary, the bride, has been living in the small whitewashed thatched cottage I have just left. Twelve children
10 have been brought up there but only two are still living at home. The eldest son, heir to the small farm, is helping his father with the farm work, (they employ no farm labourers); the youngest daughter is still at school. Two years ago, Bridget Mary went to England to take up domestic work in a hospital and it was while she was living there that she met her future
15 husband, Terry. He himself is an Irishman who used to live in Dublin and now has a well-paid job in a light engineering works in England. They got engaged and started saving. Now they are thinking of buying a small semi-detached house near Terry's factory.

The wedding ceremony was performed in the church in the nearest town
20 at half-past eight yesterday morning. Another couple were being married at the same time. Nobody worried about the cost of the celebrations: four luxurious cars brought bride, bridegroom, family and friends home, and forty people were crowded into the tiled kitchen and the tiny living-room, hung with framed school certificates and religious pictures. An enormous
25 meal was eaten; the wedding cake was cut and toasts were drunk in whisky or sherry. And while the remains of the feast were being cleared away and the rooms swept, the four cars set out again, taking the married couple and relations for a drive round the countryside.

The evening party was to have started at ten o'clock, but by nine o'clock
30 many of the guests were already arriving. A few of the nearer male relatives were looking rather awkward in evening suits with smart bow ties, and the pleasant, unsophisticated countrywomen appeared a little self-conscious in their Sunday best. By the time I arrived at eleven o'clock, the party was in full swing. Two men squeezing accordions provided the
35 music: the old Irish tunes that have been played at weddings for many years. Half the people in the room were dancing the square dances and reels which have been enjoyed even longer. Drinks were being handed round. A score of men stood in the narrow dark hall, leaning against the wall, drinking beer from bottles and speculating about crops, cattle and
40 the current political situation. And whenever the dancing stopped, somebody would start singing one of the sentimental, treasured Irish songs: the exile longing for his home, the grief-stricken lover mourning his fate. Sometimes we all joined in the chorus, sadly and solemnly, before getting up to dance again.

45 Irish weddings are almost certain to have been celebrated in this way for generations. The very old and the teenagers, the middle-aged couples who

take time off from their families, all meet together to keep up the old traditions and enjoy themselves as their ancestors did. I have been to wedding receptions where champagne has been served to the accompani-
50 ment of soft unnoticed orchestral music; I have listened to carefully-prepared speeches and eyed a little enviously the model gowns of women far more elegant than I could ever hope to be. I have been impressed, and a little bored. I have just been sitting up all night in a small, uncomfortable Irish cottage and I have been enjoying every moment of it.

Notes on the passage

Vocabulary

Title a wedding is the ceremony. a marriage is the life partnership.

3 *horizon* (N) *horizontal* (Adj) opp. *vertical*.
a precipice a very steep slope is almost *perpendicular*.

3 *eagerly* (opp. *reluctantly*): He was *eager/anxious* to help. He got up *reluctantly*.

4 a person, a car or a place can be *searched* by the police to find stolen goods. The police are *looking for, searching for, seeking* the stolen thing. At ten o'clock they were still *in search of* somewhere to spend the night.

5 *prolong* time (one's visit or stay) (N *prolongation*). *extend* a road or building (N *extension*). A passport or working permit is also *extended*. *lengthen* a dress.

5 *gossip* (V) = chat about unimportant things. gossip (Unc N) = talk about other people's affairs. *a gossip* (C N) = a person who does this.

5 *postpone* or *put off* (more colloquial) an arrangement till a later date (N *postponement*).
delay (N and V) = cause to happen later or be late: *Fog delayed the train*.
cancel (N *cancellation*) = give up or call off something planned: *cancel a meeting because nobody is interested*.

6 *undertake* (N *undertaking*) = (a) take on a job: A firm *undertakes* the production of a new type of lorry. (b) promise: I *undertake* to return all the books I borrow from the library. *An undertaker* makes all the arrangements for funerals.

8 The *bride, bridegroom, best man* (who assists the bridegroom) and the *bridesmaids* all take part in a formal wedding.

11 An *heir* or *heiress* will inherit his/her parents' property. This will be his/her *inheritance*. An *heirloom* is something valuable handed down from one generation to the next.

11 *work* (Unc N) *a job* (C N) *do* housework, homework (normally no plural).
What is your *job*? This is *a difficult job*. What *work* do you enjoy doing?
works with special meanings:
(a) gasworks, waterworks, the works (the factory)
(b) the works of a clock, watch or machine: 'something wrong with the works'
(c) public works (State building operations), road works
(d) good works, works of charity
(e) the works of Shakespeare, of Beethoven. 'Hamlet' is a work of Shakespeare.
labour = hard, heavy work (*a labourer* working on the roads). *toil* = hard work.
drudgery (*a drudge*) = hard work that is unpleasant and earns little money.

13 *domestic work* = cleaning and cooking. *cooks, maids* and *butlers* are in *domestic service*. A *daily woman* comes in for a few hours daily or weekly to help the housewife.

16 *be/get engaged (to); be married (to)/get married (to)/marry someone; get a divorce/get divorced; they are now divorced*.

17 *save* money/someone's life/time. *savings* are money saved.

spare (V) = have enough to give away some: *I have no bread. Can you spare me some? spare* (Adj) = extra: *spare time, a spare room/tyre.*

19   *a ceremony* (C N) (wedding, opening of a new building) is *performed.*
    ceremony (Unc): *The President was greeted with great ceremony.*
    A performance of a play. Also: *the actor (sportsman) gave a fine performance.*

19   *nearest next* Which? (a) my _____ relatives; (b) the _____ lesson; (c) the _____ house after the Post Office; (d) the _____ seaside place to London; (e) We must stop at the _____ filling station along this road; (f) Where is the _____ filling station to this house? (g) He ran to the _____ telephone to call the fire brigade.

20   *yesterday morning/afternoon/evening; last night; this morning/afternoon/evening; tonight;* Not: **today in the afternoon. tomorrow morning/afternoon/evening/night.*

24   *enormous, immense, huge, gigantic, tremendous* have almost the same meaning. *mighty* suggests powerful.

25   *a toast* (C N) to someone' good health or fortune. *toast* (Unc N) = grilled bread.

25   *drunk: He was drunk.* But: *a drunken man. A drunkard* is habitually drunk.

26   The *remains* of the meal were thrown away. The *rest* of the meal was now served. Three quarters of the material was used to make a dress, the *remainder* an apron. We visited the castle *ruins.*

26   *a feast* = a very fine meal. *a banquet* = a ceremonial meal. *a festival* = a special celebration, possibly with the performance of plays and music, e.g. *the Edinburgh Festival, a harvest festival.*

27   *sweep* with a broom. *dust* with a duster. *a sweep* = a man who cleans chimneys.

27   *go/take someone* for a walk, drive, picnic. *drive* a car, lorry/bus. *ride* a horse, bicycle, motor-cycle (with one's legs over it).

31   *awkward clumsy* A clumsy person tends to knock things down and bump into things. An awkward person cannot fit easily into his social surroundings. Boys and girls in their early teens can be awkward in company because they are unsure of themselves. Awkward can also be used in these ways: *A bicycle is an awkward thing to carry up steps. Getting rid of a talkative neighbour when one is in a hurry can be awkward.*

31   *a bow* /bəʊ/ = (a) a weapon used with an arrow   (b) a special knot in a ribbon used in the hair or for a tie. A man bows /baʊz/ or leans forward to show respect. A woman curtseys [kɜːtsɪz].

32   *self-conscious* = uncomfortably aware of oneself in company. *self-assured* or *self-confident* = sure of oneself. *self-centred* = interested only in oneself. *selfish* = wanting everything for oneself. *self-controlled* = keeping one's emotions in check.

34   *squeeze* = press in from either side. *squash* = force the liquid out of something or damage by pressure. Lemon or orange *squash* are types of soft drinks.

38   *a score* = 20. *a dozen* = 12. *a gross* = 144.

39   *speculate* (N *speculation*) = (a) try to decide what the future will be like (b) invest money in a risky way in an attempt to make a big profit.

39   *crops* = the produce of the farmer's work in his fields or orchards.
    crop up A subject which comes into a discussion by chance *crops up.*

39   *cattle* = bulls, cows, oxen (working animals), bullocks (raised for meat) and calves.
    poultry = chickens, ducks, geese and turkeys.

42   *exile* (N and V) An *exile* may have been turned out of his home country.
    An *emigrant* (V *emigrate*) goes of his own accord.
    An *immigrant* (V *immigrate*) comes into a country to live.
    A *migrant* (N and Adj) (V *migrate*) moves about: *migrant birds.*

42 a *grief-stricken* mother; a *panic-stricken* crowd; a *conscience-stricken* murderer.

42 *mourning* can be the expression of sorrow for loss by death or the clothes worn to show grief.

42 *fate destiny*. But: *a fatal accident* (causing death). *He at last reached his destination.*

43 The *choir* sang the verses of the hymn and the congregation joined in the *choruses*.

43 Do not confuse *get up* (especially from bed) and *stand up*.

47 *get time off* from work;   *have time off* or *take time off*.

49 *reception: the President's reception at the airport; a reception committee; a wedding reception;   the play had a hostile reception*. A *receptionist* may work for a doctor, dentist or in a hotel.

49 *accompaniment* There can also be a piano accompaniment played by an *accompanist*.

51 *envy* of someone who has something you want but cannot have.
    jealousy of a person who seems to be taking someone's affection from you.

51 *a model gown* Only one dress of this type exists.
    a model of a ship = a small replica.   *a model* student = a perfect one.

53 *bored* = having lost interest.   *annoyed* = a little angry.

53 *sit up* = not go to bed. *wait up* for someone = not go to bed before he comes.

Phrasal verbs

take   *take up* a new hobby, interest, type of work.
        take in = (a) make a garment smaller   (b) deceive.
        take away = (a) remove   (b) subtract.
        take off = (a) remove a garment   (b) (of an aeroplane) leave the ground
            (c) imitate.
        take to = like (usually a person).
        take down = (a) write, often from dictation   (b) remove from a wall.
        take over = start doing another person's job for him.

Practice

(a) _____ your shoes.
(b) My dog has _____ you.
(c) She has _____ singing.
(d) _____ one's teacher to make people laugh.
(e) _____ these old newspapers.
(f) Can you _____ my job for the next hour?
(g) _____ this letter in shorthand please.
(h) _____ three _____ from ten.
(i) Don't be _____ on the 1st April.

clear   *clear away* dishes after a meal = clear the table.
        clear up a mystery; *clear up* an untidy room; the weather *clears up*.

keep   *keep up* old traditions.
        keep away from a person with a cold.
        keep back crowds.
        keep in a lazy child who must stay longer at school.
        keep (and *keep on*) continue.
        keep bad news *from* someone.
        keep down prices.
        keep up efforts (continue to try).
        keep out = not allow to go in.

Pronunciation

Special difficulties:
choir /kwáɪə/; champagne /ʃæmpeɪn/ (English pronunciation);
awkward /ɔ́:kwəd/.

Stress changes: horizon /həráɪzn/; horizontal /hɒrɪzɒ́ntl/;
ceremony /sérəməni/; ceremonial /serəmə́ʊnɪəl/; luxury /lʌ́kʃəri/;
luxurious /lʌgzjʊ́ərɪəs/; sophisticated /səfístɪkeɪtɪd/; sophistication
/səfɪstɪkéɪʃn/; orchestra /ɔ́:kɪstrə/; orchestral /ɔ:késtrəl/;
politics /pɒ́lɪtɪks/; political /pəlítɪkəl/.

ə as in *ago:* labourers /léɪbərəz/; treasured /tréʒəd/; traditions
/trədíʃənz/; accompaniment /əkʌ́mpənɪmənt/ enviously /énvɪəsli/.

ɪ as in *city:* kitchen /kítʃɪn/; religious /rɪlídʒəs/.

Silent letters: heir /eə/; heiress /éərəs/ or /éərɪs/.

ŋg as in *finger:* younger /jʌ́ŋgə/; youngest /jʌ́ŋgɪst/.

Others: search /sɜ:tʃ/; throughout /θru:áʊt/; thatched /θætʃt/;
couple /kʌ́pl/; mourning /mɔ́:nɪŋ/; eyed /aɪd/;
quarter /kwɔ́:tə/; eagerly /í:gəli/; necessity /nɪsésɪti/;
spared /speəd/.

Grammatical and structural points

(a) He *went* to Scotland last week (and is probably still there). He *has been* to Scotland (he has visited Scotland at some time).

(b) *one ones* These pronouns can replace a countable noun and so avoid repetition:
He has a large car and I have *a small one*.
Whose is this umbrella? Oh, it's *the one* I lost.
He likes the chocolates with hard centres but she prefers *the ones* with the soft centres.
The ones I like are of course the expensive *ones*.
When an adjective of colour, a comparative or a superlative is used, *one / ones* can often be omitted:
He has a red car and I have *a green*. He has the larger and I *the smaller*.

(c) An auxiliary (helping) verb can sometimes avoid the repetition of a verb:
She speaks with a French accent in the same way as her mother *does*.
People still celebrate Christmas as their grandparents *did*.

(d) Notice this construction:
It was while she was living there *that* she met Terry.
Is it where you are born *that* decides your nationality?
It is how you behave in difficulties *that* shows what you are really like.

(e) He was born twenty years *ago*. Not: *for twenty years*. Be careful!

(f) Positions of the body are indicated by the present participle, not the past participle as in some languages: *standing* on a chair; *sitting* in a deck chair; *leaning* against a wall; *kneeling* in church; *crouching*, ready to spring.

(g) *He enjoyed the party* Not: *He enjoyed at the party*. *enjoy* must have an object: He *enjoyed himself* at the party.

59

(h) **Verbal constructions**
Infinitive: hope to be; went to England *to take up* (Purpose).
Gerund: (a) used as nouns for names of actions: *dancing, singing, gossiping*.
(b) after a preposition: *before getting, the necessity of undertaking*.
(c) The adjectives *busy* and *worth* are followed by a gerund: *busy writing letters; Is it worth going to town now?*
(d) *start saving* (*start to save* is also possible).
(e) Meaning change: *They are thinking of buying*: they have this idea in mind and may well carry it out. *They think there will soon be a water shortage*: they think this will happen.

Prepositions

(a) *at* school (learning), *at* church (worshipping), *in* prison (as a prisoner), *at* the theatre (seeing a play), *at* the cinema (seeing a film), *in* hospital (as a patient).
But: *in* the school, *in* the church, *in* the prison, *in* the theatre, *in* the cinema, *in* the hospital: visiting the building for some purpose.

(b) *over* suggests movement: Birds fly *over* the town. *above* suggests position: The sun is now *above* the horizon. *over* is however often also used for position: the light *over* the table. *above* usually suggests a contrast: above and not below, higher than.

(c) *in* the fields, *in* the country, work *in* a factory, *in* search of, join *in* the dancing (But: join a club).

(d) *at* the same time.

(e) take people *for* a drive/a walk; long *for* his home.

(f) return *from* school; drink beer *from* (out of) a bottle.

(g) the necessity *of* undertaking. (h) hung *with* pictures. (i) heir *to*.

(j) *throughout* her life. (k) lean *against* a wall.

Expressions for use in written work

(a) *throughout* (all through) most of her life/the night/his speech.
(b) *It was* while she was living there *that . . .*
(c) *perform* a ceremony.
(d) Forty people *were crowded into* the kitchen.
(e) The cars *set out* again (for . . .)
(f) *appeared a little self-conscious.*
(g) *in their Sunday best.*
(h) *by the time I arrived . . .*
(i) Drinks were being *handed round.*
(j) We all *joined in* the chorus.
(k) *take time off* from.
(l) *to the accompaniment of.*
(m) *carefully-prepared speeches.*
(n) *sit up* all night.

Spoken English

Short answers: To, so

Most of the verbs in the answers below can be followed by an infinitive and possibly additional words. However if the infinitive meaning is already clear, it need not be repeated.

Study carefully these examples:
(a) Are you taking your exam next year?
  I'd like to. I want to. I hope to. I intend to. I ought to.
  If I can manage to. If I'm able to. If I'm allowed to.

(b) May I use this dictionary of yours?
       Yes, I've already recommended/advised/told you to.

(c) Does he actually work twelve hours a day?
       He seems to. He appears to. He tries to. He likes to. He has to.
       He needs to. He pretends to. No, he refuses to.

(d) Is he being helpful to you?
       He's trying to (be).

(e) So you're buying a car after all.
       Oh, well, my wife persuaded me to.

(f) Could you help me, please?
       Yes, I'd be pleased to.

Other possibilities:
(g) Is it going to be warm tomorrow?
       I hope so. I hope not. I think/believe so. I don't think/believe so.

(h) Must we pay to go in?
       I suppose so. I don't suppose so. They say so.

(i) He often ignores what you say because he is slightly deaf.
       Oh, I see.

(j) You really must try to control your temper.
       Yes, I know.

Practice

Answer these remarks and questions, each in a different way, using the
forms suggested above.

1   Are you going skiing next winter?
2   Is Douglas buying a sports car?
3   Can you come to lunch next Saturday?
4   May I come to your lectures?
5   Is the sea warm enough for swimming?
6   Does she really clean her husband's shoes?
7   There are no trains because there's a strike.
8   Is your young sister going alone to England next year?
9   Must we give them a wedding present?
10 Will we have to pay duty on our new watches?
11 Does he really understand Anglo-Saxon poetry?
12 Could you help me with this suitcase, please?

**Giving, accepting
and refusing
invitations on the
telephone**

A   Is that Judy? Oh, hallo Judy. How are you? I do hope you're free next
     Saturday. We're giving a party to celebrate our second wedding anni-
     versary. Cheese and wine and maybe some dancing to records. All
     quite informal, so wear what you like. You will be able to come, won't
     you? (We should be so pleased if you can come. We should so like you
     to come.)

B   I'd love to come. What time would you like me to turn up?

or   Oh, what a pity! I'd love to have come, but it's my father's birthday
     on Saturday and he'd be terribly disappointed if I didn't spend the
     weekend at home. I *am* sorry.

Saying goodbye

A Oh, I hadn't realised how late it was. I'm afraid I'll have to be going.

B Oh, not yet. I'm just going to make some coffee.

A I'm sorry, but I must, though I'd really love to stay. I've got to be up by six tomorrow morning, unfortunately. Thank you for a wonderful party.

Conversation at a party

A and **B**, who are strangers to one another, get into conversation.

B Hallo, I'm Brian Chester. Let me get you some more to drink.

A Not at the moment, thank you. I'm André Laporte. Is London your home?

B No, I come from Wells, in the West Country. You speak English extremely well. Are you French?

A No, Belgian. My mother's English, though. Have you ever been to Belgium?

B Many times. I have to travel to Brussels for my firm. I'm a sales representative. How long have you been in England?

A Since September. I'm working in a hotel as part of my hotel management training. I've been a waiter, assistant cook, receptionist, secretary: what else? I can hardly remember. Later I'll be taking a course in hotel management.

B So you haven't had time to see much outside London.

A Oh, I've spent two or three holidays in England with my mother's relations who live in the Midlands so I've got to know Oxford and Cambridge, Stratford and various other places fairly well.

B Where's your home in Belgium?

A Originally in Liège, though we recently moved to Antwerp. My father has taken over a hotel there not far from the town centre. I hardly know anything about the town yet as I was helping most of the time in the hotel before I came to England.

B I'm in Antwerp occasionally for my firm. Maybe I'll try your hotel next time I'm there, if you can give me the name.

A Here's a card. And do tell my father you've met me. Tell him also that I'm behaving myself. No time not to, really.

Reading comprehension

Choice of words

In this exercise you must choose the word or phrase which best completes each sentence.

1 The police must now _____ the escaped convict in the surrounding counties.
   A search   **B** look after   **C** look for   **D** investigate

2 Your grandfather is rather tired so do not _____ your visit.
   A prolong   **B** lengthen   **C** delay   **D** shorten

3 As we can wait no longer for the delivery of your order, we have to _____ it.
   A postpone   **B** refuse   **C** delay   **D** cancel

4 He has recently got an interesting _____ in a textile factory.
   A job   **B** employment   **C** work   **D** occupation

5 Only thoroughly unpleasant people leave the _____ of their picnics to spoil the appearance of the countryside.
 A remains   B remainder   C rest   D remnants

6 Many of the earliest _____ into the United States established large plantations.
 A exiles   B immigrants   C migrants   D emigrants

7 The judge said that he was _____ by the high standards of performance of the riders.
 A excited   B impressed   C interested   D touched

8 The sky looks lighter. I think the weather is _____.
 A clearing away   B clearing   C becoming clearer
 D clearing up

9 If I had more time, I should _____ golf as a hobby.
 A take to   B take on   C take over   D take up

10 You can _____ your shorthand ability by taking notes in shorthand during lectures.
 A keep on   B keep in   C keep up   D keep

Multiple choice responses

Read the passage carefully before dealing with the questions and statements that follow it.

In Britain arrangements for inviting and entertaining guests at a wedding are usually the responsibility of the bride's family. In most cases it is mainly friends and relations of both families who are invited but when the bride's father is a businessman of some kind, the wedding reception may
5 provide a useful occasion for establishing social connections with clients or customers and other people whose goodwill may be of advantage to him. It is, however, the bride's mother who has the job of sending out the formal printed invitation cards.

 In the case of a church wedding, the vicar of each parish in which the
10 bride and bridegroom lives is normally informed about a month in advance of the ceremony so that an announcement of the coming wedding can be made in church on each of three Sundays before it takes place. Anyone who may know of an existing marriage of either partner is ordered to give information about it, though this means of avoiding bigamy must
15 have been more effective in the days when people moved about the world less than they do today. Often up to a hundred or more people attend the religious service and the bride usually wears the traditional long white dress and veil, while her bridesmaids, who are often children, wear long dresses in attractive colours. This may also happen in the case of a civil
20 wedding in a register office but is probably less usual.

 The reception which follows may be held in a restaurant, a local hall or, when there are few guests, in the bride's own home. Refreshments are provided, a special iced wedding-cake is cut (usually to the accompaniment of speeches) and distributed to the guests, toasts are drunk and
25 dancing may follow. At some point in the celebrations, the bride goes off to change into everyday clothes and then leaves the party with her husband to go on their honeymoon, the journey they will make together, often in romantic surroundings abroad.

Here are a number of questions or unfinished statements about the passage, each with four suggested ways of answering or finishing it. Choose the one you think fits best in each case.

1 It is the bride's parents who normally have to
  A make all the arrangements for the wedding.
  B provide hospitality for the people attending.
  C decide who shall be invited.
  D pay all the expenses involved.

2 According to the passage some guests may be invited because
  A they are likely to be annoyed if they are not.
  B they may give valuable presents.
  C their presence could provide future benefits.
  D they may help with the expenses of the wedding.

3 Why are the arrangements for a church wedding usually made some time before?
  A To allow the necessary length of time for publicising the wedding.
  B To provide time for organising the reception.
  C To make sure that the guests can arrange to be free on the day.
  D To ensure a thorough investigation of the couple's existing marital status.

4 What possible difference is suggested between a church and a civil wedding?
  A Civil weddings are less commonly followed by a reception.
  B It is less usual for guests to attend the civil wedding formalities.
  C Guests at civil weddings are less formally dressed.
  D There could be less attention paid at the latter to convention and picturesque effect.

5 The reception normally takes place in the bride's home if
  A this is a large one.
  B there is enough room to entertain the people invited.
  C the parents cannot afford to hire a hall.
  D there is to be no party afterwards.

6 The couple leave for their honeymoon
  A after the church or register office ceremony.
  B immediately after the cake has been cut and the speeches made.
  C at the end of the reception.
  D as soon as the bride is ready to leave.

Composition

Narrative

A narrative composition can be one of two kinds.

The first is an exact account of what happened: a report of some national or local event appearing in a newspaper, the facts of a crime given in a police court, the details of an accident or some similar record. In this kind of account it is important to state all the facts quite correctly and in the most suitable order — usually the order in which they happened. But only these facts are given and unnecessary description and imaginative impressions have no place.

The second is a story. The intention is to interest the reader, to make him want to go on reading. The writer chooses the details which help to create the impression he wants to give, builds up interest to an important moment and includes some description to make the story more vivid.

Here is an example of this second kind of narrative:

While you were waiting for a train on a station platform, something very unusual happened. Relate what it was in 120–180 words.

Plan

1   The background — miserable people on the platform.
2   The performance.
3   The effect.

It was just after five and the platform was already half filled with people on their way home from work. Most of them looked miserable or perhaps they were just tired. Some were reading newspapers. A few were standing in groups but nobody seemed to be talking. The train was due in five minutes.

Suddenly there was a movement. Two men took off their overcoats and handed them to two women standing near. Then they asked people to move back, and spread newspapers on the ground. 'Watch, everybody,' shouted one, and he jumped straight on to the other's shoulders. A wonderful acrobatic display followed: jumping, balancing, swinging, tumbling. People crowded round watching them: others who could not see properly started talking to strangers, asking what was happening and wondering why.

Immediately they heard the train approaching, the men picked up the newspapers and put on their overcoats. 'Well,' said one, 'I hope you all feel a bit more cheerful now. Life isn't all that bad, you know.' And the people got into the train actually smiling.   *(176 words)*

Practice

Exact account (120–180 words)

1   You have had some kind of accident in your home. Relate what you were doing at the time, what happened and the results.

2   You have to prepare an account of any one of the following incidents for a radio news bulletin. Choose one of the subjects and write the account.
   (a)   A famous person has made an official visit to your town.
   (b)   An important local building has been damaged by fire.
   (c)   A crowd of people have marched to the Town Hall to protest about some unsatisfactory thing in the town.

3   As he passes a shop, Police Constable Wright sees a light moving inside. He goes to investigate. Write the constable's report of the whole incident.

4   There is a statue of a well-known person in a town market-place. Write a passage for the town guide-book explaining who the person is and how he or she became famous.

Stories (120–180 words)

1   How I missed the train.

2   You were taking a neighbour's dog for a walk on a lead. Suddenly he saw another dog and pulled so sharply that he escaped. Tell the story of what happened until you caught him.

3 You were walking down an empty street very late at night when you met an elephant. Relate what happened.

4 A dream in which you found yourself doing something impossible.

Use of English

1 **Fill each of the numbered blanks in the passage with a suitable word.**

When I at last _____(1) the town, I felt _____(2) tired to go in _____(3) of a room at once so I went into the _____(4) restaurant to where I had parked my car and sat down _____(5) a table. A waitress was clearing _____(6) the _____(7) of a meal which must have _____(8) eaten by at _____(9) forty people. She gave me a menu which I examined for a minute and I then _____(10) from her fried chicken and salad and a glass of wine. The waitress _____(11) the wine at once but I had to wait a long time _____(12) the _____(13) of the meal. When it came, there was so much on the plate _____(14) it must have _____ (15) a whole bird. I _____(16) a little first and it was _____ (17) delicious that I ate all of it. I was now neither hungry _____ (18) thirsty and as a _____(19) of fact, I was no _____(20) tired _____(21).

2 **Finish each of the following sentences in such a way that it means exactly the same as the sentence printed before it.**
   Example: The mountain roads are impassable because of heavy snow.
            Heavy _____.
   Answer: Heavy snow has made the mountain roads impassable.

   1 He is back from York after three days there.
     He has been _____
   2 He wrote that book during his holiday in Wales.
     It was while _____
   3 Christopher and his father can walk equally long distances.
     Christopher can _____
   4 It started raining last Friday and has not yet stopped.
     It has _____
   5 The market is less crowded than usual today.
     The market is not _____
   6 He cannot speak because he is so angry.
     He is too _____
   7 He came home in a taxi.
     A taxi _____
   8 Jane was standing outside a shop when I saw her.
     I saw _____

3 (a) **Complete the following sentences with an appropriate word for a form of FOOTWEAR.**
   1 Anyone intending to go climbing should wear strong mountain _____.
   2 Mrs Click still insists on knitting the woollen _____ her three sons wear when they play football.
   3 He changes into a pair of comfortable fur-lined _____ as soon as he gets home from work.

66

4   A lot of women wear open-toed and backless _____ in summer.

3 (b)   Complete the following sentences with an appropriate word which has a similar meaning to CARRY.
1   The students were asked to _BRING_ a bus timetable to the following lesson.
2   This letter has been _DELIVERED_ at the wrong address.
3   The dog jumped into the water to _FETCH_ a stick his master had thrown there.
4   It's going to rain so _TAKE_ an umbrella with you when you go out.

3 (c)   Complete the following sentences with an appropriate word for a form of LINE.
1   A _ROPE_ was thrown ashore when the boat came alongside the quay.
2   There was a heavy crash as the _____ the picture was hanging from snapped in two.
3   I need some _STRING_ to tie up this parcel with.
4   Most housewives keep a needle and _THREAD_ handy in case something needs mending in a hurry.

3 (d)   Complete the following sentences with an appropriate word for a PERSON WHO MOVES.
1   The authorities are discouraging new _IMMIGRANTS_ who want to enter the country as there aren't enough jobs for them.
2   This bird is only a summer _MIGRANT_: it spends the winter in a warmer climate.
3   All _PASSANGERS_ must show their tickets at the barrier.
4   A century ago _____ in this area might be attacked and robbed by bandits.

4   **You have received four invitations for next Saturday, three at least of which sound so attractive that you have some difficulty in deciding which to accept.**

   Using the information given, continue each of the paragraph openings suggested below, stating reasons for your decisions in about 50 words in each case.

   A   A picnic (modern equipment available) with a small group of friends on a lake or sea island — relaxation, swimming, sunbathing — travel by motor-boat.
   B   A cousin's wedding reception   A formal occasion in local hotel: excellent food, dancing, opportunity to meet plenty of friends and relations. You have known your cousin most of your life.
   C   A pop festival some fifty miles away to which you will travel on your own motor-scooter or in your own or a friend's car. Likely to be crowded, noisy and unpredictable possibility of trouble with the police.
   D   A coach excursion with a party of friends to a beautiful historical town with a lot to see, followed by a visit to an open-air theatre there in the evening.

Paragraph openings:
I don't think I would enjoy _____
I'd be rather more enthusiastic about _____
I'd be even more enthusiastic _____
However my actual choice would be _____

Interview

**Talking about a
photograph**

1 What are some of the things that suggest that this might be a quiet
country wedding?
2 Describe some of the spectators.
3 How are most of the people in the picture likely to be spending the next
few hours?
4 Why do passers-by often stop to watch a scene of this kind?

Topics

Suggest some similarities between the wedding arrangements apparent in
this picture and those common in your own country.
Do you enjoy attending weddings and wedding receptions? Why or why
not?
What will probably happen later to the photographs that are being taken?

Reading aloud

Consonant practice

1 In some languages most words end in a vowel. Avoid adding a non-existent vowel to a final consonant in English: e.g. *hat, hand, Don't come home late.*

2 Distinguish between voiceless and voiced consonants:

	p/b	t/d	k/g
Voiceless: (with aspiration)	pop	tatter	kick
Voiced:	bob	dad	big

	f/v	θ/ð	s/z	ʃ/ʒ	tʃ/dʒ
Voiceless:	puff	thin	soup	shake	church
Voiced:	vivid	this	zoo	measure	jerk

3 Distinguish between /v/ and /w/: *vine/wine avoid/away   wave*

4 Remember to pronounce /h/ except in the few cases where it is silent: **H**is **h**ouse is **h**alf an hour from **h**ere. (For omission of /h/ in unstressed auxiliaries see p. 112.)

5 /r/ in Southern English is forward, not guttural as often in German. It can be rolled slightly if the frontal vowel proves difficult.

6 Light /l/ (tongue-tip forward) starts a syllable: *eleven lovely lilies.* Dark /l/ (tongue-tip drawn back) is used elsewhere: *twelve gold balls.*

Passages

Practice consonants in separate words before reading each passage aloud. Suggest a situation in which you might hear the passage spoken.

1 Yesterday I got some information from a local estate agent about two houses for sale. One's near the town centre but it's old-fashioned, in a poor condition and rather expensive. The other's in a village in the surrounding area. It's completely modernised with central heating and other recently-installed equipment, has a large kitchen where we could have breakfast, a sitting-room that we could make very comfortable and a garden suitable for growing fruit and vegetables.

2 The first Saturday in August, you say? Oh, what a pity! I can't possibly manage that day as we'll be on holiday then, or at least that's the day we'll be travelling. Yes, we're flying to Japan and we're looking forward to it enormously. It will be my first experience of such distant parts. My husband has suggested the idea though I suppose he'll want to combine business with pleasure while he's there.

3 It's my opinion this will be the most disastrous harvest of the century. Continuous rain and cold and it's little better now. Potatoes may benefit perhaps and the orchards won't do too badly. But the grain crops are almost ruined already. What a climate! And I've got a suspicion the Government's thinking of reducing the butter subsidies. Transferring them to the needs of big business I shouldn't wonder. All those overpaid officials, ignorant of everything but their own benefit!

Structured communication

Discussion of a birthday celebration

One of a group of friends has a birthday in a few days' time and is discussing with them the best way to celebrate it together. They could go to the theatre, have a meal in a restaurant, spend the evening at a disco, organise a party in someone's house, or go to the seaside or some other resort for the day.

Each of three or four students (one of whom is the 'birthday' boy or girl) chooses a different form of celebration, tries to convince the others that it is the best and defends it against the others' criticisms.

Situational responses

1   You have been invited alone to a reception organised for international students but find that the various groups of people around you are all chattering in their own languages, none of which you understand. Finally you discover a small group speaking English. Introduce yourself to them, tell them a little about yourself and discover a little about each of them. (3 or 4 participants)

2   One student invites another to accompany him/her to a party. The person asked is not an enthusiastic party-goer and asks various questions about the kind of party it will be, people likely to be there, where it will be and how long it will last etc. before deciding from the information given whether to accept or refuse the invitation.

Expressing opinions

1   What do you consider the ideal length of time for a couple to be engaged? Suggest some reasons.

2   Argue the case for and against an expensive wedding celebration with many guests.

Talking about weekend study courses

Various weekend courses on subjects of general interest are organised in Britain. The participants usually spend the weekend in a large comfortable house often in pleasant countryside surroundings.

Here is a suggested programme for one of these educational centres.

APRIL	
4 – 6	Introduction to the Home Computer
11 – 13	Creative Writing
18 – 20	Keep Fit
25 – 27	The Countryside in Spring
MAY	
2 – 4	Workshop for the Amateur Actor and Producer
9 – 11	Painting Portraits
16 – 18	Ideas on Decorating Your Home
23 – 25	Making the Most of Your Camera
30 – 2	Explorations in the World of Opera

As a student who has attended one of the above courses, you are telling the other students in your English class about how you spent your time. Before starting, you will probably need a few moments to decide some of the things a course of this kind might cover. Various students can describe other courses they might have attended.

General guidance and practice

1 Past Continuous tense: Active

> **She was living.**
>
> **They were arriving.**

The name of this tense describes its general uses which are:

(a) to indicate the longer of two actions, the action during which something else occurred:
I was crossing the road, when the traffic lights changed.
The ghost appeared as the clock was striking twelve.

(b) to indicate two actions occurring at the same time and covering a period of time:
I was trying to do some translation while he was watching television.

(c) to emphasise that an action covered a period of time:
All day yesterday I was working in the garden.

(d) Just as the Present Continuous can express an action extending through the point 'now', 'at this time', so the Past Continuous can express an action extending through a definite point 'then', 'at that time':
This time last week, I was still enjoying my holiday.

The following uses are less common and can be studied later if this is preferred.

(e) The Past Continuous can express an intended action which never happened, principally with the verbs *go, come, intend, expect, look forward to, plan, and arrange.*
She was coming to lunch yesterday, but unfortunately she was ill.

(f) The Past Continuous may be used for an action which had not yet started, but was already arranged and sure to happen:
At the airport, I met some friends who were flying to New York.

Verbs that are rarely used in the Present Continuous tense are equally rarely used in the Past Continuous form.

Practice

In the following sentences, use a suitable form of the Present Simple, Present Continuous, Present Perfect Simple, Present Perfect Continuous, Past Simple or Past Continuous tenses:

(a) This time yesterday I (sunbathe) on a Mediterranean beach.
(b) I (meet) him while I (travel) in Italy last year.
(c) It's my birthday today, and I (receive) at least ten presents.
(d) We must have looked very peaceful. My husband (read) and I (knit).
(e) I (speak just) to Mrs White for an hour. Poor woman! The whole time she (tell) me about her many troubles.
(f) As soon as the policeman (see) the stolen car, he (raise) his hand to stop it.
(g) Throughout yesterday's lecture, he (make) detailed notes.
(h) All the time he (explain) that point, I (think) about something else.
(i) He couldn't stop to talk as he (catch) the next train.
(j) (Understand) you what I (say) when we (discuss) our arrangements for yesterday evening?

(k)   As the first drops of rain (start) to fall, everybody who (watch) the procession (put) up an umbrella.

(l)   An hour ago, while the guests (put) on their hats and coats, they (chat) about their next meeting.

(m)   My husband is lazy. Yesterday, when I (think) he (work) in the garden, he (sit) in a deck chair asleep.

2   Passives: Past Continuous and Simple Infinitive

> Past Continuous: Passive
>
> **It was being cleaned.**
>
> **They were being cleaned.**

> Simple Infinitive: Passive
>
> **I want this** *to be repaired* **at once.**
>
> **He left his suit** *to be cleaned.*

Practice

The verbs in most of the following sentences are in various tenses of the Active Voice. Rewrite the sentences using, in each case, the same tense of the Passive Voice. A Passive Infinitive is needed in three sentences. Do not include the agent unless it is clear who or what it is.

(a)   Bees make honey.
(b)   They have arrested the thief.
(c)   An unemployed labourer was repairing my roof.
(d)   Floods swept away the wooden bridge.
(e)   They were drinking toasts.
(f)   They closed the shop at one o'clock.
(g)   Prisoners are building the new road.
(h)   The Mayor is judging the fancy dress parade.
(i)   They ought to finish this job by tomorrow. *(Infinitive)*
(j)   A fourteen-year-old boy was driving the car.
(k)   An unknown artist is to paint the King's portrait. *(Infinitive)*
(l)   Mice must have eaten the cheese that the maid left out on the table. *(Two verbs. Change the order of the two parts of the sentence.)*

3   Used to, would

> He used to live.   They used to sing.
> He used not to live.   They used not to sing.

The interrogative form is not common: usually the past simple *Did he live?* or more rarely the expression *Was he in the habit of singing?* is preferred.

Used to suggests:
(a)   that the action was repeated or continuous over a fairly long period,
(b)   that it no longer takes place, or its continuation is surprising.
(c)   that it happened some time ago.
    Don't you want any chocolates? You used to like them.
    When he had more time than now, he used to write long letters to the newspapers.

Notice the word order in: *He often used to write.*

The auxiliary *would* may be used to give a similar meaning. But this usually suggests that the action was deliberate or intended, and the time when it happened is generally mentioned or suggested in some way:

When I was abroad, I would read as many newspapers as possible.

Notice the difference between:

When he was a child he used to (not *would*) *live in the country.*
When he was travelling in other countries, he would always live with local families.

Practice

Use the form *used to* or *would* (or both where suitable) in the following sentences:

(a) The days (seem) much longer than they do now.
(b) Our postman (knock) loudly on our door; now he merely slips the letters through the letter-box.
(c) When I had more money, I (often travel) by taxi in London.
(d) When I was a child and asked my father questions, he (answer) them in great detail.
(e) These old houses (be) very fashionable, and a few of them still are.
(f) In the eighteenth century writers (spend) hours in coffee houses, discussing the news of the day.

4 Am to, was to

Present forms	Past forms
I am to attend.	**I said he was to listen.**
He is not to go.	**It was decided they were to learn.**
They are to obey.	**The results were to have been announced**
Are we to give it back?	**yesterday, but we have heard nothing.**

This use of the verb 'to be' with the infinitive expresses a very firm arrangement and may be a form of command that will accept no refusal:

I am to see the director this afternoon.
You are to keep quiet.
No expense is to be spared.

The past form often appears in reported speech:

The teacher told the students that they were to stop talking.

The fact that the arrangement was not observed may be suggested by the use of a following perfect infinitive:

He was to have finished it by yesterday. (but he did not)

Practice

Rewrite each of these sentences so as to use one of the forms explained above.

(a) I have ordered anyone who disobeys to be punished.
(b) Be home early without fail.
(c) He told me to report to the Police Station.
(d) The doctor says that relaxation is important for me.
(e) We thought we would get our passports last week but they were not ready.
(f) Do not tell him anything.

(g) Must my essay be finished by tomorrow?
(h) The new regulations will be introduced by next week.
(i) The examination will be held in June.

5 While, as, when

While, when

The two following examples illustrate the difference in meaning between conjunctions

While she was doing the washing-up, she was planning her holiday.

When she did the washing-up, she used soap-powder.

While suggests that the action took enough time to complete to allow something else to happen while it was going on. It really means 'during the time that'.

When, As

As I was approaching the house, the door opened.

When I got to the door I knocked three times.

As usually indicates 'at the exact moment that'. The two things happen simultaneously.

When

(a) This may mean 'whenever' as in the first example given.

(b) It often indicates an action which is followed immediately or quite soon after by another action as in the second example.

Some other examples

While the queue was moving into the theatre, the old man still went on singing.

As the queue passed through the door, the attendant counted the number of people in it.

When there was a queue outside the theatre, a man selling peanuts always appeared.

When he had taken his place in the queue, he started eating his sandwiches.

In everyday use the three conjunctions are often used interchangeably. Notice that *while* can also have the meaning 'although' and *as* can also have the meaning 'because'.

Practice

Use *while, as* or *when* in the following sentences. In some cases more than one form may be used, with different meanings.

(a) _____ he comes tomorrow, I shall ask him where he has been.
(b) _____ he was speaking, everybody listened silently.
(c) _____ he spoke to people, he seemed nervous.
(d) _____ the National Anthem was being played, the audience all stood to attention.
(e) _____ the door slowly opened, there was a hysterical scream of terror.
(f) _____ the car passed I recognised the driver.
(g) I cannot allow you to whistle _____ you are doing an examination.
(h) Enjoy yourself _____ you are young.
(i) Come to me _____ you have finished.
(j) Have a good look at that man _____ you pass him.
(k) Peter is a wrestler _____ his twin brother Paul is an artist.
(l) _____ he wants to pass his test, he is taking driving lessons.

6 Comparisons

Comparisons of equality

(a) His scientific discoveries have been *as important as* those of Sir Isaac Newton.
   The doctor came *as soon as* he could.

(b) He is *not so clever as* I expected.

(c) *as* may be used instead of *so* in negative comparisons. It is rather more common in the negative comparison of adverbs: He doesn't speak *as fluently as* he should. He can't run *as quickly as* his brother.

The formation of comparative and superlative forms

(These rules are mainly for reference.)

(a) *-er* and *-est* are added to the adjective (with certain spelling changes) when:
   (i) The adjective consists of only one syllable, e.g. *long, longer; big, biggest.*
       Notice: *far, farther, farthest* (or *further, furthest*).
   (ii) A two-syllabled adjective ends in: -y (changed to -i), -le, -er (exceptions: eager, tender), and -ow, e.g. *happier, humblest, cleverer, narrowest.*

(b) Remember the irregulars:
   good better best; bad worse worst;
   little less least; much more most.

(c) *more* and *most* precede the adjective when:
   (i) The adjective consists of more than two syllables: *more comfortable; most generous.*
   (ii) The adjective is a participle: *more tiring; most tired.*
   (iii) The adjective ends in the suffix: -ful (*harmful*), -less (*harmless*), -ant (*distant*), -ent (*silent*), -est (*honest*), -al (*central*), -id (*timid*), -ish (*foolish*), -ive (*active*), -ous (*jealous*), -ward (*awkward*), -emn (*solemn*), -age (*savage*), -ed (*sacred*).
   (iv) The adjective has a negative prefix, e.g. *kind, kinder; unkind, more unkind* (though *unkindest* is found).

(d) Both forms: *commoner, commonest* and *more common, most common* exist. Also: *politer, politest* and *more polite, most polite.*

(e) A superlative adjective or adverb is preceded by *the*: *the last train   the most intelligent   the most fluently. Most* is occasionally used with the meaning 'very' before a few adjectives. It is not then preceded by *the*: *a most interesting story*

(f) Adverbs always have comparative and superlative forms with more and most respectively.

Practice

Use the correct form of comparison in the following sentences. There may be some spelling changes:

(a) A bicycle is not (_____ fast _____) a car.
(b) An elephant is (big _____) a camel.
(c) To a European, Chinese is (_____ difficult _____) French.
(d) A vegetable is not (_____ beautiful _____) a flower, but it is (_____ useful).
(e) An apple tree is seldom (_____ tall _____) an oak tree.

(f) She is much (pretty _____) her sister, but is not (_____ attractive _____) her charming mother.

(g) Try to write (_____ much _____) possible.

(h) A boy usually runs (_____ quickly _____) a girl.

(i) Do you agree that men are usually (_____ impatient _____) women?

(j) Nothing is (bad _____) arriving late at a (_____ important) meeting in shoes that squeak as one walks to one's place.

(k) That is the (_____ extraordinary) idea I have ever heard.

7 Prepositions

Practice

Use a suitable preposition or particle in each of the following sentences:

(a) People started coming at six o'clock and _____ half past six the hall was full.

(b) I am so tired, I am longing _____ some sleep.

(c) The driver was leaning _____ the side of the bus.

(d) All the guests joined _____ the dancing.

(e) The letter should be addressed _____ this way.

(f) May I have a day _____ to visit my mother?

(g) The snow remained _____ the winter.

(h) He is the heir _____ his father's estate.

(i) Can you write with both hands _____ the same time?

(j) When English coach tourists arrive _____ an interesting town, most of them go off in search _____ a cup of tea.

(k) I am not sure whether Dr. Wright has returned _____ his holiday yet.

4   A Gentle Nightmare

The dream changed. For hours, it seemed, I had been wandering aimlessly through a silent forest of pine trees; now I was alone in a small boat which was drifting along lazily, past tree-covered islands, whose bare rocky edges rose abruptly from the transparent water. I was being carried
5   between grassy banks where meadows sprinkled with buttercups sloped to the river. Soft fluffy clouds were reflected in the velvet surface of the water. The current must have been steady and strong, for the boat kept moving forward smoothly, without meeting any obstacle, as though it were being steered by some invisible hand.
10   Soothed by the peace of my journey, I had lost all count of time but eventually I became aware that the boat was gliding slowly towards the bank. At this point, where a narrow stretch of silver sand was bounded on either side by heaped granite boulders, an old man was standing, his hand shading his eyes. As the boat ran aground, he came up to me, held out his
15   hand, and greeted me courteously.

'You have reached us at last. We have been expecting you for so long. Would you follow me, please.'

I hesitated there for a moment. I had suddenly felt a chill conviction of danger, a shiver that suggested overwhelming evil. Yet this old man with
20   the sensitive delicate features seemed kindly and gracious. He had noticed my suspicion and he smiled at me reassuringly.

'You need not be afraid,' he murmured. 'You are deeply respected, indeed reverenced, by us all. Everything has been prepared for you. We have done everything in our power to honour you. Now please come with
25   me to the place chosen for you.'

I dared not risk offending him. But for reasons I cannot explain, I avoided touching his hand outstretched to assist me as I stepped out of the boat, and I followed him reluctantly.

Our feet sank into the yielding sand as we made our way towards a low
30   flight of marble steps which led up from the beach. The steps had been polished so skilfully that they seemed to glow in soft shades of rose, lilac and ivory. At the top my guide paused and looked back at me. I gasped in amazement at the incredible beauty of the scene which lay before me at that moment. And again I shivered involuntarily with an inexplicable
35   dread.

Notes on the passage

Vocabulary   *Title*   *a nightmare* = a bad dream. a *nightmarish* journey. *have* a dream (Not: *see*). *a daydream* = a fantasy.

1   *wander* wherever one feels like it. Also: *wander* from the point when speaking about something.

stray = leave a group and get lost: A sheep *strays* from the flock. *stray* (Adj) = without a home: *a stray cat. go astray* = go off the right path with the result of getting into trouble: *The student was soon led astray by his new friends.*

ramble (N and V) = a walk in the countryside, often in an organised group; old people sometimes *ramble* (talk in a wandering way) when speaking. a *rambling* house = one without careful planning that spreads anywhere.

2   *a pine tree* is a coniferous tree (a *conifer*), so-called because its fruit is a *cone*. Other conifers, which have needles, not leaves, are *fir* or *spruce* (Christmas) trees. *Oaks, beeches, birches* and *elms* have leaves.

2   *alone   alive   asleep   afraid   awake*   are used only predicatively, that is to say, they never precede the noun. *alone* = on one's own. *lonely* = unhappy because of being alone (N *loneliness*). Dare you stay in this *solitary* house? (N *solitude*). His grandfather is still *alive*. He is one of the greatest *living* novelists.
The cat is now *asleep*. The *sleeping* cat sprawled across the rug.
Some people are *afraid* of snakes. The *frightened* child dared not touch the dog. He is still *awake*. (No other adjective has the same meaning. One would say: The old lady, *who was still awake*, heard quiet footsteps outside.) The same is true of *ajar* (a little open): We could hear voices through the door, *which was ajar* (opp. *wide open*). *aloud* (Adv): *Read this aloud* (so as to be heard). *audible* (Adj): *You must read in a more audible voice.* Notice: I *fell asleep* at half past nine. Not: *I slept at half past nine.*

2   *boat* and *ship* can both be larger vessels. But: travel *by boat* (not *by ship*). Smaller vessels are usually boats: *a rowing boat, a motor boat, a speedboat, a fishing boat. Cargo boats* can be quite large. *A ferry* is also a boat.

3   Spelling: *past* (N); (Adj) the *past* week; (Adv) he walked *past*; (Prep) he walked *past* the school. *passed* (V): he *passed* the examination (Past Simple); he has *passed* the finishing-line (Past Participle).

3   *tree-covered   grass/fur/paper-covered. A paperback* = a book usually sold more cheaply because it has a limp and not a stiff cover.

3   *bare   bareheaded   barefooted   barelegged*   The *bare* branches of trees. An unclothed person is *naked. barely, scarcely, hardly* are all adverbs with almost the same meaning: *I earn barely (scarcely, hardly) enough to live on.*

4   he spoke *abruptly* (without politeness); he spoke *sharply* (angrily); he spoke *bluntly* (without trying to soften his words). He stopped *abruptly* (suddenly).

4   *transparent* glass; a *translucent* or *frosted* bathroom window; an *opaque* wall.

5   *sprinkle* very small pieces or drops of liquid: *a sugar-sprinkler, a water-sprinkler* for the lawn in dry weather.
scatter things in all directions: *scatter* crumbs for the birds; a *scatter-brained* person = one who very often forgets things; *scattered* villages.
spray (V and N) = force tiny drops out of something: *spray roses*, (N) *sea spray, hair spray.*

5   Common wild flowers: *buttercup, daisy, dandelion, primrose, violet.*

5   *sloped   a steep/gradual slope.*

6   Some materials: *velvet* (Adj *velvety*), *wool* (Adj *woollen*), *cotton, linen, silk* (Adj *silky*). Apart from *woollen* it is the Nouns that refer to the material: *velvet curtains, a silk scarf.*

7   *steady* = uninterrupted, regular, reliable: *a steady worker/job.* A ladder must be *steady* before a person can climb it.

8   An *obstacle obstructs* (gets in the way of) progress. A *hindrance hinders* or delays progress.

9   *steer* a boat or a car   *steering-wheel.*

10   Spelling: *peace* (*peaceful*) and *piece.*

11   be/become *aware* that (of); be *unaware* of danger; *unawares* (Adj): *The photographer caught him unawares* (not expecting this).

11 *glide* = move smoothly: *The gulls glided above the ship. glider* (N) = a kind of aeroplane without an engine.
slip = lose one's footing and possibly fall: *He slipped and fell on the frozen snow.*
slide = move forward quickly over a slippery surface: *slide on an ice-covered lake.*
skid (N and V) A car may *skid* when it unexpectedly changes direction.

12 *bank* of a river; *shore* of a lake or the sea; *beach* = where people can sit by a lake or the sea, often sandy; *coast* = where the land meets the sea. *fish from a bank; swim to the shore; lie on the beach; the coast of Wales.*

12 *narrow* has two opposites: *wide* and *broad.*

12 *bounded* = with a limit to it; a *boundary* of property/a village/a county; a *border* between two states: *the Scottish border;* a *frontier* = the official dividing line between two countries.

13 *heaped* A *heap* is a collection of things without arrangement; a *pile* of things, one on top of the other; a *heap* of cut grass; a *pile* of books.

13 an enormous *boulder;* a grey *stone;* many small *pebbles. gravel* is a collection of tiny pebbles and sand.

14 *shading* A *shadow* is normally of one object and has a shape. *shade* (Unc N) is an area where there is protection from the sun. *a sunshade, a lampshade, eye-shadow.* One *shades* a drawing (*shading*), one *shadows* (follows secretly) a person.

14 *run aground   run ashore   be adrift.*

15 *courteous   discourteous;   polite   impolite.*

16 I *waited* half an hour *for* him as I had *expected* him to arrive earlier.

18 A *chill* can also be a kind of cold: *to have a chill. cool* = pleasantly cold; *chilly* = unpleasantly cool. *the cool shade of trees; a chilly Autumn day. Keep cool!* = Don't panic. *A cool distant manner.*

18 *conviction* has two meanings: (a) *convince* (V) = make a person sure that something is true: *He convinced me he was right; He has strong religious convictions* (Adj *convinced*); (b) *convict* (V and N) = prove guilty of a crime: *He was convicted of blackmail;* a *convict* has usually been in prison several times: *He has several previous convictions.* (See also Special Grammatical and Structural Points, page 83).

19 *shiver* with cold or fear; *shudder* with horror.

19 *overwhelming* One can be *overwhelmed* by work, sorrow, worry, relief.

20 *sensitive* to cold, a *sensitive* artist. A *sensible* person does not usually do *senseless* things, as he uses his *common sense.* The pedestrian lay *insensible* in the road after the accident. He had been driving so dangerously that he must have been *out of his senses.* What you have written *makes no sense.* The mouse *sensed* danger as the cat silently approached.

20 *delicate:* pale blue is *a delicate colour; delicate lace* is made with fine thread; a *delicate child* is often ill; Avoid mentioning his dismissal: it's *a delicate subject.*

20 *feature* (N) = (a) a part of the face; (b) (Sing) a characteristic: *Overcrowding may be a feature of town life;* (c) (Adj) *a feature film.*

20 *kindly* may be part of a request, possibly with some impatience: *Would you kindly be quiet.*

20 a *gracious* and charming elderly lady; a *graceful* ballerina.

20 *notice* (V) something unusual; *remark* that the weather is fine (say something unimportant). *a notice* for people to read; *a remark* about the weather. He *observed* that his friend was ill (said or noticed).

21 *suspicion* If one has *suspicions* about someone's honesty, one is *suspicious* of him and *suspects* that he is not to be trusted.

22 A gentle wind, people in church, distant bees *murmur.* Very distant thunder *mutters;* the old woman *muttered* a curse. The boy who had not learned his lesson *mumbled* indistinctly. The doctor and nurse *whispered* so as not to wake the patient.

22 *respected:* Victorian parents were highly *respected* by their children.
respectful: Their children were usually *respectful* and obedient.
respectable: Can he really be a criminal? He seems such a *respectable* man.
respective: The candidates were interviewed in turn, according to their *respective* qualifications.

26 *offend* someone, possibly by hurting his feelings, so that he behaves coldly; *take offence at* something said = be offended by it.
Parking illegally is a motoring *offence* and anyone who does it is an *offender* against the law.
After being *on the defensive*, the army suddenly *took the offensive*. He was arrested for using *offensive* language to the Mayor, who is a very quiet, *inoffensive* little man.

28 *follow* = walk behind (Not: accompany). May I *take you* (or *go with you*) *to the station?*

28 *reluctantly* opp. *willingly.*

30 *a flight* of birds; *a flight* by aeroplane. (V) *fly, flew, flown.*
a flight from danger (V) *flee, fled, fled.*
a flight of stairs (a number of stairs together).

30 a *marble, stone, brick* wall. Not: *in marble* or *of marble.*

33 *incredible* = unbelievable. *incredulous* = unbelieving.

34 *voluntarily* = of one's own free will. *involuntarily* = without intending to.
a volunteer = someone who says he is ready to do some job willingly.

Kinds of fear

uneasiness   anxiety   worry   nervousness

apprehension and *dread* are both felt when anticipating something one knows will be unpleasant, e.g. a visit to the dentist, an examination. *Dread* is the stronger of the two.

alarm is usually a sudden fear: The news of the approach of the enemy caused *alarm* among the population of the town;
alarming reports; Do not *alarm* the children.

fright has a similar meaning, but refers more to a single experience: The boy jumped out on his sister and *gave her a fright.*

panic is a desperate fear often affecting large groups, and causing uncontrolled behaviour.

terror is very strong fear.

horror is a mixture of fear, disgust and surprise.

Verbs include *to fear, to be afraid of, to be frightened of, to dread, to alarm, to frighten, to terrify, to horrify.*

Phrasal verbs

come   *come across* something when one is not looking for it.
come out = (of flowers) open; (of a newspaper) be published.
come by = obtain.
come round after losing consciousness for a while = recover consciousness.
come off = (of an arrangement or event) happen.
come into money = inherit.
come up to (go up to) someone to speak quietly to him.
come on   come along = hurry.

Practice

(a)   How did you _____ that snuff-box? I came _____ it in an antique shop.
(b)   Give him some brandy when he comes _____.

(c) He has come _____ his uncle's fortune.
(d) Snowdrops usually come _____ in February.
(e) He came _____ me and asked my name.
(f) Come _____; your father's waiting.
(g) Do you think their wedding will ever come _____?
(h) The magazine comes _____ once a week.

Notice also: the play *came to an end*; a bus *came into sight*; his dream *came true*.

<table>
<tr><td>**Pronunciation**</td><td>

Often mispronounced: surface /sɜ́:fɪs/; granite /grǽnɪt/; courteously /kɜ́:tɪəsli/; suggested /sədʒéstɪd/; delicate /délɪkɪt/; suspiciously /səspíʃəsli/.

/ə/ as in *ago:* silent /sáɪlənt/; mirrored /mírəd/; obstacle /ɒ́bskəkl/; featu*res* /fí:tʃəz/; gr*a*cious /gréɪʃəs/; murmu*red* /mɜ́:məd/; *o*ffending /əféndɪŋ/; lil*ac* /láɪlək/; ivory /áɪvəri/; inexplic*a*ble /ɪneksplíkəbl/; t*o*wards /təwɔ́:dz/.

/ɪ/ as in *city:* for*e*st /fɒ́rɪst/; velv*e*t /vélvɪt/.
Silent letters: i*s*lands /áɪləndz/; *h*onour /ɒ́nə/; sce*ne* /si:n/.

Others: wandering /wɒ́ndəriŋ/; covered /kʌ́vəd/; transparent /trænspǽrənt/; meadows /médəʊz/; steady /stédi/; dread /dred/; boulders /bə́ʊldəz/; yielding /jí:ldɪŋ/; involuntarily /ɪnvɒ́ləntərɪli/.
</td></tr>
</table>

Grammatical and structural points

(a) Verbs used intransitively and transitively:
rise rose risen; raise raised
Most verbs can be used both intransitively (with no direct object) and also transitively (with a direct object): *He was reading* and *He was reading a letter*. Some however are always intransitive: *stand, fly, sleep,* and others always transitive, that is, they must have some kind of object: *enjoy, buy, throw (something)*.
Intransitive verbs can have no passive form. *rise* is always intransitive, with no object or passive form. *raise* must have an object.

Which (with a suitable tense form)? (i) My host _____ to greet me. (ii) The people have _____ in rebellion. (iii) A lock _____ the level of water. (iv) Has the cake _____? (v) The Government has _____ the standard of living. (vi) The sun _____ yesterday at seven. (vii) Prices are _____. (viii) The bus companies are _____ their fares.

arise arose arisen (intransitive): *troubles, problems, difficulties arise. arise* is seldom used nowadays to mean *get up*.
Notice: *rise* (N) a rise in prices, in the cost of living; ask one's boss for a *rise*.

lie lay
These two verbs cause confusion even among English speakers.

lie lay lain intransitive with the meaning of 'place oneself (or be) in a flat position'.
Infinitive: I want *to lie* down and sleep.
Present Simple: Italy *lies* to the south of Switzerland.
Present Continuous: The handbag *is lying* on the table.
Future Simple: The snow *will lie* for three or four weeks.
Past Simple: The dog *lay* stretched out before the fire.
Present Perfect: My hat *has lain* on the grass all night.

lay laid laid transitive 'to put', 'to place' (and special meanings).
Infinitive: He had *to lay* the map on the table to study it properly.
Present Simple: He always *lays* his books on the floor.
Present Continuous: The waiter *is laying* the table.

Future Simple: The Mayor *will lay* the foundation stone.
Past Simple: The mother *laid* her baby in the cradle.
Present Perfect: The hen *has laid* an egg.
(Which are the objects of the verbs in this group?)

A completely different verb is *to lie* meaning 'to tell an untruth': *he lies; he is lying; he will lie; he lied; he has lied.*

Which (with a suitable tense form)? (i) A bricklayer _____ bricks. (ii) The cat is _____ on my slippers. (iii) I _____ thinking all last night. (iv) He _____ down his glasses and then could not find them. (v) The baby will now _____ quietly in her pram. (vi) Your ball-point is _____ on the sideboard. (vii) Our hens have _____ twelve eggs. (viii) He has often _____ there for hours, watching the clouds. (ix) The Shetland Isles _____ to the North of Scotland. (x) _____ the table in the kitchen for breakfast. (xi) Why are you _____ on the floor? (xii) Many wreaths have been _____ on the War Memorial.

(b) Notice the negative and interrogative forms of *need* and *dare* when followed by an infinitive, with the alternative forms of the Present Simple tense:
NEED
Negative
I do not need to help / I need not help.
They did not need to come.

Interrogative
Do I need to help? / Need I help?
Did they need to come?

DARE
Negative
He dare not stay.
Many dared not speak. / Many did not dare to speak.

Interrogative
Do you dare to jump? / Dare you jump?
Did you dare to refuse?

But: *I do not need anything more. Do you need help?*
Notice: *Fred dared his brother to steal the apples* (challenge).
Also: *My shoes need cleaning. The house does not need redecorating yet.*

(c) *all   everything   everybody (everyone)*
The pronoun *all*, with its meaning of 'the undivided total', is less commonly found than *everything* (all the things), *everybody* (all the people):
Everything is perfect. He ate everything. Everybody was surprised. He made everyone pay.
all is used when a relative pronoun follows or is understood: *All (that) I can say is (that) he has always been good to me. (Others may think differently.)* Even in this case, however, *everything/everybody* can often be used: *He destroyed all (the letters/insects) he found. He destroyed everything* (all the things) *he found.*
The expression 'all people' is rarely used: *everybody* is far more common: *Everybody has his troubles.*

Which is the more common form? (i) I saw _____ that happened. (ii) _____ you need is a good rest. (iii) _____ is/are talking about the mystery. (iv) _____ is now finished. (v) _____ I know is that he has been arrested. (vi) She never tells me _____ (vii) He knows _____ in the district.

(d) *so skilfully that*   She mended the dress *so carefully that* it looked new. He had to wait *so long that* he became impatient.

(e) *as though it were being steered*   This rare use of the subjunctive is explained on pages 214–15. *He looked at me as if (as though) I were not there.*

(f) *urge* someone *to do* something (try to make him do it): *The doctor urged the overworked businessman to rest.*

persuade someone *to do* something (be successful in making him do it): *He finally persuaded the man to have a holiday.*

convince someone *that* something is true or right: *He convinced the man that a rest was essential. Galileo was convinced that his theories were correct.*

(g) Verbal constructions

Infinitive: We have done everything *to honour* you.

Gerund: (i) after a preposition: *without encountering*; (ii) after other verbs: *keep moving; risk offending, avoid touching.*

Clause: I became aware that the boat was gliding (Compare: *I became aware of singing.*)

Prepositions

(a) drift *along* the stream; move/walk *along* the street.
(b) *between* two things; *among* more than two.
(c) sprinkled/decorated/patterned *with* flowers (But: *painted blue*).
(d) mirrored/reflected *in* water.
(e) bounded/marked *by* a large board.
(f) *on* either side.
(g) prepare/get ready *for* someone or something; choose something *for* someone; *for* various reasons.
(h) a man *with* delicate features/blue eyes/white hair/a long beard etc.
(i) (un)aware/(un)conscious *of* danger; a feeling/conviction *of* danger.
(j) smiled *at* me; laughed at me (made fun of me).
(k) step *out of* a car.
(l) walk/run/drift *past* something (Not: *pass in walking*).

Expressions for use in written work

(a) I lost all count of time.
(b) eventually.
(c) I was/became aware that.
(d) at this point.
(e) on either side.
(f) he came up to me.
(g) everything in our power.
(h) for reasons I cannot explain.
(i) we made our way towards.
(j) I gasped in amazement at.
(k) I shivered involuntarily.

Spoken English

Requesting and offering

This is an aspect of English that needs particularly careful study as it is possible to offend someone by speaking too abruptly. Practise these expressions whenever you have the opportunity.

Formal	Informal	Friendly	Helpful
May I have your name and address, please. (*an official is speaking*)	May I have another piece of cake? (*in a family*)		May (Can) I help you? May I take your case?
I'd like my bill, please. (*in a restaurant*)		I'd so (very much) like you to come and see us again.	Would you like me to help you?

Formal	Informal	Friendly	Helpful
Would you like to close the window, please. (*teacher to a student*)			
Would you like to sit down?			
	You don't mind if I hurry off, do you?	Do sit down. (*voice rising at the end*)	Why don't you let me help?
		Won't you sit down.	

Other expressions

Would you serve my salad without oil, please?
Would you be able to help me in the house for one morning a week, please?
You won't forget to post that letter for me, will you?
Could you (possibly) move your car forward a bit, please?
You wouldn't be able to spare me some butter, would you?
Would you mind changing this ten-pound note for me, please? (*to a shop-keeper*)
I wonder if you'd mind if I used (my using) your telephone?
Would you be so kind as to lend me your pen for a moment, please?

Please and Thank you

Please is used only when asking for something. *Yes, please* shows acceptance. Refusal is expressed by *No, thank you* (Not: *thank you*).
If there is a reply to thank you (usually none is in fact given) it is *That's all right* or *Not at all. I was glad to help.* There is no need to say anything when handing something to a person, though you may say *Here you are.*

Practice

Express each of the following in a politer way. Wherever possible, show how the request could be expressed in more than one way.

(a) Give me my key. (*in a hotel*)
(b) Show me those photographs you have.
(c) Tell me how to use this telephone.
(d) I want a glass of water.
(e) Weigh this parcel for me. (*in the post office*)
(f) Do you want another cup of coffee?
(g) Come nearer the fire.
(h) Tell me the time. (*to a stranger*)
(i) Drive more slowly.
(j) Get these photographs printed by the weekend.
(k) Have lunch with me tomorrow.
(l) Turn down your radio. It's very disturbing.

Excuse me and Sorry

Excuse me is an expression of politeness, often used when speaking to an unknown person: *Excuse me, can you tell me the way to* . . . It is also said when passing in front of someone or when trying to attract someone's attention.

I'm sorry is an apology for something that has caused pain, trouble or disturbance to another person. Examples: (a) on treading on someone's foot: *Oh, I'm so sorry. I hope I haven't hurt you.* (b) on being late: *I'm so sorry I'm late. I was delayed by the traffic.* (c) on disturbing someone: *I'm sorry to disturb you but you're wanted on the telephone.*

Holidaymaking

A How did you enjoy your holiday? Did you have a good time?

B I had a wonderful time but my wife was disappointed with it.

A Did the two of you go alone or as part of a group?

B We went on a coach tour organised by Faraway tours. (*Alternatives:* on a cruise, on a package holiday in Spain.) We booked through a local travel office. As in the case of a package holiday, everything — accommodation, fares, luggage transport, meals during the day, guides and tips — was included in the price.

A We went camping in the Lake District. We packed our tent, cooking utensils, some tinned food, camp beds and bedding besides the usual luggage in the boot of our small car. We stayed at two different camping sites and explored from there. Next year we'll do the same but we want to take a motor boat up the river and camp wherever we can.

Reading Comprehension

Choice of words

In this exercise you must choose the word or phrase which best completes each sentence.

1 Many difficulties have _____ as a result of the changeover to a new type of fuel.
   A raised   **B** been raised   **C** experienced   **D** arisen

2 The deep pool was so brown and weed-covered that it was almost _____.
   A transparent   **B** solid   **C** opaque   **D** invisible

3 You must remember not to _____ from the point when you write an essay.
   A go astray   **B** wander   **C** diverge   **D** go off

4 The _____ of the lake is covered with reeds and rushes.
   A beach   **B** coast   **C** shore   **D** bank

5 Paper clips, drawing pins and safety-pins were _____ all over the floor.
   A scattered   **B** sprayed   **C** dispersed   **D** separated

6 Don't _____ to correct me if I make a mistake.
   A stop   **B** mind   **C** hesitate   **D** pause

7 I wandered through the cool _____ of the forest trees.
   A shadow   **B** dark   **C** shade   **D** obscurity

8 The neighbours do not consider him quite _____ as most evenings he awakens them with his drunken singing.
   A respectful   **B** respected   **C** respectable
   D suitable

9 The autumn air felt _____ so she went to fetch a coat.
   A cool **B** chilly **C** chill **D** tepid

10 I was not _____ by his many arguments so finally we agreed to differ
   A convicted **B** assured **C** convinced **D** concerned

Multiple choice responses

Below are a number of questions and unfinished statements about the reading passage on page 77, each with four suggested answers or endings. Choose the one you think fits best in each case. Read the passage right through again before choosing your answers.

1 The sides of the islands
   A had trees on them.
   B were covered only with grass.
   C were covered with grass and flowers.
   D had no covering.

2 How did the boat move forward?
   A rapidly.
   B uninterruptedly.
   C jerkily.
   D feebly.

3 While in the boat the writer felt
   A relaxed.
   B afraid.
   C only half-conscious.
   D helpless.

4 The passage suggests
   A that the sun was shining in a clear sky.
   B that clouds hid the sun.
   C that the sun was shining but there were clouds.
   D nothing definite about the weather.

5 Why is the writer's experience described as a nightmare?
   A He had no control over his actions.
   B He was afraid of something unknown.
   C He knew that something horrible awaited him.
   D The man who greeted him looked evil.

Composition

Description

There are two main kinds of description. In the first only facts are given. A police description of a wanted man, a house agent's description of a house, the details of interesting buildings mentioned in a town guidebook are all examples.

The second kind gives impressions as well as facts, so that the reader sees through his imagination as well as his mind. The writer provides atmosphere and feeling: of a half-ruined castle, a lake shore in early morning, a town square in carnival time. He chooses details, words and impressions to awaken the reader's imagination.

Even these descriptions, however, usually include carefully-observed facts as well as impressions. So, when describing an Underground station platform, the writer gives some exact information about the tunnels at either end, the rails, the platform and waiting passengers, the lights, seats, station names, advertisements and so on, besides impressions and atmosphere (of an enclosed space completely isolated from daylight, growing things and fresh air, clean, efficient, cold and inhuman, symbol of a technical age).

The following description combines facts and impressions. Notice that a plan has been made first.

Describe an open-air café using between 120 and 180 words.

Plan
1 The weather. The café itself.
2 The waitresses. Other people.
3 The surroundings.

A few lazy clouds were passing slowly over a sunlit blue sky. Scattered over the smooth green grass there were about twenty tables with green and white plastic tablecloths fastened on them, and brightly-coloured sunshades above. Plastic and metal chairs of various colours stood round them and in the centre of the lawn, water from a fountain splashed into a pool in which goldfish were swimming.

The waitresses, pretty girls in light summer frocks, were bringing ice-creams, cool drinks and cream cakes from the kitchen of the house at one side. Half the tables were occupied: several women were sitting talking and a few men were enjoying the sunshine.

On two sides roses bloomed against an old wall with beds of June flowers in front. On the others, tall trees sheltered lawns white with daisies. Bees were buzzing and birds were singing. Work, cold, reality perhaps, no longer existed. *(149 words)*

Practice

Write between 120 and 180 words on the following:

1 An English friend wants to buy three useful things in your country to take home with him or her. Describe three things you would recommend and the special qualities each has that make you choose it.

2 An English friend is coming to live in your home town. Give him some idea of what it will be like living there.

3 Turning out a cupboard you come across something you have not seen since your childhood and it brings back memories. Describe the object and some of your memories.

4 Two dogs are waiting with their owners in a veterinary surgeon's waiting-room. Describe each dog and its owner.

5 Compare your journey to school on a delightful summer day and on a cold unpleasant winter day.

6 Describe an ideal bed-sitting-room for yourself as a single person.

Use of English

1 **The word in capitals at the end of each of the following sentences can be used to form a word that fits suitably in the blank space. Fill each blank space in this way.**

  1 The judge was caught _____, admiring himself in the mirror in his new wig. AWARE

  2 His examination results were so unsatisfactory that it seemed _____ for him to continue studying. POINT

  3 The ambulance-men carried the injured man into the hospital on a _____. STRETCH

  4 Some people are more _____ to cold than others. SENSE

  5 The new au pair girl proved to be quite different from the family's _____. EXPECT

  6 The scientific explanation was too difficult for me. I was quite out of my _____. DEEP

  7 He was bound hand and foot and so was quite _____ to escape. POWER

  8 It is thoroughly dishonest and _____ to cheat in an examination. HONOUR

2 **Rewrite each of the following sentences, replacing each of the italicised words or phrases with its opposite.**
Example: He *went up* the stairs *quietly.*
Answer: He came down the stairs noisily.

  1 He has *ordered* us to move *quickly.*

  2 The food was so *well-cooked* that he ate *a lot.*

  3 He was so *hard-working* that he *passed* the examination.

  4 He has *a lot of* clothes on because of the *cold.*

  5 In some parts where the river was *narrower*, it was very *deep.*

  6 He *refused* the *sweet* grapes I offered him.

  7 He had *got up* an hour before and now he was *wide awake.*

  8 He *refused* to *put down* the two *heavy* cases.

3 **For each of the six phrases in italics in the sentences below, four suggested explanations are given, from which you must choose the correct one, A, B, C or D.**

  1 Tom is late home today. He has probably *been kept in.*
    A He has been asked to do extra work in the office.
    B He has to stay longer at school because of misbehaviour.
    C He has attended a works conference that has lasted longer than expected.
    D Somebody has asked his advice just as he is leaving.

  2 Some people can easily *be taken in.*
    A They are easily tricked.
    B They are pleasant guests.
    C It is easy to like them.
    D They are easily found accommodation for.

  3 I hope the house-warming party *will come off.*
    A will not happen.
    B will happen.

    C will be successful.

    D will be arranged.

4 Far too many crimes are never *cleared up*.

    A prevented from happening.

    B given enough attention.

    C dealt with successfully.

    D made known to the public.

5 If only the public *keeps up* its present interest, we should be able to raise the money we need.

    A continues to show.

    B increases.

    C renews.

    D expresses.

6 Don't worry. Perhaps you'll *come across* it later.

    A understand.

    B find.

    C be successful with.

    D get back.

4 **You are one of a group of four students in an English-language class. Your teacher has asked each of you to write a paragraph of about 50 words stating what you want to give most time and attention to in the lessons. Below are the notes that each of the other students makes before writing the paragraph.**

    Write the paragraph that each student produces, starting with the suggested openings below. Then write a final paragraph of the same length suggesting your own preferences, which may combine some of the others or differ from them.

A **Hilary**

    Preference: speaking

    only opportunity for practice;

    planned visit to England;

    wide variety of subjects possible;

    everyday language is more enjoyable.

B **Francis**

    Preference: grammar

    understanding of how language works;

    useful in constructing new sentences;

    helps to avoid mistakes;

    also reading comprehension introducing new vocabulary.

C **Jean**

    Preference: reading with discussion and writing

    widens vocabulary and ideas;

    what is read remembered better;

    write at home: time to think and use dictionary;

    learn useful expressions.

Paragraph openings

Hilary would like to spend most of the time speaking _____

Francis considers grammar the most important thing to study as _____

Jean learns most by reading which provides opportunities _____

For my part I think _____

Interview

Talking about a photograph

1 Describe what is happening in this picture.
2 How will most of the photographs and films being taken be used later?
3 How are the new arrivals being photographed likely to spend the next few hours or days?

Topics

What different kinds of people are usually welcomed with flowers and photographers?

Is there any useful place for ceremony (including military parades, carnival processions, receptions at airports) in the present-day world?

Suggest the short speech that might have been made by the lady receiving the flowers.

Reading aloud

Syllable weakenings

Most English words have one stressed syllable though sometimes there are two, one of them slightly stronger than the other.
Examples: *còmpośition mànufácture* and many negative forms: *ùnmiśtákable dislíke ìnconvénient.* Usually vowels in unstressed syllables are pronounced /ə/ or /ɪ/ or apparently disappear altogether.

Passages

In the following passages weakened syllables are in italics. Read and practise the words indicated before reading the whole passage aloud. Then suggest a situation in which each passage might have been spoken.

1   I've sel*dom* had such a frigh*tening* experi*ence.* I was attending an *opera* per*for*mance at Co*vent* Gar*den* Theatre: I was *apparently a*mong the audi*ence* in the bal*cony.* People *a*round me were whis*pering* and chat*tering;* my seat was uncom*fortable* and nothing was hap*pening* on the stage *except* that the ac*tors* were quar*relling* vio*lently.* Sud*denly* I found myself on the stage: I was *sup*posed to be the princi*pal sop*rano but I had *for*gotten my part and the oth*er* per*formers* were threa*tening* me. The peo*ple* in the audi*ence* were furi*ous* and started throwing rot*ten to*matoes and *po*tatoes and half-ea*ten* sau*sages.* I was hit by a huge bar of cho*colate* and then I woke up.

2   The *police* have *suggested* that we should put out a warning to our list*eners* to keep an eye op*en* for *sus*picious-looking cha*racters* in their neigh*bour*hood. You'd be *sur*prised — or maybe you wouldn't — at the num*ber* of bur*glaries* that have hap*pened recently, particularly* in the early af*ter*noon when resi*dents* are working or out shopping. No*body* looks for*ward* to going home to find cu*pboards* and draw*ers* op*en* and their *posses*sions scat*tered* and bro*ken,* with je*wellery,* valu*ables,* bank *certificates* and oth*er* pro*perty* sto*len.* You can *pro*tect one *a*nother by *pro*viding immedi*ate* in*formation* to the *po*lice about anyone you *sus*pect is up to no good.

3   33344. Mrs Par*sons* speaking. Oh, it's you Eli*zabeth.* Where are you? At Harwich? Did you have a good crossing? And your break*fast*? Good. Now, have you got much lug*gage*? A suitcase and a tra*vel* bag? Can you ma*nage* it yourself? You've car*ried* it all the way from Cen*tral* Fin*land*? My good*ness*! Now there'll be a train to Li*ver*pool Street, but I don't know the *de*par*ture* time. Oh, in five m*inutes'* time. Then you'll have to hurry. Now we'll come and meet you at Li*ver*pool Street Sta*tion.* I do hope we'll be in time. If we're not at the barri*er,* wait un*der* the clock. *Sup*pose there are two clocks? We'll look for you un*der* both.

Structured communication

Discussion of unusual holidays

Here are a few suggestions for some holidays which might seem unusual. Can you suggest some more?
    Travelling with a donkey or pony through a remote part of your own or another country and staying at farms or small inns on the way.
    Joining a safari group visiting a large game reserve or conservation park and taking photographs.
Discuss one of the holidays suggesting why you would or would not like to take part in it and some of its unpleasant aspects.

Action situations

1 You are hurrying along a busy road late in the evening on your way to an appointment. You are the only pedestrian until you see coming towards you a child of about four with no coat on. There is still no one else in sight. What would you do?

2 You live alone in a block of flats in an area where there have been several recent burglaries. In the middle of the night you hear screams for help from the person living above you. What would you do?

Opinions

Express your opinions on one or more of the following subjects.

1 What do you think are some of the causes of different types of dreams?

2 What are some of the things that might help you to judge a person's character on a first meeting?

3 What things might offend you?

Topics for a prepared talk

Prepare to talk for about two minutes on one of the following topics.

1 A vivid dream you have had.

2 A description of something dangerous or frightening you have had to do and what it was like doing it.

A press interview of someone famous

A famous person (real or imaginary) is being interviewed by one or more student journalists. Either the examiner or a student can be the famous person. Questions are asked about the celebrity's life (past and present), opinions, present programme, interests and future plans. The interview may be preceded by suggestions about what kind of famous person is being interviewed: statesman, artist, fashion designer, sportsman, film/theatre/TV personality, etc.

General guidance and practice

1 Past Perfect Simple and Continuous tenses

> *Simple form*
>
> Active: **I had experienced.**
> **He had spoken.**
> Passive: **The steps had been polished.**

> *Continuous form*
>
> Active: **I had been wandering.**
> Passive: very seldom used.

(a) The Past Perfect tense indicates an action which had happened before something else happened — in other words it expresses a time farther back than a certain point in the past.
Certain conjunctions: *when, as soon as, immediately, after, because, even though* are followed by the Past Perfect when there is a need

to emphasise that the action expressed had happened (or the state had existed) at an earlier time than another action or state in the past:

He joined the class a fortnight after it had started.
He joined late because he had been on holiday.

(b) The Past Perfect is far less commonly used when the sentence consists of two main clauses:

He finished his breakfast and then went to school.

(c) It often replaces the Present Perfect or Past Simple tenses in changes from direct to reported speech:

I have lost my ticket.
He said he had lost his ticket.

(d) It forms part of the *if* clause in a third conditional (see page 165):

If you had left earlier, you would have been in time.

(e) The Past Perfect Continuous shows that the earlier action had covered a period of time:

He had been staying in Paris before he came to London.
The old man told me he had been living in the same house all his life.

Practice

The following passage is a well-known problem story. Copy it out, using the correct form of the verbs shown. The verb forms may include gerunds, participles, infinitives and passive forms. When you have finished, answer the question, using the correct tense in your answer:

A certain man, who was the manager of a firm which (undertake) road repairs, (intend) to travel by train to Manchester. Before (set) out, he (look) up the times of the trains, and (discover) that there (be) three: one at seven, one at eight and one at nine o'clock. He (know) he (miss) the seven o'clock train, so after (pack) a small suitcase, he (start) out (catch) the eight o'clock train.

As he (walk) to the station, he (notice) one of his night-watchmen, who (sit) by his fire at the side of the road. (Know) that the man (work) for the railways previously, the manager (ask) him whether the eight or nine o'clock (be) the faster train.

The man (shake) his head solemnly. 'Usually the eight o'clock (be) very good,' he (say). 'But last night as I (sit) here, I (have) a terrible dream. In my dream I (see) a wrecked train. I (know) it (be) tonight's eight o'clock train I (can) see. There (be) a dreadful accident and everyone in the train (kill). (Go) not on that train tonight.'

The manager, who (be) superstitious, (decide) (wait) for the next train, which (travel) by a different route. It (be) a long journey, and after he (travel) all night, he (reach) Manchester. There, to his horror, he (learn) that the night-watchman (be) right. The eight o'clock train (have) an accident, and all the passengers (be) killed.

So he (put) a fifty pound note in an envelope and (send) it to the man, together with a note (dismiss) him from his job.

Why did he do this?

2 Revision of Passives

Revise the rule for forming the Passive from the Active Voice as shown on page 29.

Practice

Express the following sentences in the Passive Voice (the Past Perfect form is shown on page 164). Be careful to give the correct tense.

(a) People had seen him behaving in a very suspicious manner.
(b) A wasp has stung me.
(c) My landlady does my washing.
(d) The cat laid the half-eaten mouse on the doorstep.
(e) They had decorated the room beautifully.
(f) Someone had obviously offended her.
(g) A young boy was steering the car.
(h) A hat shades his eyes.
(i) The mother soothed the frightened child.
(j) He is sprinkling pepper all over your meal.

3 Should, ought to, must, have to

(a) *should   ought to*
Both these verbs, which are usually interchangeable, express duty, though often with a suggestion of failure in carrying out the duty:
I should work harder. (Perhaps I will but I doubt it.)
I shouldn't waste so much money.

They are used in giving advice:
You should/ought to take more exercise.

should may express probability:
That programme should be interesting.

A following perfect infinitive usually, though not always, suggests failure:
You should have told me before. (but you didn't)

(b) *must*
This suggests a much stronger feeling of personal duty, applying either to the speaker or to someone else:
I really must keep this room tidier.
You/Jane must be quieter: I've got to work.

must can express a future idea:
I must leave earlier tomorrow.

The past forms are:
I had to help my mother yesterday.
I've had to open a window: the room's so stuffy.
He was late because he had had to mend a puncture.
Past forms are explained on page 150.

Negatives of *must*:
You mustn't shout at me. (I forbid it.)
You needn't shout at me: I can hear you all right. (It isn't necessary.)

must can express near certainty. The negative form is *cannot* or *can't* (near impossibility):
It must be quite late now. It's already dark.
He can't be ill. I was speaking to him only a moment ago.

(c) *have to   have got to*

have to suggests necessity:

All children have to go to school nowadays.

have got to more commonly refers to one particular situation:

I'm sorry. I've got to go now. I've got to be home by one o'clock.

In everyday speech *must* and *have to* are often used interchangeably.

Practice

1 Complete the following sentences with a form of *should, ought to, must* or *have to*.

    (a)   I _____ go and visit my sister-in-law but I am too busy.

    (b)   Every weekday most people _____ get up early in order to get to work in time.

    (c)   You _____ do your homework more regularly. I insist.

    (d)   He _____ pay duty on his new camera on his return home last year.

    (e)   As it was raining hard, I _____ catch a bus.

    (f)   The pupils _____ have been quiet while the teacher was away, but there was pandemonium in the room.

    (g)   A specialist _____ keep up to date with the latest medical developments in his field, but if he is busy, this is difficult.

    (h)   Do come and have tea with me. I _____ tell you about my holiday.

    (i)   He _____ have a tooth out yesterday.

    (j)   I _____ write three letters already today.

2 Express the following sentences in the negative and also in the interrogative. In the case of *must* give both forms of the negative, explaining the difference in meaning.

    (a)   I must telephone the manager this morning.

    (b)   Wild animals should be kept in cages.

    (c)   The gardener will have to mow the lawn.

    (d)   The explorer had to face many dangers.

    (e)   Farm labourers have to work longer hours than factory workers.

    (f)   They have had to widen the lane.

    (g)   That stove should have been cleaned out yesterday.

    (h)   The examination must be written in pencil.

    (i)   The Prime Minister has to appoint a new Foreign Secretary now.

Note: The last sentence is a clear example of the possible difference between the present forms of *must* and *have to*. If he must appoint a new Foreign Secretary, someone is saying that this is his duty. But the previous one has retired, and it is necessary for him to appoint a new one; he *has to* do it.

3 Re-write the following sentences in a slightly different way using *must* to suggest near certainty or *can't* to suggest impossibility.

    (a)   He is so fair that he almost certainly comes from Scandinavia or Germany.

    (b)   But there surely isn't a bus strike today. I've just come here by bus.

    (c)   It's obvious that that man working in the garden is our new neighbour.

    (d)   I probably appear somewhat stupid but I'm a bit deaf today.

    (e)   Surely you don't feel tired already. You've only just started working.

4 Word order: adverbials of manner, place and time

Notice the order of adverbs and adverbial phrases in these examples:

The boat was gliding *slowly towards the shore. (manner, place)*
I hesitated *there for a moment. (place, time)*

When more than one adverb or adverbial phrase follows the verb, the usual order is: manner, place, time.

Often, when there are two or three adverbial expressions, one of them, usually a time adverb, is placed at the beginning of the sentence:

At that time I was living in Paris.
Before long you will be speaking quite fluently.
In the trees the birds were singing sweetly *(adverb of place)*.

The order of words may change the emphasis in the sentence. If one of the adverbial expressions is especially important, the normal order may be changed. The one that is most emphasised comes *last*:

The cat went out reluctantly *into the freezing night*.
The cat went out into the freezing night *reluctantly*.

Practice

Write the following sentences so that the words are in a suitable order. There may be more than one alternative.

(a)   She waited (impatiently) (in the bus queue).
(b)   I get up (during the winter) (reluctantly) (in my cold room).
(c)   He walks (to the station) (slowly) (at the end of a long day).
(d)   Wild animals go seeking their prey (after dark) (in the jungle).
(e)   The snow fell (for thirty-six hours) (over a wide area) (continuously).
(f)   The ship will dock (at Tilbury) (at eight o'clock).
(g)   The water continued to pour (steadily) (into the tunnel).
(h)   The discontented inhabitants start rioting (dangerously) (now and again) (in the streets).

5 Interrogative pronouns and adjectives: what?, which?

What is used when the choice is unlimited. *Which* suggests a known or limited number.

Practice

Use what or which in the following sentences:

(a)   _____ shoes did you take to be repaired?
(b)   _____ of your three sisters are you most like?
(c)   '_____ can I get for you, Mrs. Adams?' said the grocer.
(d)   He is so worried that he doesn't know _____ to do.
(e)   _____ is the correct way to address a duke?
(f)   _____ London park do you consider the most beautiful?
(g)   I really don't know _____ his name is.
(h)   _____ side of the street do you live on?

6 Who, whom, which

Each of these may be used interrogatively:

Who is there?
Whom have they chosen?
Which of us is right?

or as a relative form:

There is the actress who has just had a nervous breakdown.
Mary is the sister (whom) you have met.

She is the one (whom) you were speaking about.
That coat (which) you bought is very smart.
(See page 168 for a note on the omission of *whom* and *which*.)

Who is used for the nominative (subject) form. *Whom* is used for the accusative form (object of the verb or governed by a preposition). *Who* is often used for *whom* in conversation, but *whom* is normal in written English.

Practice

Insert *who, whom* or *which* in these sentences. Use the pronoun in each case, even where it may be omitted.

(a) _____ will they elect as President of the Sports Club?
(b) Nobody knows _____ is the most likely candidate.
(c) Mr. Smith is the one _____ most people seem enthusiastic about.
(d) I don't know _____ I shall vote for.
(e) _____ suggested Mr Brown?
(f) _____ of them is the most popular?
(g) The election, _____ will take place on Friday, will be quite exciting.
(h) The results, _____ the local newspaper will publish the next day, may cause some ill-feeling.
(i) _____ are you working for now?
(j) _____ of these newspapers have you finished with?

7 The semi-colon and the colon

The semi-colon is used to separate two parts of a sentence, each of which is complete in itself:
I had been in a silent forest; now I was alone in a small boat.

A colon may be used for the same purpose, but in this case, each part of the sentence expresses essentially the same idea:
Christmas is becoming increasingly commercialized: shops and business interests see it merely as a way of making money.

A colon may introduce a list:
All cycles sold at this price have the following equipment: three-speed gearing, a carrier, a dynamo-operated lamp and a pump.

Practice

Insert semi-colons or colons in the following sentences.

(a) The gale inflicted terrible damage roofs were torn off and crops were flattened.
(b) The escaped prisoner scrambled over the wall beyond he caught sight of the river.
(c) Tomorrow is a bank holiday all shops and businesses will be closed throughout the day.
(d) I should like these special items delivered today a tin of coffee, a bar of household soap and a jar of marmalade.
(e) Far into the night he worked as day dawned he sank back into the chair, exhausted.

5 Shelter for the Night

The rain started as dusk was falling. He had been walking since ten o'clock and he was beginning to feel extremely tired. Overhead, heavy grey clouds were gathering rapidly; a few streaks of what had been a fiery sunset gleamed for a while on the dark bog puddles ahead, but these soon faded,
5 leaving a uniform greyness of earth and sky.

The narrow muddy path twisted to avoid large rocks on either side and the few scattered bushes. As the rain had now obviously set in and was falling with increasing determination, he wearily unfolded his raincoat and put it on. He felt in his pocket for his small torch, which he would
10 probably need before long. He was getting hungry so he greedily munched some of his stock of ginger biscuits and chocolate. He had no idea of how far he had still to walk; so far as he was concerned he was the sole inhabitant of a deserted world of gigantic cloud continents, damp gloomy wastes of moorland, tiny streams and driving soaking rain.

15 Suddenly he felt the path descending steeply. Peering through the darkness, he could discern lights. By switching on his torch, he was able to walk faster and within a quarter of an hour was striding briskly along a paved street between rows of houses. At the crossroads he noticed a small public house with a board outside announcing that there was accommodation
20 available on the premises. He pushed open the door, went through a dimly-lit passage and entered a smoke-filled bar. Men were leaning against the counter, arguing about business and betting, cricket and crime; a group of three in the far corner, who looked like commercial travellers, were very nearly quarrelling over politics, while a third group, quietly
25 playing dominoes, seemed completely absorbed in their game.

The cheerful-looking woman serving behind the bar said good-evening to him in a friendly way but shook her head discouragingly when he asked for a room.

'I'm sorry,' she said, 'the local race week is starting tomorrow and every
30 room has been taken. But it's bad weather to go hunting for rooms in. I suggest you go and see Mrs. Parkins next door. Since her son has been working away, she usually has a spare room, and she never minds helping anyone who has nowhere to sleep, provided he's respectable.'

Notes on the passage

Vocabulary

Title *shelter* (V): trees *sheltered* the house; he *sheltered* from the rain. *a shelter* (N): the cave provided *shelter*; a bus *shelter*. a *sheltered* spot (Adj).
a refuge (N) = a safe place: seek (take) *refuge from an advancing army*.
a refugee = someone who takes refuge in another country for political reasons.

1 *dawn* (daybreak), *sunrise, daylight, sunset, dusk* (twilight), *darkness* (the dark). *twilight* can refer both to morning and evening. day *dawns*; dusk *falls*; night *falls*; a mist *thickens*. Notice: Gradually *it dawned on me* that I had taken the wrong road.

2   *fairly, quite, very, extremely/exceedingly, excessively* (too much).

2   *overhead   underfoot   ahead.*

3   *rapidly, swiftly, quickly, fast:* all with similar meanings; *quickly* and *fast* are the more commonly used. *fast* may be (a) an adjective: *a fast train, fast colours* (that do not come out when washed) (b) a verb: go without food (Note: breakfast) (c) an adverb: *Don't speak so fast.*

3   *a streak* = a narrow irregular strip: *a streak of paint; a streak of cruelty in someone's nature.*
a *striped* dress; a tabby cat has *stripes*. a gold *band* round the cuff of a uniform.
a *strip* = a fairly long but narrow piece: *a strip of paper/material; a comic strip* (in the newspaper). *strip* (V) = take off a covering: *strip the bark from a tree-trunk; the doctor told the patient to strip.*

4   *gleam* (N and V): polished metal and a lake surface in moonlight *gleam*. There was *a gleam of interest/excitement* in his eyes.
dazzle (V) = shine so brightly as to make it impossible to see. *blinding* is even stronger than *dazzling*.
sparkle (N and V): a stream in sunlight *sparkles*.
glitter (N and V): diamonds *glitter* (a hard bright light).
glow (N and V): a dying fire *glows*.

4   *for a while* = for a time. *a little while. meanwhile* = while this was happening.

4   *bog* = wet, muddy earth that can be dug out and burned as *peat*. a *marsh* and a *swamp* are dangerously wet and muddy: the *swamps* of the Amazon; the Essex *marshes*; an Irish *bog*.

4   a *puddle* in the street; a duck *pond*; a swimming *pool*; a *lake*.

5   *uniform* (Adj) = all the same. A soldier wears a *uniform* (N).

6   a *muddy* path; *sandy* soil; a *rocky* valley; *stony* ground; a *pebbly* beach; a *grassy* slope; a *mossy* bank.

6   *twist:* a corkscrew into a cork; one's ankle.
wind wool into a ball; *wind up* a clock; a *winding* road (*wind   wound   wound* /waund/). (Do not confuse: *wound* /wu:nd/ *wounded   wounded*).
revolve: the earth *revolves*; a *revolving* door; a *revolver*.
a *revolution* is in effect a complete turning around or change.
roll: a ball *rolls*, a *roll* and butter.

7   *fall:* rain *falls. fall down: a child falls down;* (something already standing on the ground falls down). *drop* = let fall: *He dropped his stick* (Not: *let fall*).

8   *increase* = get or make more: *increase one's income.*
grow: plants, animals, profits grow (N *growth*).
extend = get or make longer: *extend a road, a large building; the extension of the motorway.*
expand = get or make bigger: *metals expand when heated* (N *expansion*).
swell = get bigger (especially parts of the body): *a painful swollen wrist* (N *swelling*).

8   *unfold/fold up   undo/do up.*

10   *munch* an apple; *crunch:* the dog *crunched* a small bone; *chew* food for some time (*chewing gum*); *lick* with the tongue: the dog *licked* my hand; *lap:* a cat *laps* milk; *snap:* the parrot *snapped* at my finger; *suck* a sweet.

11   *stock:* The shopkeeper has no atlases *in stock:* they are *out of stock.*
store (V): goods are *stored* in a warehouse; (N): *a store of food for the winter.*
a department store = a large shop selling many different things.

11   *ginger* is a spice. Other spices are *cinnamon, nutmeg, cloves* and *pepper* and they are added to food to give extra flavour.

13   *desert* (N): *the Sahara Desert;* (V): *he deserted* (abandoned) *his friends when they were in danger.*

a deserter = someone who runs away from the army; a *deserted* house.
dessert = the sweet course at the end of a meal (for pronunciation see page 101).

13 *gigantic* (Adj)   Opp. *tiny, minute. giant* (N and Adj). *dwarf* (N) But: *a dwarf tree or plant.*

13 Asia is a *continent.* The rest of Europe is sometimes referred to by British people as *the Continent.*

13 *damp* (N *dampness*): *a damp climate; damp clothes* (slightly wet in an unpleasant way).
moist (N *moisture*): *bread should be kept moist* (not quite dry).

13 *gloomy: a gloomy dark room; a gloomy outlook, face, mood.* a *dismal* expression on someone's face; *dismal* weather. a *dreary* life, day, lesson.
gloomy suggests darkness; *dismal* sadness and depression; *dreary* monotony.

13 *waste* (V): *waste time/money;* (N): *a waste of time; desert wastes;* (Adj): *waste land; a wastepaper basket.*
the waist = part of the body.

14 *stream* = a small river, a brook. In a school, *streaming* is the division of children into classes according to their ability.

15 *descend/descent   ascend/ascent.   Ascension Day* is a religious festival.

15 *peer* = look with difficulty. *discern* = see with difficulty.

17 *stride* (N and V) = walk with long steps. sit *astride* a horse.

18 *crossroads* or *road junction;* a road can also *fork;* a *bend* in the road: *Turn left at the crossroads, then bear to the left where the road forks.*

18 In a *public house* people can drink beer, wine and spirits.
An *inn* is a country *pub,* sometimes offering *accommodation* for travellers.
A *hostel* (e.g. *youth hostel*) provides cheap accommodation.
A *boarding-house* is a kind of family hotel. *full board* is accommodation and all meals.

20 *available* = can be obtained or used. *accessible* = within reach. Venice is *accessible* by one road only. Cooking *facilities* are available.

22 *argument:* in which people take sides. In a *quarrel* they get angry. A *discussion* is an exchange of opinions.

22 *betting* on horses. *gambling* with cards or in a casino. *Football pools. 'Let's have a bet on it.'*

26 A *shop assistant* stands behind a *counter* and *serves* the *customers.*

27 *shook her head* to say no. *shook her fist* to show anger (at someone). *shook hands with* someone.
She *nodded* to say yes. She *nodded* because she was almost asleep.

31 *next door* = in the next house. *our next-door neighbour.*

32 *spare* (Adj) = extra because not in use; (V): *I can't spare the money* (I haven't enough). Compare: *save* money in a bank (*savings*).

Phrasal verbs   set   bad weather *sets in.*
set out for the place one is going to.
set up a business; *The father set up his son in business.*
to be *set upon* by criminals and robbed of one's money.

Other uses of set
a *set* of glasses/artificial teeth; a tea/coffee *set* (or service); a radio/television *set*; a *set* in tennis.
setting: music composed for certain words; frame in which a jewel is set; surroundings or background for a play, book etc.: The story is *set* in Mexico, with exotic and dramatic *settings.*

look　*look like* another person/being a fine day.

look down on someone considered inferior.

look at a picture.

look for something lost.

look into a matter that needs explanation or investigation.

look forward to something pleasant.

look after children.

look out of a window; *look out!* (a sudden warning of approaching danger).

look up the meaning of a word in a dictionary; *look up* to someone very much respected.

look away from an unpleasant sight.

look over someone else's book.

overlook (not notice) a mistake, or something one should have done and has forgotten to do, or something that deserves punishment but will be passed over on this occasion; *overlook* or *look out on* a park.

look upon (regard) someone as an expert.

look on (as an *onlooker*) without taking any active part.

look round in a shop.

look through something written, possibly to find any mistakes; *look through* a window.

Pronunciation

Special difficulties: fiery /fáɪəri/; ginger /dʒíndʒə/; biscuits /bískɪts/; chocolate /tʃɒklət/; giant /dʒáɪənt/; gigantic /dʒaɪgǽntɪk/.

Sound changes: desert (N) /dézət/; desert (V) /dɪzɜ́:t/; dessert (N) /dɪzɜ́:t/.

Stress: overhead /ə́ʊvəhéd/.

ə (as in *a*go): moorland /mʊ́ələnd/
*a*ccommodation /əkɒmədéɪʃən/; commercial /kəmɜ́:ʃəl/.

ɪ (as in city): premis*e*s /prémɪsɪz/; discour*a*ging /dɪskʌ́rɪdʒɪŋ/.

Others: streaks /stri:ks/; gleamed /gli:md/; puddles /pʌdlz/; uniform /júːnɪfɔ:m/; torch /tɔ:tʃ/; peering /píərɪŋ/; discern /dɪsɜ́:n/; quarrelling /kwɒrəlɪŋ/; cheerful /tʃíəfəl/.

Grammatical and structural points

Present participles

In some places in the passage the present participle is used adjectivally: *a board announcing* (a board which announced); *a group playing dominoes* (who were playing); and in others the effect is that of an adverb: *peering through the darkness, he saw* (when he peered); *these faded, leaving a uniform greyness* (when these faded, they left . . .).

The present participle is found in written English, but rarely adverbially in spoken. 'Walking along the High Street, I met an old friend' would sound odd in conversation. It would be expressed as: 'I met an old friend as I was walking along the High Street.' In any case, do not overdo the use of the present participle, as even in written English it often sounds strange. One would be unlikely even to write, for example: 'Going into his room he turned on the light' but: 'He went into his room and turned on the light.' Use participles only in cases where you have already met and learned them in English.

Uncountable and Countable nouns

Uncountables: *determination, darkness* (abstract); *accommodation* (general); *rain, mud, ginger; cricket* (a game); *betting* (a gerund).

101

With meaning change: *crime* (in general)/*a crime; business/a business; light/a light; chocolate/a chocolate.*
Plural: *premises.* Plural form but singular meaning: *Politics/the news/mathematics/physics is worth studying. It is interesting.*

Provided (that)/providing

These two terms are interchangeable. They can often replace *if* when the idea of fulfilling a certain condition is especially strong. They can begin a sentence but more often follow a main clause:
> *I'll come if I can. I'll come provided you pay my fare.*
> *Take these tablets if you feel ill.* ('provided' would be impossible)
> *Provided you continue taking these tablets, you will not be ill.*

Adverbial phrases

Several adjectives end in *-ly.* These include:
> *friendly, chilly, leisurely, lovely, kindly, silly, jolly.*
A very few writers use the adjectives as adverbs, but a far pleasanter effect is produced
(a) by using an adverbial phrase such as: *in a friendly way;*
(b) by avoiding the adverb in some way: *he went for a leisurely walk through the town;*
(c) by using another adverb: *he sang beautifully.*

Some adjectives, including most participles, have no adverbial form:
> *difficult, determined* and *interested* are examples.
Where there is a corresponding noun, a 'with' phrase can sometimes be used adverbially:
> *He spoke with difficulty. He listened to the speech with interest.*
Even when an adverb exists, the 'with' phrase can sometimes be used when the adjective is modified by another adverb:
> *The rain was falling with increasing determination* (no adverb).
> *He greeted me unenthusiastically* (with little enthusiasm).
> *He awaited the results pessimistically* (with increasing pessimism).

Alternative verbal constructions

Infinitive/Gerund	*begin/start to write/writing* (little meaning change)
Gerund	*finish/stop writing*
Gerund	He *suggested (our) hiring* a car.
Clause	He *suggested (that) we (should) hire* a car.
Gerund	Would you *mind waiting* a few minutes?
Clause	Would you *mind if I use* your telephone?
	Mind how you go.

Prepositions

(a) *put on/take off* a garment; *put/turn/switch on/off* a light; *switch on/off* a torch; *turn on/off* a tap/the gas (Not: open and close).
(b) *covered with/by* moss.
(c) *before* long.
(d) *waiting for* a quarter of an hour.
(e) *on* the premises.
(f) enter a room (Not: *in*).
(g) hunt animals (But: hunt *for* a room).
(h) ask/argue *about* (But: discuss something).
(i) no idea *of* how far.

Expressions for use in written work

(a) overhead, underfoot, ahead (*A short way ahead, I could see . . .*).
(b) for a (long) (short) (little) while; meanwhile.
(c) The rain had set in.
(d) This will need repairing before long.
(e) He had no idea *of* (the way etc.) but: He had no idea what to do next.

(f) be/get/feel hungry, thirsty, tired, angry, bored etc.
(g) So far as I am concerned, a sandwich would be enough, but Dick wants a cooked meal.
(h) He will telephone within a quarter of an hour.
(i) She never minds helping.
(j) accommodation available on the premises.

Spoken English

Common colloquial expressions

The following words appear quite frequently with various meanings in spoken English.

mind
Would you mind waiting a few minutes? No, *I don't mind* in the least.
Mind how you go (advice to someone driving or cycling).
Mind that step! *Mind* the doors! (on the London Underground).
She *minds* the children while I'm at work. *Mind your own business.* (impolite).
Oh, it's just starting to rain. *Never mind*, we're nearly there.

manage
Can you *manage* that suitcase?
Can you *manage* to be there at seven? No, I'm afraid *I can't manage it*.
He can't *manage* his own affairs, let alone a shop.

wonder
I *wonder* where he is.
I *wonder if* I could do something to help you?
I *wonder if* you could let me have a stamp for this letter?

afraid
I'm afraid I can't tell you.
I'm afraid he's ill.
Will it be cooler tomorrow? *I'm afraid so/I'm afraid not.*

trouble
bother
Sorry to *trouble/bother* you but I think I left my gloves here.
May I trouble you to move your chair a little? It's/that's *no trouble at all.*
Don't *trouble/bother* to knock.
I hope I'm not *giving you too much trouble.*
What's the trouble? Oh, the engine's *giving trouble.*
If you say that to them, you'll *cause trouble.*
He's always been *a trouble to* his mother.
The trouble is that you're downright lazy.
Bother, I've dropped it!

chance
Is there *any chance of* getting a ticket?
Are you *by any chance* Barbara's sister?
Have you *by any chance* got a key like mine?
It was quite *by chance* that we stayed in that hotel.
So you think all accommodation will be taken? Well, we'll have *to chance* that / Well, *let's chance it.*
I'll go if I *get the chance.*

good
bad
harm
It's no good complaining. You'll have to put up with it.
A holiday will *do you good.* It'll *do you good* to have a rest.
A little hard work would *do you no harm.*
It might *be a good idea*/mightn't *be a bad idea* to take some food.

I don't think we'll be allowed to go in, but *there's no harm in asking*.

How about taking a camera? Yes, *that's a good idea/That's not a bad idea*.

doubt   *I've not the least doubt* he can do it.
There's no doubt he's a great actor.
There's no doubt about it.
I doubt whether we've got time.
Will he ever finish writing his book? *I doubt it.*

various   I just *can't help* making mistakes.
What on earth are you doing?
I dare say you'll manage to pass the exam, though it's a bit doubtful.
Thank goodness I've found my purse!
It's a job to manage to live on £40 a week.

Emphasising

The auxiliaries *do* and *did* can be used to express strong emphasis:
I *do* wish you'd hurry!
I tell you he *did* say that!

Other auxiliaries, such as *will* and *would*, can be used to give similar emphasis:
She *will* shout when she gets excited.
He *would* keep thanking me for my help.

Practice

Express these ideas emphatically. The new subject is given. In some cases the new sentence will be much shorter.

(a) make a lot of mistakes (you).
(b) contradicting the statement that I had not telephoned (I).
(c) complimenting someone on a new hair style (it).
(d) missing you while you were away (your dog).
(e) on expressing dissatisfaction with some new shoes somebody had insisted on buying (you).
(f) expressing irritation with a cat who always lies on your flower beds (she).
(g) expressing liking for a good detective story (I).

Asking the way

In the country

A Excuse me, could you tell me the way to Sheepcote, please?
B I'm afraid you're going in the wrong direction (going the wrong way). Follow this path back for about a mile. You'll pass a farmhouse on your right and just after that, you'll see a path branching off to the left. Follow that, and you should reach the village in about half an hour.

In a town

A Excuse me, could you direct me to the General Post Office?
B Go straight along this street to the traffic lights. Turn left there, and a short way along on the left, you'll see a cinema. Take the next turning on the right and you'll see the Post Office. It's a small building facing a big supermarket. It'll take you about ten minutes

to get there. You could go by bus but it's hardly worth it. (Grey-chapel Avenue? I'm afraid I've never heard of it. Are you sure you've got the name right?)

Practice

Ask someone the way to and then give directions for finding:

(a) the nearest post office from your place of work or school.
(b) a cottage about two miles from a village you know of.
(c) the nearest hospital from your own home.
(d) the nearest large car park to the Town Hall where space will certainly be available.

Reading comprehension

Choice of words

In this exercise you must choose the word or phrase which best completes each sentence.

1 Make sure you _____ your food properly before you swallow it.
   A eat **B** crunch **C** chew **D** bite

2 Many separate strands were _____ together to make the rope really strong.
   A twisted **B** woven **C** rolled **D** wounded

3 The melting of the snow has caused flooding by _____ rivers.
   A increased **B** expanded **C** overgrown **D** swollen

4 The headlights of the approaching car were so _____ that the cyclist had to stop riding.
   A gleaming **B** dazzling **C** visible **D** light

5 A leopard has spots and a tiger has _____.
   A strips **B** streaks **C** stripes **D** bands

6 Some useful ideas were suggested while the social committee was _____ the club's programme for the coming season.
   A arguing about **B** discussing **C** quarrelling about
   D disputing about

7 With an eighty-hour week and little change or enjoyment, life must have been very _____ for the nineteenth-century factory worker.
   A weary **B** anxious **C** dark **D** dreary

8 He is paving the garden _____ with flat stones of various shapes.
   A way **B** track **C** path **D** alley

9 Weeks later he had still not found a job and he began to feel _____.
   A sorry **B** displaced **C** displeased **D** discouraged

10 A long line of traffic had to wait at the _____ until the train had passed.
   A crossroads **B** junction **C** level crossing **D** bridge

The following extracts are taken from an information booklet about Youth Hostels in Great Britain.

Hostel buildings vary from cottage to castle. Most have been adapted to hostel use though some have been specially built for the purpose. As it is impossible to put identical facilities into such a wide range of buildings, hostels have been divided into four grades so

5 that members pay an overnight fee roughly corresponding to the facilities provided. Nevertheless, whatever the architectural differences, all hostels offer accommodation with the following facilities.

Sleeping in dormitories normally with 2-tier beds. Mattresses,

10 blankets and pillows are provided but you take your own sheet sleeping bag or hire a freshly laundered bag at the hostel.

Washing Washing facilities are provided, and at hostels where stated there are also baths or showers. You provide your own toilet articles including soap and towel.

15 **Common Room** All hostels have a common room. At some hostels this also serves as a dining-room.

Meals At most hostels hot meals can be provided by the warden. (The Hostel Details state where this is not the case.) Meals cannot be guaranteed unless paid for in advance. Lunch packets should also be

20 booked in advance whenever possible: it is easier to provide appetising fare when the warden knows beforehand how many lunch packets will be required. (Please note that lunch packets do not include any drinks.) Breakfast is usually cereal or porridge and a cooked dish followed by bread and marmalade and tea. Evening meal

25 is a 3-course meal usually consisting of soup, a meat course, a sweet or pudding and tea. A number of hostels now have a cafeteria service or provide snack meals.

Members' Kitchen At all hostels except some temporary hostels there are facilities for members to cook their own meals, including

30 cooking points, pots and pans. There is no charge for the use of these facilities.

Small Store Where the Hostel Details state that there is a small store it means there are sufficient foodstuffs on sale to enable self-cookers to prepare a meal. The following list of a typical small store

35 gives you a good idea of what you can buy, though every small store may not necessarily offer you these exact items. If ordered in advance: milk, bread, potatoes, margarine. Without ordering in advance: tins of beans and/or spaghetti, soup (or packets), condensed or evaporated milk, meat or meat pudding, fish, vegetables, fruit, steamed

40 puddings. Small jars of jam and marmalade. Small packets of tea, coffee, sugar and cornflakes or other cereal. Matches. Chocolate. Packets of crisp bread or oatcakes and dehydrated potato powder.

Store Where the Hostel Details state that there is a store there is an extensive range of foodstuffs available. It is likely that such stores will

45 have all the goods listed above and also the following: Greater variety of tinned goods. Packets of cheese, oats, biscuits and dates. Meat extract cubes. Milk, bread, potatoes and margarine should be ordered in advance.

Cutlery and crockery are supplied whether you have meals

50 provided or prepare your own.

Hostel telephones Telephones are primarily provided for administrative use and urgent business, not for social purposes. Wardens will pass on urgent messages, but cannot always locate a member to bring him to the telephone. It is helpful if you tell your friends and family
55 "Don't ring me — I'll ring you," and then use a public call box. If a warden allows you to use the telephone for an outgoing call, please be brief — there may be a member in difficulty, urgently trying to contact the warden. Bookings can be made by telephone. The telephone may be used for enquiries.

Here are a number of unfinished statements about the passage each with four suggested ways of finishing it. Choose the one you think fits best in each case.

1   The price of a night's accommodation
    A is related to the kind of building in which members stay.
    B varies according to the region.
    C is the same in all hostels.
    D depends on standards of convenience and comfort.

2   People spending a night in a hostel
    A have to use a sheet sleeping bag.
    B are provided with a free sheet sleeping bag.
    C have to bring their own sheet sleeping bag.
    D must use only a newly washed sheet sleeping bag.

3   Meals in hostels
    A may be available in the evening to those who arrive early enough.
    B are provided three times a day.
    C have to be booked in advance.
    D are cooked only for hostellers who arrive before 6 p.m.

4   All hostels provide
    A plates, knives and forks.
    B certain kinds of foods in packets.
    C bread and milk for self-cookers.
    D tins of beans and of soup.

5   The information about hostel telephones is included to
    A warn members against using them except in emergencies.
    B explain why their use is forbidden.
    C make clear both how and when to use them.
    D discourage hostellers from taking their use for granted.

Composition

Explanations

The most important qualities of a good explanation are clearness, accuracy and careful arrangement.

Below is an example of a short explanation. Certain facts are made clear first in the opening paragraph and then the other details are arranged so that the ideas follow one another logically.

Write a short report of the climate of the area you live in. This should include general information about temperatures, rainfall and wind directions, but it is not necessary to give any figures. Use between 120 and 180 words.

Plan

1 Position of Great Britain.
2 Winter climate.
3 Summer climate.
4 General tendencies.

Great Britain lies to the west of the Continent of Europe and has the Atlantic Ocean to the west. Winds most often come from that direction and are therefore damp and not too cold. The Gulf Stream, which flows around all coasts, helps to raise temperatures.

Winters are chilly and often damp but seldom really cold. There is some frost and occasional snowfalls, but normally the snow soon disappears. In some years there are longer periods of frost and snow.

Summers are fairly warm but never very hot though there may be occasional heat waves. It is often cloudy. Rain may fall at any time.

This is an island climate, with very changeable and moderate heat, cold and rainfall. It is impossible to give exact information about any period of the year.

(132 words)

Practice

Write between 120 and 180 words on the following.

1 Give an account of the main ways in which the people in your town or village earn their living.
   Here is a possible plan:
   (a) The most important industries (or kinds of farming)
   (b) Trade and business
   (c) Professional and general

2 Explain briefly how you celebrate any one of the following in your country:
   a wedding
   a twenty-first or other special birthday
   Christmas Eve (or Christmas Day)
   any national festival

3 Explain why you are learning English.

4 Explain the main difficulties you have had in learning English.

5 What are the advantages and drawbacks of living in a flat?

6 Explain why you enjoy or dislike living in the town or village where your home is.

7 As Secretary of a Youth Club you have to prepare an account of the aims, activities and meeting-times of the club. Write this account.

8 As a prospective Town Councillor you are preparing a letter to be sent to all the town residents. This mentions three things in the town which you think need improvement and how you think these improvements could be carried out. Write the information given in the letter — there is no need to put an address. You can write about an imaginary town if you wish.

Use of English

1 **Fill each of the numbered blanks in the passage with one suitable word.**

Thoroughly tired he _____(1) down on the bed and _____(2) asleep almost immediately. He was _____(3) by the sound of heavy footsteps in the attic _____(4). He took his torch and crept up the steep _____(5) of stairs, _____(6) the attic door silently. There were some cupboards inside but otherwise the room was _____(7) empty. He _____(8) on his torch now and started to examine _____(9) carefully, but found _____(10) to explain the sounds. He leaned _____(11) a large wardrobe and _____(12) his head disbelievingly. He had no _____(13) _____(14) to do next. Then he noticed that the _____(15) of the floor was completely covered with dust apart from _____(16) own footprints. He made his _____(17) downstairs again but he _____(18) little that night. He kept _____(19) to every sound and wondering _____(20) the house might be haunted.

2 (a) **Complete each of the following sentences with an appropriate word for a type of BUILDING.**
1 When he was set free after twenty years in _____, he was amazed at the changes he found.
2 Students can save money and make friends by living in a university or college _____.
3 An elderly or handicapped person is better off in a _____ with no stairs to climb.
4 He keeps his tools and equipment in a _____ he has put up in his garden.

2 (b) **Complete each of the following sentences with an appropriate word for an area of WATER.**
1 After the heavy shower, the _____ in the street soon dried up in the warm sunshine.
2 It takes about three hours to walk round the shore of the _____.
3 The river is fed by a number of small fast-flowing _____.
4 There's a _____ of water in the hall where you left your wet umbrella.

2 (c) **Complete each of the following sentences with an appropriate verb having the meaning FALL/GO DOWN.**
1 Wood will float but iron will _____.
2 Overnight the temperature _____ by ten degrees.
3 The lift _____ slowly, stopping at every floor.
4 The water-bird _____ into the water and came up with a fish in its beak.

2 (d) **Complete each of the following sentences with an appropriate word for a form of FORWARD MOVEMENT.**

1 These shoes are so uncomfortable that I can hardly _____ in them.
2 Never _____ when under the influence of alcohol.
3 Can you _____ a bicycle?
4 Do you see that: a small cat _____ after a large dog?

2 (e) **Complete each of the following sentences with an appropriate word expressing DISTANCE.**

1 Some of the mountains in this range are over three thousand metres _____.
2 These old streets are so _____ that pedestrians can pass along them only in single file.
3 The room had a length of four metres and a _____ of three.
4 This huge lake is nowhere more than three metres in _____.

3   **The reading passage described the experiences of a walker who was in fact offered accommodation in Mrs Parkin's house. That night he wrote a letter home.**

The following word groups, when extended into complete sentences, form part of the letter. Make all the changes and additions necessary to produce grammatical and well-constructed sentences. Note carefully some of the types of changes that may have to be made.

Example: This evening / I / find / pleasant place / spend / night.
Answer: This evening I have found a pleasant place to spend the night.

Dear Mum and Dad,

1 I / now complete / first half / my journey / and I / feel / little tired.
2 After / I / leave / home / Sunday / I / walk / more / eight hours.
3 Next day / I / leave / hostel / where / spend / night / seven o'clock / morning.
4 It / rain / so hard / I / travel / bus / instead / walk.
5 Today / weather / be / better / and I / spend / day / walk / beautiful mountain country.
6 It rain / when I / reach / this town / and / first / I / be / worried / find / accommodation.
7 I / tell / go / Mrs Parkins' house / as / son / be not / at home / now.
8 I / just / promise / good supper / and while / I / wait / it / I / write this letter / you.

More news soon.
Mark

Interview

Talking about a photograph

1 Suggest several ways in which this picture is related to the reading passage *Shelter for the Night*.
2 What was each of the domino players actually doing at the moment the photograph was taken?
3 Describe the type of interest in the game that each of the people behind the bar is showing.

Topics

Compare this pub with a café or similar place in your country where people can go to relax.

Various kinds of social life: coffee parties, dinner-parties, dances, meeting friends in cafés etc. Which do you most enjoy taking part in and why?

Suggest some ways of 'wasting time'. How would you define 'wasting time'?

Reading aloud

Meaning in spoken English is conveyed by the more essential words in a sentence, usually nouns, main verbs, most adjectives and adverbs. These are pronounced clearly, their unweakened vowels (see the reading passages in the previous section) being given their full value. Less essential words, including some auxiliary and modal verb forms, a few non-quality adjectives, certain pronouns such as *her, us, them,* the relative pronoun *that* and a few short conjunctions, may be spoken very quickly and lightly, with their vowel sounds weakened to /ə/ or /ɪ/, and initial *h-* (e.g. in *have*) and final *-d* (as in *and*) omitted.

Some commonly weakened forms

Auxiliaries: are /ə/, was /wəz/, were /wə/, has /əz/, have /əv/, had /əd/.

Modals: (unemphasised) must /məst/, could /kəd/, should /ʃəd/, would /wəd/.

(The above verbs are not weakened in negative or interrogative forms)

Pronouns: that /ðət/, her /hə/, us /əs/, them /ðəm/.

Adjectives: some /səm/ followed by an uncountable or plural: *I had some (səm) tea.*

Prepositions: to /tə/, at /ət/, of /əv/, for /fə/, from /frəm/.

Conjunctions: and /ən/, but /bət/, as /əz/.

Before reading aloud the following passages, underline the words you think are likely to be weakened and practise reading each in the word group where it belongs, using the weakened form.

Example: I left *as* early *as* I *was* able.

When you are satisfied with the results, read each passage through before suggesting the kind of situation in which it might have been said.

Passages

1   I left as early as I was able: I'd say it was about a quarter to seven. The sun had risen about an hour before but it was still a bit misty in low-lying places. I climbed to the top of Roman Beacon and from there I could see for miles. There was a long line of hills in front of me that stretched farther than I could see, with a few scattered villages on their slopes. I followed the ridge for a considerable distance and then stopped for a cup of thermos-flask tea and a sandwich at the highest point. At that time it was very warm but, as the afternoon went on, I noticed that some clouds were gathering and soon after sunset it started to rain. Fortunately I was only a short way from the town and had brought a good raincoat with me so I didn't get wet. But now I'm really tired and am looking forward to a good night's sleep.

2   Well, my opinion is that you can't trust any of them. They're all of them out for themselves. Look at that fellow Strongman that's standing for the Selfhelp party in this area. What's he but a lazy so-and-so that's never done a hard day's work in his life and depends for his keep on his well-off mum and dad? And that Mrs Sweet of the Social Welfare party. As hard as nails: if a starving beggar were to ask her for a crust of stale bread she'd turn her back on him and as likely as not have him arrested. Politicians! For all I know there may be some of them that are worth their weight in gold but I've never met any of

them. Most of those that I've ever met are in the game for what they can get out of it.

Structured communication

Talking about a regional map

Below is a map of Croyshire. Examine it for a minute or two and then express your ideas on one or more of the given topics.

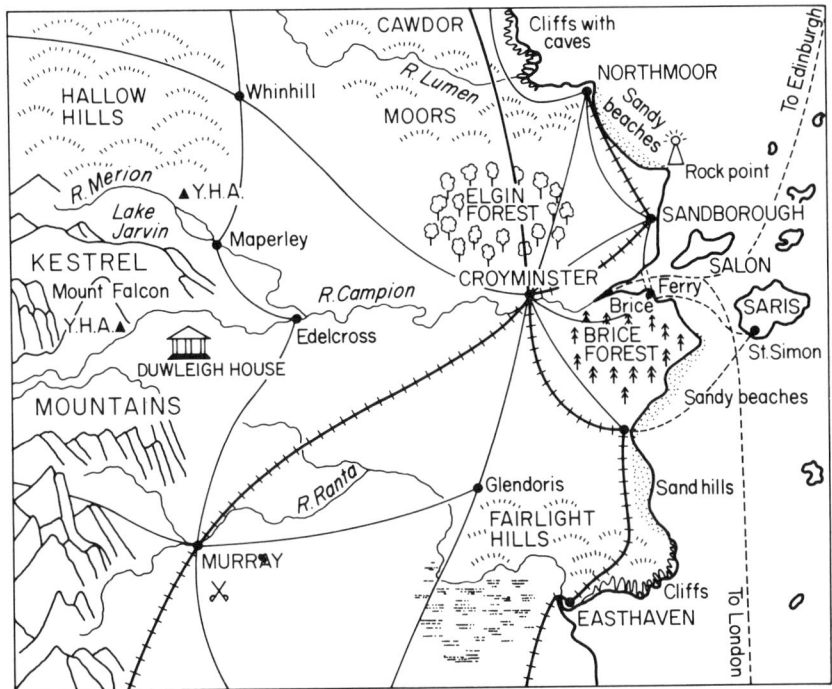

1 inch = 10 miles

🌳🌳 Deciduous forest	🏛 Historic house	—— Main road
⭡ ⭡ Coniferous forest	▲ Youth hostel	++++ Railway
= = Marsh		- - - - Shipping
ˌˌˌˌ Moors and hills	🔆 Lighthouse	✗ Battlefield

Some additional information

Croyminster: Capital of the area. Interesting historical city with some light industry.

Murray: A small but beautiful old market town.

Sandborough: A large seaside resort with sandy beach and many forms of amusement.

(a) Suppose you've retired from work and want to write a book, where in this area would you choose to live? Give several reasons for your choice.

(b) A foreign friend is staying with you in Croyminster. How do you spend each of seven days?

(c) Where could a motel most suitably be established? Why?

(d) Where would you establish a children's holiday camp? Why?

(e) How does this area differ from the area you live in?

(f) Describe any part of the coast of your country or of any nearby country.

Speech situations

1 You have been asked for advice about interesting places in your area. Suggest a few, explaining why you are recommending a visit.

2 You have been asked to recommend a local restaurant. Justify your choice.

Expressing opinions

1 What things can make a pub, café or restaurant attractive besides the food and drink served there?

2 Do you enjoy walking in the countryside? Why or why not?

3 If you could choose the weather throughout the year, what kind of weather or varieties of weather would you choose? Explain why.

Description of objects

The following objects are all mentioned in the reading passage 'Shelter for the night'. Describe each of them in such a way that the other students can guess what it is. Special reference should be made to its uses and what it is usually made of.

(a) a raincoat (b) a pocket (c) a torch (d) a biscuit (e) chocolate
(f) a house (g) a (shop) counter (h) a domino

Discussion of youth club programme

A youth club committee under its full-time organising chairman is discussing the club programme for the next few months. Some two hundred young people are members and there are five rooms of various sizes on the premises. Indoor arrangements can cover every evening in the week and additional off-the-premises activities can be organised in the afternoons at week ends.
Suggest some ideas for activities, including social and educational activities, sports, social service in the community (old people etc), theatre visits, coach outings, weekend camping etc.

General guidance and practice

1 The infinitive

Uses

1 Subject of a verb: the gerund is commonly used as a subject of a verb but the infinitive so rarely that an intermediate student should avoid it entirely.

2 The infinitive follows various kinds of main verbs

    (a)   without the preposition *to*:
        (i)   modals such as *can, may, might, must, should, need, not*
        (ii) *had better, would rather: You'd better hurry.* (see page 170)
        (iii) *make, let: They made/let me help.*
        (iv) verbs of seeing, hearing, feeling: *I saw him stop.*
        (v) After the preposition *but: They did nothing but laugh.*

    (b)   with the preposition *to*:
        A large number of main verbs, many of which are introduced in

different parts of this book. It is impossible to suggest any guidance in the use of the infinitive or gerund after other verbs; each example has to be learned as it occurs. There is a summary of most of the common uses on page 263.

Forms

Notice the following infinitive forms:

	Active	Passive
Simple	**to take**	**to be taken**
Continuous	**to be taking**	—
Perfect	**to have taken**	**to have been taken**
Perfect Continuous	**to have been taking**	—

The form of the infinitive used suggests either time or duration (often both), as shown in the following examples:

He likes *to lie* in the sun. (habitual action)

He wants *to take* a photograph. (in the immediate or distant future)

He seems *to be taking* a photograph. (at this moment)

He seems *to have taken* a photograph. (he has just finished)

He is said *to have taken up* politics. (action in the past)

He must *have been taking* photographs all day. (emphasis on a period of time)

The sentry told us we ought not *to have taken (been taking)* photographs of the aerodrome. (the perfect infinitive used with 'should' or 'ought to' — the photographs were actually taken.)

We should *have asked* him about it. (perfect infinitive — in fact we did not ask him.)

Practice

1 Express these sentences with a suitable infinitive form of the verbs in brackets.

(a) Why is Grandfather working in the garden? He should (rest) on a hot afternoon like this.

(b) Why aren't you ready? You could (finish) your packing this morning.

(c) Further information can (obtain) at the Citizens' Advice Bureau.

(d) I'd like (visit) Athens during my coming holiday.

(e) You seem (carry) a lot of luggage. Where are you going to?

(f) In the circumstances there was nothing I could do but (leave) the shop.

(g) He can't find his wallet. He thinks it might (steal).

(h) I might (enjoy) myself at the seaside if I hadn't been preparing for this exam.

2 Replace the words in brackets in the following passage with any suitable verbal form, active or passive, you have learned in this or a previous chapter:

Mrs. Parkins proved to be a motherly woman of about fifty. An apron (tie) round her neat blue skirt and she (seem) (smile) even before she (open) the door.

'I (just come) from next door,' he (explain). 'I (tell) that you some-times (let) your spare room.'

Her face (cloud) over. '(Be) not that a pity!' she (exclaim). 'I (just promise) it to one of my husband's friends. He (send) here by his firm today to survey a new housing site.'

He (just turn) away, when she (stop) him. 'I (must) (think),' she (say). '(Come) in and (sit) down.'

He (lead) into a cosy sitting-room where a fire (burn). She (watch) television when he (knock), but after she (put) a kettle on in the kitchen, she (come) and (switch) the television off.

'I (think) of an idea,' she (inform) him. '(Mind) you sleeping on a camp bed in the attic? The mattress (air) two days ago, and the sheets (can) (air) now while you (have) some supper. What (think) you of that?'

He (say) this (be) a very good idea, and in less than half an hour an enormous supper of eggs, bacon and tomatoes (set) in front of him. As soon as he (eat) it, he (go) thankfully to bed. He (seem) (discover) a very comfortable lodging.

2 The gerund

The gerund is a noun formed by adding -ing to a suitably adapted verbal infinitive form:

sing   singing,   write   writing,   run   running.

It can be qualified by an adjective and modified by an adverb:

Clear thinking/Thinking clearly is essential in an emergency.

Though a noun it can take an object:

Eating too many sweets is bad for the teeth.

Note: A true gerund is uncountable: *He is studying building.*
But the product of a gerund is countable: *two buildings.*

(a)   A gerund can be the subject of a verb:
    Smoking (cigarettes) can be harmful.

(b)   It can be the object of certain verbs:
    He has stopped/given up smoking.
    Children enjoy running about.

(c)   It often follows a preposition:
    You can learn a lot by keeping your eyes open.

(d)   It can follow the adjectives *worth* and *busy*:
    This isn't worth reading.   She's busy typing.

(e)   As a noun it may be preceded by a possessive adjective:
    Do you mind my smoking? (*me smoking* would suggest that the speaker is on fire.)

As in the case of the infinitive, verbs taking a gerund object must be learned individually; a few verbs can be followed by either, with or without meaning change.

Practice

Suggest suitable gerunds to complete these sentences together with additional words where appropriate. Say which of the uses listed above the gerund is serving.

(a)   _____ is my favourite summertime occupation.
(b)   A dog enjoys _____
(c)   Old people spend a lot of their time _____

116

(d)   In late spring families start looking forward to _____
(e)   That film on at the Regent Cinema is well worth _____
(f)   _____ makes me very tired.
(g)   The weather had cleared up so I suggested _____
(h)   The cook was busy _____
(i)   Having no coins for the telephone I asked a passer-by if she'd mind

_____

(j)   _____ is more interesting than _____

3   Direct and indirect objects

There are three groups of verbs in which the construction involving direct and indirect objects differs.

(a)   *I sent/wrote/gave him a letter:*
        I told him a story.
        I bought him a present.

The forms *me, him, her, it, us, you, them* are all used to express the direct and indirect object. When the indirect object precedes the direct object it has no preposition (*to* or *for*) before it. It may however follow the direct object — usually for emphasis — and in this case is preceded by *to* or *for* as suitable. This applies also to noun objects:
        He gave his son/him a gold watch.
        He bought a gold watch/it for his son/him.
        They have awarded this year's Nobel prize to a blind poet.

Other verbs in this group include: *take, bring, show, make, sell.*

(b)   In the case of the verb *ask*, the indirect object is never accompanied by the preposition to:
        I asked him a question.
        Never **I asked a question to him.*

(c)   In the case of *say, explain* and *describe*, the indirect object is always accompanied by *to*, and must therefore always follow the direct object:
        I said goodbye to him.
        The teacher explained the rule to the students.
        The guide described the historic battle to the tourists.

All verbs indicating ways of speaking (e.g. *shout, whisper, mutter*) belong to this group.

Practice

Arrange the direct and indirect objects correctly in the following sentences, adding any necessary prepositions. Indicate where there is a possible alternative and suggest any difference in meaning this may result in:

(a)   The postman gave / a registered letter / me
(b)   The man gave / a bone / his dog
(c)   Why have you sent / this / me
(d)   The scientist explained / the experiment / me
(e)   One of the audience asked / a question / him
(f)   Have you told / everything / them
(g)   Why did you say / that / him
(h)   The retired colonel wrote / a letter / the editor

(i)   Why didn't you send / a postcard / her
(j)   The witness described / the accident / us

4 Countable and uncountable nouns

The passage on page 98 includes: some nouns that are always uncountable, some that are uncountable or countable according to their meaning and some that are always plural. Others are included in the lists below.

Practice

1   Use each of these nouns in sentences so that its meaning and use are made clear. Those in the middle list have at least two meanings.

Unc	Unc/C	Plural
information	rubber	clothes
machinery	tea	police
furniture	wit	goods
advice	hair	surroundings
shopping	cold	premises
money	work	scissors
gambling	iron	
luggage	sense	
news	manner	
knowledge	force	
magic	pastry	
applause	tin	
elastic	wood	
dust	glass	
progress	ice	
water		

2   What are:
   (i)   a compass
   (ii) a pair of compasses.

5 Word order: pre- and inter-verb adverbs

(a)   Single word adverbs of frequency: *always, usually, often, frequently, sometimes, occasionally, seldom, rarely,* and *never* may precede the verb when this is in the Present or Past Simple Tense (for exceptions see (e) below.) *Very often, very frequently, very seldom, very rarely, hardly ever, scarcely ever* may do the same.

Among the other adverbs to which this rule may apply are:
   (i)   *soon, still, now, then, recently, possibly, obviously, evidently.*
   (ii)   many adverbs of manner when they are not emphasised in any way: *He entered the room and quietly sat down.* (Cf. He entered the room noisily but sat down *quietly.*)
   (iii) Most other unemphasised adverbs.

(b)   A few adverbs indicating definite time like *yesterday, today, tomorrow, nowadays* never stand between subject and verb. The same applies to *early* and *late.*
   He arrived here yesterday.

(c)   When single adverbs modify other words than main verbs they should normally stand as near the word modified as possible:
   That dog is very badly trained.
   You promised never to stay out late.

The day was almost over.
The same applies to the adverbial *only* which is often misplaced especially in speech.

Practice

Suggest six different meanings of the following sentence expressed by the six positions of *only*:
(Only) the solicitor (only) showed (only) the farmer (only) the paper (only) he had (only) to sign.

(d)   In a few phrases where the adjective is used adverbially it never comes between the subject and verb. Two examples are *to work hard, to stay long* (a long time).

(e)   The exact position of the adverb depends on the form of the verb.

    (i)   Except in the case of the verb 'to be' and also when there are two verbs together, when the verb is a single word (Present and Past Simple tenses) a suitable adverb can be placed between the subject and the verb:
He never answers my questions.
The maid quietly left the kitchen.
But: *She is never late.*
Such adverbs usually follow the verb 'to be' immediately.

    (ii)   When the verb is made up of two or more words, a suitable adverb can be placed between the first two of these words:
He must always salute his superior officers.
I have sometimes been annoyed with him.
She is now making a speech.
He can soon come out of hospital.

All these adverbs may come at the end of the sentence when they are specially emphasised:
This is not his first time in prison: he has been there often.

Note: The whole subject of the order of adverbs is a difficult one as word order depends very much on sentence meaning and emphasis rather than rules. However, the above rules should help a little.

Practice

In the following sentences, indicate the different places where the adverb may be placed, making it clear where the position would be an expected one and where the position indicates special emphasis.

(a)   He goes to the cinema. (often)
(b)   He is selfish. (sometimes)
(c)   He has completed his novel. (now)
(d)   They are opening a new school here. (soon)
(e)   The rain has set in. (probably)
(f)   The audience went home. (then)
(g)   The old man went up to the window. (slowly)
(h)   He was tired out. (obviously)
(i)   Are you sitting there doing nothing? (still)
(j)   The coach tourists have been allowed time to write letters. (occasionally)
(k)   The small boy was feeding the monkey with peanuts. (busily)
(l)   The waiter spilt the soup on her new dress. (clumsily)

(m)　He likes to get his newspaper. (early)
(n)　Go and wash your hands. (now)
(o)　Have you seen a pink elephant? (ever)
(p)　The milkman forgot to call. (yesterday)
(q)　I am afraid he is not working. (hard)
(r)　Owls can see in the dark. (only)
(s)　He has been spoilt. (completely)
(t)　The stepfather treated the child. (cruelly)

Note:　The word *ever* is normally found only in interrogative and negative sentences, or in what are in effect reported questions:
　　I wonder if he will ever come.
It is however found with *hardly* or *scarcely* in affirmative statements:
　　He is hardly ever away.

6 Inverted commas

(a)　Inverted commas may be used either in pairs or singly.

(b)　Where the direct speech begins, the inverted commas are usually upside down ['']; where it closes they are the right way up [''].

(c)　They are always above the line:
　　'Good morning,' he said.

(d)　If the inverted commas open in the middle of the sentence for the first time in that sentence, they are usually preceded by a comma and followed by a capital letter:
　　Mrs. Bates glared at her husband and said, 'You need a haircut.'

(e)　Direct speech ending in the middle of a sentence is followed by a comma.

(f)　If the same person starts to speak a second time in the same sentence, it is usual to open with a small letter:
　　The ticket collector said: 'You've just missed the train,' and added unsympathetically, 'and that was the last one tonight.'

(g)　Questions and exclamation marks come inside the inverted commas:
　　'Where have you been?' he asked. (no comma in this case)

(h)　A new paragraph should be started with each fresh speaker:
　　She turned on him indignantly. 'It isn't true,' she said. 'They will never believe that.'
　　He shrugged his shoulders. 'Whether it is true or not,' he assured her, 'they can be persuaded to believe it.'

Practice

Punctuate the following passage, inserting inverted commas, commas, question and exclamation marks and capital letters, and also starting new paragraphs where necessary:

The shop assistant eyed me sulkily as I went up to the counter. Have you any of those reversible mackintoshes you had last week I asked. No madam she answered they are sold out. What a pity I exclaimed. But perhaps I can take a nylon one. Have you one in blue? No madam said the assistant only yellow. I felt I was making no progress. Well I said I must have something. It's pouring now. Perhaps I can manage for the present with a cheap plastic one. You'll need outsize madam the assistant replied and they are in our stock room. Could you fetch me one I asked. No madam, it's my lunchtime now. Sorry. She examined herself in the shop mirror for a moment and then walked off, leaving me unattended.

Unusually annoyed I asked to see the manager. He was very apologetic. I'm sorry he said we are always having complaints about that assistant. And yet you keep her I remarked. Yes but she's leaving tomorrow he replied. She says she has found a much better job as a receptionist in a luxury hotel. I am wondering about two things I meditated aloud how she got such a job and how long she will keep it.

(Do you need a question mark at the end?)

7 Some spelling rules

(a) Doubling of final consonants

(i) Single syllables containing one vowel and ending in a single consonant (with the exception of -*w* and -*y*) double the final consonant before a suffix beginning with a vowel:

stir   stirred   stirring   big   bigger   biggest
hat   hatter   rot   rotten

(but notice: *bus, buses; gas, gases*).

(ii) Words of more than one syllable with a single vowel in the last syllable and a single final consonant double the final consonant when the stress is on the last syllable, provided that the suffix begins with a vowel. There is no doubling when the final consonant is -*w* or -*y*.

When the stress is elsewhere there is no doubling, except when the final consonant is -*l*, which is always doubled so long as there is a single vowel in the last syllable, and the suffix begins with a vowel. Three exceptions to this rule are: *worshipped, gossipped* and *kidnapped*.

Examples:

begín   begínning   begínner
tátter   táttered
refér   reférring   reférred   but réference
cáncel   cancellátion   cáncelling
instál   instálling   instálled   but instálment

Practice

Complete the following words by adding the suffixes indicated:

stop	-ed	-ing	-er	
rub	-ed	-ing	-er	
heat	-ed	-ing	-er	
gallop	-ed	-ing		
quarrel	-ed	-ing	-some	
confer	-ed	-ing	-ence	
conquer	-ed	-ing	-or	(*qu* are together a
offer	-ed	-ing		consonant)
shut		-ing	-er	
signal	-ed	-ing	-er	
regret	-ed	-ing	-able	
open	-ed	-ing		
admit	-ed	-ing	-ance	
happen	-ed	-ing		
appear	-ed	-ing	-ance	
matter	-ed			
compel	-ed	-ing		
transfer	-ed	-ing	(*transferable* is an exception)	
benefit	-ed	-ing		

Remember: write   wrote   written
a dining-room   a dinner table

(b)   *ie   ei*

(i)   English schoolchildren learn this rule as: 'i before e except after c'. This applies only when the sound corresponds to the phonetic / i:/, as in *brief, chief, belief, grief, thief, piece, niece, priest, hygiene, shriek, receive, deceive, ceiling, conceit.* There are two exceptions: *seize, Sheila* (a girl's name).

(ii)   The sound 'ei' is sometimes expressed by the letters 'ei' or 'eigh': *rein, vein, weigh, eight, reign.*

(iii)   The following words are sometimes misspelt: *height, foreign, forfeit, friend.*

(c)   Noun: *-ce* Verb: *-se*
Compare the spellings of the following nouns and verbs.
Nouns: *advice   practice   licence   device   prophecy*
Verbs: *advise   practise   license   devise   prophesy*

Practice

Complete the following with the correct spelling.

(a)   You need more practi__e in speaking.
(b)   advi__e to school-leavers
(c)   licen__ed for the sale of alcohol
(d)   Experts prophe__y a growing fuel shortage.
(e)   an anti-thief devi__e on cars
(f)   a driving licen__e
(g)   You must practi__e daily.
(h)   I advi__e you to wait.
(i)   His prophe__y did not come true.
(j)   a doctor's practi__e
(k)   Can you devi__e a method of improving my spelling?

(d)   Final *-ce/-ge* before a suffix beginning with *a* or *o*. The final *-e* is not dropped in such cases before *-ous* or *-able*. Examples: *courageous, noticeable* (cf. *notable*), *changeable.*

General practice   Complete the following words, adding or deleting letters as necessary.

(a)   rel__f   (b)   tap (ing)   (c)   manage(able)
(d)   perc__ve   (e)   peace(able)   (f)   conceal(ed)
(g)   prefer(ence)   (h)   compar(able)   (i)   s__ge
(j)   begin(ing)   (k)   f__ld   (l)   label(ing)
(m)   matter(ed)   (n)   coat(ing)   (o)   rec__pt
(p)   challeng(able)

122

6 Fear for Company

By the time she had finished tidying up, Bill was almost ready to go. He
was looking for his gloves, which turned up eventually under a cushion.

'You need not worry about me, Mum,' he declared. 'If the fog thickens,
Harold will put me up for the night. In that case, I promise I'll give you a
5 ring as soon as we decide. But even if I didn't get into touch with you,
you'd know I was all right. I give you my word I'll take no risks.'

'I hope not,' she said bluntly. 'I shall be waiting up till you call. You'll
be better off staying the night anyhow, if they don't mind.'

He grinned affectionately. 'I'll see,' he said. 'How about your dropping
10 in to see Aunt Maggie when I've gone? She'd be only too pleased.'

He kissed her goodbye, strode out to his motor cycle and swung one leg
over the saddle. The engine roared into life and she watched him move off
noisily down the road. He turned, waved, swerved to avoid a wandering
dog and disappeared into the mist which was blotting out all but the nearer
15 houses.

She had always enjoyed being alone. Bill had had the radio repaired and
if she felt like it, she could listen to whatever play was being broadcast that
evening. She had the chance of trying out the new record she had been
given for Christmas. And inevitably there was a pile of washing that
20 needed ironing; there were clothes to be mended and patched, socks to be
darned. Had she wanted company, she would have taken Bill's advice and
called at her sister's, who would have been delighted to have someone to
share her solitude. But she was reluctant to go; she could not get rid of the
persistent feeling that if she were to leave the house, she would have cause
25 to regret it bitterly.

'It's absurd to be having such fancies,' she said to herself. 'I've
obviously been overworking and am tired out. I could do with a sleep. I
shall feel better when I wake up.'

She made up the fire with a few logs of wood and lay back in the
30 rocking-chair. The clock ticked rhythmically; the logs crackled and flared.
Her eyelids drooped and she dozed peacefully.

She awoke with a sick feeling of dread. The room was in darkness, with
a heap of dying embers in the grate. Before turning on the light, she groped
her way to the window. Fog, yellow and opaque, was pressing against the
35 panes, muffling all sounds of the few pedestrians whom circumstances
compelled to be out of doors. She drew the curtains to shut out its grimy,
dreary ugliness.

Her uneasy feeling of imminent catastrophe was increasing; she pulled
herself together firmly and went to stoke the fire, this time with lumps of
40 coal. Heavy steps were approaching the house; there was a single com-
manding knock. With the shovel still clutched in one hand, her fingers
automatically loosening her apron ribbons, she went to open the door.
Blocking the open-sided porch, framed by the enveloping fog, stood a tall
grave-faced policeman.

Notes on the passage

Vocabulary

Title   *company* (Unc) = having people with one: *He likes company.*
a company (C) = a group of people associated for business: *a limited company; a theatrical company.* Notice: *an acquaintance; a friend (a school-friend).*
a companion = somebody with one. *a fellow-student. comrade* is rare in English.

1   *tidy (up) a room, tidy up; She always looks neat and tidy. wash clothes (do the washing); wash up (do the washing up).* Also: *do the ironing.*

2   *eventual/eventually*   final/finally.

5   *touch: get in touch with; be in touch with; keep in touch with; be out of touch with; lose touch with. Some people keep in touch with old friends by sending Christmas cards. Doctors must keep in touch with new developments in medicine.*

6   Spelling: *all right.*

9   *grin* (N and V) = smile broadly like a schoolboy.
sneer (N and V) = smile cruelly and contemptuously (can also be used for an unpleasantly critical remark).
beam (N and V) = smile with great enjoyment.
giggle (N and V) = laugh in a silly way (*snigger* has a similar meaning but includes furtive mockery).
chuckle (N and V) = laugh quietly with great enjoyment.

11   *swing* = move like a pendulum.
sway = with the upper part moving from side to side, as trees do in a wind.
swerve = change direction suddenly to avoid something. A person sitting on *a swing* moves backwards and forwards. At fairs there are *swings* and *roundabouts.*

12   Animal noises: a lion or tiger *roars;* a dog *barks,* and when angry, *growls* or *snarls;* a cat *meows,* and when pleased, *purrs;* a cow *moos;* a pig *grunts;* a sheep *bleats;* a hen *clucks;* a cock *crows;* a duck *quacks;* some birds only *twitter;* bees *buzz;* crickets *chirp;* snakes *hiss.*

12   *look at* something still (a picture). *watch* something moving (a game).

14   *a blot* is an ink stain on paper, and it can be partly removed by the use of *blotting-paper. to blot out* is to make disappear.

17   a play is *broadcast* on the radio but *shown* on television.

18   *try out* some new thing to see whether it is satisfactory.
try on a new dress to see whether it fits and suits you.

18   This is a new *recording* of the concerto. *a record-player.* Also: *sports records; a record* of what has happened.

20   *patch* (N and V) = cover with material a worn place in a garment. Also: *a patch* of blue sky, of woodland.

23   *get rid of* something by throwing it away or giving it away, of unwelcome people by sending them away.

26   *a fancy* = something vaguely imagined. *fancy* (V): *What do you fancy for dinner?* (What would you like to have?) *Fancy that!* (an exclamation of surprise). (Adj): *a fancy cake* (not plain but decorated); *a fancy handkerchief; a fancy-dress party* (when unusual costumes are worn).

27   *overwork* (N and V) = do more work than is good for one's health.
overdo things = do more than is good for one. Also: this meat is *overdone/underdone. overrated* = thought too highly of; *overpraised.* Also: *overcharge; overeat; overflow; overload; oversleep; overstrain; overweight.* Notice: *do overtime* = do extra work; *overtime pay.*

27   *tired out* = completely tired. A *worn* coat may be repaired; a coat that is *worn out* cannot. *eat up/finish up/use up* = completely.

29 *make up* a fire with extra fuel: coal, coke, logs of wood.

30 dry sticks burning may *crackle;* badly-fitting windows *rattle* in a strong wind; leaves *rustle;* old wooden stairs may *creak;* coins in a bag or glasses may *clink;* heavy iron chains *clank;* a heavy noisy bell *clangs;* a heavy silk skirt may *swish.*

31 *eyelids eyebrows* are sometimes plucked. *eyelashes* are sometimes false.

31 *droop* = sink slowly: unwatered plants may droop.

31 *doze* = sleep lightly or have a nap (a short sleep). Notice: *a dose* of medicine.

33 *embers* = the glowing remains of a fire. *cinders* = pieces of burnt-out coal. *ashes* = the cold remains of something burnt. *an ash-tray* for *cigarette ash.*

35 *muffling A muffler* is a thick scarf worn to protect the throat and neck; a person is then *muffled up.* When noise is *muffled,* the sound appears to have a thick muffler over it. Notice: *a muff* (to keep the hands warm). *A shawl* is considerably larger than *a scarf.*

38 *a catastrophe (catastrophic)* is *a disaster (disastrous).*

38 *pull yourself together* = take control of yourself: *I have relaxed for an hour but now I must pull myself together and do some work. I know this has been a shock to you but you must pull yourself together and face it.*

41 coal is carried in a *shovel;* lumps of coal (and sugar) can be picked up in *tongs;* a fire is poked (pushed into) with a *poker;* a garden is dug with a *spade* and dead leaves are brought together with a *rake* and carried away in a *wheelbarrow.*

41 *clutch* something = seize it wildly. *grasp* something = seize it firmly. *cling (to)* with the fear of losing. *grip* = hold very tightly. *clasp* = have one's arms or hand round. *a clasp* = a fastener not unlike a buckle on a belt.
Which? _____ an opportunity; _____ the banisters when falling downstairs; a child _____ a puppy; some people _____ their lost youth; he could not escape from the policeman's _____.

42 *lose keys. loose* (set free) a guard dog. *loose* (Adj) (opp. tight). *loosen* = make less tight. (Be careful with spelling.)

42 *an apron* covers the front of the clothes. *an overall* covers the clothes completely. A comprehensive insurance policy provides *overall protection.*

44 *grave* (Adj) = serious. *grave* (N) = a hole in the ground where a dead person is buried.

Phrasal verbs

turn *turn against* someone = take a dislike to someone known.
turn away from an unpleasant sight. *turn away* people for whom there is no room.
turn back and go home again.
turn down an offer or suggestion = refuse it.
turn in = go to bed. *He turned the garage into a workroom .*
turn on/off the light/the radio/the T.V./the gas/a tap.
turn out an unwelcome dog. *The weather turned out fine. The boy turned out better than his parents had expected.*
turn over a page. *The small boat overturned in the sea.*
He *turned around* to write on the blackboard.
turn up at a meeting.

Practice

(a) _____ and see who is behind you.
(b) Be sure you _____ for our party.
(c) _____ to the next page.
(d) Ambulancemen cannot _____ from horrible sights.
(e) It's getting a bit late: I'll soon have to _____.
(f) He used to like you: why has he _____ you?

125

(g) The barman _____ the drunken man. *TURNED OUT*
(h) She _____ his invitation to dinner. *TURNED DOWN*
(i) The ugly duckling eventually _____ a swan. *TURN OUT*
(j) The film _____ to be utterly boring. *TURNED OUT*
(k) Very cold water eventually _____ ice. *TURNS IN*

Other uses of *turn*:
(a) He turned pale. His hair turned grey.
(b) The weather turned (became) cool. (*turned out* suggests there had been some doubt.)
(c) It has turned eight (is a little after eight).

Pronunciation

These need care:

ʊ (as in good): b*u*sh /bʊʃ/, c*u*shion /kʊʃn/, p*u*sh /pʊʃ/, f*u*ll /fʊl/, p*u*ll /pʊl/

ʌ (as in sun): br*u*sh /brʌʃ/, cr*u*sh /krʌʃ/, r*u*sh /rʌʃ/, R*u*ssian /rʌʃn/, g*u*ll /gʌl/, l*u*llaby /lʌ́ləbaɪ/

eɪ (as in day): *a*pron /éɪprən/, *a*pricot /éɪprɪkɒt/, *a*corn /éɪkɔːn/, *a*lien /éɪlɪən/, *A*sia /éɪʒə/, *A*von /éɪvɒn/, *a*viation /eɪvɪéɪʃn/, *a*viary /éɪvɪəri/

Stress changes: récord (N) /rékɔːd/; recórd (V) /rɪkɔ́ːd/.
Similar cases of noun and verb stress changes: permit, ally, conduct, contract, envelope, convict.

Sound changes: cycle /sáɪkl/, bicycle /báɪsɪkl/; dropped /drɒpt/, drooped /druːpt/; dosed /dəʊst/, dozed /dəʊzd/; lose /luːz/, loose /luːs/, loosen /luːsn/.

Silent letters: ironing /áɪənɪŋ/; rhythmically /rɪ́ðmɪkəli/.

ə (as in *a*go): *a*ffecti*o*nate /əfékʃənɪt/; inevit*a*ble /ɪnévɪtəbl/; persistent /pəsístənt/; *a*bsurd /əbzɜ́ːd/; pedestrians /pədéstrɪənz/; circumstances /sɜ́ːkəmstənsɪz/; curtains /kɜ́ːtənz/; automatic /ɔːtəmǽtɪk/; policeman /pəliːsmən/ or /pliːsmən/; Christmas /krísməs/; obviously /ɒ́bvɪəsli/; gramophone /grǽməfəʊn/.

Others: shovel /ʃʌ́vl/; tidying /táɪdɪŋ/; ready /rédi/; flared /fléəd/; opaque /əʊpéɪk/; grimy /gráɪmi/; catastrophe /kətǽstrəfi/; porch /pɔːtʃ/; muffled /mʌ́fəld/; ugliness /ʌ́glɪnɪs/; broadcast /brɔ́ːdkɑːst/; solitude /sɒ́lɪtjuːd/; clutched /klʌtʃt/.

Grammatical and structural points

(a) *whatever*   anything that, it doesn't matter what; of any kind:
   You can do whatever you like.
   He has no sense whatever.

whichever   it doesn't matter which:
   Choose whichever you like

whoever   anybody that:
   Whoever said that must be mad.

whenever   any time that:
   Come whenever you feel like it.

wherever   any (every) place that:
   Sit wherever there is room.
   Wherever he goes, he causes trouble.

however   in any way, it doesn't matter how:
  However much he tries, he still makes mistakes.

Each of these can be a stronger form of the corresponding interrogative pronoun or adverb:
  Whatever are you doing? Wherever have you been?
  However may also have the meaning of *yet*.

(b) Reflexive pronouns are much less common in English than in many other languages. Be careful with these verbs:
  he hid; he feels tired; he remembers; he escaped; he ran away; he hurried; the flower opened; the museum opens on Sundays; the door opened/closed.

Here are one or two English uses:
  he enjoyed himself (enjoyed the party); *he washed himself* (he got washed); *he cut/hurt/injured/killed himself.*
Remember: *he combed his hair; he broke his leg; he washed his face.*

Notice these reflexives with prepositions:
  talk to herself; look after himself; take care of yourself; pull yourself together; do it for myself; look at herself; he did/made it for himself.

Notice the difference between: *he did it by himself* (without help) and *he lived by himself* (alone).

(c) Participles: active and passive
The Present Participle is active in meaning:
  an interesting book (the book provides the interest).
The Past Participle is passive in meaning:
  an interested reader (the reader is interested in or by something).
Examples from the passage: *Fog, . . . muffling all sounds . . . the shovel still clutched in one hand.*

(d) *all but; nothing but; everything but; anything but; nobody but; anybody but. but* is often (though not necessarily) used in these cases instead of *except*.

(e) Infinitives: active and passive
In many cases, when the infinitive is adjectival, either the active or the passive can be used: *clothes to be mended/clothes to mend; socks to be darned/socks to darn.*
But usually: *a house to let; a book to read; time to waste.* Notice: *a house for sale.*

(f) Verbal constructions
Alternative constructions:
  like/love/hate to *do/doing* (with little meaning change)
  but: should like *to do;* enjoy/dislike/detest/loathe *doing*
  stop doing something *to do* something different: *He stopped climbing to admire the view* (purpose).

Infinitive:	Subject	to be	adjective	infinitive
	He	*is*	*ready*	*to go.*
	They	*will be*	*sure/pleased/*	*to come.*
			in a hurry	*to leave.*

Gerund: *How about your dropping in to see her?*
  She had the chance of trying it out.
  You will (would) be better off staying the night.

Prepositions

(a) *for:* a tie *for* Christmas; go to Wales *for* a holiday (but: he is now *on* holiday); go to a concert *for a change;* do something *for a bet.*
(b) called *at* her sister's; but: called *on* her sister.
(c) *in/out* of touch with.

(d) worry *about*.

(e) get rid *of*.

<table>
<tr><td>Expressions for use
in written work</td><td>

(a) *By the time* you get there, it will be dark.

(b) It may rain. *In that case*, we shall have to cancel the picnic.

(c) *Even if* you leave at once, you will still be late.

(d) *I give you my word* (I promise).

(e) He *had the chance of* appearing on television.

(f) She would *have cause to* regret it/be thankful.

(g) She *pulled herself together*.

(h) You will *inevitably* fail because you are so lazy.

</td></tr>
</table>

Spoken English

Making suggestions

Each of the following opening statements can introduce some kind of recommendation or idea of something that might be done.

> *What do you think of (about)* seeing the football match tomorrow?
> *Wouldn't it be a good (better) idea* to reserve seats in advance?
> *It might be a good idea* to wait and see what the weather's like.
> *Would you like* to go on a river-trip up the Thames?
> *Shall we* have lunch at the 'Good Cheer' restaurant?
> *How about* having some wine with our lunch?
> *Let's* have a party.
> *Why not* put off your visit till next week?
> *We'd (we had) better* leave now.
> *We might as well* sit down while we're waiting.

Practice

(a) Express each of the above as it would follow the words 'He has suggested'. The first will be: *He has suggested our seeing the football match tomorrow.*

(b) Express each of the following ideas as a suggestion, using as many ways of doing so as are suitable in each case:
  let our friends know we're coming; have the car serviced before our holiday; consult a doctor; throw all these old newspapers away; have the house redecorated; take an umbrella.

Colloquial expressions from the passage

I'll give you a ring. I'll ring you up. (I'll (tele)phone you.) (*I'll drop you a line* = I'll write to you.)

He's *well off* (a) He has a lot of money. (b) He's always grumbling: he doesn't know when he's *well off*.

He's *better off*/than I am/without your useless advice/living at home. It's *better for* you to live at home. You'll be *better off* living at home.

He'd be *only too pleased* to see you.

I *could do with* a fortnight's holiday.

I see = I understand. *Do you see?*

I'll *see* = I'll think about it.

I'll see about it = I'll think or do something about it.

I'll see to that splinter in your finger = I'll do whatever is necessary to put things right.

Practice

Use one of the above expressions with *see* to complete each of the following.

(a) Can we go to the circus next week? _____
(b) This tap needs a new washer. All right, _____
(c) You see, he's so terrified of water because years ago he nearly drowned. Oh, _____
(d) Could you knit me a pair of warm gloves? Well, _____
(e) It's already one o'clock. _____ lunch.

On the telephone

R Admass Publicity. Good afternoon.

P Good afternoon. This is Miss Pelham speaking. May I speak to Mr. Tavistock, please?

R I didn't quite catch your name. Would you spell it, please? . . . Thank you. Would you wait a minute, please. I'll see if he's in. . . . I'm sorry, I'm afraid he isn't in just now. Can I put you through to his secretary?

P If you would, please.

S Miss Somerset speaking. Mr. Tavistock isn't in now but perhaps I can help you.

P This is a personal matter which is rather urgent. If Mr. Tavistock will be in soon, perhaps he can ring me back.

S I'm afraid he's in Bristol today.

P Is it possible to get in touch with him there?

S No. You see, he'll be making calls all day and then going on to Cardiff.

P This is really an emergency. Are you his private secretary? Can I tell you something in confidence?

S Most certainly you can.

P I'm the Nockling probation officer. His son has been arrested for robbery with violence and as his mother's in hospital, I've been asked to get hold of his father, needless to say, as soon as possible. Is there any way at all of getting a message to him?

S I could ring one or two of our clients in Bristol to ask about his whereabouts. I'll do my very best to make contact. What number should I give him?

P I'd be so pleased if you would. It's 67890/54321. Miss Pelham. Thank you.

A conversation about health

A I'm sorry. I feel a bit faint and giddy (dizzy). My head's swimming. Do you mind if I sit down?

B Of course not. Here, sit in this armchair. Now relax. It might be a good idea to put your head down. I'll get you some water. Would a drink of brandy help?

A No, it's all right. I feel a bit better now. It's a touch of the sun, I think.

B Lie back quite still for a few minutes. I should take it easy for the rest of the day and stay in the shade.

Reading comprehension

Choice of words

In this exercise you must choose the word or phrase which best completes each sentence.

1 I want to rent a flat, _____ one reasonably near our school.
  A eventually **B** in fact **C** if possible **D** really

2 One of the tigers has got _____. Warn everyone of the danger.
  A lose **B** loose **C** loosened **D** lost

3 Now that they are engaged, they are both _____ some of their earnings for their future home.
  A saving **B** sparing **C** sharing **D** keeping

4 With the spring here you can _____ these ski boots till you need them again next winter.
  A give away **B** get rid of **C** put away
  D do away with

5 After the children's party she had to spend two hours _____ the sitting-room.
  A ordering **B** arranging **C** tidying up
  D clearing away

6 He _____ the tap but could get no water.
  A opened **B** adjusted **C** controlled **D** turned on

7 I _____ the blouse in the fitting-room but it was obviously too small.
  A tried on **B** tried **C** wore **D** tried out

8 The Andersons have not _____ yet and I doubt if they will now.
  A turned up **B** turned in **C** come up **D** come in

9 I should like to _____ with old friends but I have so little time.
  A be in touch **B** keep in touch **C** write **D** speak

10 Wolves were _____ in the nearby forest.
  A roaring **B** barking **C** howling **D** growling

Forgetfulness and the elderly

The following extract from a pamphlet describes some ways in which the relatives and friends of elderly people can help them keep in touch with what's going on.

Be patient
Elderly people respond best to a calm and unhurried environment. This is not always easy to provide as their behaviour can sometimes be irritating. If they get excited or upset then they may
5 become more confused and more difficult to look after. Although sometimes it can be extremely difficult, it is best to be patient and not to get upset yourself. You should always encourage old people to do as much as possible for themselves but be ready to lend a helping hand when necessary. At the same time it is also
10 important that you don't make them feel like children

Give information
Failing memory makes it very difficult for the person to recall all the basic kinds of information we take for granted. The obvious way to help in this situation is to supply the information that is

15   missing and help them make sense of what is going on. The information has to be constantly repeated to make up for the poor memory. You must use every opportunity to provide information but remember to keep it simple and straightforward.

20   The kinds of information that may be required are (1) *who* you are (2) *where* you are (3) *where* you are going (4) *what's* happening and why and (5) *what's* to be done, e.g.,

"Good morning Mum. This is Fiona your daughter. It is eight o'clock so if you get up now we can have breakfast downstairs."

25   When the elderly person makes confused statements e.g. about going out to his or her old employment or visiting a dead relative, correct in a calm matter-of-fact fashion: "No, you don't work in the office any more. You're retired now. Will you come and help me with the dishes?"

Provide memory aids

30   We rely heavily on the information provided by signposts, clocks, calendars and newspapers. These assist us to organise and direct our behaviour. Confused old people need these aids all the time to compensate for their poor memory. Encourage them to use and refer to reminder boards or diaries for important forthcoming

35   events and label the contents of different cupboards and drawers. Many other aids such as colour coding, cards of information, photographs, scrap books, addresses or shopping lists could help in the individual case. You will probably have to encourage the elderly person to use these aids at first.

Below are a number of questions or unfinished statements about the passage, each with four suggested answers or endings. Choose the one you think fits best in each case.

1   The main subject of the pamphlet about elderly people is
    A   their general care and welfare.
    B   promoting their physical and mental health.
    C   how they can be helped to look after themselves as far as possible.
    D   assisting physically handicapped people to live a normal life.

2   The pamphlet gives help for anyone responsible for an elderly forgetful person by
    A   removing some of his or her worries about the job.
    B   suggesting sensible things to do in these circumstances.
    C   providing ideas that will help in recovering the lost memory.
    D   explaining the causes of loss of memory.

3   A difficulty experienced by friends and relatives is that they may
    A   worry too much about the old person's condition.
    B   try to do too much for the person concerned.
    C   find it difficult sometimes to deal with matters calmly.
    D   fail to understand the old person's problems.

4   How should confused statements and ideas be dealt with?
    A   plainly and sensibly.
    B   by a detailed explanation of the mistake.
    C   by showing sympathy and understanding.
    D   by ignoring them and talking about something else.

5 Visual aids can give practical help to elderly people by

    A bringing back to mind various kinds of useful information.

    B informing them about what has to be done next.

    C helping them to revive old memories.

    D clearing up their mistakes and confusion.

Composition

Dialogues

There are two ways of writing a dialogue:

1 In the form of a conversation:

> 'Good morning,' said the waitress. 'What would you like?'
> 'Just a cup of coffee, please,' said Anne.
> 'Black or white?' asked the waitress.
> 'Black, please,' Anne replied, and then added, 'and I'd like a biscuit with it.'

2 As dialogue in a play is written:

    A Excuse me. Can you tell me the way to St. Peter's Church?

    B I'm sorry, I'm afraid I can't. I'm a stranger here. Oh, but wait a moment. It's about five minutes down this road.

    A Thank you very much.

    B No, it isn't St. Peter's. I remember now it's St. John's. Have you any idea what it looks like?

    A No, I've never seen it. I'm really looking for the house just opposite it.

    B Then it isn't the church I passed before that. That was opposite a hospital. Let's ask that man coming along.

The question itself should suggest which of these forms is wanted. If nothing is suggested, the second form may be accepted as a dialogue, the first one as a conversation.

Points to remember

(a) Read the question carefully. Make sure that all the necessary ideas are included in the dialogue and that this is a suitable length.

(b) Try to write really natural conversation. Remember the following points:

    (i) Verbal and negative abbreviations are normal in dialogue and conversation — in contrast to their use in formal written English.

        These include: *I'm, don't, can't, there's, How's?*

    (ii) Short simple constructions. People often answer in only one or two words or perhaps an incomplete sentence. 'And' and 'but' join parts of sentences: the more complicated constructions are far less common.

    (iii) Simple colloquial forms. Have you noticed how often people say 'Well', 'Oh', 'I'm afraid —', 'I wonder if —', and many similar forms with no very definite meaning?

    (iv) Short answers.

    (v) The many other expressions and constructions which make conversation sound more natural.

    (vi) In the case of a conversation, be careful to punctuate according to English convention (see pages 120–21).

Here is an example of a dialogue which includes several of the things mentioned above:

A car has been stolen. The owner is telephoning the local Police Station to report the theft. Write the dialogue that takes place in 120–180 words.

A Updown Police Station. Can I help you?

B John Driver of 1 Highlands Road, Updown, speaking. I've just discovered my car's been stolen.

A Can you give me details of the car, sir? What make is it?

B It's a red Lightning sports car.

A What's the registration number?

B 65432 ABC.

A When did you lose it?

B I've just come out of Updown General Post Office. I left it outside but it has gone now.

A I see. You didn't lock it, I suppose?

B Well, no, I'm afraid I didn't. And what's worse, I'd left the keys inside. I was in a bit of a hurry.

A Well, that's asking for trouble, isn't it. Anything special inside?

B Yes, there was. My golf clubs and two bottles of brandy.

A Well, we'll see what we can do. Have you a telephone number?

B Updown 6420.

A Thank you. By the way, you realise it's a no-parking area outside the Post Office, don't you?

B Er . . . yes. I believe so. I'm in trouble, aren't I?

A It does seem so. We'll be getting in touch with you as soon as possible.

B Thank you. Goodbye.

Subjects for practice

Each dialogue should consist of between 120 and 180 words.

1 A conversation between a door-to-door salesman and a lady whom he is trying to persuade to buy an encyclopedia.

2 You are in a hurry to catch a train. On the way to the station you run into an old acquaintance whom you have not seen since you both left school some eight years before. You have only one minute to spare. Write the conversation that takes place.

3 While you are exploring an unknown town, you see an interesting-looking building, so you stop a passer-by and ask about it. Write the conversation in the form of a dialogue.

4 You are walking along the street when you are stopped by a radio interviewer and asked your opinion about whether space travel is a waste of money. Write what is said in the form of a dialogue.

Use of English

1 **Finish each of the following sentences in such a way that the new sentence means exactly the same as the one before it.**

   1 It is unnecessary for you to change your dress.
      You need _____

   2 You'll be better off staying the night.
      It will _____

   3 Bill had had the wireless repaired.
      Bill had asked _____

4   I could do with a sleep.
    A sleep _____
5   She awoke with a feeling of terror.
    When she _____
6   With a lot of luck, you may get your novel published.
    If you _____

2   **The meaning of the sentence 'She is too lazy to make much progress'
    can be expressed instead by a negative sentence using 'hard-working'
    and 'enough'. Change each of sentences 1–5 below in the same way.**

1   The light is too dim to read by properly.
2   He is too miserable to be popular.
3   She is too rough to take care of her baby brother.
4   The book was too boring for me to enjoy reading it.
5   The actor was too ugly to take the part of Orlando.

3   **The word(s) in italics in the following sentences can be replaced either
    by a form of the word in brackets or by a phrase containing this word,
    and in some cases other minor changes may have to be made in the
    sentence. Rewrite each sentence accordingly.**

1   He *is often* shy in the presence of strangers.   (TEND)
2   He *asked for several pieces of information* in the tourist office.
    (ENQUIRIES)
3   He *has been back from Berne for two days.*   (RETURN)
4   *Could you* change a twenty-pound note for me?   (KIND)
5   He *probably can't* speak English.   (WONDER)
6   *Why not spend* tomorrow at the seaside?   (HOW ABOUT)
7   *Please close the door* quietly when you go out.   (MIND)
8   *Would you recommend me to read* that novel?   (WORTH)
9   *Writing to him won't help.* He never answers letters.   (GOOD)

4   **The policeman referred to in the reading passage had come to ask
    about a car parked outside without lights. Later in the evening Bill tele-
    phoned his mother.**

    **In the following conversation, finish suitably the incomplete
    sentences.**

Mother: 321   7654. Mrs Mackintosh speaking.
Bill: Hallo, Mum. Bill speaking. I'm here at Harold's.
Mother: Oh, thank goodness. (1) How long _____?
Bill: Round about two hours. Double the usual time.
Mother: (2) What's _____?
Bill: The weather? Still pretty awful. Visibility only a few metres.
Mother: (3) Was there _____?
Bill: There were a few cars and other motor-bikes at first but no
    lorries or buses. I was only afraid of running into a tree or
    getting lost.   (4) What _____?
Mother: Nothing very much. I did some mending and read a book
    for a while but most of the time I've been asleep.
Bill: How about Aunt Maggie? (5) I suppose you _____.
Mother: No, I stayed indoors. I'd have got lost in the fog myself.
    (6) Are _____?
Bill: Yes, I am. He's asked me to stay.
Mother: (7) What time _____?
Bill: I'll wait and see what the weather's like. Not before break-
    fast in any case.

Interview

Talking about a photograph

1 What is the relationship between this picture and the reading passage on page 123?
2 What differences are there?
   Suggest why the woman has opened the door before the policeman has had time to ring the bell.
3 Describe the expression on the policeman's face.

Topics

What are some of the reasons for the police to visit someone's home?
Suggest some of the jobs the police have to do.
What is your own most likely reaction when you open your door to find a policeman standing there?
What qualities of physique and character are desirable in a policeman?

Word linking

English is spoken in groups of words linked according to meaning, with pauses separating the meaning items. Within groups, words are not separated but run together into continuous sound. As a result final consonants are transferred to the beginning of following words with an initial vowel sound.

Example: It isn't at all an unusual incident.

This applies also in the case of a normally silent final -*r*.

Example: For further information, enquire in the newspaper office at the far end of this street.

Before reading the following passages, look through them silently, pencilling in final-consonant initial-vowel links with a pencil. Notice, however, where a pause is appropriate and accordingly no link is made. Practise the linked word groups aloud before reading aloud each whole passage. Suggest a situation in which each passage might have been spoken.

Passages

1   This is Mrs Anne Adams speaking. My home number is 444 9988, though I'm speaking now from a call-box as my own phone's out of order. I haven't had an incoming call for the past two days and today there's no sound of any kind when I lift the receiver. Perhaps you could test it in about five minutes' time when I'm back indoors again. I'll have to go out again in half an hour. Could you send someone to repair it this afternoon or at any time after eight o'clock tomorrow morning?

2   Put up your hands those of you who came to school on a bicycle. I see. About eleven of you. And how many more of you have got a bike at home? Quite a lot of you. Who cycles along any kind of main road on the way to school? Most of our cyclists. Now I want you to think a bit and then each of the eleven of you who come by bike will let us know which of the various traffic rules he or she thinks is the most important when riding.

3   Good evening, madam. I'm sorry to disturb you on such an unpleasant evening but I've got to find the owner of that black car that's parked in the road just outside your house. It hasn't even got any parking lights on, and in a fog like this it's a danger to every form of traffic on the road. If it isn't yours perhaps you can identify it: would it belong to one of your neighbours by any chance?

Giving encouragement in worrying situations

Suggest what you could say to calm down and/or encourage someone in each of the following situations.

1   A mother whose young son or daughter usually arrives home at five in the evening but is already two hours overdue.

2   A friend or relative who is sitting for an exam the following day and is in a bad state of nerves, revising frantically and unable to eat or sleep.

3   A neighbour whose cat has not been home for the past two days.

4   A companion on a journey who's worried because he/she can't remember having turned off the gas before leaving home.

Discussion of children's instructional traffic area

This is a plan of a children's playground and traffic instruction park in the town of Heinola in Finland. Here young cyclists can become familiar with traffic signs and the rules of the road in safety.

Here are some subjects of discussion based on the plan.

(a) Some of the signs are warnings for road-users. Describe the signs and suggest what warnings they are giving. What action must the road-users take when they see each of these signs?

(b) What mustn't road-users do when they see these signs?

(c) There are a number of pedestrian crossings shown on the plan. What advice would you give to a child about using a pedestrian crossing?

(d) What are some road-signs you can't see on the plan?

(e) Why are roundabouts constructed at some road junctions?

(f) What is the rule for using a roundabout in your country?

(g) What do traffic lights look like and how do they control the traffic?

(h) What is your opinion about compulsory traffic light restrictions for pedestrians?

(i) What other ways can children enjoy themselves in this park?

(j) How are children trained to behave sensibly in traffic in your country?

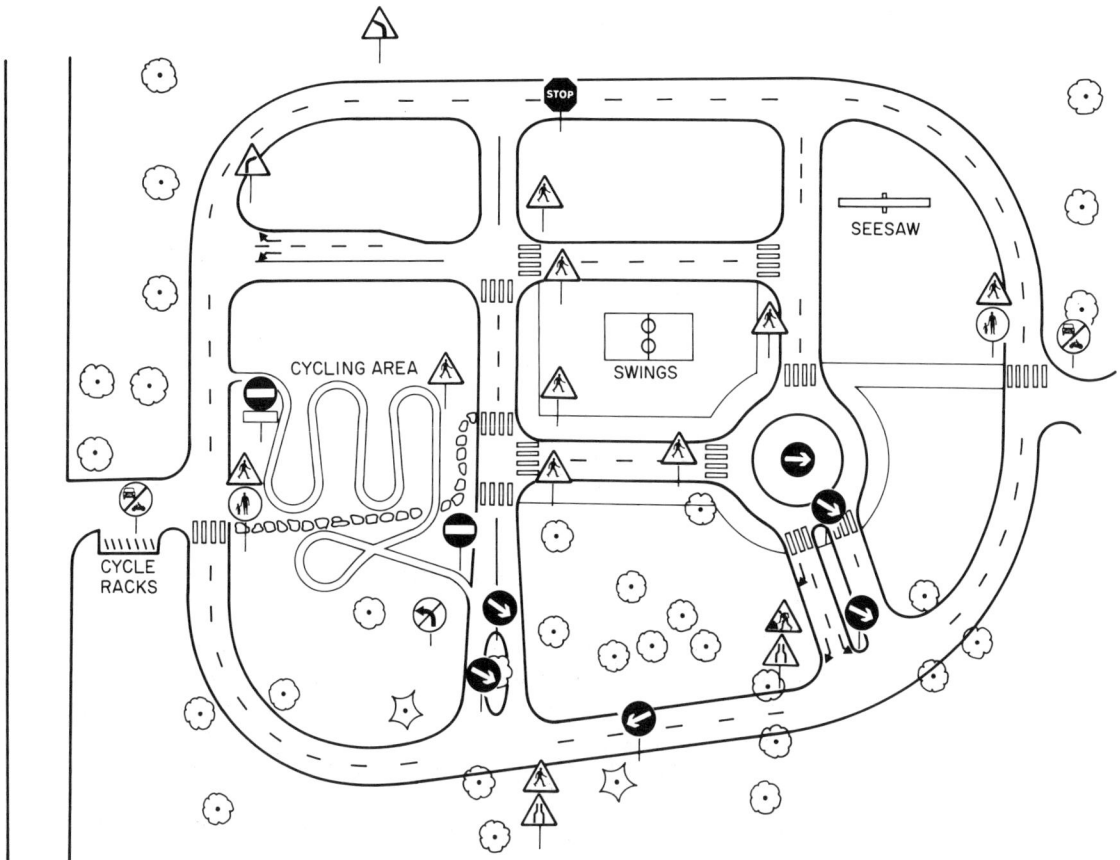

137

Action situations

What would you do in each of these situations?

1   You are returning alone from a weekend in the country when you get a puncture in a tyre of your bicycle. You haven't got a repair outfit and in fact have never mended a puncture yourself.

2   You are stranded alone in a mountain hut after a heavy snowfall. You've got plenty of wood for a fire, candles, food and water. You have to remain there two or three days.

Expressing opinions

1   If you were a parent living near the centre of a large busy town, what would be your attitude towards providing your son or daughter with a bicycle or motor-scooter to go to school on?

2   What is your opinion of premonitions (strong unreasonable feelings that something disastrous is soon going to happen)?

Topics for a prepared talk

Make short notes on one of the following topics and use them in giving a talk that should last about two minutes.

1   An experience you may (or may not) have had in unusually difficult weather conditions (e.g. a thick fog, icy roads, a gale, a thunderstorm).

2   A strange-looking vehicle lands in a field near you and two extra-ordinary individuals emerge from it and come towards you. What happens next?

General guidance and practice

1   Future Simple

Forms

Written Affirmative	Spoken Affirmative
I/we shall take **he/you/they will take**	**I'll/we'll take** **he'll/you'll/they'll take**
Written Negative	Spoken Negative
I/we shall not take **he/you/they will not take**	**I/we shan't take (won't take)** **he/you/they won't take**
Passive **shall/will/'ll be taken**	

Shall is most commonly used in the first person of the interrogative: *Shall I take?* The difference between *shall* and *will* in spoken statements is apparent only in the negative forms when *won't* is more common in all forms than *shan't*.

Note: *You/he shall do it:* the speaker is determined that this must happen — it can be an order.

I will/won't do it: I am determined about this. Both *shall* and will would be stressed in speech.

Uses

The Future Simple expresses

(a) Willingness and refusal: *Peter will carry it for you. I won't help you.*
(b) A promise: *I'll do it without fail tomorrow.*
(c) A decision, intention or idea: *I'll do it now before I forget.*
(d) Possibility or probability: *I think it will be fine tomorrow.*
(e) First Condition (result clause): *If those clouds clear away, it will be fine tomorrow.*
(f) Announcement of a future event: *The meeting will be held on Saturday.*

Practice

Complete each of the sentences below with several words including a future form of the verb in capitals (affirmative or negative). The sentence should express the idea in the following brackets.

Example: In any case I _____. TELEPHONE (promise)
            In any case I'll telephone you this evening.

(a) The football match _____. TAKE PLACE (announcement)
(b) I _____. TAKE (refusal)
(c) You _____. FINISH (order)
(d) Your shoes _____. BE READY (promise)
(e) If you don't hurry, you _____. BE (result after condition)
(f) That's quite enough noise. You _____. BE (quiet)
(g) Are you hungry? All right, we _____. HAVE (willingness)
(h) Don't you understand? I _____. TRY (intention)
(i) I should think that all you students _____. PASS (probability)

2 Other Future Forms

Future Continuous

The Future Continuous expresses

(a) An arranged future action:
     He *will be attending* a conference in Milan next week.

(b) An action that will be happening at a certain future time:
     This time tomorrow *I shall be swimming* in the Mediterranean.

(c) A future action whose duration is stressed:
     The miners *will be working* all through the holiday.

The following two examples make clear a main difference in use between the Future Simple already explained and the Future Continuous:
     I *am/shall be telephoning* her tomorrow, so I can tell her the news then.
     Hasn't she heard the news? I *shall telephone* and tell her as soon as possible.

Future Perfect

This expresses an action which will have been completed by a certain future time:
     By Saturday they *will have repaired* the television. (Active)
     By Saturday the television *will have been repaired*. (Passive)

Future Perfect Continuous

This expresses a continuous action which comes up to (though is not necessarily completed by) a certain future time:

When he takes his driving test, he *will have been learning* for six months.

An arranged future action can be expressed both by the Present Continuous and Future Continuous tenses. In the latter the speaker may be imagining himself already at the future time referred to, but any real differences between these tenses is slight.

Practice

Use the correct Future form of the verb in brackets in the following sentences:

(a) I (make) a cup of tea in a few minutes; would you like one?
(b) I intended to write him a letter this afternoon. I (do) it tomorrow.
(c) By this time next week the new scheme (introduce). (Passive)
(d) Who (win) the hundred metres in the next Olympic Games?
(e) Many more tourists (arrive) by the time the week is over.
(f) By next June you (live not) here long enough to become naturalised.
(g) If the publishers agree about the need for revised copies, more editions of that book (produce) than any other he has written. (Passive)
(h) The retired statesman (spend) next winter in Southern Spain.
(i) If my money continues to disappear like this I (beg soon) in the streets all day.
(j) By the time he sits for the examination, he (learn) English for ten years.
(k) Next September all bus fares (increase). (Passive)
(l) (Go) you to the library this afternoon?

3 Verb tenses in adverbial time clauses

In adverbial clauses of time beginning with such conjunctions as *when, before, until, as soon as* etc., the Present Simple, Continuous or Present Perfect are used in English where logically the Future might be expected:

As soon as the ship *docks*, the passengers will be allowed to land.
I shall be pleased to see the photograph, *when it has been printed.*

This does not apply to a noun clause object of a verb:

Do you know *when he will return?*

Practice

Use the correct form of the verb in brackets in the following sentences:

(a) He will expect dinner to be ready when he (come) home.
(b) Immediately the sun (rise), the priests will offer a sacrifice.
(c) As soon as the referee (appear), the game will begin.
(d) You will not begin eating until after everybody (sit) down.
(e) It will be raining before they (be) ready.
(f) Will you have completed the course when you (sit) for the examination?
(g) While he (enjoy) a holiday in Italy, I shall be doing night work in Birmingham. (Continuous)
(h) When you (read) the newspaper, please let me have it.
(i) He has not told me when he (write).

(j) After the bus company (introduce) the new timetable, there should be a better bus service.

4 The Future in the Past and in Conditional Forms

These forms are very similar:

	Active	Passive
Simple	**I would/should tell**	**I would/should be told**
Continuous	**I would/should be telling**	—
Perfect	**I would/should have told**	**I would/should have been told**
Perfect Continuous	**I would/should have been telling**	—

The first person forms of the Conditional usually have the auxiliary *should*, the second and third person forms *would*.
 Would is normally used in all persons of the Future in the Past tense, which is used in reported speech (see pages 191–193).
 Notice the spoken forms which replace both *should* and *would*:
I'd, you'd, he'd, she'd, we'd, they'd.

Introductory conjunctions in Conditions

If, Unless (= if not)
 She never answers the door *if* you ring only twice.
 She never answers the door *unless* you ring three times.
Unless stresses that the condition must be fulfilled.

Even if: the condition is unlikely with a possibly unexpected result.
Even though: the condition is true and the result unexpected.
 Even if you've got the qualifications (unlikely), you won't get the job.
 Even though you've got the qualifications (true), you won't get the job.

Provided (that): the force of the condition is stronger.
 We can offer you a university place *provided* you pass the school-leaving examination.

Habitual Condition

 If he *feels* tired, he *spends* the day indoors.
  (present)   *(present)*

If can normally be replaced by *when/whenever*, though *if* stresses the fact that this is a condition.

Imperative as a result

 If you *feel* tired, *don't do* any work.
 If you *don't feel* tired, *do* some work.
  (present)   *(imperative)*

First Condition

(any present tense)	*(Future Simple/Continuous)*
If he *feels* tired tomorrow,	he *will spend* the day indoors
If he *is working,*	he *won't be listening* to the radio

141

| If he *has gone* back to the cafe, | he *will have found* his coat there. |
| If she *has been shopping* today, | she *will have* no money left. |

All these conditions express a **possibility**.

Second Condition

(Past Simple/Continuous)	*(Conditional Present/Continuous)*
If you *worked* here,	you *would/could earn* more.
If you *were working* for them,	you *would earn/be earning* much less.

These conditions are **unlikely** or **unreal** ones: the person spoken to is not working here, though on hearing this he might decide to.

The Second Condition is often used in persuading people to do something.

The Third Condition in which the passing of time has made **the result impossible** is explained on page 165.

Notice that *could* may be a Past Simple or a Conditional form:

I *could* understand everything he said.

If you gave him a lift, he *could* be here earlier.

Practice

1   Pick out examples of First and Second Conditions from the reading passage on page 123 and say which type each of them is.

2   Finish the following sentences:

(a)   If the train is late, _____
(b)   If it rained, _____
(c)   If she needs more money, _____
(d)   Even if it stops raining _____
(e)   Even though she comes from Wales, _____
(f)   Provided I've got some free time, _____
(g)   If the weather hasn't changed by tomorrow, _____
(h)   If you explained this to us again, _____
(i)   If I sent the letter by express post, _____
(j)   If I had some eggs, _____
(k)   If you could give me some help, _____

3   Finish these sentences with a conditional clause:

(a)   I shall be very pleased with you if _____
(b)   I never go swimming even though _____
(c)   I wouldn't fly to Australia even if _____
(d)   I shan't forgive you unless _____
(e)   You can join the library provided _____
(f)   He wouldn't accept your help even if _____
(g)   I'd take up chess as a hobby if _____
(h)   He'll deliver the goods to your house if _____

5 Have something done

Examples:

I am *having* a dress *made*.
He *had* his shoes *repaired*.
He has *had* his photograph *taken*.
They will *have* their house *redecorated*.
She should *have* her eyes *tested*.
We want to *have* the money we paid for our tickets *refunded*.
Nobody enjoys *having* a tooth *drilled* and *filled*.

In spoken English *get* often replaces *have*. It may suggest that the subject is taking an active part in any arrangement made:

I am *getting* a dress made.

Construction and word order

have (in a suitable tense and form) + something + Past Participle
    have   *a dress*   *made*

Meaning

The past participle shows the real action being carried out. The subject of the sentence is not doing this action, but is causing someone else to do it for him. In the first example above, I am not making the dress but arranging for someone else to do this for me.

Practice

Rewrite the following sentences with the italicised form serving as or suggesting the new subject of the sentence. The main verb *have* will have the same tense or form as the verb in **bold type**.

Example:

They **are building** a new house for *us*.
We are having a new house built.
They **must check** *your* brakes as soon as possible.
You must have your brakes checked as soon as possible.

(a)   They **are cleaning** *William*'s suit.
(b)   They **are installing** a refrigerator for *our neighbour*.
(c)   They **are shortening** *his* overcoat.
(d)   They **were copying** the documents for *the lawyer*.
(e)   They **fitted** a new lock for *my landlady*.
(f)   They **will wash** *Giles*'s car tomorrow.
(g)   They **are going to train** *Elizabeth*'s voice.
(h)   They **have set** *your* hair.
(i)   *He* **is arranging** for them to publish his eight-hundred-page novel.
(j)   I think that they **can develop and print** *your* films at Mitchell's.

6 Be, feel, have, suffer from

In the reading passage Bill's mother was tired out but hoped she would feel better after a sleep. *Be, feel, have* and *suffer from* are commonly used in referring to illness or discomfort. Here are some examples:

to have: a toothache,   ear-ache,   aching feet,   a sore heel (a blister),   a sore throat,   a temperature,   a cold, a cough,   hay fever,   a pain in one's back,   a pain in one's stomach,   indigestion,   a heart attack,   a stroke, a skin disease,   a fit,   a nervous breakdown,   influenza, appendicitis,   bronchitis,   measles.

to suffer from: rheumatism,   arthritis,   heart trouble,   deafness,   high blood pressure — all normally chronic complaints.

to feel: ill, tired, depressed, well, better.

to be: ill, seriously ill, in poor health, run down, unconscious, convalescent.

To *lose weight* it may be necessary to *go on a diet*; otherwise *weight* may be *gained* or *put on*.

Treatment of injuries and diseases

Cleanse the wound thoroughly and apply an *antiseptic* to counteract *germs* which spread disease. A *disinfectant* is normally for household purposes. Otherwise the wound may *fester*. *Sticking plaster* may be applied or the wound may be *bandaged* (with a bandage). *Ointment* may be smeared over the skin.

A *surgeon sets* a broken bone. He *operates on* a patient only after an *anaesthetic* has been *administered*. The patient *has an operation* (it is machines and schemes that are *operated*).

Infectious diseases are spread by air-borne germs; *contagious* ones by actual physical contact.

One *registers with* a doctor and is given free treatment as part of the *National Health Service*. When ill, one *consults* (*goes and sees* or *sees*) a doctor who *examines* his or her patient. The doctor may write a hospital letter to arrange for *specialist* treatment. The patient may have to go into hospital as an *in-patient* or attend at intervals as an *out-patient*. He may go in for *observation*.

Illnesses

Answer the following questions.

(a) When do you have to use your handkerchief very often? What do you use your handkerchief for?
(b) What is almost certainly true of a person with a flushed face and a hot forehead? What does a doctor use a thermometer for when examining a patient?
(c) What might be the cause of a sore heel?
(d) What painful complaint do people risk suffering from by sleeping in damp sheets?
(e) What has to happen in hospital to a person suffering from acute appendicitis? What does one call the doctor qualified to do this job?
(f) What does the ordinary person often use an antiseptic for?
(g) What may happen to a person who works and worries too much?
(h) What may happen to a person who eats too much (i) at one meal? (ii) over a long period? What can a person do to lose weight?
(i) What are some of the symptoms of being run down?
(j) What conditions may cause one's feet to ache?

7 Revision of phrasal verbs

Complete the phrasal verbs in the following sentences:

(a) He has taken _____ several new hobbies since his retirement.
(b) Will they ever clear _____ the matter of the missing secret papers?
(c) You shouldn't have taken _____ so many responsibilities.
(d) A small boy came _____ to ask the time. (*3 words*)
(e) This rose has come _____ since yesterday.
(f) I'm still looking _____ my watch. It must be somewhere.
(g) She's turned _____ a marriage proposal from a multi-millionaire.
(h) The weather has turned _____ better than expected.
(i) Thank you but I don't want to buy anything now. I'm only looking _____.
(j) While she was looking _____ the window she saw a car draw up outside. (*2 words*)
(k) You look _____ you need a good meal. (*2 words*)
(l) He turned _____ to see who was following him.

7 Originality is Not Everything

There were once three sons of a wealthy businessman. Whenever they met, the two eldest, who were twins, used to quarrel about which of them should be his father's heir. The youngest, who was not in the least ambitious, took no part in their arguments. As soon as they left home, the father arranged for an adequate income to be provided for each of them, but insisted that apart from this they were to be financially self-supporting.

The elder twin, who had the advantage of good looks and a striking personality, decided that he would take up the stage as a career. He joined a small repertory company, acted in minor parts, was invariably unpunctual at rehearsals and was accordingly unpopular with his fellow-actors. He earned little and so had to live mainly on his allowance. He occasionally thought of changing his profession, but always put off making a decision, and he became increasingly bored and disillusioned.

His twin brother considered himself unconventional and original, so he set up as an artist. He rented a large dirty attic, which he converted into a studio, grew a beard and haunted the cafés patronised by similar young men, who would sit for hours condemning contemporary standards and declaring themselves the pioneers of the school of 'Neo-Revelationism'. He earned nothing, spent all his allowance, ran up a very large number of bills and was accordingly always in debt.

The youngest son, who had no special artistic talent, worked hard and was awarded a University scholarship. After taking his degree, he decided he would like to be a teacher, and having completed the necessary training, he obtained his professional diploma. He was appointed to a teaching post in a Grammar School, where he earned enough money to live on and was able to save his allowance.

After years of failing health, the father eventually died. The will, which had been drawn up some years previously, was read to the family. The elder twin had inherited his father's business, the younger was to receive all the money that was not invested in the business, while the youngest boy was left his father's house and estate as his share of the property.

Unfortunately an actor who cannot even be punctual should not be expected to manage a business, and it was not long before the firm went bankrupt. The artist had no doubt that within a short time he would be making a fortune by speculation. He believed in taking risks, the more spectacular the better, and he invested in schemes which should have provided an unusually large profit. They failed completely in their purpose, and in less than a year he was penniless. Nobody knows now what became of either of the brothers who were always hoping for too much.

But the youngest brother was able to fulfil his own modest ambition. With the capital he had saved, he converted the house into an orphanage. He gained the approval of the Local Authority, who made a grant large enough to provide for its upkeep. Influential people contributed donations, and with the help of a few assistants he was able to care for homeless and backward children. He achieved contentment.

This is a story that has the old-fashioned moral that thrift may bring more rewards than material ones. No genuine neo-revelationist would accept so outworn a philosophy, which, nevertheless, resulted in a surprising amount of happiness for a considerable number of people.

Notes on the passage

Vocabulary

1   The word *merchant* is not often used nowadays except for a *coal merchant* (who sells coal) and the *Merchant Navy* as distinct from the Royal Navy. The following words, each with a more exact meaning, have replaced it: *a businessman, a shipping agent, an exporter and importer, a shipowner, a shopkeeper, a wholesaler* (selling large quantities), *a retailer* (selling small quantities), *a dealer* (a general term for one who buys and sells things).

3   The expression **in the youngest time* does not exist in English. '*in former times*' refers to the distant past. *recently* is used for a short time ago.

4   Do not confuse: please *take a seat*; the meeting will *take place* next Monday; he is *taking part* in the play/in the meeting; *take your place* in the procession; he will *take the place of* the absent performer; nothing can *take the place of* a good home.

5   A *salary* and *wages* are *earnings:* a *salary* is usually an annual amount, paid in twelve equal monthly parts; *wages* are paid for the hours worked or the amount achieved — usually weekly.
Income is all the money received, from earnings, investments, rents, pension etc. *Income tax* is paid on it to the Government. *Rates* are paid to the Local Authority. *Duty* is paid on imported goods and *Value Added Tax* on other goods and services. *Interest* is paid on some bank accounts and dividends on shares.

7   *striking* = catching the eye. Workmen *strike (go on strike)* for better conditions. People *strike* matches. *It struck me* that he had changed a lot recently. *struck by lightning*.

8   *career* = an occupation, often extending throughout life. Not merely an occupation offering prospects of promotion.

9   *repertory company* = a group of actors who present plays which are changed frequently, often once a week. Such companies are more often found in provincial towns.
A West End company usually gives performances in well-known London theatres.
A repertoire is a collection of plays, songs or other forms of entertainment that a performer or group of performers knows well enough to present to an audience.

10   *a rehearsal* of a play   *A dress rehearsal* is the final practice with the conditions of an actual performance, ready for the first night.
repetition is merely repeating: *repetition aids memorising*. (Adj *repetitive*).
recite a poem (speak it formally) (N *recitation*).

11   *mainly* = principally, chiefly. *a main road; a main line* (railway); *the main imports*. *mostly* is more common in speech than in writing.

11   *an allowance: His father allows him a certain sum each month: he gives him an allowance.*
permission: He allows his daughter to use his car: she has his permission to use it. He has permission to stay away from school.
A soldier's holiday is *leave*. *leave* may sometimes mean permission: *He gave me leave to remain seated.*

13   *increasingly bored* sounds better in written English than *more and more* bored.

13   *disillusioned* (N *disillusionment*) = having lost one's illusions. *An illusion* of something that does not exist; *an optical illusion*.
a delusion (deluded) is similar, but with a strong idea of deception, a definite falsifying of things. A sick person may have delusions.

15   *rent* (V) for a period: *rent a house, a television;* (N) pay/charge *rent*.
     hire (V) for short time only: *hire a bicycle, car, boat*.
     The owner of a house may become a *landlord* or *landlady* by *letting* the house to a *tenant*.

15   *an attic* may be a room that is lived in; things are stored in a *loft*. Both are at the top of a building. Below a building, a *basement* may be lived in or be part of a shop; a *cellar* however is used for storage. A *garret* is a poor unpleasant room under the roof.

15   *convert* (V) = to change: He *converted* his house *into* separate flats. He *converted* some of his investments *into* ready cash. (N *conversion*.) Also, to *convert* someone to a (new) religion (N *cónvert*). Missionaries are people who try to convert other people to their own faith. Atheists do not believe in a god.

16   Spelling: Plurals of words ending in -o: *studio, soprano, concerto, piano, solo* and similar words that are still clearly Italian in origin add -s: *studios, pianos*. Other words, more completely absorbed into the language, add -es: *potatoes, tomatoes, heroes, echoes, mottoes*.

16   A *patron* is an influential and wealthy person who takes an interest in a society or a charity or (especially in eighteenth-century Europe) a person's creative work, and provides money and other help. *to patronise* can mean to treat someone considered an inferior with obvious kindness: *He examined my work in a patronising way and said that it was not bad for a beginner*. St. George is the *patron saint* of England, St. Andrew of Scotland, St. David of Wales and St. Patrick of Ireland.
     In the passage, *patronise* means visit and make use of (a café, club, shop).

17   *condemn* (V) = say something is thoroughly bad: *condemn cruelty to animals; condemn someone to death*. (N *condemnation*.)
     blame (V and N) = say someone is the cause of a bad thing: *He was blamed for the accident. He took the blame*. (But: it was his *fault*.)
     criticise = give an opinion about the value of something (often concentrating on faults): *criticise a film*. (N *criticism, a critic*.) Adj *critical: a critical moment in his life*. Newspapers publish *reviews* of books, plays, films and concerts.

17   *contemporary* (Adj and N) = of the same period: *Shakespeare and Bacon were contemporaries*. Often the adjective means 'of the present time': *contemporary or present-day furniture*.
     modern is a wider term: *the modern age*. *up-to-date* is emphatically modern (opp. *old-fashioned*).
     fashionable suggests a short period only, as fashions soon change. Avoid 'today's' as an adjective: '*present-day* English styles/opinions' is more usual.

20   When a person *owes* money he is *in debt*. If he cannot pay his debts when these must be paid, he is/goes *bankrupt*. He is then *a bankrupt*.

22   Prizes are *awarded* when the decision is made about who shall receive them. They are *presented* when they are actually given. Money and marks are also *awarded*.

22   A *scholarship* is a payment of money to enable a clever student to undertake a certain course of study.

22   A *degree* is a title given by a university to a student who has reached a satisfactory standard in certain subjects. He is then a *graduate;* before he gets his first degree and while he is studying at university, he is an *undergraduate*. Notice that a graduate must have a university *degree*, with which he *graduates*.

24   A *diploma* is a title awarded by a university, school, college or professional society. Diploma subjects are often practical ones such as Domestic Science, Architecture, Social Studies, though diplomas and degrees may sometimes be awarded in the same subjects.

24   One *applies for* a post or job, and, if successful, one is *appointed*. On leaving the job, one *resigns* (sends in or hands in one's *resignation*), or *is dismissed*. When one reaches a certain age one *retires* from work. One may then receive a *pension*. Nouns: *application, appointment, resignation, dismissal, retirement*. An *old age pensioner* (or *senior citizen*).

25 *live on* the money one earns; he *makes his living* by giving private lessons. What do you *do for a living?*

27 One *fails* or *passes* an examination. Notice however: *fail* to do something. But: *succeed in* doing it.

27 Do not confuse: he *died* and he *is dead*. Also: *disease* (illness) and *decease* (death).

27 A *will* states money and property arrangements to be carried out after a person's death. This is sometimes entitled 'Last Will and Testament'. The *Old Testament* and the *New Testament* are the two divisions of the Bible.

31 An *estate agent* arranges the buying, selling, letting and managing of houses etc.

32 *punctual* = coming at the right time. *exact* = precise: *the exact number*. The train arrived *on time*. Jane had arrived *in time for* it.

35 a *fortune* = a lot of money. *fortune* (Unc) = luck: *good or bad fortune*. (Adj *fortunate*) (Adv *fortunately*). A *fortune-teller* tells *fortunes*.

35 I *believed* his story. He *believes in* enjoying life, in astrology, in God.

37 *on purpose* = intentionally, deliberately. Opp. *accidentally, unintentionally. You broke that cup on purpose. No, it was accidental (an accident).*

38 '*What has become* of your silver brooch? I haven't seen you wearing it lately.' 'I don't know *what has become of it*'. This expression is used only in questions.

39 She *wants* a new dress. She *wishes* she could travel. She *hopes* to visit London next Easter.

40 *modest* In the passage the opposite of this word would be *excessive* or *exaggerated. They manage on a modest income.*
A different opposite is *conceited: He is modest/conceited about his achievement.* (N *modesty/conceit*.)
proud and *humble* are opposites (N *pride/humility*): *He bowed humbly before the proud king.*

41 *interest* is earned on *capital* invested. Vienna is *the capital* of Austria. Adj: *a capital letter, capital punishment* (punishment by death).

41 An *orphanage* is a home for *orphans*, children without parents.
A child is *adopted* by another couple or family.
A parent's remarriage may give a child a *stepfather* or *stepmother* (a *stepchild*).
A *foster child* is temporarily part of another family.
A *guardian* may take the place of dead parents and the child is then a *ward*.

42 A *local authority* = the local Town Council or County Council. Some people *have authority* over others, who must obey. He is *an authority on* Roman coins.

42 A *grant* is a sum of money awarded for some special purpose, often by a local authority, e.g. a grant to maintain a student at University. *to grant* a request = to agree to it. A *loan* (V *lend*) must be given back: *the loan of money, of a book.*

43 *provide* help, money, goods. *provide for* a family = work to let them have what they need. provisions = food, especially taken on a journey.

43 A *donation* is usually money donated to some useful cause. *a blood donor/donation. charity* (Unc) is giving to those in need and a *charity* organises this.

44 *care* I don't *care* (it is nothing to me). He only *cares about* football. I don't *care for* that colour. A mother *cares for* her children. *Take care* of your handbag/the children. Her address is *care of (c/o)* Mrs. Smith.

45 *achieve* success, happiness, an ambition, fame (all abstract and needing effort to obtain). His discovery/invention/election was a great *achievement*.

46 *thrifty* opp. *extravagant. thrift/extravagance. meanness/generosity.*

47 *reward* (N and V) = (give) a kind of prize for a special service or action: *Lost: a three-month-old tortoiseshell kitten: reward offered.*

47 *material* (Adj) opp. *spiritual*.

47 *genuine* = true: *a genuine antique, picture* (opp. *fake*). A *genuine* person is *sincere*.

48 *accept* a present, an idea (opp. *refuse*). *agree to* a suggestion. *agree with* a person, an opinion. *acceptance. agreement. sign an agreement.*

Phrasal verbs

put *put off* (postpone) an arrangement till a later date.
put up friends for the night.
put a pen *down* on the table.
put food *away* in the larder.
put forward a suggestion at a meeting.
put back a book on the bookshelf.
put by money for one's old age.
put on a coat; *put on/off/out* a light.
be *put out* (either offended or given trouble) by someone's annoying behaviour.
put up with small inconveniences without doing anything about them.
output the amount produced.

Practice

(a) He is putting _____ as much money as possible in case he loses his job.
(b) The firm has doubled its _____.
(c) He has put _____ some excellent ideas.
(d) Put _____ that carving-knife at once.
(e) Put the light _____.
(f) Don't put _____ your visit too long.
(g) He was quite put _____ by your criticism.
(h) Poor woman, she has a lot to put _____.
(i) Put the sugar _____ in the cupboard when you have finished with it.
(j) She is putting _____ the dog's collar before he goes out.
(k) As the last bus had gone they put me _____ in their spare room.

run *run up* bills by not paying for the items bought.
The car *ran into* a tree.
He returned from his holiday early because his money *ran out*.
A car may *run out of* petrol and stop.
run away from an angry bull.
The dog *ran after* the cat.
He was *run over* by a car.
He is always *running down* his boss.

Practice

(a) The unhappy child ran _____ from his home.
(b) I wish he didn't run _____ his friends.
(c) He is careful never to run _____ bills.
(d) Four cars ran _____ one another on the motorway.
(e) He nearly ran _____ three chickens in the country lane.
(f) Owing to the strike, the factory has run _____ essential supplies.
(g) The small brave explorer was running _____ a large terrified tiger.

Other meanings of *run*: Colours can *run into* one another. A manager *runs* a business or a hotel. A boy of sixteen can *outrun* (run faster than) a younger brother.

Pronunciation

Be careful: career /kəríə/; repertory /répətəri/; contemporary /kəntémpərəri/; pioneers /paɪəníəz/; considerable /kənsídərəbl/.

Stress changes: variety /vəráɪəti/; invariably /ɪnvéərɪəbli/; various /véərɪəs/; contribute /kəntríbju:t/; contribution /kɒntrɪbjú:ʃn/; moral /mɒ́rəl/; morale /mɒrá:l/; patron /péɪtrən/; patronise /pǽtrənaɪz/.

Do not confuse: dingy /díndʒi/; dinghy (small boat) /díŋgi/.

ə (as in *a*go): stand*a*rds /stǽndədz/; tal*e*nt /tǽlənt/; schol*a*rship /skɒ́ləʃɪp/; diplom*a* /dɪpláumə/; previo*u*sly /príːvɪəsli/; p*u*rpose /pɜ́:pəs/; backw*a*rd /bǽkwəd/; phil*o*sophy /fɪlɒ́səfi/; s*u*rprising /səpráɪzɪŋ/.

ɪ (as in *ci*ty): r*e*hearsals /rɪhɜ́:səlz/; mod*e*st /mɒ́dɪst/; orphan*a*ge /ɔ́:fənɪdʒ/; r*e*wards /rɪwɔ́:dz/.

ʃ (as in *sh*ip): ambi*tio*us /æmbíʃəs/; finan*ci*ally /faɪnǽnʃəli/ or /fɪnǽnʃəli/; influen*ti*al /ɪnflʊénʃəl/; profe*ssio*n /prəféʃən/.

ʒ (as in plea*s*ure): occa*sio*nally /əkéɪʒənəli/; deci*si*on /dɪsíʒən/; disillu*sio*ned /dɪsɪlú:ʒənd/.

ju: (as in *u*se): unpop*u*lar /ʌnpɒ́pju:lə/; spectac*u*lar /spektǽkju:lə/; gen*u*ine /dʒénju:ɪn/.

Others: wealthy /wélθi/; beard /bɪəd/; condemn /kəndém/; debt /det/; awarded /əwɔ́:dɪd/; schemes /ski:mz/; accept /əksépt/ or /æksépt/.

Grammatical and structural points

(a) *Missing tense forms of defective verbs*

	Infinitive	Pres. Simple	Past S.	Pres. Perf.	Future S.
can	**to be able**	**can**	**could**		**can**
		is able	**was able**	**has been able**	**will be able**

He would like *to be able* to play the piano.
He *can/will be able* to come tomorrow.
He *has been able* to eat a little today.
Notice: *enable:* A wheel chair *enables* a handicapped person to get about.

	Infinitive	Pres. Simple	Past S.	Pres. Perf.	Future S.
must	**to have to**	**must**			**must**
		have to	**had to**	**has had to**	**will have to**

He is said *to have to* work fifteen hours a day.
All her life she *has had to* work hard.

	Infinitive	Pres. Simple	Past S.	Pres. Perf.	Future S.
may	**to be allowed**	**may/might**	**might** (reported speech)		**may**
		is allowed	**was allowed**	**has been allowed**	**will be allowed**

You ought *to be allowed* to stay out later.
My boss said I *might* have the day off.
I *was allowed* to have the day off.

(b) *the more . . . the better*
Notice these constructions: *the more spectacular, the better; the smaller, the better; the more he had, the more he wanted; the older he grew, the worse he looked; the less he spoke, the more he heard.*

(c) *having completed his training* or *after completing his training*. It is clumsy to write: *after having completed*.
Rewrite each of these in two different ways: after having completed his novel; after having written his letter, he went to post it.

(d) There is a considerable difference between: *he worked hard* and *he hardly worked*.

(e) Two uses of the *reflexive pronoun* in the passage: *he considered himself intelligent* (cf.: *he considered buying a flat*); *they declared themselves pioneers of a new school* (cf.: *they declared (that) they were pioneers*).

(f) *He earned nothing* is more emphatic than 'he did not earn anything'.
Rewrite each of these statements to emphasise the negative meaning: I didn't touch anything; he hasn't got anywhere to live; he doesn't ever complain; we don't know anybody in town

(g) *Verbal constructions*
Infinitive: he arranged for an income *to be provided;* he expects (is expected) *to manage;* enough money *to live on;* too poor *to be happy*.
Gerund: believe in *taking* risks; put off *making*.
Alternatives: he insisted *on their being;* he insisted *(that) they must be*.

Prepositions

(a) *in* debt; invest *in* a business; result *in* happiness for.
(b) the approval *of;* the (dis)advantage *of* good looks; with the help *of*.
(c) unpunctual *for (at)* rehearsals.
(d) live *on* his allowance.
(e) appoint *to* a post.
(f) (un)popular *with*.

Constrasting forms: he is *acting in a play;* the group are *acting a play.*
convert someone *to* one's own ideas; *convert* a house *into* flats.
provide someone *with* a meal; *provide* a meal *for* someone.
fail an examination; *fail in* one's purpose.
believe a story; *believe in* taking risks.
similar to; different from; in contrast to.

Expressions for use in written work

(a) *not in the least* ambitious/interested/important.
(b) *take (no) part in* a discussion.
(c) *Apart from* his occasional forgetfulness, he is very reliable.
(d) *had the (dis)advantage* of good looks/a wealthy family/a good education.
(e) He was *appointed to* a post.
(f) *draw up* a will.
(g) Parents *should not be expected to* pay for expensive schoolbooks.
(h) Jane paid ten pounds *as her share of* the expenses.
(i) He *believed* in enjoying life.
(j) He succeeded *in his purpose* of becoming a doctor.
(k) I wonder *what has become of* all that money I drew out of the bank.
(l) His suggestion *gained the approval of* the committee.
(m) He climbed the tree *with the help of* a ladder.
(n) *a considerable amount of* money/*a considerable number of* expressions to learn.
(o) He became *increasingly annoyed.*
(p) He is *invariably* polite.

(q) He is a bad driver and *accordingly* has had several accidents.
(r) *Unfortunately* he is a bad sailor.
(s) but *nevertheless* he usually travels by sea.

Spoken English

Question tags

These short forms, added at the end of a sentence, are common in spoken English.

Formation

Question tags consist of two words: a main verb or suitable auxiliary followed by a pronoun. In many cases, a negative question tag follows an affirmative main verb in the preceding statement and vice versa.

Examples: I am right, *aren't I.* (Notice the first person interrogative form.)
Your father isn't ill, *is he?*
You can't understand this, *can you.*
The children take after their father, *don't they.*
Your friend had a shock, *didn't he.*
You won't be there before Tuesday, *will you.*
You did ask him, *didn't you.*

An extra auxiliary is sometimes used in the opening statement.

Uses

1 Seeking confirmation of what is being said. No question mark, and a falling intonation at the end. The answer is expected to agree with the suggestion in the statement.
    You were dismissed from that job, *weren't you.*
    He wouldn't give a definite answer, *would he.*

2 As a surprised question. A question mark and a rising intonation at the end.
    The school children aren't going on strike now, are they?
    You won't give up your job, will you?

3 As a special request. No question mark and a falling intonation.
    You will help me, *won't you.*

4 As a challenge. No question mark, and a falling intonation.
    You stole that money, *didn't you.*

Practice

Complete the following to make statements followed by question tags. The subject and verb tense are suggested.

1 Seeking confirmation:
    (a) make some tea (*you*, Past Simple)
    (b) need more petrol (*we*, Present)
    (c) your birthday tomorrow (*it*, Future)
    (d) come from Norway (*Kurt*, Present Simple with extra auxiliary)
    (e) like porridge (*the children*, Conditional)
    (f) may still come (*he*, Present)
    (g) stop here (*train*, Present with extra auxiliary).

2 A surprised question:
   (a) not speak Portuguese (*Robert*, Present Simple)
   (b) not do the journey in one day (*they*, Future)
   (c) have your breakfast before you left (*you*, Past Perfect)
   (d) not buy a sports car (*your sister*, Present Continuous)
   (e) not a storm last night (*there*, Past Simple)
   (f) write to you (*I*, Past Simple with extra auxiliary)
   (g) not get loose again (*the dog*, Present Perfect)
   (h) not exceed the speed limit (*Aunt Matilda*, Past Continuous).

3 A request:
   (a) write to me (*you*, Future)
   (b) not lose your keys (*you*, Future).

4 A challenge:
   break that window (*you*, Past Simple).

Talking about the weather

Sunshine: It's a lovely day today, isn't it. What a glorious day! Scorching hot. Sultry/Close (Adj). It's a bit cloudy but it won't rain.

Rain: It looks like rain. It's just starting to rain. It's pouring with rain. It's only a shower. It'll soon pass over. Dull/Wet.

Wind: It's very windy today. A strong wind. A gale.

Storm: I think there'll be a thunderstorm. What a vivid flash of lightning! That was a loud clap of thunder. He was struck by lightning. The ship was caught in a storm.

Cold: It's bitterly cold. There's a hard frost. It's freezing hard.

Talking about one's job

A   What's your job? (What do you do for a living?)
B   Oh, I'm (the) secretary to the sales manager of a food processing factory.
A   Do you get good pay? (a good salary?) (Is the job well paid?)
B   Pretty good, though I have to work hard for what I get. And there's quite a lot of overtime.
A   What qualifications have you got? (What are the qualifications needed?)
B   I got a degree in Economics and then took an intensive course in shorthand, typing and various forms of office practice. There aren't many opportunities for women in Management: secretarial work seems to be the only thing available.
A   How about holidays?
B   Only a fortnight a year. But I have to travel sometimes with my boss and I enjoy that.
A   Do you think I'd make a good secretary?
B   No, I'm sure you wouldn't. You're not methodical enough and you're far too forgetful and untidy.
A   Thank you. Well, you wouldn't make a good artist and that's what I'm going to be. You've got no imagination.

Talk about your job: pay, duties, hours, holidays, conditions of work, sickness and pension benefits, why you like or dislike it, the type of person best suited for it.

Reading comprehension

In this exercise you must choose the word or phrase which best completes each sentence.

1 Now that he has retired, he lives partly on his pension and partly on the _INTEREST_ on his post office savings account.
   A income   **B** wages   **C** interest   **D** salary

2 Every day thousands of _____ fly the Atlantic for negotiations with American firms.
   A merchants   **B** dealers   **C** businessmen
   D tradesmen

3 He _____ spends his holidays in the mountains though occasionally he goes to the seaside instead.
   A usually   **B** invariably   **C** rarely   **D** always

4 She worships the sun and _____ she always spends her holidays in Greece.
   A nevertheless   **B** accordingly   **C** yet   **D** however

5 _____ to leave early is rarely granted.
   A allowance   **B** permission   **C** leave   **D** a permit

6 She is leaving her husband because she cannot _____ his bad temper any longer.
   A put down   **B** put away   **C** do away with
   D put up with

7 The weather was _____ the exceptionally poor harvest.
   A blamed for   **B** condemned for   **C** accused of
   D criticised for

8 Before you _____ down other people, it is as well to consider your own faults.
   A turn   **B** bring   **C** run   **D** send

9 You must have _____ the examination before Friday, so bring your money to the office as soon as possible.
   A passed   **B** taken   **C** sat for   **D** entered for

10 His _____ for his loyal support of the party was a seat in the Cabinet.
   A recompense   **B** repayment   **C** reward
   D compensation

Below are a number of questions or unfinished statements about lines 1–26 the reading passage on page 145, each with four suggested answers or endings. Read through the section of the passage again, then choose the best answer or ending in each case.

1 The youngest brother did not quarrel with the others because
   A he disliked arguments.
   B he was much younger than they were.
   C he was not interested in the subject of their quarrels.
   D he was quiet and shy.

2 When the brothers went out into the world, the father
  A expected them to be independent.
  B gave them the money they wanted.
  C gave them money to be independent and then no more.
  D saw to it that they had just enough for food and accommodation.

3 Which of these adjectives describes the eldest brother?
  A weak-willed.
  B ambitious.
  C unattractive.
  D extravagant.

4 The second brother became an artist because he believed that
  A he had talent.
  B his ideas were new and different.
  C he should help to reform society.
  D this was a worthwhile career.

5 Why did the youngest son decide to take up a teaching career?
  A It was what he wanted to do.
  B It would provide him with a living.
  C He had a special talent for teaching.
  D It was the only career open to him.

Composition

Letter writing

Each country has its own conventional system of setting out a letter and addressing an envelope. The British system differs in several details from those of other countries. Here is a summary of the most important requirements.

The envelope

(a) It is not usual for the sender's address to be written on the back of the envelope (though this is a good idea) provided the address is on the letter itself. Many people keep letters and throw away envelopes.

(b) The name and address are usually written on the lower half of the envelope.

(c) A man is usually addressed either as:
Mr. J.A. Brown or *J.A. Brown, Esq.,* (the full Christian name is sometimes used). His wife is *Mrs. Brown*, his daughter *Miss Brown*, and his young schoolboy son *Master Brown*. The full stop after *Mr.* and *Mrs.* is optional and may be omitted. There is no stop after *Master* or *Miss*.
Letters signifying military, civil or academic honours may follow the name, if the addressee prefers this or the contents of the letter make these appropriate.

(d) The name of the house occupies the next line if the house has no number.

(e) On the next line the house number followed by the street is written. According to correct business convention, 'Road', 'Street', etc., are not abbreviated. The comma after the number is optional.

(f)   The town and county (the latter in the accepted abbreviated form) follow. If the town shares the county name as in the case of York, Warwick, Hertford and several more, the county is usually omitted.

(g)   Each line can begin immediately below the beginning of the one above, or a short equal space may be left each time.

(h)   For maximum clearness block capitals can be used.

(i)   A comma follows the surname and ends each line except the last.

```
┌─────────────────────────────────────┐
│                                      │
│        J. A. Brown, Esq.,            │
│        12, Green Street,             │
│        DANBY,                        │
│        Hants DY9 9XZ                 │
│                                      │
└─────────────────────────────────────┘
```

(Hants stands for the county, Hampshire.)

The letter superscription

(a)   This is written at the top of the letter at the right-hand side.

(b)   It consists of the address of the sender (but not his name), followed by the date.

(c)   It is arranged in a similar way to the address on the envelope.

(d)   The date is normally written: day, month (in full), year (in full): 8th February, 19--. (Remember the abbreviations: 1st, 2nd, 3rd, 4th, 21st, 22nd, 23rd, 31st.) The full stop after the year is optional but there is usually a comma after the month.

(e)   In a business letter the name and address of the receiver of the letter usually follows, but on the left-hand side. (It may be written at the end of the letter.)

(f)   The letter opens: *Dear Sir, Dear Madam, Dear Mr. Brown, Dear Mary* — according to how well the person is known by the writer. Notice there is no exclamation mark.

(g)   The letter itself begins a short way below at some distance from the side.

The ending

The letter ends *Yours faithfully, (Yours truly,)* in business correspondence where the opening phrase was *Dear Sir* or *Dear Madam. Yours sincerely* indicates some degree of acquaintance. In this case the opening will have been *Dear Mr Brown* etc.

Any other ending which seems appropriate may be used in letters to close friends or relations.

Here is a possible example of the superscription and ending of a letter to an acquaintance.

1, West Avenue,
Bolchester,
Lancs. BH1 1VQ

22nd November, 19___.

Dear Patrick,
    It . . .

Yours sincerely,

The letter

(a) Paragraphing is important. Plan out what you intend to say before you begin writing. A short letter may introduce two, three or four subjects. Each should be dealt with in a separate paragraph. Each new paragraph may begin a short distance from the side.

(b) Clearness and conciseness (shortness) are important, especially in business letters. A friendly letter may of course spread indefinitely (unless you are in an examination and required to write a certain number of words).

(c) Simplicity is equally important. Do not try to be ambitious.

(d) It is possible to introduce conversational abbreviations in a letter to a friend to give the effect of conversation, but never in a business letter.

(e) The adjective 'nice' is commonly used in speech but it is best avoided in writing as it tends to be overused and often a more exact adjective such as 'interesting', 'enjoyable', 'attractive' or the more generalised 'pleasant' or 'delightful' would provide variety.

(f) If an examiner asks you to write a letter, he wants to see whether you know how to set it out correctly, paragraph and punctuate it and write clear, simple English in well-constructed sentences on the subject set. He also wants to see whether you understand instructions. Accordingly if limits to the number of words are mentioned, you must keep within these limits.

An example of a letter to an acquaintance

An English correspondent has written to say that his/her middle-aged parents would like to spend a holiday in your country. They wish to stay in a place that is beautiful, reasonably quiet and with plenty of opportunities for excursions. You have also been asked to recommend a small hotel or pleasant boarding-house for them. Write your reply in between 120 and 180 words. You should make the beginning and ending like those of an ordinary letter but the address is not to be counted in the number of words.

Here is a suggested paragraph plan for your letter.

1 Reference to the letter received.
2 The place recommended and its surroundings.
3 The inn suggested.
4 Offer to call on them and give further help.

14 Parnassus Avenue,
Lindenbaum,
Ruritania.
22nd February, 19___.

Dear Shirley,

I am very pleased to hear that your parents intend to spend their holiday in Ruritania. There are so many delightful places here that it is difficult to choose the most ideal.

My own choice would be Montamare, a medieval walled city by the sea with a castle and small cathedral. There are long sandy beaches and a harbour with red-sailed fishing-boats. Forest-covered hills rise behind with vineyards and orchards on their slopes. There are castles, deep blue lakes dotted with islands, caves and several picturesque old towns in the surrounding area.

Near the harbour stands a three-hundred-year-old smugglers' inn, with low beamed ceilings, wooden balconies lined with flower-boxes and lovely old polished furniture. It is comfortable and spotlessly clean. The food is excellent and the price reasonable. I can certainly recommend it and I enclose the address.

Please let me know when your parents are coming. I should be delighted to call on them and show them some interesting places. Can't you possibly manage to come with them?

Yours sincerely,
Helena

(174 words)

Practice

Each of the following subjects should be dealt with in a similar way using between 120 and 180 words, apart from the address. You are recommended to work out a plan for your letter first.

1   You have recently changed your address and wish to inform a friend. Write a short letter in which you say why you have moved and what your new home is like.

2   Write to a friend inviting him or her to spend a few days in your home and suggesting some of the things you can do during the visit.

3   You have recently had a telephone installed in your home. Write to a friend who lives in a nearby town and is not on the telephone explaining why you decided to do this, giving your number and suggesting that you would like to hear from him or her sometimes. Add any other news.

4   You are returning by post a friend's book you have kept far too long. Write a letter apologising for and explaining the delay and expressing your good opinion of the book.

5   You have been successful in an examination. Write to the teacher who prepared you for it, thanking him or her for helping you to achieve this result. Include some news about what you are now doing.

6   You have taken an 'au pair' job with an English family. The English lady has written to you in your own country, giving details of your duties which will allow no regular time for classes. Write a reply suggesting politely that, as your main purpose in coming to England is to study, you will need a definite period each day free for attending classes. Ask for one or two pieces of additional information.

7   A holiday cottage you have rented has proved quite unsatisfactory. Write to the owner, explaining the reasons for your dissatisfaction and asking for some kind of compensation.

Use of English

1   **Finish each of the following sentences in such a way that it means the same as the sentence printed before it.**

1   According to his arrangement, a pension will be provided for everyone over sixty.
He has arranged _____
2   Our teacher insists that we write all our essays on alternate lines.
Our teacher insists on _____
3   After many years of hard work, he retired.
After he _____
4   With the money he has saved, he can buy a house.
His savings will _____
5   It was not long before he had an accident.
His _____
6   It would be better for you to work in a bank.
You would be _____
7   He thinks it is a good idea to eat a lot of fruit.
He believes _____
8   It might be a good idea for you to ask for the day off tomorrow.
How _____?

2   **Notice these two expressions: the more spectacular the better; the less noise you make, the less possibility of your discovery. Add similar comparative forms to complete the sentences below.**

1   The _____ I teach him, the _____ he seems to understand. It is hopeless.
2   The _____ you work, the _____ you will earn. So work harder.
3   The _____ south one travels, the _____ the temperature becomes.
4   The _____ the price, the _____ the quality.
5   I want to buy a good watchdog, the _____ the _____.
6   The Government must do something to control rising prices, the _____ the _____.

3   **Complete each of the following sentences suitably, using not more than five words.**

1   He would eat something if he _____
2   I shall not be able to carry this unless _____
3   We shall have dinner as soon as it _____
4   He would have lit the fire if it _____
5   I can't do the washing-up until _____
6   There will be an open-air performance of 'Twelfth Night' this evening provided _____
7   I should go to the theatre more often if only _____
8   He still speaks hardly any German even though _____

4   **Adam Kresus owns a chain of hotels, a large country house, a collection of valuable pictures and investments worth around five million pounds. On making his will he decides to divide his possessions among the following:**

(a)   His son, who, while intelligent, has no interest in business and spends his time wandering around the world and his daughter, who has just graduated from university in Economics and Business Studies.

(b)   A residential clinic for drug addicts which he has established and now helps to maintain.

(c)   The establishment of what will be called the Adam Kresus Gallery where his pictures can be on display to the public.

(d)   A scientific institute carrying out cancer research.

Explain what your arrangements would be if you were Adam Kresus, giving reasons for your decisions. Use one paragraph of about 50 words for each of the above four possible recipients, using the following openings:

I have decided that my son _____

In my clinic _____

I've long wanted to establish a gallery _____

The work carried out by the cancer research institute _____

Interview

Talking about a photograph

1   Where was this photograph taken? Why do you think so?
2   Describe what you can see of the room, including the desk.
3   What problem(s) has the child got and how is the teacher trying to overcome them?

Topics

What other kinds of handicapped children need special provision in education?
What qualities are specially needed in a teacher of handicapped children?
Do you think handicapped children are better off in special purpose-built schools or should they be educated with other children with extra lessons provided?
What are some of the things that are being done nowadays to make life easier for people handicapped in various ways?

Reading aloud

Word grouping and pausing

When conversing or reading aloud the speaker normally expresses himself in meaning groups with a slight pause between each. As explained in the previous section, within the meaning group, words are joined by final to initial sound links which produce a continuous flow of sound, interrupted momentarily only at the end of the group. A comma or other punctuation mark could mark the end of the group but often this is determined only by meaning and in fact different readers could interpret meaning breaks in different ways and accordingly vary the positions of pauses.

A full stop, colon or semi-colon indicates a more definite pause. Here is a passage marked for pausing. Some of the pauses, marked (/), are optional according to the reader's interpretation.

Unfortunately / an actor who cannot even be punctual (/) should not be expected to manage a business / and it was not long (/) before the firm went bankrupt. The artist had no doubt (/) that within a short time (/) he would be making a fortune by speculation.

Passages

Read through each passage silently before reading aloud to give yourself the opportunity to decide on the position of pauses. Remember to link words when reading aloud to ensure smooth continuous reading. Suggest a situation in which each of the three passages might be heard.

1   You are after all only three quarters of an hour late so I suppose you think we should all be very grateful to you for turning up at all. And I wonder if it worries you in the least that for the past forty-five minutes eleven people who've taken the trouble to be here on time have been sitting around with nothing to do waiting to see whether you'd think it worth your while to put in an appearance at all.

2   Have you had the chance yet of going along to see what that idiot Beverley Primwell is showing in his exhibition in the Sisley Gallery? Well, all I can say is that if you haven't, don't bother to waste your time going: it's utterly dreary, mediocre and without a single new idea.

And he it was who dared to condemn us, the only group around now-adays who've got anything original to exhibit to the public, or at least to those members of the public who've got the taste and intelligence to make the effort to understand us.

3   I'm very sorry to take up your valuable time Mr Goldhart but this is a welcome opportunity for me to explain some of the things we're trying to do in the four children's homes we've established. I know the State has provided some excellent institutions for orphan children and has arranged foster homes for them too. Our special concern is for children who have got homes already but they're so unsuitable that the children are better off out of them. Parents who are in and out of prison, are violent, perpetually drunk or drug addicts, or haven't the least idea how to look after children. These are the children we've made it our job to care for.

Structured communication

Speech situations

Suggest what might be said in each of the following situations.

1   Through no fault of your own you're late for work for the second time in a week. Your boss is annoyed about your lateness which has caused a good deal of inconvenience.

2   While shopping with a friend you see something you'd very much like to buy but you haven't got enough money with you to pay for it. You hate borrowing money but decide to ask your friend to lend you what you need.

3   You have lent something to a friend who seems to have forgotten all about it. Make a tactful request for its return.

4   Express your annoyance with a friend who has kept you waiting for a long time and on turning up has made no attempt to apologise.

5   You are asking your bank manager for a bank loan of £10,000. Explain what you want it for.

Expressing opinions

1   What are some of the attractions and drawbacks of a stage career?

2   What is your opinion of teaching as a career?

3   Would you prefer a career involving plenty of adventure and possibly some risks or one which guarantees security?

4   What conventions do you regard as really useful ones?

5   What would constitute happiness in life for you?

Topics for a prepared talk

Prepare to speak on one or more of the following topics for about two minutes. Think over the topic for a few moments, possibly making a few notes on it.

1   Your tastes in art, music, sport or reading together with reasons for the appeal of the subject you prefer.

2   Some of the achievements of pioneers.

3   Some ways in which people can satisfy a taste for adventure.

A job interview

One student (or possibly more than one) is being interviewed for a holiday job which involves looking after children between eight and twelve years of age in a holiday activity camp. The interviewer (interviewers) question(s) the candidate(s) about his/their background and interests to decide on job suitability, while each candidate asks questions about the type of work, hours, pay, accommodation etc. that are to be expected.

Discussion on the role of schools

An exchange of opinions on the role of schools in present-day society. Points covered could include:

(a) The main purpose of schools
  (i) Preparation for a career
  (ii) Preparation for life in general
  (iii) Social training: working and cooperating with other people
  (iv) Preparation for the effective and enjoyable use of leisure etc.

(b) What kinds of subjects should be taught.

(c) Streaming or mixed-ability classes.

(d) Discipline.

(e) Out-of-school activities: clubs, sports contests etc.

General guidance and practice

1 Revision of tenses: Active Voice

	Past	Present	Future	Future in the past
Simple	I told	I tell	I shall tell	I would tell
Continuous	I was telling	I am telling	I shall be telling	I would be telling
Perfect	I had told	I have told	I shall have told	I would have told
Perfect Continuous	I had been telling	I have been telling	I shall have been telling	I would have been telling

Infinitives	
Simple	to tell
Continuous	to be telling
Perfect	to have told
Perfect Continuous	to have been telling

Participles	
Present	telling
Past	told

Practice

Use the correct form of each of the verbs shown in brackets.

(a) I know how I (spend) the money you (give) me last Christmas. I (keep) it till now in my Post Office Savings Account. I (just see) a beautiful cameo brooch in a jeweller's shop. I (go) to the Post Office tomorrow, and when I (draw) out the money, I (buy) the brooch.

(b) If the milkman (call) before I (come) back, (ask) him if he (bring) me some cream tomorrow. I (already use) up what I (buy) yesterday.

(c) Milton (write) much of his greatest poetry after he (become) blind and while he (live) in lonely and unhappy retirement. We (owe) the poem 'Samson Agonistes' to the fact that he (suffer) so intensely.

(d) By this time tomorrow I (buy) my ticket and at this very moment I (sit) in the train before it (leave).

(e) The experts (say) that people (use) far more electricity during the last few cold days, and there (be) further power cuts if the public (not economise) more. Last winter the electricity authorities (say) that more power (be) available this year, but recently they (not be able) to keep up with the extra demand.

(f) My family (do) all the packing for the holidays this morning while I (still sleep). They (open) drawers and cupboards all the time, but I (hear) nothing.

(g) I have never seen such a long queue before. By the time we (reach) the box office they (sell) all the tickets. We (queue then) for five hours and I (be) sure we (get) nothing.

2 Revision of tenses: Passive Voice

	Past	Present	Future	Future in the past
Simple	I was told	I am told	I shall be told	I would be told
Continuous	I was being told	I am being told	—	—
Perfect	I had been told	I have been told	I shall have been told	I would have been told
Perfect Continuous	—	—	—	—

Infinitives	
Simple	to be told
Continuous	—
Perfect	to have been told
Perfect Continuous	—

Participles	
Present	being told
Past	having been told

Practice 1

Convert these sentences from the Active to the Passive Voice. In sentences (g)–(j), there are two verbs to change. Be careful to use the same tense.

(a) They have made mistakes before.
(b) An old man was sweeping up the dead leaves.
(c) We are preparing a room for you.
(d) They recorded the broadcast speech.
(e) Some of the workers have organised an unofficial strike.
(f) A panel of distinguished authors will judge the literary competition.
(g) Experts will have examined the newly-discovered prehistoric wall-paintings before they give an opinion.

(h) They estimate that the new oil-wells will yield millions of gallons annually.
(i) They would have completed the investigations into the causes of the air disaster by tomorrow, but the injured pilot has now revealed new facts.
(j) They had checked the cargo carefully before they unloaded it.

Practice 2

Convert the following into the Active Voice. In some cases the new subject will have to be chosen in accordance with the meaning of the sentence.

(a) The men were being paid much better by the new boss.
(b) The job was done by a skilled workman.
(c) The corn was being harvested early this year.
(d) The garden has at last been weeded by my husband.
(e) The bridge had been washed away by floods and the fields were covered by water.
(f) Their new premises will be designed by an architect and constructed by a well-known firm of builders.
(g) All the sheep will have been sheared by the end of this week.
(h) The logs are floated down the river to the sawmills in summer and autumn.
(i) Beautiful articles of porcelain have been produced by that firm for nearly two centuries.
(j) The railway line was being electrified and it was hoped that a faster train service could be introduced.
(k) The letter would have been registered if the envelope had been properly sealed.
(l) That tap ought to have been turned off properly.

3 Conditions: revision and Third Condition

Practice

Use a suitable form of the verb in capitals in each of the following conditions.

(a) (Habit) If she FEEL depressed, she GO for a long walk.
(b) (Result, imperative) If you HAVE some free time, DROP in and have a chat.
(c) (First Condition) If he DRIVE at that speed, sooner or later he HAVE an accident.
(d) (Second Condition) If he WRITE today, he GET an answer this week.
(e) (Habit) He never COME by car even though he HAVE one.
(f) (Result, imperative) ASK me to repeat it if you NOT UNDERSTAND.
(g) (First Condition) You NOT MAKE much progress if you NOT MAKE an effort.
(h) (Second Condition) You NOT BE home before dark unless you LEAVE by three.

Third Condition

If you **had sent** it by air mail, it **would have reached** there in four days. (but you didn't send it by air mail and it is too late now)
If it **hadn't been raining**, he **wouldn't have taken** his car.
(Notice the affirmative alternative: **Had you sent** it by air mail, . . .)

Practice

Express the following as if they were Third Conditions.

(a) If he goes climbing, he wears his heavy boots.
(b) If I see him, I'll warn him not to say anything.
(c) If he doesn't enjoy the play, he will leave before the end.
(d) He won't pay me if I don't ask him.
(e) She writes to me on my birthday if she remembers the date.
(f) You will sell your house easily if you don't ask too high a price for it.

4   Modal verbs in conditions

can   If you **can** come today, you **can/will be able to** meet him.
If you **could** come today, you **could/would be able to** meet him.
If you **could have** come today, you **could have** met him. *or:*
If you **had been able to** come today, you **would have been able** to meet him. (Either form can be used in either clause.)

must   If you **must** be there by five, you **must/will have to** take a taxi.
If you **had to** be there by five, you **would have to** take a taxi.
If you **had had to** be there by five, you **would have had to** take a taxi.

The use of were with a singular subject

Were is sometimes used in a Second Condition:
   If I were you . . .   If he were interested, . . .
This is a normally accepted form even in everyday speech.

The form *were to* used in the Second Condition suggests less likelihood.
   If he *were to* find out about this, he'd be furious.

Would in a conditional clause

When *would* expresses willingness, it may appear in the conditional clause:
   I'd be very grateful if you *would (you'd)* post this letter for me.

Practice

Suggest a result of these conditions, using a suitable form of the verb in brackets.

(a) If you want to read this book, I (let) _____
(b) Unless the light improves, we (can not) _____
(c) If I were to win the competition, I (buy) _____
(d) If you hadn't offended him, he (help) _____
(e) If you had lost that ticket, you (must) not _____
(f) If I wanted to do the journey in one day, I (must) _____
(g) I should be so pleased if you (come) _____
(h) I shouldn't touch that if I (be) _____
(i) I wouldn't have been able to find my way if I (had not) _____
(j) I wouldn't need to wear glasses if I (can) _____

5   May, might

May and *might* can have two different meanings:
(a) Permission
      You *may* smoke if you wish.
      The head teacher said that the children *might* leave school early.

(b) Possibility

May and *might* suggest 'perhaps', 'possibly'. *May* suggests a stronger possibility than *might*, but, in effect, there is little difference in meaning. *Might* is normally used when the rest of the sentence is in the past.

He *may* be right. (He is perhaps right).

You *may* get the job: you're quite well qualified.

You *might* get the job but they're really looking for someone with more experience.

The plan *might* work if we tried it soon enough.

In some cases either meaning may apply. The appropriate one becomes apparent only in speech.

He *may* come tomorrow. (Permission)

He *may* come tomorrow. (Possibility)

In connection with the second of these uses, *might* is sometimes used in making a request.

You *might* help me with this box.

The speaker suggests that the person addressed will perhaps be kind enough to help.

It can also be a reproach.

You *might* listen while I am speaking.

Here are some infinitive constructions following *may* and *might*:

You *may be lucky* in the football pools. (Simple Active)

They *may be moving* soon. (Continuous Active)

He *may have had* an accident. (Perfect Active)

She *may have been staying* in a hotel. (Perfect Continuous Active)

The house *may have been destroyed*. (Perfect Passive)

That was dangerous; the mixture *might have exploded*. (Perfect Active)

He said he *might be coming* late. (Continuous Active)

The door *might have been locked*. (Perfect Passive)

Notice that when *might* is followed by a Perfect Infinitive there is in most cases the suggestion that the possibility was unfulfilled.

Practice

Rewrite each of the following sentences, introducing some form of *may* or *might*. Certain words will have to be left out.

(a) You could perhaps have been more careful.
(b) Am I allowed to help you?
(c) Would I be allowed to open a window?
(d) If you had sent your letter yesterday, it could perhaps have been delivered by today.
(e) The ship will perhaps leave this evening, but I doubt it.
(f) Our neighbours are allowed to use our telephone if they ever need to.
(g) Unqualified persons are not allowed to practise as doctors.
(h) Fancy travelling at that speed! You could possibly have been killed.
(i) They are possibly coming tomorrow.

6 May as well, might as well

Notice these uses of *may as well* and *might as well*:

I *may/might as well* finish now that I have started.

You *might as well* be dead as live in such a small place.

The first example suggests, though with no great enthusiasm, that this is worth doing. The second gives the impression that one idea is so unpleasant or fruitless that the new suggestion could not be much worse.

Here are two further examples:
    You *might as well* see him now he is here.
    I *might as well* have been speaking to a brick wall. He took no notice at all.
Notice that when *might as well* is followed by a Perfect Infinitive, the suggestion normally is that the action of the Infinitive did not actually happen.

Practice

Rewrite the following sentences, using one or the other of the above phrases. Part of each sentence will be changed considerably. The new subject is in italics in sentences (a)−(d).

(a)   It would have been just as satisfactory if *I* had stayed at home. I learned nothing in the class.
(b)   It will be just as useful for *you* to save your breath. He won't listen to you.
(c)   It will be a good idea for *you* to get some sleep while you have the chance.
(d)   I suggest *you* sit down. You have a long time to wait.
(e)   Why not bring your fishing rod too? We may have some spare time.
(f)   It could have been a good idea to stay the night there. We gained nothing by returning a day earlier.

7 Defining and non-defining clauses

Notice these two sentences:
    The youngest, *who was not in the least ambitious*, took no part in their arguments.
    An actor *who cannot be punctual* should not be expected to manage a business.

Each introduces an adjectival clause, but the relationship of this clause to the rest of the sentence is different in each case.

In the second case, the adjectival clause defines the actor, not an actor who is successful, nor an actor who cannot remember his lines, but *an actor who cannot be punctual*. The clause defines or explains what actor is meant and is therefore a *defining clause*.

In the first case, the adjectival clause merely adds a piece of description: it does not define who the youngest is or which youngest he is as we know who he is already. It is a *non-defining clause*.

A non-defining clause is:
(a)   separated from the rest of the sentence by commas.
(b)   always introduced by *who, whom, whose* or *which* and these are never omitted.

A defining clause is:
(a)   not separated off by commas.
(b)   sometimes introduced by *that* instead of *who, whom* or *which*. If a preposition immediately precedes the pronoun, *that* cannot be used.

Notice: The pronoun may be omitted when it is:
 (i)   the object of the following verb or:
(ii)   governed by a preposition.
The brackets below show where a pronoun could be omitted.
    With the capital (that/which) he had saved he set up a business.

The student (that/whom) I was discussing the problem with . . .
The student with whom I was discussing the problem . . .

Practice

Insert the relative pronoun in the following sentences, putting brackets round it if it may be omitted. Put in commas where these are necessary.

(a) Here is the medicine _____ does you good.
(b) Our little puppy _____ David adores is always in mischief.
(c) The socks _____ she was knitting were for the Red Cross.
(d) The aged man in a wheel-chair _____ is talking to the hospital matron was once a great surgeon.
(e) The gate _____ you came through must be kept shut.
(f) The pen with _____ he wrote so many great novels is now carefully preserved.
(g) The American ambassador _____ you were speaking to a moment ago will be returning home soon.
(h) The beauty queen _____ was elected in last year's competition is now a rising film star.
(i) The news of his death _____ has shocked the whole nation has been reported throughout the world.
(j) The waiter _____ you were enquiring about has been dismissed.

8 Too, enough

Too suggests more than is needed or wanted:
I'm sorry I can't come. I've got *too much* to do.
He's now *too old* to be included in the team.

Enough suggests just as much as is needed or wanted:
Have you got *enough bread*?
You don't speak *clearly enough* for me to hear you properly.
Note: *enough* precedes a noun but follows an adjective or adverb:
enough bread, tall enough, clearly enough.

Do not confuse *too* with *very*:
He's *too ill* to attend the meeting.
He's *very ill* so he won't be able to attend the meeting.

Too suggests some comparison: *too much/many/large* for some purpose.
Notice however the occasional response to a gift or compliment:
That's really *too kind* of you.

Too and *not enough* are in effect opposites:
It's *too warm* to go for a long walk.
It's *not warm enough* to go for a long walk

Any verb directly following *too* or *enough* takes an infinitive form:
He's *too young to take part.*
He's *not old enough to take part.*

Practice

1 Express each of the following sentences in another way but with the same meaning using *enough* and the opposite of the adjective or adverb.

(a) I'm too poor to own a car like that.
(b) You type too slowly to qualify as a secretary.
(c) This room is too dark to work in.
(d) The flat is too far from my place of work.

2   Complete each of these sentences with a suitable infinitive and other words.

(a)   Jane says she hasn't got enough courage _____
(b)   The party won't get enough votes _____
(c)   The bus was too crowded for me _____
(d)   I've got too little time _____

9   Fairly, quite, rather

Each of these adverbs is used to modify an adjective or another adverb, indicating the degree to which it applies.

Fairly suggests a reasonable level; *rather* suggests a more decided or definite level. *Rather* is often used to modify adjectives or adverbs indicating undesirable qualities.

His drawings are *fairly* good, but I doubt whether he will ever become a famous artist.

This photograph is *rather* good. It would be a good idea to enter it for the competition.

I am afraid he is *rather* dishonest.

She spoke *rather* sharply.

Quite is a little more definite than *fairly*, especially if emphasised in speech:

Your last piece of work was *quite* good.

Quite can also mean completely:

I haven't *quite* finished yet.

Notice the difference in meaning here:

The film is *fairly* long; it lasts about two hours.

The film is *rather* long: some cutting might have improved it.

Rather often precedes a comparative form:

The dress is *rather* longer than I expected.

Practice

Insert *rather* or *fairly* in each of the following sentences. Suggest also those cases where *quite* could be used either with the meaning 'fairly' or with the meaning 'completely'.

(a)   I'm sorry. I'm _____ tired. I think I'll go to bed.
(b)   It would be as well to bring an overcoat: it's _____ cold today.
(c)   She is _____ pretty, but not exceptionally so.
(d)   That remark was _____ unkind, wasn't it?
(e)   I have been _____ free from colds this winter.
(f)   The details are _____ accurate but there are a few errors.
(g)   You had better behave yourself; he is _____ strict.
(h)   The accident was _____ serious: in fact it was fortunate nobody was killed.
(i)   He is _____ more intelligent than the average ten-year-old.

10   Had better, would rather

You had (You'd) better hurry = I advise you to do this.
I should (I'd) rather take my time = I prefer to do this.

Practice

In each of the following sentences insert either the phrase *had better* or *should/would rather* as appropriate.

(a) We _____ play chess than bridge.
(b) You _____ hurry up. It is early closing day today.
(c) There are stinging nettles either side of the path. We _____ be careful.
(d) _____ you _____ have rice pudding or cherry tart?
(e) He _____ not light the geyser until he knows how to use it.
(f) Would you prefer to visit Kew Gardens or Hampton Court Palace? I _____ see Kew Gardens today.

11 Various verbal constructions

These are common constructions and quite important, so careful attention should be given to them.

Notice these verbs which are normally followed by an infinitive or a noun clause.

He decided to go.   He decided that she should go.
He determined to go.   He determined that she should go.
He proposed to go.   He proposed that she should go.
He arranged to go.   He arranged that she should go.
                          He arranged for her to go.

But: He thought he would go/He thought of going. (*Not:* *He thought to go.)

He suggested she should go/He suggested her going. (Not: *He suggested her to go.)

Here are some verbs followed by the infinitive and not the gerund:

He failed to go.   (He missed going.)
He managed to go.   (He succeeded in going.)
He meant to go.   He hoped to go.
He wanted to go.   He wished to go.
He planned to go.

Remember the construction with *want: He wanted me to come.* (Not: *He wanted that I come.*)

Practice

Use the correct verbal form in these sentences.

(a) The firm decided (start) a new advertising campaign.
(b) The woman determined (her husband buy himself) a new suit.
(c) They managed (rescue) all the sheep stranded in the snow.
(d) The explorer succeeded (discover) an unknown tributary of the river.
(e) The woman wants her husband (buy) her a new electric cooker.
(f) The team failed (score) another goal.
(g) The salesman thought (persuade) the housewife to buy a vacuum cleaner.
(h) I missed (see) the almond blossom this spring.
(i) He hopes (get) a good mark for his essay.
(j) He suggested (invest) our money in a building society.
(k) The electric cooker firm arranged (present) a cookery demonstration to housewives.
(l) They arranged that the demonstration (take place) in their new showrooms.

12 Revision of prepositions

Insert the correct prepositions in the following sentences.

(a) Do you believe _____ ghosts?

(b) He converted the barn _____ a small theatre.

(c) He is saving money to provide _____ his future.

(d) Are you taking part _____ the concert they are giving in the Parish Hall next week?

(e) He has invested most of his capital _____ oil shares.

(f) I don't know what has become _____ the scarf I was given for my birthday.

(g) A spider lives _____ (or feeds _____) flies caught in its web.

(h) The game resulted _____ a draw, two all.

(i) He trod _____ my toe _____ purpose.

(j) He is very extravagant and is always _____ debt.

(k) A circus clown is usually popular _____ children.

(l) The producer has himself acted _____ many outstanding roles.

(m) The antique dealer was patronised _____ many connoisseurs.

(n) Judging by the meal she gave us, she might profit _____ attending a course in cookery.

(o) They were defeated _____ their purpose.

(p) We are hoping _____ a change in the weather.

8 Pity for a Stranger

The little man came up to me as I was about to enter the telephone box and asked me whether I had a match.

'I'm sorry,' I said. 'I don't smoke, so I haven't any. You had better ask someone else.'

5   He looked rather disappointed, hesitated, and then turned away. I watched him walk slowly down the street before I picked up the telephone directory to look up the number I meant to dial.

I am not used to a public call box so, at my first attempt to get through, the warning pips had stopped before I realised I had to insert a coin.

10   When I was at last able to speak, I was told that the person whom I urgently wanted to give a message to had just that minute gone out.

Swearing slightly under my breath, I emerged from the box and came face to face with the little man, who was looking as pathetic as a stray dog. As he raised his hat again, I could see he was quite bald. A thin line,

15 resembling a duelling scar, crossed one cheek. He spoke nervously.

'Excuse my troubling you again,' he said. 'May I walk along with you a little way? I must confide in someone. I need help desperately.'

He had an unusually deep voice which suggested a strange combination of shyness and self-confidence. I was conscious of a fairly strong foreign

20 accent and I wondered what country he had actually come from. I said that I had to catch a train in twenty minutes' time, but that he might accompany me to the station.

'I am going to shock you,' he said suddenly, after a moment's silence. 'Can you lend me five pounds? I have no money at all.'

25   I have come across many queer characters during my life and plenty of people have tried to borrow money from me. I have generally managed to avoid lending them any. But, perhaps because of the very directness of his appeal, I somehow had the impression that his need might be desperately urgent.

30   'I'm sorry,' I replied. 'I'm afraid I can't lend you anything, as I'm not in the habit of carrying much money about with me. Don't you think that the police might be the best people to ask for help? They could tell you the address of some hostel or organisation you could go to.'

He hesitated. 'I dare not go to the police,' he said quietly. 'If I do go,

35 they will have to send me home. That is what I'm afraid of. I don't know what to do.'

'Why did you come here?' I asked. 'How did you come? And surely you must have some money.'

'I did have a little money,' he replied, 'but it was stolen from my room in

40 the hotel and I dared not complain. As to how I came here, I should rather not say anything about it. I cannot accept the system of government under which I have had to live and life in my own country has become unbearable to me. A friend of mine, to whom I am eternally grateful, agreed to help me to escape.'

45   Naturally I tend to distrust stories like this, but the little man's quiet firm manner of speaking had impressed me. I felt half inclined to let him

have a few pounds on the chance that he was telling the truth, but I was rather short of ready cash anyhow, and might have needed what I had with me on the way home.

50 'I'm sorry,' I said again. 'Why don't you try the police in any case? The authorities usually deal sympathetically with people who have troubles like yours.'

He shook his head rather sadly, raised his hat and left me. I caught my train and soon forgot the incident.

55 It was three weeks later that I happened to glance at an old evening paper and caught sight of a small paragraph at the bottom of the front page: 'The unidentified body of a short bald man, with a deep scar across one cheek, was recovered from the River Thames yesterday. The police believe he had committed suicide.' I then noticed the date: just two and a

60 half weeks before.

I suddenly remembered talking to the little man. It was I who might have been the final cause of this terrible tragedy. For days afterwards the cruelty of my refusal made me suffer continual shame and remorse. I swore that I would never again refuse any appeal for help.

65 It was some time during the following week that I was coming down another street on my way to an appointment. Two men were in the street, one of whom seemed slightly familiar. The shorter one, whom I seemed to know, was standing by the telephone box, feeling in his pockets. As the other man was about to enter the box, the short man spoke to him, and

70 then lit a cigarette from the lighter he was offered, before strolling away for a short distance, apparently waiting for someone. As I approached on the other side of the road, I noticed a long scar across one cheek.

I need not have reproached myself so bitterly.

Notes on the passage

Vocabulary

1 *box* (N) *a telephone box; a pillar box* (for posting letters — *a letterbox* is also possible); *a box in a theatre* (at the side of the stage); *a box office* (where one buys theatre and cinema tickets — but *a booking office* for travel tickets); *a box number* (used instead of an address in newspaper small advertisements); *a matchbox* (the container), *a box of matches.*
Boxing Day = the 26th December. *box* (V) = fight with the fists; *boxing gloves; a boxer.*

2 *match* (N) = (a) a safety match that strikes (b) a competitive game (c) an equal: *The champion has met his match* (d) something similar or in harmony: *These cushion-covers will be a good match for the chairs* (e) a marriage: *a matchmaker* is someone who enjoys bringing likely marriage partners together.
match (V) = be similar to or harmonise with: *She had a blue hat and blue gloves and a scarf to match.*

5 *disappointed* (N *disappointment*) = unhappy because some pleasant thing has not happened: *He was very disappointed by his failure to get the job he wanted.*
deceived (N *deception*) = given a wrong idea: *The shop-keeper deceived the customer into thinking he was getting a bargain.*
pretend (V) (N *pretence*) = try to give the idea of being or knowing something when this is not true: *The other guest pretended that he knew all about business but in fact he was only a young office clerk.*
claim (V and N) = say that one has the right to something, say that something is true: *He claimed the watch that had been found; he claimed that it belonged to him.*

6 *pick* a flower in the garden/an apple on the tree; *pick up* a flower that has fallen on

the ground/a book lying on the table. *pick* one's favourite chocolate from those in the box (= choose); *pick up* a language by using it, without methodical study.
fall from above the ground: *an apple falls from a tree; fall down* when already standing on the ground: *He fell down while playing football.*

6 *telephone directory   a library catalogue* containing names of books; *a furniture catalogue; a brochure* = a very small book (*booklet*) giving information; *a pamphlet* or *a leaflet* is usually a single sheet giving information.

7 *mean* (V)   (a) What does this word *mean*? (b) I *mean* what I say, and nothing will make me change my mind. (c) I *mean* to finish this before tomorrow. (d) I *meant* to write to you but I had no time (so I did not).
(Adj) (a) He is so *mean* that he grudges the cost of the polish on his door knocker (opp. *generous*). (b) It was a *mean* thing to try to get me into trouble like that. (c) the *mean* annual rainfall (*average*)
(Pl N) (a) to have *means* = to have plenty of money (b) The only *means* of getting there is by boat. He would use any *means* to get rich. (*way*)

11 *urgently*   An *urgent* matter is one that must receive immediate attention. An envelope may be marked URGENT — the letter must be dealt with at once. (N *urgency*).
An *emergency* is a state of affairs needing urgent attention. An *emergency operation* must be performed at once. Buildings where many people gather together have *emergency exits* in case of fire.

12 *swear* = (a) use bad language (b) give one's solemn word that one will do something: *He swore that he would take revenge.* A witness in a law court has to *swear* (take an oath) to tell only the truth.
vow (V and N) has a similar meaning to (b): *He vowed never to forget.* Monks, nuns and often people being married take *vows*.
curse (V and N) may mean 'use bad language' or 'wish evil things to happen to one's enemy': *He uttered a curse on those who had destroyed his home and family.*

12 *under my breath* = in a whisper. *out of breath* or *breathless* = having no breath after running (but: *breathless with excitement*).
panting = breathing quickly. *gasping* = drawing in air with difficulty.

13 *face to face (with); back to back; side by side* (four *abreast*); *shoulder to shoulder; hand in hand; arm in arm.* put on a dress *inside out/back to front.* hang a picture *upside down.*

15 *duel* (V and N) = an organised fight between two people.
dual (Adj) = double: *dual controls in a car.*

15 *a scar* (from an old wound); *a bruise* (blue-brown); *a bump* on the head; *a spot* on the nose; *a swelling; a blister* (from walking); *a corn* (hard skin, often on the foot); *a scratch* (from something sharp). *He has a black eye because he bumped into a lamp-post.*

17 *confide* (in someone) $\doteq$ tell something secret, hoping for sympathy. say something *in confidence*, trusting it will be kept secret. *a confidential* secretary/document. *confident* = (sure) of one's success. *a confidence* (C N) = a secret exchanged; *confidence* (Unc N) = sureness: *A mountain-climber must have confidence in his ability. self-confidence; over-confidence.*

17 *desperate* (Adj) = not knowing what to do because no hope is left and so possibly violent. *despair* (V and Unc N) = lose all hope; *in despair: He was so hopeless at housekeeping that, in despair, he decided to get married.*

18 *combination.* An *alliance* between countries (*allies*). A *union* = a combined group: *the Soviet Union; the United States.*

19 *shyness* = quietness and reserve with people. *timidity* = fear of people.

19 *conscious of* = aware of. *unconsciousness* = unawareness of one's surroundings.

20 a foreign *accent;* a local *dialect.*

20 *actually* = really. Not: *at that time.*

24 *borrow* something from another person. *lend* something to another person; *a lending library*.

27 *very* (Adj) is emphatic: *The very idea! I should never dream of it. That was the very thing I was going to say.*

28 *appeal* (V and N): *an appeal for money and food for famine victims.*
call (V and N) = a loud cry: *The drowning man called for help.*

31 *a habit* is personal: *Smoking is a bad habit.* (Adj *habitual*).
a custom is a practice observed for generations by a group of people (Adj *customary*).
a tradition is similar but with a stronger idea of the past. (Adj *traditional*).

40 *complain about* the bad food or the noise; *complain of* a headache.
A complaint may also be an illness, often one that lasts for a considerable period: *Bronchitis and rheumatism are common complaints.*
One can *reclaim* money (demand to have it back) but *reclamation* usually refers to bringing back useless land into cultivation.

42 *unbearable* and *intolerable* are of similar meaning. *tolerant* = accepting willingly that other people may have opinions different from one's own.

46 *feel (be) inclined to / tend to:* both these suggest that the following action happens naturally, easily or often: *He is inclined to (tends to) exaggerate.* The very slight difference in meaning can be seen best in the related nouns.
A *tendency* is a general likelihood. It may well express the general or abstract though this is not always the case. An *inclination* suggests a personal feeling of wishing to do something.
to *tend to* may therefore more often be found in connection with more general or abstract cases; to *be inclined to* in more personal and voluntary ones:
  Mathematical figures tend to be misleading in the study of human behaviour.
  He is inclined to be lazy.
Another less common expression is to *be prone to: He is prone to argue. Children are prone to various childish illnesses.*
In very many cases the three expressions can be used interchangeably, *tend to* being probably the most common.

47 *tell the truth*   But: *tell a lie.*

48 *short of* money/time = not having enough to spare. *Short of stealing a car, there seemed to be no way of getting home*   apart from, other than by.

49 *on the way* home; your bicycle is *in my way* so you'll have to move it; you can reach the village only by car as it is a very *out-of-the-way* place; he isn't the type of person I admire but *in a way* I like him; oh, *by the way*, I nearly forgot to tell you that Martin asked to be remembered to you. *incidentally* can usually replace *by the way*.

55 *I happened to* glance = I glanced by chance. *I happened to meet him.*

55 *glance* (V and N) quickly; *gaze* (V and N) for a long time; *stare* (V and N) with surprise or curiosity, possibly rudely; *glare* (V and N) angrily; *peer* (V) look with difficulty; *peep* (V and N) take a quick look at something; *catch sight of* = see suddenly; *catch a glimpse of* = see suddenly for a very short time.
Which? (a) _____ sadly at a departing ship (b) _____ ahead through thick fog (c) a teacher may _____ at a talkative student (d) _____ at someone wearing extraordinary clothes (e) _____ a friend travelling in a fast car (f) The old lady _____ through the closed curtains at her new neighbours (g) _____ at newspaper headlines when in a hurry (h) _____ a waiting friend as the train stops.

58 *recovered from*   One also *recovers from* an illness (N *recovery*).

59 *commit* suicide/murder/robbery/theft. *A crime* is *committed.*
commission (N) may be: (a) the sum charged by an agent for doing some service such as buying shares: *a ten-per-cent commission;* (b) the special authority given to an officer in the armed forces. A sergeant is a *non-commissioned* officer.

62   *a tragedy* (Adj *tragic*). *A comedy* (Adj *comic*). *A comedian* is the kind of performer who makes people laugh.

63   *continuous* = continuing without a break. *continual* = extending over a long time. Which describes (Adj or Adv): a railway line? a dog barking? a child asking for sweets? the prairies stretching across Central Canada?
constant can have a similar meaning to *continual*.

63   *ashamed of* a bad action; feel *shame* because of it; a *shameful* action is one to be really ashamed of; a *shameless* person is one who does not seem to feel shame whatever he does.

70   *stroll* and *saunter* (V and N) both mean to walk in a leisurely way. Cf. *march* (as soldiers); *stride, pace* (backwards and forwards); *strut* (proudly and often foolishly). All except *strut* are nouns and verbs. *A march* can also be a musical composition.

Phrasal verbs

give   *give away* without payment; a secret.
       give back = return something to its owner.
       give in   your homework to the teacher; allow an opponent the victory.
       give off   smoke, heat, a bad smell.
       give out = distribute to people e.g. books to students; the sun gives out heat; supplies give out (come to an end).
       give up   a habit such as smoking; trying to do something.

Practice

(a) Uranium _____ radio-activity.
(b) Food is _____ to starving people.
(c) Her patience finally _____.
(d) He _____ trying to find the answer.
(e) I _____ to their demands.
(f) He _____ what he had borrowed.
(g) We shall never _____ to the enemy.

go   With expressions connected with movement, meanings are obvious; these include: *go away, in, back, round, out, forward, backward.*

  go into a matter = investigate it.
  go for = attack as a dog might; fetch.
  go over = examine and check a second time.
  go with = harmonise, e.g. Some colours *go with* one another well.
  go without (do without) = manage without having something e.g. *go without* food.
  go in for an examination.
  go up = rise, e.g. prices.

Pronunciation

Distinguish between: dial /dáɪəl/; duel /djúːəl/; dual /djúːəl/; mean /miːn/; meant /ment/; deal /diːl/; dealt /delt/; bold /bəʊld/; bald /bɔːld/; breathe /briːð/; breath /breθ/.

ə (as in *a*go): urgently /ɜ́ːdʒəntli/; emergency /ɪmɜ́ːdʒənsi/; famili*a*r /fəmílɪə/; trag*e*dy /trǽdʒədi/; dist*a*nce /dístəns/; for*ei*gn /fɒ́rɪn/ or /fɒ́rən/; symp*a*thetically /sɪmpəθétɪkli/; *a*pparently /əpǽrəntli/; consci*ou*s /kɒ́nʃəs/; desp*e*rate /déspərət/; conscienti*ou*s /kɒnʃiénʃəs/; commit /kəmít/; system /sístəm/.

Others: directory /dɪréktəri/ or /daɪréktəri/; unidentified /ʌnaɪdéntɪfaɪd/; suicide /súːɪsaɪd/; accent /ǽksənt/; Thames /temz/; approached /əprə́ʊtʃt/; swear /sweə/.

Grammatical and structural points

(a) He *used to get* up early but he no longer does; he *is used to (accustomed to) getting* up early so he does not mind. It is wrong to say: *He uses to get up early.* This should be: *He gets up early* or *He is in the habit of getting up early.*

(b) He is *my* father. He is a friend *of mine* (one of my friends). The use of the possessive pronoun after *of* suggests one of a number; one could not therefore speak of *a father of mine.*
Other persons: some notes *of yours;* an idea *of his;* a habit *of hers;* a relation *of ours;* a dream of *theirs* to live in a country cottage; a mistake *of Jock's;* a suggestion *of the Greys'.*

(c) The adjective *own* must always be preceded by a possessive adjective: *my, his, our* etc. or a possessive form of a noun: The dog sits on *his (its) own* chair. Is this *Caroline's own* car?

(d) *might have needed*   Notice the following constructions and meanings:
You *must have* seen him (almost certainly)
You *might have* lost it (this is possible)
You *might have* told him (but you did not)
You *need not have* told him (but you did)
You *should (ought to) have* told him (but probably you did not). (See also page 94.)

(e) someone *else*, everywhere *else*, nothing *else* etc. Do as you are told *or else* you will be in trouble.

(f) I have to catch a train *in twenty minutes' time.* Not: *after twenty minutes.*

(g) *about to* do something: *He was about to go out when he had second thoughts and turned back.*

(h) *The police are* investigating the crime: this is a plural noun.

Prepositions

(a) No preposition: *enter* a room; *resemble* another person.
(b) conscious/aware *of;* in the habit *of* talking; afraid *of* meeting; short *of* food; the cause *of* his failure.
(c) emerge *from* (come out of); money stolen *from* her purse.
(d) He stood face to face *with* his hated enemy; carry money about *with* him.
(e) I telephoned him *on* the chance that he might be in.
(f) confide *in* his best friend.
(g) muttering *under* his breath.
(h) grateful *to* him *for* his help.
(i) *As to* the other two bags, we can carry those ourselves.

Expressions for use in written work

(a) I was *about to* speak when I sneezed.
(b) look disappointed.
(c) *insert* a coin.
(d) He had *just that minute* gone out.
(e) He said something *under his breath.*
(f) He *came face to face with* a bull.
(g) *Excuse my* troubling you.
(h) I was *conscious of* a strange silence
(i) *in* twenty *minutes' time.*
(j) I *had the impression that* he was afraid.
(k) *As to* tomorrow's arrangements, we can discuss them later.
(l) He *tends to* argue.
(m) I *felt half inclined to* leave at once.
(n) He stayed *on the chance that* he might hear something.
(o) I met her *on the way home.*
(p) I *happened to* meet him.
(q) I *caught sight of* a stork flying.
(r) *For days afterwards* he stayed indoors.

Spoken English

Most languages have their one-word exclamations that can express many different feelings. These are the three main ones used by English speakers. They are sometimes similar in use and the same situation could cause different people to use one or another of these.

Well

These are some of the many ideas which can be expressed by *well:*

Surprise: Well, I am surprised to see you!
Challenge: Well, what do you want from me?
Hesitation: Well, I'm not sure. We'll have to think it over.
Relief: Well, thank goodness we've arrived safely.
Decision: Well, I know what I'll do. I'll ask William to give me a lift.
Qualified (slightly unsure) *approval:* Well, perhaps it will do.
Resignation: Well, I suppose there's nothing we can do about it.
Sarcasm: Well, well, look who's come to help — now we've finished!

Practice

Explain the meaning suggested by *well* in each of the following:

(a)   Well, and what are you going to do about it?
(b)   Well, in some ways we enjoyed it.
(c)   Well, let me think. Yes, I remember. His name was Alvar.
(d)   Well, you *are* early for breakfast today. It's only ten o'clock.
(e)   Well, that's settled. Now we know what we'll be doing.
(f)   Well, I'm glad that's over.
(g)   Well, I never thought she'd grow up to be so beautiful!

Oh

Oh can have these uses among others:

Alarm: Oh, you frightened me!
Delight: Oh, what a wonderful present!
Pain: Oh, that hurts!
Protest: Oh, that's not fair.
Calling someone's attention: Oh, Miss Smith, can you spare a minute, please?

Ah

Ah is a more controlled expression of feeling. It is less often used by young people.

Ah, so that's what he told you.
Ah, you see. I've known him much longer than you have.

**Further question
tags**

In a few cases affirmative tags follow affirmative statements and negative ones negative statements.

(a)   To soften a command: Open a window, *will you? (would you?)*
(b)   To show interest: So your brother has directed a film, *has he?*
(c)   To express a challenge: So you think you can do it better than I can, *do you?*
(d)   To show sarcasm: Dad, I want to borrow your car. Oh, *you do, do you?* And what happened to it last time you had it?

Reading comprehension

Choice of words

In this exercise you must choose the word or phrase which best completes each sentence.

1 She felt very _____ when her husband forgot her birthday.
   A deceived   **B** deserted   **C** desperate
   D disappointed

2 This was one of the few crimes he did not _____ .
   A make   **B** perform   **C** commit   **D** achieve

3 As a result of their _____ the three small independent countries felt less afraid of their powerful neighbour.
   A combination   **B** alliance   **C** partnership   **D** union

4 I _____ to my office as it is so near my home that I don't need to drive there.
   A use to go   **B** go on foot   **C** walk   **D** go

5 As a result of the radio _____ for help for the earthquake victims, over a million pounds has been raised.
   A appeal   **B** call   **C** programme   **D** advertisement

6 An ambulance must have priority as it usually has to deal with some kind of _____ .
   A urgency   **B** crash   **C** crisis   **D** emergency

7 I have a number of _____ to make about this hotel so I wish to see the manager.
   A complaints   **B** claims   **C** reclamations
   D accusations

8 The road lay ahead of him, a _____ grey line stretching to the horizon.
   A continual   **B** constant   **C** continuous
   D prolonged

9 If you are so senseless as to go on long walks in tight-fitting shoes, you must expect to get _____ .
   A scars   **B** scratches   **C** bruises   **D** blisters

10 After his prolonged dive in search of the ring he emerged from the water _____ .
   A breathtaking   **B** gasping for breath   **C** panting
   D without breath

Multiple choice responses

Read the following passage before dealing with the questions and statements that follow it.

Using a public telephone may well be one of the minor irritations of life, demanding patience, determination and a strong possibility of failure, together on occasion with considerable unpopularity.

5 The hopeful caller (shall we call him George?) waits till six o'clock in the evening to take advantage of the so-called 'cheap rates' for a long-distance call. The telephone box, with two broken panes of glass in the side, stands at the junction of two main roads with buses, lorries and cars roaring past. It is pouring with rain as George joins a queue of four depressed-looking people. Time passes slowly and seems to come to a standstill while the

10 person immediately before George carries on an endless conversation, pausing only to insert another coin every minute or so.

Eventually the receiver is replaced and the caller leaves the box. George enters and picks up one of the directories inside, only to discover that someone unknown has torn out the very page he needs. Nothing for it but

15 to dial Directory Enquiries, wait patiently for a reply (while someone outside bangs repeatedly on the door) and finally note down the number given.

At last George can go ahead with his call. Just as he is starting to dial, however, the door opens and an unpleasant-looking face peers in with the

20 demand, 'Can't you hurry up?'. Ignoring such barbarity, George continues to dial and his unwanted companion withdraws. At last he hears the burr-burr of the ringing tone, immediately followed by rapid pips demanding his money, but he is now so upset that he knocks down the coins he has placed ready on the top of the box. Having at last located

25 them, he dials again: the pips are repeated and he hastily inserts the coins. A cold voice informs him, 'Grand Hotel, Chalfont Wells.' 'I've an urgent message for a Mr Smith who is a guest in your hotel. Could you put me through to him? I'm afraid I don't know his room number.'

The response appears less than enthusiastic and a long long silence

30 follows. George inserts more coins. Then the voice informs him, 'I've been trying to locate Mr Smith but the hall porter reports having seen him leave about a minute ago.'

Breathing heavily, George replaces the receiver, just as the knocking on the door starts again.

Here are a number of questions or unfinished statements about the passage, each with four suggested answers or endings. Choose the one you think fits best in each case.

1   The main intention of the passage is to provide
    A   instructions about how to use a public call box.
    B   advice about how to deal with public telephone problems.
    C   criticism of the efficiency of the telephone system.
    D   an account of possible annoyances in using a public telephone.

2   Which of the following calls are you unlikely to make at the 'cheap rate' referred to?
    A   to discuss your account in a bank in Scotland.
    B   to have a chat with an elderly relation.
    C   to ask about a friend in hospital who has just had an operation.
    D   to express Christmas greetings to cousins in Australia.

3   George can at least be thankful that
    A   the call box is in a convenient position.
    B   the telephone itself is working.
    C   he can use the directory in the box to find the number.
    D   he is able to give his message to the hotel receptionist.

4   Why does George have to dial a second time?
    A   He hasn't remembered to put the money in the box.
    B   He hasn't got enough money with him.
    C   He has got to find the money to put in the box.
    D   He can't find the number he wants in the directory.

5 What are George's feelings when he completes his call?
   A He has some difficulty in controlling his annoyance.
   B He is very disappointed at missing his friend.
   C He is annoyed with himself for being so stupid.
   D He is depressed at the thought of having to try again to get through.

Composition

Business letters

The main qualities of a good business letter are clearness (which depends partly on the logical arrangement of ideas), exactness and concentration on the subject matter to be dealt with. Before you start writing the letter, think over carefully the ideas you have to convey, and how best to arrange them and, when you write, express these ideas briefly and exactly.

The language of a business letter is necessarily more formal than that of a letter to a friend but it is still clear, straightforward English. Expressions such as 'we beg', 'we tender our thanks', 'your esteemed favour', 'inst', 'ult', and 'prox' are very old-fashioned and should never be used. On the other hand the language is that of formal written English, not that of everyday conversation.

Here is an example of a topic for a more formal letter.

A large British travel association has established a centre for British tourists in your town. An advertisement has appeared in one of your local newspapers asking for applications from suitably qualified people to be responsible for the welfare, entertainment and guiding of the visiting tourists. You are interested in this post. Write a letter of application (inventing the name of a Travel Association) in which you state your qualifications and ask for further details. The letter should be headed and ended suitably and, apart from the heading and ending, should be expressed in between 120 and 180 words.

Here is a suggested plan:

1 Expressing your interest in the posts

2 Qualifications related to these posts

3 Personal qualifications and experience

4 References

5 Request for further information

The letter is on the facing page.

Schloss Bellarosa,
Ruusulinna,
Arkadia

1st April, 19—

The Personnel Manager,
The Daydream Tourist Association,
3, Factory Street,
Grimesborough,
Murkshire,
England

Dear Sir,

I am interested in your advertisement in the 'Arkadia Morning Mail' for hostesses to be responsible for the welfare, entertainment and guiding of British guests in your holiday centre in Ruusulinna.

I am now a third-year student of English and History in the University of Gardenia but am free from early June till late September. I have spent one year in London working in an English family and attending courses in English so I can speak this language fluently.

My father has been a guide and I have often accompanied him and also myself acted as guide to English-speaking groups. My studies and experience have familiarised me with the many interesting places in my country. I am sociable, really interested in people and, I believe, at the same time reliable and sensible.

I enclose the address of the Manager of the local Tourist Information Office who is willing to supply further information about me.

If you are interested in my application, I should welcome further information about these posts, including the salary and general conditions of employment.

Yours faithfully,

P Cosmos

(Miss P. Cosmos)   *(179 words)*

Subjects for practice

Write a suitable letter of between 120 and 180 words on one or more of the following subjects. The beginning and ending should be that of a business letter but should not be included in the number of words. Where details are not given you can supply your own ideas.

1 You are the secretary of a society. Write a letter to a well-known English-speaking person living in your town asking him/her whether he or she would be willing to lecture to the society. Explain something of the aims and interests of the society and suggest a time, place and a general idea of a possible subject for the lecture.

2 You have to attend a conference in Birmingham in a month's time. A friend has recommended the Belflair Hotel and you are writing to book a room. Give details of the type of room you want (single/double, with or without shower or bath etc.) and ask about terms for bed and breakfast and full board.

   You would also like information about the position of the hotel (in a quiet or busy street), how near it is to the Conference Centre and whether there is a car park or garage. There may be other information you need.

Ask for confirmation of your booking as soon as possible and state that you will not be arriving until late in the evening.

3   Before leaving England you had bought a large box of chocolates for your mother. Shortly after your return, she opened them, only to find that they were stale and uneatable. Write a letter of complaint to the British manufacturers, giving all necessary details.

4   Home circumstances force you to give up an office job you have taken in England. Write a letter of resignation, giving your reasons for leaving, asking for a testimonial and expressing your regret.

5   In an English newspaper you have read an article stating that, owing to their school education, only young English people are really willing to take an interest in welfare problems throughout the world. Write a letter to this paper in which you set out the attitude of the young people of your own country to these matters.

Use of English

1   **Fill in each of the numbered blanks in the following passage with one suitable word.**

The unaccompanied tourist _____ (1) is visiting a town _____ (2) the first time may have to deal _____ (3) various unexpected and sometimes unpleasant situations. Some of these may be the _____ (4) of his or her own ignorance. Without a map it is only _____ easy (5) to get _____ (6) in a maze of streets and to wander about _____ (7) hours, unable to ask the _____ (8) in an unknown _____ (9). In some large cities, it is not uncommon for tourists to have their money _____ (10) by thieves. A woman who is _____ (11) of her handbag may _____ (12) the same time _____ (13) her passport, travel tickets or possibly her driving-_____ (14) and she may get little help or sympathy when she calls at the local police _____ (15). Some people may be _____ (16) ill after _____ (17) too much of the local overrich food. Others may buy so many expensive souvenirs to _____ (18) home with them that they run completely _____ (19) of money and have to return home _____ (20) than they had intended.

2   **The word in capitals at the end of each of the following sentences can be used to form a word that fits suitably in the blank space. Fill each blank in this way.**

1   There isn't much _____ of refreshment: there's either weak tea or lukewarm beer.   CHOOSE
2   His stroke has resulted in the temporary _____ of his power of speech.   LOSE
3   You have to ask the _____ of the Company before you can take on additional part-time work.   PERMIT
4   The _____ of the thousands of starving refugees shocked even the hardened relief workers.   SEE
5   He is a very _____ person whose feelings are easily hurt. SENSE

3   **For each of the following sentences, four explanations are given, from which you must choose the correct one.**

1   You had better improve your writing.
   A   Your writing was better earlier.
   B   It has got to be better.
   C   You are succeeding in your efforts to do this.
   D   I advise you to do better writing.

2   Anne always confides in her sister.
   A   Anne trusts her in everything.
   B   Anne feels safe in telling her her secrets.
   C   Anne feels safe and protected with her sister.
   D   Anne gives her sister all the advice she needs.

3   I have come across many unusual people in my travels.
   A   I have met them.
   B   I have quarrelled with them.
   C   I have succeeded in finding them.
   D   I have known them for a short time only.

4   He was not inclined to pass over the matter unnoticed.
   A   He did not intend to do this.
   B   He did not feel like doing this.
   C   He did not enjoy doing this.
   D   He refused to do this.

5   He might have forgotten your request.
   A   But he has not.
   B   This could be an explanation.
   C   He should have done this.
   D   If only he had forgotten it!

6   I shall buy some extra food in case they all come.
   A   provided they come.
   B   if in fact they come.
   C   to provide for this possibility.
   D   on condition that they come.

7   He must pull himself together.
   A   He must take more exercise.
   B   He must take more share in our work.
   C   He must improve his figure.
   D   He must control himself and start doing something useful.

8   He says he will continue to use his old car for the time being.
   A   for at least a short time ahead.
   B   so long as it lasts.
   C   at the moment.
   D   because he already has it.

9   I dare say the police will do nothing about it.
   A   I am not afraid to say.
   B   I think it could happen that.
   C   I think it likely.
   D   Even though it seems impossible, this is what I think.

10   She enjoys making believe she is a great actress.
   A   giving this impression.
   B   imagining that she is one.
   C   deceiving people by pretending that she is one.
   D   working to achieve this.

4 **Mirja and an English lady, who are sitting at the same table in a café, have got into conversation. Complete the dialogue below by supplying the English lady's missing words.**

    E How are you getting on in London?
    M I'm really not very happy here.
1 **E** _____
    M It's so difficult to get to know people. I often feel lonely.
2 **E** _____
    M I'm working as an au pair with a family, looking after two small children.
3 **E** _____
    M Yes, they're quite pleasant but I don't see much of them. Both of them work all day and watch television every evening.
4 **E** _____
    M No, they seem to have very few. Almost nobody visits them.
5 **E** _____
    M I suppose they just don't have time to make friends.
6 **E** _____
    M Yes, at a local College. But I'm the only one in my class from my country. And I'm a bit shy and don't like to be the first one to speak.
7 **E** _____
    M Well, I've walked in the parks and visited the Tower and Westminster Abbey. But I don't live near the centre and bus and underground fares are rather expensive.
8 **E** _____
    M I'm free every afternoon and all day Sunday.
9 **E** _____
    M I have a lot of studying to do and I read a good deal.
10 **E** _____
    M Oh, I should enjoy that. Which afternoon would that be?
11 **E** _____
    M Thursday, yes. What is your address?
12 **E** _____
    M Oh, thank you. I'll be outside this café at quarter-past four then.
13 **E** _____
    M I shall look forward to that very much.

5 **Using the passage on page 180 about some of the inconveniences of using a public telephone call box, write four paragraphs, each of about 50 words, in which you explain the various stages and possible problems involved in making a call. Begin each paragraph with one of these openings.**

1 When you have to use a public call box, be prepared for various inconveniences. You _____

2 If you don't know _____

3 When you are ready to make the call _____

4 The person who replies will first _____

Interview

1 Describe the woman at the end of the queue.
2 Describe the expressions on the faces of the various people.
3 What different things make this a rather depressing picture?
4 How does the telephone box in this picture resemble or differ from those most common in your own country?

Topics

On what occasions do people have to use a public telephone even when they have a telephone of their own?

What are some of the advantages of the telephone for a private person (as distinct from a businessman etc.)?

Discuss the relative advantages of communicating by letter and by telephone.

Reading aloud

Intonation practice

English intonation, the rise and fall of the voice to express meaning and feeling, is complicated and subtle: the theory can be mastered but it needs a good ear for pitch and tone and considerable practice with tapes or records or everyday contact with English speakers to achieve ease and naturalness in speaking. However a few basic patterns are given here.

Tune 1 — the voice falls at the end of a word group:

I can't come now.

Tune 2 — the voice rises at the end of a word group:

Is it?

Tune 1 is the more definite of the two. Besides expressing finality, it suggests a plain statement.

Jane isn't here.

Tune 1 normally ends a question beginning with an interrogative pronoun, adjective or adverb.

Why don't you help?

Tune 2 may mark

(a)   Incompleteness: at the end of a word group it suggests that something else will follow.

If you need any help (⌣), don't hesitate to ask (⌐).

(b)   A question that has no interrogative form before it.

Are you there?

(c)   Politeness, often turning an order into a request.

Sit down.   (an order)   Sit down.   (a request)

Passages

Read through the following passages silently, dividing longer sections into word groups as you do so and deciding which of the two patterns should mark the final word. Then read the passages aloud, suggesting a situation in which the words might be spoken.

1   Oh, I'm so glad you're there now Martin. I've been trying to contact you all day. Where have you been for the past few hours? Never mind. I've got something very important to tell you. Have you found a job yet? You haven't? Well, I ran into Harry Hall today. Do you remember him? Yes, he was at school with us. He says his firm is taking on a dozen new building apprentices. Yes, a dozen. Why don't you ring them first thing tomorrow morning?

2 This is Mrs Jane Jones speaking of 99 Laburnum Lane. I've been standing at my window for the past ten minutes: I wasn't able to sleep. Five minutes ago I saw a dark-coloured car draw up a hundred yards down the street. Two men in dark suits got out. I couldn't see them clearly: only that they were of medium height and build. There's a detached house about twenty yards from here, number 94. The occupants are away on holiday now. The men went round to the back of the house and I haven't seen them since. You may like to investigate.

3 This is an additional item that has just come in. The two brothers, Peter Lucas, aged nine, and Jim, aged seven, who disappeared last Saturday afternoon, have returned home safe and well. They've been spending the past two days in a barn near a farm five miles from their home. Peter admits that he stole some food from the farm kitchen. When they'd finished eating that, they said they felt rather cold and lonely so they decided home might be more comfortable. Needless to say, their parents, who had reported their disappearance to the police on Saturday evening, were extremely relieved.

Structured communication

Requests for service in a hotel

While you are staying in a British or American hotel, you find a paper with the following pictures on it to be used by non-English speakers in indicating things in their rooms that need attention or repair. Your English however is good enough to manage without the pictures. Suggest what might actually be wrong in each case and ask politely for the matter to be put right.

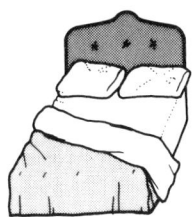

(a)

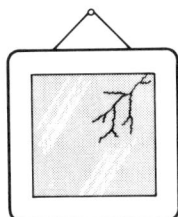

(b)

(c)

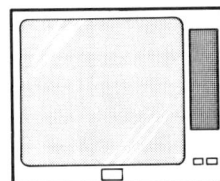

(d)

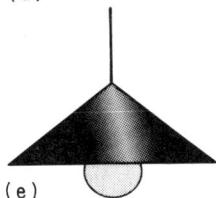

(e)

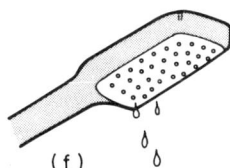

(f)

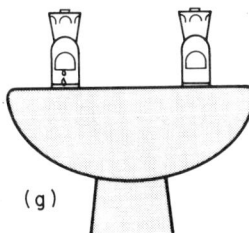

(g)

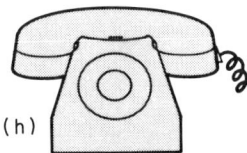

(h)

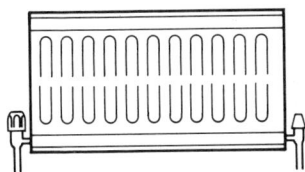

(i)

402

(j)

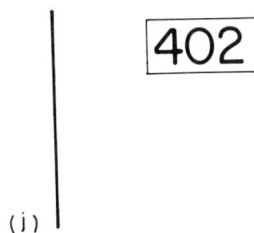

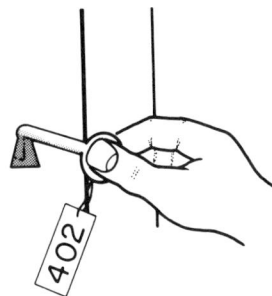

Speech and action situations

1 A stranger asks you for money. What is he like? What are you doing at the time? How does he introduce the subject? What reason does he give for asking? What is your reaction?

2 What do you do and say in each of the following cases?

(a) After you have had an expensive meal alone in a restaurant, the bill is presented. You then find you have left your wallet or hand-bag at home and have no money and also no means of identification. You have never been in the restaurant before.

(b) You are touring by car a country whose language you do not speak. After a long day's journey, you find you have left your passport in the previous hotel. You had intended to cross the frontier the following day.

(c) You return after midnight on a Sunday morning to a house where you live alone and find you have no key with you. All doors are locked and windows firmly shut and the neighbours are all in bed.

(d) After posting a number of letters together, you remember that you have not put a stamp on the most important one, an application for a secretarial post.

(e) A stranger in a train, a pleasant and likeable person, persists in talking to you when you want only to read.

(f) Somebody knocks at your door and with great sincerity tries to convince you of something you are not in the least interested in. You are too well-mannered to shut the door in the person's face.

Expressing opinions

1 What is your opinion of the habit of swearing? Is it a useful outlet for strong feelings, a form of rebellion, a survival of a forgotten childish desire to shock? Could there be some other reason for it and do reasons vary in different people? Give reasons for your opinion.

2 Nowadays very much is spoken of equality for everyone. Can there be equality resulting from appearance or will there always be a type of person one admires and other types one feels pity for, despises (feels contempt for) or dislikes because of something in his/her appearance?

3 What is your attitude towards lending and borrowing money?

4 What are some of the ways in which the police can help the individual person?

5 What is your attitude to appeals for financial help (a) from individuals (b) from charitable organisations?

A group story

A stranger approaches a couple of people walking along a street and makes an unexpected request. By means of answers to a series of questions asked by the teacher, the class creates a story about this incident, leading up to the request, explaining what it was and what happened after.
The teacher's questions could include the following:

Where were the people at the time?
Describe them.
Where were they going to?

What was the weather like at that time?
What kind of street was it?
What had the stranger been doing before he/she came up to them?
Describe the stranger.
What was he/she wearing?
What was his/her voice like?
How did he/she speak? softly? loudly? any unusual accent?
What did he/she say?

And then?

General guidance and practice

1 Reported statements

Study these two examples, the first of direct, the second of reported or indirect speech.

'I'm sorry,' said the man. 'I don't smoke, so I haven't any.'
The man said he was sorry. He did not smoke, so he did not have any.

When converting from direct to reported speech, the following rules usually apply:

(a) Conversational abbreviations are not used.

(b) Verb tenses normally shift to the past. The usual changes are:

Present Simple   to   Past Simple
Present Continuous   to   Past Continuous
Present Perfect ⎫
Past Simple   ⎭   to   Past Perfect
Present Perfect Continuous ⎫ to   Past Perfect Continuous
Past Continuous   ⎭
Future forms   to   Future in the Past forms

(c) Pronouns often change. First and second person pronouns may shift to the third person; second person pronouns may change to the first person. The same applies to possessive adjectives. Changes may depend on other words in the sentence.

The old man said, 'I can remember the early aeroplanes.'
The old man said he could remember the early aeroplanes.

He shouted, 'You are telling lies.'
He shouted at me, saying that I was telling lies.

(d) Certain other appropriate changes are also made. Here are few:

today	to	the same day, that day
yesterday	to	the day before, the previous day
tomorrow	to	the day after, the next day
this, these	to	that, those
now	to	then, at once, at that time
ago	to	before
the day after tomorrow	to	in two days' time
last week	to	the week before, the previous week
next week	to	the week after, the following week
this week	to	the same week

It is impossible to give all changes, which, in any case, depend on the meaning of the passage, and may usually be decided by common sense.

(e) If only the actual words spoken are given, it is necessary to supply a suitable introductory phrase, e.g. *He said; The speaker suggested; The teacher explained. That* may often be omitted. The introductory phrase, when supplied in this way, is usually in the past simple tense and has a third person subject:

'The medicine is to be taken every three hours.'
The doctor gave instructions that the medicine was to be taken every three hours.

'I shall arrive tomorrow.'
My sister wrote to say (that) she would arrive the next day.

Practice

Change the following examples of direct speech into reported speech.

(a) 'I need help desperately,' he said.
(b) 'I'm sorry,' he replied. 'I'm afraid I can't lend you anything.'
(c) 'I had some money,' he replied, 'but it was stolen from my room.'
(d) 'We shall write to you this week,' they promised.
(e) 'I am coming now,' he said. 'Perhaps I can give you a lift?'
(f) 'My car has been stolen,' he said. 'I shall have to telephone the police.'
(g) 'My father came to England fifty years ago, and has been living here ever since,' said Mary.
(h) 'I don't need your help today. I shall be busy tomorrow however,' said Mrs Fowler.
(i) 'You are not to forget what I have told you. You can't go the day after tomorrow,' said Father.

2 Reported questions and commands

The following sentences illustrate the basic changes necessary when converting direct questions and commands into reported speech. Notice that verb tenses and pronoun changes are similar to those in statements.

(a) 'Why did you come here?' I asked. 'How did you come?'
I asked him why he had come there and how he had come.

(b) 'Do you know your way home?' he asked me.
He asked whether I knew my way home.

(c) 'Go to the police for help,' he said.
He told the man to go to the police for help.

(d) 'Don't go to the police for help,' he said.
He told the man not to go to the police for help.

(e) 'Are you warm enough?' she asked.
She asked me if I was warm enough.

(f) 'Are you coming or not?' he asked me.
He asked me whether I was coming or not/whether or not I was coming.

(g) 'Come next week,' he suggested.
He suggested my coming/that I should come the following week.

Practice

Change the following into reported speech. Supply a suitable introductory phrase where this is not given.

(a) 'Can you help me?' I asked the porter.
(b) 'See me tomorrow afternoon,' he ordered his secretary.
(c) 'What shall we do this evening?' the children asked their mother.
(d) 'Don't look now,' said my friend, 'but I think the woman who has just come in is the star of that film we saw yesterday.'
(e) 'Will you be coming with me?'
(f) 'How do you spell your name?'
(g) 'Lie down and stop barking.'
(h) 'What is the time? Is your watch right?'
(i) 'Do you agree or not?'

3 Ways of expressing the future

The following ways of expressing the future have already been explained.

(a) *We shall deal with that tomorrow.*
(A plain statement of the future in most cases with some suggestion of willingness, decision, intention or probability/possibility.)

(b) *We are dealing with that tomorrow.*
(It is arranged and settled.)

(c) *We shall be dealing with that tomorrow.*
(The same, but with emphasis that this will happen in the future.)

It is also possible to express the future in other ways:

(d) *to go* with the infinitive, suggesting either
  (i) intention or determination
      They are going to let off fireworks tonight.
  (ii) great probability (often with verbs of thinking or anticipating, expressed or understood)
      (I think that) prices are going to rise soon.
      (I anticipate that) we are going to have a wonderful day.

Notice that happenings expected in the natural course of events are not expressed with *go*.
    Tomorrow will be/is Sunday.
    It will soon be dark.

(e) *to mean, to intend*
      He means to build up a large fortune within the next ten years.
      I do not intend to put up with any nonsense.

(f) *to be about to*
    This expresses an action which will happen almost immediately.
      The race is about to start.
      He looked as if he were about to burst into tears.

(g) *to be bound to, to be sure to*
    This expresses certainty about the future.
      The bus is bound to be late; it always is.
      Don't worry! He is sure to remember.

Practice

Write the following sentences in as many ways as you can, using the above forms. Give the exact meaning of each form.

(a) The Sports Club (hold) a social next Saturday.
(b) He (be) ninety on his next birthday.
(c) The storm (break).
(d) (Make) you any pancakes on Shrove Tuesday?

(e) The film (be) popular.
(f) He (die), unless help comes quickly.
(g) He (find) out what you said.
(h) Tomorrow's journey (take) five hours.
(i) The river (rise) as a result of all this rain.
(j) Why (not give) you him a birthday present?

4 Simple and perfect infinitive after modal verbs

must
All the evidence suggests that the statement is true.
>He *must be* very old: he remembers the First World War.
>Margaret *must be using* her telephone: the number's engaged.
>It *must have rained/have been raining* during the night: the pavements are still wet.

needn't have   didn't need to
needn't have: Something that was done was unnecessary and possibly unpleasant.
>You *needn't have* walked here: I could have fetched you in my car.
>You *needn't have* shouted: I'm not deaf.
not need to: Something was not done as it was unnecessary to do it.
>I *didn't need to* walk: Jill took me there in her car.

can't
The evidence suggests impossibility though there is sometimes a suggestion that the idea is true.
>He *can't be* ill: I saw him playing tennis a few minutes ago.
>He *can't be* ninety. He runs up the stairs like a two-year-old.

couldn't   +a simple infinitive
This suggests greater impossibility.
>He *couldn't still be alive:* he was born in 1870.

can't have   couldn't have   +perfect infinitive
All the evidence suggests impossibility.
>You *can't have walked* here from Brighton: it would take ten hours.
>You *couldn't have seen* me yesterday: I was in London all day.

should   could   +simple infinitive
This expresses probability though not certainty.
>He *should/could be* home by now, so I'll telephone.
>How strange! There's no answer. He *should be* home by now.

should   could   +perfect infinitive
This expresses uncertainty which is stronger with the use of *should*.
>He *should/could have left* home by now. (but I'm not sure that he has)
>You *should/could have told* me before. (but you didn't)

may   might
These usually suggest possibility, though this is less strong in the case of *might*.
>I think that's the answer though I *may/might* be wrong.
>I should ring the bell again. He *may/might* not have heard it.
might followed by a perfect infinitive sometimes expresses reproach.
>You *might have written* to let us know you were coming. (but you didn't)

Note also: *was going to   was to* (non-modal)
>He *was going to be here* by nine o'clock
>He *was to be here* by nine o'clock.
Both of these constructions suggest almost certain failure.

Suggest what could be said in each of these situations using the verb in italics.

1 Mrs White's comment when a neighbour says she has seen her son Roger fishing during school time. *should*
2 Matilda expresses sympathy for her husband after he has had an exhausting day at the office. *must*
3 Anne, who has been worried that her daughter may have pneumonia, is assured by the doctor that the girl has only a severe cold. *need not*
4 Linda's reply to a question about why she hadn't been shopping the day before. *need not*
5 What you say to a friend who claims to be tired after a completely lazy day. *can't*
6 Your reply to someone's suggestion that you might have left your lost gloves in a certain café. *can't have*
7 Your answer to an accusation that you've written a certain letter that isn't in fact in your handwriting. *couldn't have*
8 You're suggesting the time when lunch will be ready. *should*
9 You're explaining why lunch wasn't in fact ready owing to a power cut. *should have*
10 You're suggesting why an acquaintance has ignored you when meeting you in the street. *might have*
11 You are reproaching someone who has failed to write to you while on holiday. *might have*

5 Some, any

The basic rule for the use of *some* and *any* and their compounds is that *some* is used in an affirmative statement and command, *any* in an interrogative form and after a negative. Verbs such as *to be unable, to fail, to deny, to refuse*, and the conjunction *if* may have a negative force.

I must have put my key *somewhere*.
The child has bought *some* sweets.
You should take *something* to cure that cough.
Do *something* quickly.
Will you need *any* of these old magazines?
He had never met *anyone* like them.
Haven't you *anything* to do?
He denied that the story had *any* truth in it.

Some and its compounds may be used in interrogative sentences when an affirmative answer is expected, and also when the idea is more exact.

Would you like *some* fruit?
Have you found *somewhere* to live?
Have you found *anywhere* to live?

Any used in an affirmative statement or command can suggest an indefinite idea.

Ring me up *any* time you like.
You can ask *anyone* you know.

Practice

Use *some, any* or one of their compounds in each of the following sentences.

(a) I knew there was _____ I forgot to put in the cake.
(b) The police have been unable to find _____ trace of the criminals.
(c) Is there _____ that I can find peace?
(d) I picked _____ mushrooms yesterday morning.
(e) They failed to discover _____ who could translate the message.
(f) The student was looking for _____ to sit down.
(g) May I have _____ more potatoes please? I have used up all those I bought yesterday.
(h) She can't find her powder compact _____.
(i) Take _____ one which you think will fit.
(j) I am sure there wasn't _____ left over yesterday.
(k) Sit _____. There is plenty of room.
(l) During the winter there isn't _____ to do in the garden.

The negative forms of the above are *no* (Adj), *none* (Pronoun), *nowhere, no one, nobody, nothing*. In which of the above sentences could one of these negative forms be used? In which would it be slightly unnatural?

6 Word order: objects of phrasal verbs

When a phrasal verb has a noun as its direct object, the noun in most cases can stand either between the verb and the particle or after the particle:
He is putting on his hat. or: *He is putting his hat on.*

When the direct object is a pronoun it usually stands between the verb and the adverbial particle:
He is putting it on. Not: **He is putting on it.*

Notice that the verb 'look' is often followed by a preposition which is not a particle. In this case the preposition must be followed by the noun or pronoun it is governing — neither can come before it:
I am looking at it.
His mother is looking after him.
You must look for them.

'Look up' is, however, a phrasal verb. It is therefore wrong to say 'I must look up it'. This should be 'I must look it up'.

Practice

In the following sentences, put in its correct place the noun or pronoun object in brackets at the end of each, and indicate in which cases this could stand in more than one position:

(a) Put down on the floor. (the basket)
(b) He is bringing back tomorrow. (them)
(c) You can hang up in the corner. (it)
(d) Write down in your notebook. (the words)
(e) They are putting off until next Friday. (it)
(f) Are you looking after carefully? (her)
(g) Look at carefully and then put away. (the picture) (it)
(h) Your shoelace is undone. You must do up. (it)
(i) They are looking up in the dictionary. (the spelling)
(j) You can either undo your coat or take off. (it)
(k) Give back. (it)

(l) Fill in. (the form)
(m) Give in. (your work)
(n) Please pick up. (the chalk)
(o) Be careful when you pick up. (it)
(p) I am ringing up. (him)
(q) Throw away. (it)

7 Revision of prepositions

Practice

Insert the correct preposition (single word or phrase) in each of the following sentences:

(a) You will find the answer _____ the bottom of the page.
(b) That sharp bend has been the cause _____ many accidents.
(c) The referee glanced _____ his watch.
(d) _____ the question of refreshments, I should think lemonade and sandwiches will be sufficient.
(e) We shall resume the programme _____ ten minutes' time.
(f) The terrified sheep were conscious _____ the presence of the wolf.
(g) I shall next deal _____ the suggestion to set up a new recreation centre.
(h) The Society is appealing _____ half a million pounds in aid of the flood victims.
(i) I am grateful _____ you _____ your assistance.
(j) The landing-stage is being constructed _____ the other side _____ the river.
(k) He was muttering terrible curses _____ his breath.
(l) The firm has agreed _____ supply the newspaper syndicate with newsprint.
(m) Our business rivals have agreed _____ our terms.
(n) Neither of the hostile groups could agree _____ the other and the meeting broke up in disorder.
(o) We are running short _____ petrol. We must find a filling station.
(p) He was so afraid _____ being found out that he refused to confide _____ anyone.
(q) The defeated team challenged its opponents _____ a return match.

9 Picnic in the Dining Room

'We shall be having a picnic tomorrow afternoon,' said my hostess, Mrs. Brown. 'It will be quite simple and we shan't make any fuss. I think an afternoon in the open air will do us good, don't you? Would you like to come with us?'

5 I had already made an appointment with the hairdresser but I weakly agreed to cancel it. Mrs. Brown smiled graciously.

'I shall be making some cakes this afternoon,' she explained, 'so I shan't have any free time. I wonder whether you would mind doing some shopping for me during your lunch hour, that is, if you can fit it in.'

10 She handed me a typewritten list made up of twenty-four separate items, from shrimps to sugared almonds, including an order for a chicken, four sliced loaves, a half-litre of fresh cream and some Camembert, all to be delivered at the house before five o'clock. That still left me with plenty to carry myself, and it seemed that if only I could manage to stagger home

15 with my load, there would be no danger of starving the next afternoon.

That evening a violent thunderstorm broke. Rain poured down; the sky was split by terrifying flashes of forked lightning while peals of thunder drowned conversation. But Mrs. Brown was not upset.

'It will have cleared up before morning,' she prophesied. 'When this
20 storm has passed we'll have ideal weather, you'll see. The B.B.C. weather forecast has promised sunshine, and they don't often make mistakes.' She was right. The following morning was glorious. Early in the morning I could hear her moving about in the kitchen. Breakfast was late and consisted of corn flakes and toast.

25 'I must apologise for neglecting you,' said Mrs. Brown. 'So much to do! You won't mind making your bed this morning, will you? I'm so busy. I'm afraid we shall have to make do with cold meat and potatoes for lunch.'

The whole morning seemed to be spent in loading the car with a variety of bags, baskets and mysterious parcels. After a lunch of cold mutton,
30 boiled potatoes, and limp damp lettuce, we took our raincoats and umbrellas and fitted ourselves into the car. I was in the back seat, squeezed uncomfortably in the midst of a mountain of equipment.

We crawled for the next two hours along a main road where a line of traffic was wedged so tightly together that it was almost stationary. Mr.
35 Brown was in charge of the steering wheel but Mrs. Brown controlled the driving. At last we turned down a narrow lane and started looking for a suitable place for tea. Each one that we saw had its drawbacks: too sunny, too shady, too exposed, too sheltered. 'If we were to picnic there, we should be too hot, cold, conspicuous, shut in,' declared Mrs. Brown as she
40 inspected each in turn.

At last she decided that a certain meadow (in reality no different from any other meadow we had examined) would do. Mr. Brown opened the gate and drove the car inside. We started to unload.

I had never in my life realised that so much stuff could be required for a
45 simple picnic. A folding table was produced together with a clean glossy tablecloth, folding chairs (with cushions), enough crockery and cutlery for

a banquet and more than enough food for six courses, paper serviettes, a transistor radio, half a dozen illustrated magazines and even soap, a towel, water and a bowl for washing our hands after the meal. I half expected a
50 crimson carpet, possibly footstools for our feet, with red candles as tasteful table decorations. I did discover a tin of fly killer, a bottle of ammonia for the treatment of stings and even some indigestion tablets.

For a whole hour we made our preparations and at last everything we needed was ready. As we were enjoying our first mouthful of thermos-
55 flask soup, a stout man opened the gate and came towards us.

'Sorry to make a nuisance of myself, but in five minutes we shall have finished milking the cows,' he announced. 'They'll be coming back here directly after.'

Mrs. Brown gazed at him speechless for a moment. At last she found
60 words. 'But you can see we've only just started eating,' she protested indignantly, 'Surely you can delay sending them in for an hour or so?'

'Sorry ma'am, we've other jobs to do. We'll give you time to clear up: that's the most that we can allow. Say twenty minutes. You know you're trespassing, of course?'
65 Mrs. Brown seemed to collapse in her chair. I wished I were fifty miles off. Mr. Brown was the only one that accepted the situation philosophically. 'It seems to be high time we departed,' was his only comment.

Half an hour later we moved off as the cows were wandering down the lane and as the first drops of rain were falling. We joined the traffic jam in
70 the main road. Three hours later we unpacked again and had our picnic in Mrs. Brown's dining-room — with a carpet underfoot but still no candles. We were strangely silent but our deep sense of grievance did not in any way prevent us from eating a great deal.

Notes on the passage

2 *make a fuss* = cause a lot of disturbance and excitement about unimportant things. *fussy* (Adj) about one's food, clothes, small details in other people's behaviour.

9 *fit* (N) = (a) a sudden attack of illness consisting of convulsions (as in epilepsy); *a fit* of coughing. (b) a coat or dress should be *a good fit* (the right size). *a fitting* = the trying on of a garment that is being made. Also: the size of a garment: *We supply overcoats in various fittings.* *fit* (V) = (a) be the right size: *These shoes don't fit me.* (b) occupy a certain place among other things: *Can you fit this into your suitcase? The solicitor is very busy but he can fit you in at two o'clock.* *fit out* = provide all the necessary equipment for something: *to fit out a climbing expedition.* *fit* (Adj) = (a) healthy: *Although he is eighty, he is still quite fit.* (b) suitable: *Is he fit to undertake such a responsible job?* (c) in the right condition: *A drunken man is not fit to drive a car.*

11 Some *shellfish:* shrimps, prawns, crabs, lobsters, oysters.

13 *deliver* letters, parcels, goods to the house (N *delivery*).

14 *stagger* = walk or stand unsteadily so that one nearly falls, often because one is overloaded or ill. *staggered* (Adj) may mean 'extremely surprised'. Periods of work may be *staggered* so that the workers are free at different times; they may have *staggered* holidays. Sometimes the working-day of twenty-four hours in divided into three periods of work: each of these periods is *a shift.*

16 storms *break.* wars and epidemics *break out. an outbreak* of measles.

17   forked and sheet *lightning*. peals (more prolonged) and claps of *thunder*. Thunder may gradually become louder: it *mutters, growls, rumbles and crashes*.

20   *B.B.C.* = British Broadcasting Corporation.

21   *promise* usually suggests pleasant things to come (not, in this case, extreme cold or fog).
forecast (V and N) the weather, results of races and matches, success and failure, future possibilities.

29   *a parcel* is usually larger than *a packet. parcel post. a packet* of soap powder.

30   *limp* (Adj) = the opposite of stiff or crisp. *limp* (V) = walk lamely and with difficulty because of a foot or leg injury. A *lame* person may walk with the help of *crutches*.

30   *lettuce*   Note that *a salad* contains several kinds of vegetable or fruit.

32   *in the midst of*   among, not necessarily in the middle of.

33   *crawl* = move in an almost flat position or very slowly. *crawl* (N) = a stroke used in swimming, with the head low in the water.
creep most often suggests moving very quietly: *I crept upstairs so as not to disturb the sleeping family.*
crouch = remain still, with one's body near the ground and hands and feet close together: *The cat was crouching, ready to spring.*

34   *wedged*   A *wedge* is a small, triangular-shaped block, used for keeping a window or door in position.

34   Spelling: *stationary* = without movement. *stationery* = notepaper and envelopes; *a stationer* sells these in a *stationery shop*.

35   *Parts of a car:* the steering wheel, the engine (not: the motor), headlights, the bonnet, the windscreen, brakes, gears, the clutch, the accelerator, the boot. A car is powered by (runs on) *petrol*.

39   a *conspicuous* building or other object; an *outstanding* statesman or other well-known person.

41   *a meadow* where cattle may graze or grass is grown; *a field* of corn.

44   *realise* = become aware of an idea: *realise that one's watch has stopped.*
recognise = know the identity of someone seen: *She's lost so much weight, I hardly recognised her.*

45   *fold* a letter or tablecloth in two or four; a dress or skirt may have *pleats;* a dress taken out of a suitcase may have *creases;* he *crumpled* the letter into a ball and threw it away. *crumple* is a verb only; the other three are nouns and verbs. *A deck chair* is a kind of *folding* chair.

45   Photograph prints may be *glossy* or *matt*.

46   *cushions* lie on chairs or sofas: *a cushion-cover. pillows* lie on beds: *a pillow-case*.

46   *crockery* = cups, saucers, plates, dishes and other china tableware.

46   *cutlery* = knives, forks and spoons. A *cruet* may include salt, pepper, vinegar, mustard. *A salt-cellar; a pepper-pot*.

47   paper *serviettes;* linen *table-napkins*.

48   A transistor radio *is portable*. A typewriter may also be *portable*.

48   A *magazine* is a *periodical*, a publication appearing at intervals of a week or more. A *review* is more often a critical article on a book, play, film or concert though it may be a general account of something: *a review of the week's news.*
A revue is a form of satirical entertainment.

50   A *carpet* covers most or all of the floor surface of a room;
a rug is smaller, and often very thick (a hearthrug);
a mat is similar to a rug but of thinner material. *A travelling rug* is like a blanket.

51 *decoration* = making something look bright and pleasant; *a decoration* is anything that does this, e.g. *Christmas decorations*. They are *redecorating* the sitting-room.

52 A wasp or bee *stings*. A mosquito *bites*. Thorns and needles *prick*.

54 *a mouthful, spoonful, cupful, handful, pocketful, roomful* (of people).

54 *a thermos flask* is sometimes called a *vacuum flask*. A *vacuum-cleaner* removes dust from a carpet.

56 *a nuisance* This is a common word in spoken English. It refers to a small thing or a person that causes inconvenience and irritation. Missing a bus can be a nuisance and a person who is often unpunctual is also a nuisance.

60 *protest* (N and V) In origin the word *Protestant* referred to those people who protested against the Roman Catholic Church. A *Non-conformist* is a person belonging to a religious group that does not accept the doctrines of the Church of England.

64 *Trespassers will be prosecuted* may be written on a board outside private property. A trespasser invades other people's property and is threatened with some kind of legal punishment.

67 *a comment* = a remark. A *commentary* is a continuous description of something happening at that time: *A football match commentary. A radio commentator.*

72 *grief* = sorrow. *grieve* over someone's death. *a grievance* = unfair treatment causing feelings of resentment: *The men's grievances include low wages, long hours and badly-cooked food in their canteen.*

Phrasal verbs

break a storm *breaks*, but a war/an epidemic *breaks out* (starts); (*an outbreak*).
break up into pieces; also: finish the school term.
break down = stop functioning (a machine); lose control of one's feelings on hearing bad news (*a nervous breakdown*).
break into a building to steal.
break away = get free of.
break bad news to someone; *break* a promise.

Pronunciation

Sound and stress changes: separate (Adj) /sépərɪt/; separate (V) /sépəreɪt/; prophecy (N) /prófɪsɪ/; prophesy (V) /prófɪsaɪ/; prepare /prɪpéə/; preparation /prepəréɪʃən/; philosopher /fɪlósəfə/; philosophic /fɪləsófɪk/.

Notice the stress: ideal /aɪdíəl/; magazines /mǽgəzíːnz/; serviettes /sɜːviéts/

ə (as in *ago*): items /áɪtəmz/; sugared /ʃúgəd/; almond /áːmənd/; violent /váɪələnt/; breakfast /brékfəst/; apologise /əpólədʒaɪz/; potatoes /pətéɪtəʊz/; mysterious /mɪstíərɪəs/; stationery /stéɪʃənəri/; suitable /súːtəbl/; conspicuous /kənspíkjʊəs/; dozen /dʌ́zən/; crimson /krímsən/; ammonia /əmə́ʊnɪə/; nuisance /njúːsəns/; collapse /kəlǽps/; grievance /griːvəns/; illustrated /íləstreɪtɪd/.

ɪ (as in *city*): lettuce /létɪs/; banquet /bǽnkwɪt/; tablets /tǽblɪts/; speechless /spíːtʃlɪs/; carpet /káːpɪt/.

Others: mackintoshes /mǽkɪntóʃɪz/; towel /táʊəl/; indigestion /ɪndɪdʒéstjən/; directly /dɪréktli/ or /daɪréktli/; ma'am /mæm/ or /maːm/; situation /sɪtjʊéɪʃən/; comment /kóment/.

Grammatical and structural points

(a) 'The B.B.C. weather forecast has promised sunshine and they don't often make mistakes' (11.20-21).
they is often used to indicate some vague authority, group or source of information: *They say that they have already arrested the gang leader.*

When using a pronoun, make sure that the noun it refers to is clear. Here is an example of unsatisfactory use of a pronoun: *Long lines of people were waiting at the barriers while worried officials were surrounded by angry passengers. They did not know what do to.*

The impersonal pronoun *one* is less often used in conversation. The pronouns, *we, you,* or *they* are used instead:
Nowadays we tend to prefer comfort to adventure.
You seldom see taxis in this part of town.
They have built too many high blocks of flats and not left enough space for children to play in.

(b) The following time expressions contrast with usage in some other languages:
early this morning; early in the morning; late last night; early tomorrow; during the last few days; the other day (a few days ago); *the trial will take place in a week's time.*

(c) an hour *or so;* a dozen *or so*   This phrase, meaning 'about', is most often used with expressions of time or round numbers.

(d) *Verbal constructions*
Infinitive: it is time to go; have time to enjoy life.
Gerund: apologise for neglecting; prevent us from eating (or: prevent our eating); danger of starving.
Clause: realise that so much stuff could be required.

Prepositions

(a) *in* the open (fresh) air (indoors; out of doors); *in* the midst of; each *in* turn; *in* reality; *in* my life.
(b) an appointment *with;* this left me *with* plenty to carry; make do *with;* load *with* (*loaded with shopping*); together *with.*
(c) an order *for* a chicken; apologise *for;* required (needed) *for;* a bowl *for* washing in; enough *for.*
(d) danger *of;* consist *of;* make a nuisance *of* oneself; a sense *of* loss.
(e) twenty-four items, *from* shrimps *to* sugared almonds (suggesting a wide range); prevent *from.*
(f) *including* an order.

Expressions for use in written work

(a) a day *in the open (fresh) air.*
(b) a list *made up of* twenty items.
(c) There would be *no danger of* losing my way.
(d) Breakfast *consisted of* corn flakes and toast.
(e) Each one *had its drawbacks.*
(f) She inspected *each in turn*
(g) I have *never in my life* realised.
(h) I *half expected* a carpet.
(i) *for a whole hour.*
(j) At last *she found words.*
(k) an hour *or so.*
(l) It seems to be *high time we departed.*
(m) our *deep sense of grievance.*

Spoken English

Now, what shall we do next?   Something has been finished and there is a
   slight pause for thought.
Be careful now.   Warning or advice.
Now what's (has) happened?   Impatience.
Now do as I tell you.   Introducing an order.
Now then, leave that ladder alone!   Introducing a sharp order or
   warning.

Practice

Explain the use of *now* in each of the following.

(a)   Now, what did I tell you? Didn't I warn you?
(b)   Now say that again more carefully.
(c)   Now, how about having a little rest?
(d)   Look before you cross the road now.
(e)   Now then! We're not having that noise here.

Why expresses gentle surprise: *Why, that's just like the one I bought!*

What expresses slightly shocked or horrified surprise: *What, is that all the
work you're done in three quarters of an hour?*

Here, give that to me. I can put it right.   A way of drawing someone's
attention.
Here, this won't do. I want a better one.   A challenge.

Look is used to draw someone's attention to something that will be said
(not 'Hear' as in some languages): *Look, we could make do with a snack
now and have a meal later.*

Look out! is a shouted warning of immediate danger (not 'Attention',
which is used mainly when drilling soldiers). But, before an announcement: *May I have your attention, please.*

Shop Assistant	Good morning. Can I help you?
Customer	Not at the moment, thank you, I'm just looking round. I'm really looking for a bookcase, glass-fronted and with about three shelves.
SA	How about this one? Is this the kind of thing you're looking for?
C	Well, it's got a mahogany veneer, hasn't it. I'd prefer walnut.
SA	We haven't any walnut ones in stock at the moment. We could order one in this style though, if you like.
C	How long would I have to wait for it?
SA	Four to six weeks, probably, though I can't guarantee any particular date.
C	Would you be able to deliver it to my house when it comes in?
SA	Yes, madam, if you live locally. Our vans deliver every day.
C	Please order one for me then. And may I have one of these blue rugs. I see the price has been reduced. I can carry that myself.
SA	They're a very good bargain, madam. I'll wrap it up for you. There. There's a loop in the string for you to hold it by. Would you be willing to pay a small deposit on the bookcase?
C	Yes, I suppose so. How much would you like it to be?
SA	Say five pounds. Would that suit you? Thank you. Here's your receipt

for the deposit, your bill for the rug and your change. If you'll leave your name, address and telephone number, I'll get in touch with you as soon as the bookcase comes in.

Reading comprehension

Choice of words

In this exercise you must choose the word or phrase which best completes each sentence.

1 Mrs. Brown was very _____ when she broke her beautiful Wedgwood teapot.
   A disturbed   **B** deranged   **C** upset   **D** damaged

2 The school is half empty as a serious epidemic of measles has broken _____.
   A up   **B** out   **C** in   **D** down

3 Swarms of ants are always invading my kitchen. They are a thorough _____.
   A nuisance   **B** disturbance   **C** trouble   **D** annoyance

4 There is something wrong with his vocal chords and, as a result, he has always been _____.
   A silent   **B** dumb   **C** speechless   **D** deaf

5 As the fat man sat down, the deck chair _____ under him, with a loud noise of tearing canvas.
   A fell   **B** sank   **C** dropped   **D** collapsed

6 By nine o'clock I _____ that my guests were not coming.
   A realised   **B** recognised   **C** understood
   D noticed

7 He is looking after three orphans _____ his own six children, so now he has nine children to provide for.
   A besides   **B** except   **C** beside   **D** instead of

8 We have little _____ information about developments in this field.
   A actual   **B** present-day   **C** up-to-date   **D** modern

9 A walk in the fresh air will _____.
   A better you   **B** heal you   **C** do you good
   D make you good

10 Don't annoy that wasp. It will _____ you.
   A sting   **B** prick   **C** bite   **D** stick

Multiple choice responses

Read through the passage carefully before dealing with the questions which follow it.

"of merchantable quality"

"fit for the purpose"

Keep calm!

1..8..9.

What the law says about buying things

When you buy something you and the seller make a contract. Even if all you do is talk! The seller — not the manufacturer — must sort out your complaint.

The law has three rules:

1 Goods must be **of merchantable quality.** This means that they must be reasonably fit for their normal purpose. Bear in mind the price and how the item was described. A new item must not be broken or damaged. It must work properly. But if it is cheap, second-hand or a 'second' you cannot expect top quality.

2 Goods must be **as described** — on the package, a display sign or by the seller. Shirtsleeves must not be long if marked 'short' on the box. Plastic shoes should not be called leather.

3 Goods must be **fit for any particular purpose** made known to the seller. If the shop says a glue will mend china, then it should.

All goods — including those bought in sales — are covered (food too) if bought from a trader — for example, from shops, in street markets, through mail order catalogues or from door-to-door sellers.

Please note: If you are entitled to reject something, take it back yourself if you can. It is quicker and you can discuss it face to face. Strictly speaking the seller should collect it. You may be able to claim extra compensation if you suffer loss from a faulty buy. For example, when a faulty iron ruins clothes.

Making your complaint

To make a complaint:
* stop using the item
* tell the shop at once
* take it back (if you can)
* take a receipt or proof of purchase (if you can)
* ask for the manager or owner
* keep calm

If it is a tricky problem it may be better to write. To be on the safe side it is better to use recorded delivery. Keep copies of all letters. Do not send receipts or other proofs of purchase — give reference numbers or send photo-copies.

If you phone:
* first make a note of what you want to say
* have receipts and useful facts handy
* get the name of the person you speak to
* jot down the date and time and what is said
* keep calm!

If you see the notice NO REFUNDS you can do two things
1. Ignore it.   2. Tell your Trading Standards Department.
Such notices are illegal, even for sales goods. A trader cannot wriggle out of his responsibility if he sells you faulty goods.

Below are a number of questions or unfinished statements about the information, each with four suggested answers or endings. Choose the best answer or ending in each case.

1 The subject of all the information above is
   A advice about when and how to complain about goods bought.
   B warnings about problems that may arise in buying things.
   C instructions about the best way of making a complaint about unsatisfactory goods.
   D protection offered by the law against a dishonest shopkeeper.

2 According to the information given, the law protects the buyer if
   A goods bought are not in perfect condition.
   B he or she has been overcharged.
   C instructions how to use the goods are misleading and cause damage.
   D goods bought are below the standard to be expected.

3 You may be able to get extra compensation if
   A you take the goods back yourself.
   B defective goods have caused damage.
   C there is something seriously wrong with the goods.
   D you put the complaint in writing.

4 You are not entitled to compensation if you have obtained the article
   A by post.
   B from a friend or neighbour.
   C in an open-air market.
   D in a sale.

5 What additional action is recommended if the complaint is made by telephone?
   A Keep a record of the circumstances of the call.
   B Refer to what is written on the receipt.
   C Ask for the person who was responsible for the sale.
   D Describe exactly what is wrong with the unsatisfactory article.

6 The notice 'No Refunds' suggests that the trader will refuse to
   A acknowledge that goods bought from him are below standard.
   B exchange faulty goods.
   C pay for damage caused by faulty goods.
   D return the customer's money.

Composition

Giving instructions

Instructions may be written in two different ways: (a) in paragraph form, (b) as separate points or instructions, possibly listed with numbers.

(a) *Instructions about how to make an omelette.*

A PLAIN OMELETTE FOR ONE PERSON

Break two eggs into a basin. Beat them a little till the whites and yolks have mixed properly. Add a little salt and pepper and a tablespoonful of water and mix these in.

Melt a little fresh butter in an omelette pan, remembering that too much butter will make the omelette greasy. When the butter is hot, pour in the eggs, stir twice in the centre and cook the eggs over a low heat. Loosen the edges with a knife to allow the uncooked part to run underneath.

When the under surface is firm, double the omelette over with a knife so that it is crescent-shaped and allow any loose egg to cook. Lift it out on to a hot dish covered with paper with the side that was nearest the pan on top. Serve it at once.

A well-cooked omelette should have a firm surface but be creamy inside.

(149 words)

In this example commands are used throughout. It is possible to use the passive (*The eggs are broken into the basin . . .*) but this is less definite.

Subjects for practice (instructions in paragraphs)

You should use between 120 and 180 words in each of the following.

1   Give instructions about how to fry chips or how to make coffee.
2   Give advice about how to keep healthy and comfortable either during a very cold winter or a very hot oppressive summer.
3   A young friend who lives alone says he feels feverish and thinks he may have flu. You are sure he should not be at work (or school). Write down the advice you give him about looking after himself at home, including calling a doctor if necessary. Offer to do what you can to help him yourself.
4   Give instructions on how to keep a dog in first-class condition.
5   Write down the advice a teacher might give students before they sit for the First Certificate examination.
6   Advise a student how to use a dictionary intelligently when doing a translation.

(b)   Instructions that could be placed in each room of a hostel for students and young workers

NOTICE

1   Meals are served at the following times:
     BREAKFAST 7.30-9.00
     LUNCH   12.00-14.00
     DINNER   18.30-20.00
2   Residents are expected to make their own beds but rooms are cleaned daily by the hostel staff.
3   Please be as quiet as possible after 23.00 as others may already be asleep.
4   Food should not be kept in rooms as this encourages mice.
5   Do not stay in the bathroom for more than twenty minutes as other people may want to use it.
6   Laundry should be taken to the Linen Room before 10.00 on a Monday morning. It can be collected from there on Friday. A list of charges is in the Linen Room.
7   Facilities for washing and drying small items of clothing are available in the Drying Room. An iron is also provided.
8   There is a public telephone in the entrance hall.
9   Payment for accommodation must be made in the Warden's Office every Saturday morning between 9 and 12.
10   A week's notice of departure must be given.

Though polite, these instructions are brief and plain. They include the

following kinds of instructions:
(a) Commands (3 and 5).
(b) The use of 'should', 'must', 'are expected to' (2, 4, 6, 9, 10). Other possibilities are 'may', 'can', 'are advised to', 'may wish to', etc.
(c) Statements of fact (1, 7 and 8).

Subjects for practice (listed directions)

The following exercises should be dealt with in the same way as the one above. You are advised to use between 120 and 180 words in each case.

1 A woman calls twice weekly to help in your house. She usually stays two hours each time. You are going to be away for one week so you leave polite instructions about what should be done during the week. One or two details need special attention. Write the list you make. (Remember to be polite and pleasant and not to overwork her.)

2 Mrs. Baker is sending her husband shopping. She wants some meat, bread, cheese and oranges, an electric light bulb and a special magazine. A parcel (not yet stamped) has to be posted. A complaint must be made to the window-cleaner about having failed to come for some time. An appointment with her dressmaker must be cancelled. (Neither of these has a telephone.) Finally she wants the kind of book she enjoys from the Public Library. Write the list she gives him.

3 Mrs. Mason is going on holiday for a month. As she is very forgetful, she makes a list of things she must remember to do before leaving home. Write down eight possible items in her list. (These should not include the actual packing and getting ready.)

4 The instructions normally found in a public telephone box.

Other subjects for composition

1 It is the evening before the picnic. Mrs. Brown is trying to persuade her husband to go on the picnic. He is not at all keen and makes various objections and excuses before being finally persuaded. Write the dialogue that takes place in between 120 and 180 words.

2 It was such a beautiful afternoon that you decided to have tea or some other light meal in the garden. Unfortunately while you were eating, circumstances forced you to go indoors again. Write about your decision to have tea outside, your preparations and what happened, in between 120 and 180 words.

3 The writer of the comprehension passage had to put up with many inconveniences and disappointments. Explain what these were in two paragraphs, using between 175 and 200 words. The first paragraph should deal with the inconveniences she experienced the day before the picnic, the second those experienced on the day of the picnic.

Use of English

1 **Finish each of the following sentences in such a way that it has the same meaning as the sentence before it.**

1 He was about to tell me something when he changed his mind.
He was on _____

2 I advise you not to annoy him.
   You had _____

3 It wasn't necessary for you to come so early.
   You _____

4 Living alone is normal and natural to him.
   He _____

5 Having had his supper he went to bed.
   As soon _____

6 If you have higher qualifications you will get a better job.
   The higher _____

2 **Use a form of the verb in capitals to complete each of the following sentences.**
   Example: My mother _____ the ironing when I got home.   DO
   Answer: was doing.

1 The post _____. Here are two letters for you.   ARRIVE

2 I shall show you my photographs as soon as they _____.
   ready.   BE

3 A talkative stranger tried to convince me that we _____
   before.   MEET

4 Someone _____ you about an hour ago.   TELEPHONE

5 He _____ for his firm for ten years but now he is looking for
   another job.   WORK

3 **Choose the best explanation, A, B, C, or D, that applies to each of the following sentences.**

1 You won't mind making your bed this morning, will you.
   A This is a very polite request.
   B A question is being asked.
   C It almost taken for granted that the person asked will agree to this.
   D It is uncertain whether the person asked will agree.

2 Can you make do with half a litre of milk today?
   A Can you find a use for it?
   B Can you let me have it?
   C Can you manage with only this amount?
   D Can you do without it?

3 If we were to picnic there, we should be too hot.
   A in this unlikely case.
   B if we had to do this.
   C if this had been arranged.
   D though this is quite impossible.

4 She decided that a certain meadow would do.
   A It would be quite suitable.
   B It would be good enough.
   C It would be used only as a last hope.
   D It would be less unpleasant than the others.

5 I did discover a tin of fly-killer.
   A This is not so fantastic as the other two suggestions but extra-ordinary enough.
   B In addition to all the other things.
   C This must be emphasised.
   D This is a colloquial use of the past tense.

6 Say twenty minutes.
   A This is a suggestion to be accepted.
   B This is a plain statement.
   C This is a command.
   D This is a polite request.

4 **When doing his or her shopping each of these people prefers a different one of the following shops.**

A **Hilary**, a man or woman living alone, who has a full-time job.
B **Mrs Candy**, who has a large young family and not much money.
C **Salome Siddons**, actress wife of a film producer, who does a lot of entertaining.
D **Mrs Meek**, an elderly widow, who lives alone.

The local shops they can visit are:
1 **Berkeley and Claridge**
   Self-service and counter service. Specialists in unusual inter-national foods not obtainable elsewhere. Wide variety of pre-cooked frozen food. Large stock of first-class wines, liquers, exotic fruits, pastries etc. Excellent service but prices averaging 10% to 20% higher than elsewhere. Car park.

2 **Widerange Supermarket**
   Large self-service shop with wide variety of British and European foods at average prices. Emphasis on cleanliness, quality and courtesy. Café for tea, coffee and snacks.

3 **Plainfare Hypermarket**
   Self-service for foods, household goods (including fridges and tele-visions) and cheap utility clothes for adults and children. Little shelf display: most goods are taken from price-marked cartons. Almost no staff service. Prices average 10% below normal with many even cheaper special offers. Often overcrowded. Car park. Supervised playroom for customers' children.

4 **The Corner Shop**
   A small owner-managed shop (with one assistant). Counter service only. Good stock of everyday foods, household cleaners etc. Average prices. Owner will obtain special goods ordered by regular customers. Slow service but a friendly atmosphere and personal interest. Deliveries made to homes on request. No car park.

Write a paragraph of about 50 words to suggest and give reasons for the choice of shop of each of the people named above. Begin the paragraphs with the following openings.

Hilary does most of his/her shopping at _____.

Mrs Candy finds it most convenient to shop at _____.

Salome Siddons makes a habit of shopping at _____.

Mrs Meek much prefers _____.

Interview

Talking about a photograph

1 What various things suggest that this is an old picture?
2 Compare the clothes with those that would be worn today.
3 Why do you think this spot has been chosen for the picnic?
4 Suggest some of the ways in which Mrs Brown's picnic differed from the one shown here.

Topics

What is your own attitude towards going on picnics?
Why do some people (especially families) enjoy picnics?
What are some of their possible drawbacks?

Reading aloud

Further intonation practice

1 *Statement-question change*
A statement may serve as a question if it ends with an upward (Tune 2) intonation. This form sometimes expresses surprise and one or more words may be emphasised (see page 234).

You didn't actually see him.	(Statement: Tune 1)
You didn't actually see him?	(Question: Tune 2)

He's coming back tomorrow.	(Statement: Tune 1)
He's coming back tomorrow?	(Question suggesting surprise: Tune 2)

2 *Question tags*
Type 1   expecting confirmation of what has been said:
It's cold today, *isn't it.*   (Tune 1 at the end)
Type 2   expressing a (frequently surprised or disbelieving) question:
This wine wasn't produced in England, *was it?*   (Tune 2 at the end)

3 *Implication*
A Tune 1 ending expresses a plain statement:
That's not what I think.
A Tune 2 ending implies an additional meaning besides the obvious one:
That's not what I think.   (I disagree with your opinion)
Note: This use of Tune 2 to express implication may prove difficult for Intermediate students and is best picked up by imitation of the class teacher and taped dialogue.

Passages

Read through each of the following passages silently before reading it aloud. While noticing the various details of sounds and phrasing that have been referred to earlier, pay special attention to the use of intonation in expressing meaning and the linking within word groups. Suggest a situation in which each of the passages might be spoken.

1   Is that the Eatwell Supermarket? It's Mr Stewart on the telephone, isn't it. Oh, isn't it? Mr Macdonald, is it? Well now, I'd like you to deliver some provisions to me urgently. Yes, I am indeed Mrs James of 8 Jordan Avenue, not number 6 where you delivered them last time. I'd like a fair-sized frozen chicken though not too big, a large tin of tomato soup and, if you've got any, two punnets of strawberries. And you've got a medium-sized carton of double cream, haven't you. Good. Would you be able to send the things this afternoon? This morning? Oh yes, that would be even better. Thank you very much. Goodbye.

2   How do you like that red dress with the white spots, Amy? Yes, it is a bit bright I suppose, but cheerful on a cloudy day. You don't like it, do you. Well, perhaps not. You're not really suggesting that dark brown one, are you? It's a bit depressing, isn't it. You don't think so? Well, tastes differ of course. How about the pale pink one over there? Too young for me? Well, that is unkind, isn't it. You're only a year younger and you're wearing light blue. Well otherwise there's only the cream one left in my size so I suppose I'll have to have that.

3 Excuse me, you wouldn't know where the bus for Amberwell stops, would you. Oh, it's this stop, is it? Thank you. Have you any idea when the next one leaves? Oh there's a timetable here is there? So there is. Oh, yes, it goes every half hour, doesn't it. So the next one will be here in twenty-five minutes. That will be a long wait, won't it. Oh, you think the one before hasn't arrived yet, do you? And you're quite right. Here it comes.

Structured communication

Discussion of a plan of a bungalow

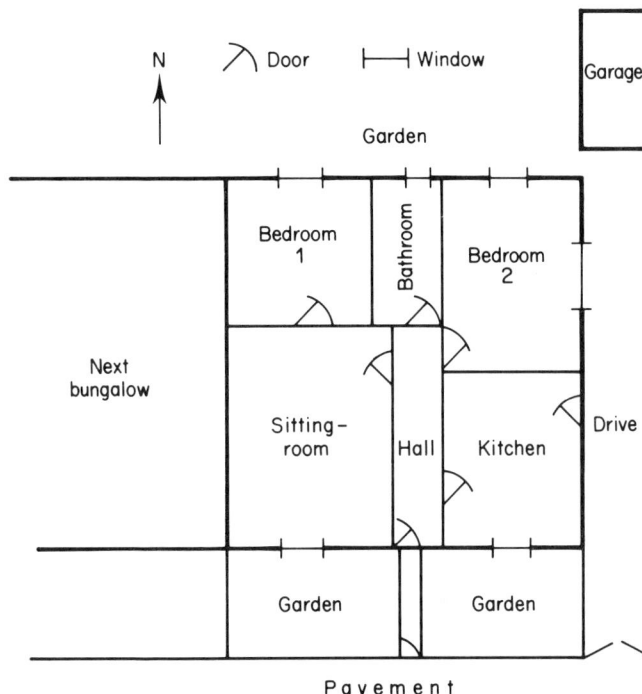

Pavement

This is the ground-plan of a semi-detached bungalow (it is joined on the left to another similar bungalow). Mr. and Mrs. Bridges, a young married couple, are now living in it. Study the plan carefully and then suggest answers to the following questions.

(a) Explain the quickest route by which the Bridges could go from the garage to Bedroom 1.
(b) Where is the kitchen? Is this an ideal position for it?
(c) What are two disadvantages of the hall?
(d) The garage might have been built farther forward, at the side of Bedroom 2. Suggest an advantage and disadvantage of this arrangement.
(e) What is a possible advantage of having the bedrooms at the back of the house?
(f) Why do you think two houses are built side-by-side in this way? What is the main disadvantage of this arrangement?
(g) Suggest why you would or would not find the bungalow a pleasant and convenient place to live in.
(h) Describe a typical small modern house and its surroundings in your country.

Action situations

1 You're getting ready to go away on holiday and have left most of your preparations till the last minute. On your last day at work you decide to go without lunch and do as many jobs as you can fit in. In fact you do five useful things, all quite different, during the free hour. Suggest what these might be.

2 You have to travel for at least eight hours in a car with two children between the ages of five and eight. What preparations do you make to ensure their good behaviour and comfort and what do you do about this during the journey? (You aren't driving yourself.)

3 What do you do if you cut your hand while working?

4 You hear a noise during the night and bravely go to investigate. You find two burglars in your living-room, searching it and causing considerable damage. What do you do?

Speech situations

What would you say if you were in any of the following situations?

1 On paying your hotel bill, you find you have been overcharged on two or three items. Protest politely, pointing out where mistakes have been made.

2 Your dog has run out without his collar and has been missing for two days and you are now ringing the police station to ask whether he has been brought in.

3 Your teenage nephew or niece has complained that there is nothing interesting for young people to do nowadays. Remind him/her of the many ways in which he/she could spend the time.

Topics for a prepared talk

Prepare to talk about one or more of the following topics for about two minutes. You can jot down a few notes to help you.

1 Some of the benefits and drawbacks of owning a car.
2 Your choice of menu for an ideal meal.
3 Kinds of weather that make things difficult for the motorist, suggesting effects and reasons.

Expressing opinions

1 Describe an ideal place for a picnic.
2 Do you enjoy a thunderstorm or are you slightly afraid of storms? In either case, try to explain your feelings.
3 What effects has the private car had on the countryside?

General guidance and practice

1 The subjunctive

A few remnants of the subjunctive are still to be found in English. The most obvious affect the verb *to be* and though even these are disappearing, they are normally retained in the speech of educated people. In most cases what is apparently the plural form *were* is used with a singular subject. This occurs mainly in the following three cases:

(a) After *if* as used in the second type of condition, especially when some doubt is implied. After *as if* or *as though* in comparisons:

If I *were* cold, I should put a jumper on.
If his pension *were* to be withdrawn, he would be penniless.
He ran as if/though he *were* being chased by devils.
Compare: I asked him if he *was* happy. (reported speech)
The mother told the child to call her if he *was* afraid. (a reasonable possibility)

(b) After the verb *wish*:

I wished I *were* fifty miles off.
He wishes he *were* handsome.

The past tense which normally follows this verb is sometimes explained as a form of the subjunctive:

I wish I *lived* nearer.

(c) After the words *supposing* and *suppose*:

Supposing I *were* to confess everything.

A past form of any verb may follow *supposing*:

Supposing he *came* now!

(d) Old uses of the subjunctive remain in phrases like *'God save the King!', 'Long live the President!', 'Thy will be done!', 'If it be possible.'*

(e) Certain other unexpected past forms after a few introductory expressions, including some of those above, may be examples of survivals of subjunctive forms:

I think it would be a good idea if we *went* home.
It is high time/about time that fence *was* mended.
I'd rather you *did* it.
If only I *had* more time!

Practice

Use the correct form of the verb in brackets in each of the following.

(a) He would be more popular if he (be) less argumentative.
(b) He behaves as if he (own) the earth.
(c) Our service engineers could come immediately if there (be) a breakdown.
(d) I'd rather he (say) nothing about it.
(e) I think it would be a good idea if you (get) on with your work.
(f) He felt so depressed that sometimes he wished he (be) dead.
(g) Supposing Father (say) we couldn't go!
(h) It is really time we (have) a holiday.
(i) We wish you (come) more often.
(j) She screamed and laughed wildly as though she (be) mad.
(k) If only you (not snore)!

2 Tense changes in reported speech

Here are some more things to remember when changing from direct to reported speech.

Modal verbs

Some modal forms never change their tense.
These are: *ought*, *should* and *might*.
'You *ought to/should* rest more.'
The doctor told me I *ought to/should* rest more.

215

'There *might* be a storm.'
He was afraid (that) there *might* be a storm.

Conditions

Study the following examples of the three main conditions:

(a) 'If you *are* not quiet, you *will be sent* to bed.'
The mother threatened that if the children *were* not quiet, they *would be sent* to bed.

(b) 'If there *were* a revolution, everybody *would get* enough to eat.'
The speaker told his audience that if there *were* a revolution, everybody *would get* enough to eat.

(c) 'If the moon *had been shining,* you *would have seen* the old windmill.'
Our host told us that if the moon *had been shining,* we *should have seen* the old windmill.

The first condition follows the normal tense change rules.
The verbs in the second and third conditions do not change.

Must

The changes affecting this verb depend on the way it is used.

(a) A habitual but not eternal action: *must* becomes *had to.*
'In my job, I *must* speak English every day.'
The secretary said that in her job she *had to* speak English every day.

'We *must* catch a bus whenever we go to the station.'
My cousins complained that they *had to* catch a bus whenever they went to the station.

(b) A future action: *must* becomes *would have to.*
(The subject may be just about to do the action but it has not yet happened.)
'I *must* look up his number in the telephone directory.'
The matron said she *would have to* look up his number in the telephone directory.

'You *must* speak more clearly if you want to be understood.'
I told him he *would have to* speak more clearly if he wanted to be understood.

(c) An eternal action: no change.
'Swallows *must* migrate in winter.'
The teacher explained that swallows *must* migrate in winter.

'Every living creature *must* have food.'
He stated that every living creature *must* have food.

(d) *Must not:* no change
'You *must not* forget what I have said.'
The old woman warned us that we *must not* forget what she had said.

(e) *Need not* becomes *did not need to* or *did not have to* according to meaning.
'You *need not* work so hard.'
My brother told me that I *did not need to* work so hard. (there was no necessity)

My brother told me that I *did not have to* work so hard. (there was no compulsion)

Can Could

Can becomes *could, could* becomes *had been able to/would be able to,* according to meaning.

'Jeremy *can* now count up to twenty.'
Jeremy's mother said that her son *could* now count up to twenty.

'We *could not* make ourselves understood in that restaurant.'
The tourists said that they *had not been able to* make themselves understood in that restaurant.

'I *could* do it on Monday.'
He said he *would be able to* do it on Monday.

3 Further aspects of reported speech

Confusion of meaning

In converting from direct to reported speech, changes in pronouns may lead to confusion in meaning.
Study this example:

'Mr. Reed, when can I come to your house for my lesson?'
If we change this automatically into reported speech, it may read:

The student asked Mr. Reed when he could come to *his* house for his lesson.
Common sense will adjust this to:

The student asked Mr. Reed when he could come to *Mr Reed's* house for his lesson.

Change of introductory verb

Study this example:

'*I'm going* to have fish and chips,' announced the stout woman. '*What do you want?*'
In this case a direct statement is followed by a direct question. Two different verbs will be needed in the corresponding reported speech:

The stout woman announced that she *was going to* have fish and chips and asked her companion *what she wanted*.

Say Tell

Tell normally needs an indirect object, that is, the person who is told. If there is no indirect object *say* is used.

He *told me/his wife* (that) he was going out.

He *said* (that) he was going out.
Exceptions: An indirect object is not necessary in these cases: *tell a story, tell the time, tell the truth, tell a lie, tell the difference between.*

Some other points

Certain ideas expressed in direct speech cannot be conveyed exactly in reported speech. Here again common sense is required. Here are some examples:

'Would you give me your name, sir?' said the policeman.
The policeman politely asked the motorist for his name.

'Help!' he shouted.
He shouted for help.

'You idiot,' John yelled, 'you've spoiled everything.'

John yelled that his friend, whom he called an idiot, had spoiled everything.

General uses of reported speech forms

We have been dealing with reported speech as it represents the re-telling of direct speech. Remember however that reported speech forms may appear in any kind of sentence or passage. Here are only a few cases:

They knew that they had not a chance.

He wrote about what he had seen.

We had no idea when we would return.

I could not think what his name was.

I hoped the weather would be fine, but I was afraid it would rain.

Reported to direct speech

This is of course a reverse process to the one already described. Remember especially the following points:

(a) The use of inverted commas (page 120).

(b) Certain tenses in reported speech have two possible forms in direct speech, depending on their meaning.

The **Past Perfect Simple** may change to the **Present Perfect Simple** or **Past Simple**.

The **Past Perfect Continuous** may change to the **Present Perfect Continuous** or **Past Continuous**.

The motorist told me *he had left* his licence at home.

'*I've left* my licence at home,' said the motorist.

The motorist told me *he had not seen* the traffic lights.

'*I didn't see* the traffic lights,' said the motorist.

(c) Direct speech often opens with the words spoken and ends with the main verb and the speaker. The subject and verb here may be reversed in order when the subject is a noun, as in the example above.

(d) Colloquial abbreviations are used in direct speech.

Practice

1 Convert the following sentences into reported speech. Suggest a speaker where necessary.

(a) 'I am sorry to disturb you, sir,' said the policeman. 'I shall have to ask you a few questions.'

(b) 'I must admit that what you say may be true,' said my wife.

(c) 'Do you regret coming to live in this small town?' asked my neighbour.

(d) 'I protest against your intolerable interference in my affairs,' said the angry tenant to his landlord.

(e) 'Lie down!' he told his dog. 'Now be a good dog and don't get up till I tell you.'

(f) 'Why didn't you come and see me yesterday? I was expecting you.'

(g) 'He will be making a speech here next Friday,' said the election agent. 'Do try to come and hear him.'

(h) 'Next time you drop in, you must tell us about your holiday,' my friend suggested.

(i) 'If I overslept, I should miss the train.'

(j) 'You must speak more politely when you answer your teacher.'

(k) 'You must not forget to send us a postcard.'

2 Convert the following examples of reported speech into direct speech:

(a) The tramp said he had had nothing to eat since the previous Monday.

(b) He told me he had been an invalid ever since an accident which had happened three years before but the doctor now had hopes that he would recover.

(c) The foreman asked the apprentice whether he had seen the slide rule that the foreman had been using earlier that morning.

(d) The sergeant told the soldiers to report for duty the next day. They were not to leave the barracks that evening as there might be trouble in the town.

(e) The porter asked me where I wanted him to put my luggage. He wanted to know whether it would be all right in my compartment or whether he should put it in the guard's van.

(f) Christopher offered me a cigarette explaining that he had another packet in his pocket.

4 Verbal constructions with see, hear, feel and smell

Verbs of seeing, hearing and feeling can be followed either by the Present Participle or by the Infinitive depending on the meaning expressed:

He saw/noticed the light *disappear* from inside the room.
He observed/watched the daylight gradually *fading*.

She heard the man *whistle* twice.
She heard the man *whistling* a tune.

I smelt the potatoes *burning*.
I could feel the dog *shiver* as I touched him.
I could feel the dog *shivering* with cold.

Where the Infinitive is used, the action happened and was completed. Where the Present Participle is used, the action was continuous and the emphasis is on the doing of the action.

Practice

Use the correct form of the verb in brackets, Present Participle or Infinitive, in each of the following sentences.

(a) There is often a crowd standing watching men (dig) up the road.

(b) I jumped up from my chair when I heard the doorbell (ring).

(c) You must have heard the telephone (ring) but you couldn't be bothered to answer it.

(d) I saw him (shut) the book impatiently and (put) it back on the shelf.

(e) He felt the intense cold (creep) into his very bones.

(f) Can you smell the dinner (cook)?

(g) Did you notice the cat (crouch) just near the mousehole?

(h) We felt the ship (give) a violent lurch.

5 Do and make

Broadly, *to make* implies the creation of something new; *to do* implies the carrying out of some action. One *makes* a cake, a dress, a sound; one *does* homework, knitting, a kind action.

But it is often very difficult to decide whether or not a new thing has been created or an action done, and there are a considerable number of exceptions to this statement. It is therefore advisable to notice and remember each individual case of one or other of these verbs.

Here is a list of a few cases:

Do	*Make*
do work (homework, housework, etc.)	make a dress, a cake, coffee
	make a mistake
do a job, an exercise, an examination, a test	make an appointment
	make the beds
do the washing-up	make a fortune
do shopping	make money (become rich)
do lessons	make friends with
do a translation (or, make a translation)	make an enemy of
	make a noise
do one's hair	make peace
do good	make an agreement
do harm, evil	make a will
do a good turn	make a bargain
do one's best	make improvements
do one's duty	make progress
	make the most of
	make a copy
	make preparations
	make an arrangement
	make a fuss, make a fuss of
	make a nuisance of oneself
	make trouble
	make a fool of
	make fun of
	make up one's mind
	make sure
	make sense
	make time (find time)
	make a difference
	make haste
	make allowances for
	make changes

Notice these expressions:

Yes, those gloves will *do*. I'll take them.
This meat is only *half done*. I don't like underdone food.
It really isn't *done* for you to sit there with your hat on.

Phrasal forms of do and make

do   It is time you *did away with* that filthy old hat. Why not burn it?
They have bought some paint and intend to *do up* their house.
There is no jam left. You will just have to *do without* it.
I can't *do up* this button. It will just have to stay undone.
I've had little to *do with* him. We seldom meet.
What has dressmaking *to do with* algebra?
Don't trust that waiter. He *did* me *out of* ten pence last week.

make   Nothing in a child's life can ever *make up for* the lack of a good home.
He is *making up* a parcel of small presents.
She is *making up* her face ready for the party.

That story isn't true. You *made it up*.

Thank goodness, they have *made up* their quarrel.

I can't *make out* this illegible writing.

What is paper *made of?* It is *made by* machinery.

Flax is *made into* linen. Linen is *made from* flax.

That beach bag was *made out of* an old cotton frock.

If you can't get exactly what you want, try to *make do with* the next best thing.

The thieves *made away with* a thousand pounds' worth of jewellery.

Practice

Rewrite the following sentences using some form of *do* or *make*.

(a) He has committed an error in this exercise.
(b) Try not to be a trouble in the class.
(c) Boy Scouts should perform a kindness every day.
(d) Can you produce good coffee?
(e) He has caused a lot of misfortune to his country.
(f) He has gone forward during the last few weeks.
(g) Will you please produce another letter like this one?
(h) The pirate captain decided to attack the treasure ship.
(i) The Transport Board are raising fares to compensate for their recent losses.
(j) The fishmonger hadn't any plaice today. We'll have to be content with cod.
(k) Workmen are redecorating my room.
(l) Why doesn't the Corporation get rid of those obsolete trams?
(m) The imaginative child invented a vivid story about a kindly dwarf.
(n) What confusion and trouble you are causing just because you have lost a cheap ballpoint pen.
(o) I have forgotten to write my homework.
(p) This message is almost impossible to read. Can you understand it?
(q) Some people do not wish to have any relationship with their neighbours.
(r) You are laughing at me!
(s) Hurry up! You'll miss the train!

6 Quantities

Much is used for quantity, *many* for number:

He hasn't *much* money, but he seems to have *many* friends.

The same applies to *little* and *least* (quantity) and *few, fewer* and *fewest* (number):

He eats *little* chocolate and *few* sweets.

Write a summary in *fewer* than eighty words.

You have *less* patience than I have.

Fewest is seldom used. It is usually replaced by *the smallest number*:

This is *the smallest number* of students that have ever attended.

Much before a noun or modifying a verb is rarely used in an affirmative statement or command. It is replaced by *a lot, a good deal* or *plenty*:

I have spent *a lot of* money.

I enjoyed it *a great deal*.

Very much, too much and *so much* are more commonly used:

I have spent *too much* money.

I enjoyed myself *very much*, or I *very much* enjoyed myself.
There is *so much* to do.

Much is used in negative and less commonly in interrogative sentences. It can follow verbs of a negative meaning like *deny, forbid, doubt* even when these are used affirmatively:
You won't find *much* left.
Have you *much* to do?
I doubt if I'll have *much* success with my new book.

Practice

1   Use a suitable expression in the following sentences from among those that have just been mentioned. In many cases more than one would be possible.

(a)   He has _____ worries or responsibilities. How lucky he is!
(b)   I can't come now. I have _____ to do this morning.
(c)   We must expect _____ people than usual in such bad weather.
(d)   He doesn't take _____ care of his bicycle.
(e)   He looks half-starved. I'm sure he eats _____ food than he ought.
(f)   I use my vacuum cleaner _____.
(g)   Do you smoke _____ cigarettes a day?
(h)   He buys _____ tobacco, and has _____ pipes.
(i)   In our house there are _____ rooms but oddly enough, not _____ space.
(j)   He eats _____ fruit as he says it doesn't agree with him.

2   Rearrange list B below so that the objects correspond with the words in list A.
Example: *a ball of string.*

A   a ball, a cake, a tin, a pair, a packet, a bar, a skein (ball), a reel, a bunch (bouquet), a bundle, a pack, a coil.

B   cotton, flowers, sardines, wire, wool, toilet soap, chocolate, cards, shoes, firewood, envelopes, string.

7   There is, it is

It is basically easy to distinguish between these two expressions.
It is/they are normally introduces something already known or that has at least been mentioned or suggested:
   'What's that?' '*It's* a baby tortoise'
There is/are introduces something new:
   There is a canary in the garden.

It is may also introduce ideas not previously referred to.
These include expressions dealing with:
(a)   the weather: *It was a hot day.*
(b)   time: *It is six o'clock* (possibly answering the question, *What is the time?*) *It is a long time to wait till supper.*
(c)   a journey: *It is a long way to London.*
Many other expressions are introduced by *It is* such as:
   It is a pity that . . ., It is essential that . . ., It is easy to . . .

Perhaps the two following examples best show the difficulty of distinguishing between these two introductory expressions:
   It is a long journey from London to Edinburgh.
   There is a long journey ahead of you.
Students normally pick up the correct usage by reading or listening.

222

Practice

Replace the spaces in the following sentences by *it is, they are, there is* or *there are*.

(a) _____ far too much spice in this cake. _____ not necessary to use so much.

(b) _____ a year since we met.

(c) Please try this chocolate. _____ a free sample from the makers.

(d) _____ time to go now. No, it isn't. _____ still time to have a cigarette.

(e) Don't eat that. _____ a poisonous berry. _____ many of them in these parts.

(f) _____ a frog on the edge of that pool. _____ one of those creatures that do not appeal to me.

(g) _____ a train leaving at nine o'clock. _____ a fast one.

(h) _____ often a difficult job to trace the owner of lost property.

(i) _____ a shame that even today _____ so many homeless people.

(j) _____ no time to stop and talk. _____ a bus to catch. _____ a fair distance to the terminus.

(k) _____ (Future tense) an hour to wait for the train and _____ a twenty-minute walk to the station.

(l) _____ (Present Perfect tense) a big fire in the warehouse. _____ (Past Simple tense) a great pile of timber stored there.

(m) _____ (Past Perfect tense) a tiring day and _____ (Past Simple tense) still a lot do to.

(n) _____ (Conditional Perfect tense) thousands more visitors to the exhibition if _____ (Past Perfect tense) more widely advertised.

8 Revision of prepositions

Use a suitable preposition in each of the following sentences.

(a) Concrete consists _____ sand, gravel, cement powder and water.

(b) If you can improve this _____ any way, please do so.

(c) Have you enough room in that tiny garage of yours _____ your enormous car?

(d) We cooked our meal over a fire _____ the open air.

(e) Sarah came home from the party, loaded _____ sweets and toys.

(f) A rabbit is different _____ a hare.

(g) I have made an appointment _____ the optician to choose new frames for my glasses.

(h) He apologised _____ his sarcastic remarks.

(i) The coach party had salmon and cucumber salad _____ lunch.

10 Ghosts for Tea

'Fifty pence for a view over the bay,' said the old man with the telescope. 'Lovely clear morning. Have a look at the old lighthouse and the remains of the great shipwreck in 1935.'

Fifty pence was sheer robbery, but the view was certainly magnificent.
5 Cliffs stretched into the distance, sparkling waves whipped by the wind were unrolling on to the beach, and a few yachts, with creamy-white sails, were curving and dodging gracefully on the sea. Just below, a flock of sea-gulls were screaming at one another as they twisted and glided over the water. A mile out to sea, the old lighthouse stood on a stone platform on
10 the rocks, which were being greedily licked by the waves. In no way indeed did I grudge my money. As I directed the telescope towards the lighthouse, the man beside me tapped my wrist.

'Have you heard about the terrible tragedy that occurred there in that lighthouse?' he asked in a hushed whisper.
15 'I imagine there may be plenty of legends attached to such a dramatic-looking place,' I suggested.

It's no legend,' declared the old man. 'My father knew the two men involved. It all took place fifty years ago today. Let me tell you.'

His voice seemed to grow deeper and more dramatic.
20 'For a whole week that lighthouse had been isolated by storms,' he began, 'with terrifying seas surging and crashing over the rocks. People on shore were anxious about the two men working there. They'd been on the best of terms until two or three weeks before, when they had quarrelled over cards in the village inn. Martin had accused Blake of cheating. Blake
25 had vowed to avenge the insult to his honour. But thanks to the wise advice of a man they both respected, they apologised to each other, and soon seemed to have got over their disagreement. But some slight resentment and bitterness remained, and it was feared that the strain of continued isolation and rough weather might affect their nerves, though, needless to
30 say, their friends had no idea how serious the consequences would be.

'Fifty years ago tonight, no light appeared in the tower, and only at two o'clock in the morning did the beam suddenly start to flash out its warning again.

'The next morning the light was still visible. The storm had almost
35 blown itself out, so a relief boat set out to investigate. A grim discovery awaited the crew. The men's living-room was in a horrifying state. The table was overturned; a pack of playing cards was scattered everywhere; bloodstains splashed the floor. The relief men climbed the winding stair to the lantern room and there discovered Martin's body, crouched beside the
40 burning lamp. He had been stabbed and was dead. Two days later, Blake's body was washed up, scratched, bruised, and terribly injured.

'Only then could we really start guessing what had happened. This great tragedy could only have been due to a renewal of their quarrel. Bored and depressed as a result of their isolation, Martin and Blake must have started
45 to play cards. Again suspecting cheating, Martin had accused his former friend of dishonesty; a fight had broken out and Blake had seized his

knife. In a fit of madness he had attacked his companion, who had fallen mortally wounded. Then, appalled by what he had done, the loneliness, the battering of wind and waves, Blake had rushed to the parapet and
50 flung himself on to the rocks below, where the sea had claimed him.

'But Martin was still alive. Hours later, after darkness had fallen, he had recovered consciousness. He remembered his job of lighting the lamp; suffering intense pain, the poor wretch crawled slowly up the winding staircase, dragging himself from step to step till he got to the lantern. At
55 his last gasp he managed to light this before finally collapsing.

'For years afterwards it was said that the lighthouse was haunted, and, owing to these stories, they didn't have any applicants for the job of light-house-keeper from among the superstitious local inhabitants. And now they say that on every anniversary of that day, especially when the sea is
60 rough, you can stand in the living-room, hear the cards falling and the sound of angry cries, see the flash of a blade, and then glimpse a figure rushing to the parapet. And then you hear the slow dragging of a body from step to step towards the room above.'

The old man paused and I turned to go.
65 'By the way,' he added, 'have you any free time this afternoon? If so, why don't you have tea in the lighthouse? We are putting on a special boat trip today. We're charging five pounds. And my brother, who bought the old lighthouse when they built the new one just on the point, can serve very good teas there, included in the price of the boat trip — a bargain, con-
70 sidering the problem of obtaining the food. And if you are at all sensitive to the supernatural, you're likely to have an unusual, perhaps an uncanny experience there.'

I eyed him appreciatively. 'You're wasting your talents,' I said. 'You should have been a fiction writer.'
75 'You don't believe it?' exclaimed the old man indignantly.

'I'd find it a job,' I answered. 'My father, Henry Cox, started as keeper of that lighthouse fifty-two years ago, and he and Jim Dowley, now retired on a pension, were in charge for ten years. Come and see my dad one day with that tale; he'd enjoy it.'
80 But the old man had already turned his attention to a more likely client.

Notes on the passage

Vocabulary

1 *a view* = (a) the area seen from a certain point: *the view from my window* (b) an opinion: *one's political views*.
a viewpoint = a place from which a view is seen.
a point of view = an opinion on a particular matter.
a sight = something seen: *The ceremony was an interesting sight*.
an outlook = (a) what can be seen when looking out (b) what seems likely to happen: *the weather outlook*.
scenery = the general appearance of the countryside.
a landscape = scenery seen as a kind of picture.
a scene = (a) a division of an act of a play (b) a view, usually having a definite quality: *the breath-taking scene of the moon rising over the sea* (c) the place where something happened: *the scene of the crime* (d) an unpleasant display of bad temper or emotion: *to make a scene*.
the countryside = the characteristic region away from the town. This is similar in meaning to 'the country'.
Nature = the natural creative force as part of the countryside (not *the Nature*).

Which? (a) He enjoys wandering in the _____. (b) The mountain hotel offered magnificent _____. (c) The spoilt actor enjoyed making awkward ___·___. (d) He has no political _____. (e) the romantic _____ of Norway. (f) The _____ in the motor industry is depressing. (g) This is the _____ of the accident. (h) The very _____ of food made him feel worse. (i) The _____ from his room is far from cheerful. (j) I prefer his _____ pictures to his portraits. (k) _____ has adapted these creatures to their surroundings. (l) The Coronation was a brilliant _____.

Notice the following expressions: *a bird's-eye view; the view-finder* (part of a camera); *in view of (= because of): In view of the dangerous condition of the building, the public cannot be admitted; the sights of London; come into sight; go out of sight; know someone by sight; fall in love at first sight; sight-read* (music); *lose sight of.*

1 *telescope telegram, telegraph, television, telepathy* (*tele-* means 'distant'). *microscope periscope, horoscope* (*-scope* in each case means 'see'). *scope* can also mean the range of a person's opportunities: *His present job provides little scope for his artistic talents.*

4 *sheer* (a) *a sheer drop of eight metres:* a vertical drop (b) *sheer silk:* so light and delicate that it is transparent (c) *a sheer waste of time:* complete, absolute.

5 *a whip* is sometimes used when horse-riding. Other equipment is: *the harness, the saddle, the reins, the bridle.* At one time *spurs* were used to urge the horse on: *Ambition spurred him on. whipped cream* has been beaten to make it firm.

6 *a sail* of a ship; the *sale* of a house; spring *sales* in the shops. Even a steamer can *sail: The cruise liner will sail at four o'clock.*

7 *curve* (N and V) = a rounded line. *bend* (N and V) = a line which turns in another direction; also *bend down, bend forward. fork* (N and V) = a division of a line into two directions. A road can *curve, bend* and *fork.*
An *S-bend;* a *hairpin bend;* a *roundabout* (a large island in the middle of a road junction); *a turning; a cul-de-sac* or *no thoroughfare.*

12 *wrist* = part of the arm. *fist* = the clenched or closed hand.

15 *attached to* = joined to: *A label was attached to the string. Also* fond of: *She is very attached to her cat.*

23 *terms* (Plural) = (a) items agreed to in a contract or treaty (b) a price, especially for a service: *hotel terms* (c) conditions: *We did not agree to his terms of the release of the hostages.* (d) personal relations *They are on good (bad) terms with each other.* Cf. *term* = a period of time: *There are three terms in the school year.*

29 *affect* (V only) = influence: *The dry weather has affected the quality of the fruit.* Cf. *effect* (N) = result: *It has had a bad effect on the quality of the fruit.* *effect* (V) = cause a certain result: *Certain changes have been effected.* Note: *to have a good (bad) effect on.*

32 *a beam* of light, *a sunbeam.* He *beamed* (smiled happily) with pleasure. A beam can also be a strong supporting bar of wood below a ceiling.

35 *relief* (N) = the taking away of a heavy burden or worry: *There is no danger of my losing my job after all. What a relief!* Also: *The drug provided a temporary relief from pain.*
relieved (Adj): *She was relieved to find her children safe.*
relieve (V) = take over someone's job to allow him to rest: *The sentry was at last relieved and could eat and sleep.*
relief (Adj) (a) *a relief fund:* for flood, famine or earthquake victims to provide them with food and shelter (b) *a relief bus:* to take home the large crowds (c) *a relief map:* showing comparative heights by colours.

40 *stab* Here are a few ways in which the victim in a detective story can be murdered: He may be *stabbed* (with a knife), *poisoned, strangled, suffocated, hanged, gassed* or *pushed over a cliff.* As a result, he dies and when he is *dead* there is an *inquest*

presided over by a *coroner*. The doctor who has carried out the *post-mortem* to discover the causes of death will give evidence, in a *law court*.

41 *scratch* (N and V): people *scratch* with their *nails;* cats with their *claws*. This causes *a scratch* on the skin. Furniture may get *scratched*. Potatoes are *scraped* or (like apples) *peeled*. Floors are *scrubbed* with a *scrubbing brush* or washed with some kind of mop. A table is *polished* by *rubbing* polish over it on a cloth.

45 *play cards, football, chess. play the piano, the violin, the trumpet. play a game. act on the stage. act or perform in a play. play the part of* Hamlet.

53 *intense* pain, effort, heat, light. an *intensive* course of study (lasting a short time).

58 *superstitious* people never walk under ladders. *superstition* (N).
suspicious can describe a feeling: *The dog was suspicious of strangers* and also what causes the feeling: *A suspicious-looking man seemed to be watching the house.*

61 *a knife blade* and also *a blade of grass.*

69 *a bargain* = (a) an agreement in which each person may give up something: *We made a bargain that I should cook dinner and he would wash up after.*
(b) something of good value that is bought cheaply: *It is sometimes possible to find a good bargain in the sales.*
to bargain: to discuss the price of something: *After a lot of bargaining, he bought the ring at a satisfactory price.*

76 *I'd find it a job* = I should find it difficult.

80 a shopkeeper has *a customer;* a solicitor has *a client;* a doctor has *a patient.*

Pronunciation

ə as in *a*go: occurred /əkɜ́:d/; legend /lédʒənd/; isolated /áɪsəleɪtɪd/; *a*pologise /əpɒ́lədʒaɪz/; parapet /pǽrəpɪt/; superstition /su:pəstíʃən/; *a*ppreciatively /əprí:ʃətɪvli/; indignantly /ɪndígnəntli/.

ɪ as in *ci*ty: television /telɪvíʒən/; imagine /ɪmǽdʒɪn/; declare /dɪkléə/; consequences /kɒ́nsɪkwensɪz/; bargain /bá:gɪn/.

Others: view /vju:/; yacht /yɒt/; wretch /retʃ/.

Grammatical and structural points

(a) *each other   one another*

each other refers to only two people; *one another* can be used to refer to three or more people. Notice the following expressions:
They looked at *each other/one another* in surprise.
They did a lot for *each other/one another.*
They are not speaking to *each other/one another.*
They had to be separated from *each other/one another.*
They have little confidence in *each other/one another.*

(b) *Verbal constructions*

Infinitive: vow *to avenge.*
Infinitive expressing purpose: a boat set out *to investigate.*
Gerund: accuse someone *of doing* something.
Clause: I imagine (that) there may be many legends . . .
I had no idea *of how* late it was.

Prepositions

(a) *in* a whisper; *in* a loud voice. Notice: say something *aloud*. (Not: *in a high voice.*)
(b) *on* good terms with; *on* every anniversary of that day.

(a) have a look at.
(b) on the best of terms.
(c) needless to say.
(d) the storm had blown itself out.
(e) set out to investigate.
(f) recover consciousness.
(g) retired on a pension.
(h) turned his attention to.

Spoken English

Expressing certainty and doubt

Certainty

I'm convinced/(quite) certain/(quite) sure things will improve.
I refuse to/can't believe you're doing your best.

Doubt

I doubt whether I'll understand much of this evening's play.
I wonder whether he'll remember it.

Mixed probability and doubt

I can't help thinking that it'll be a mistake to buy that car.
I suppose you could call her a good cook but she's got no imagination.
I imagine (= I think it likely) he'll have finished by five o'clock.
I dare say (= I think it possible) the play will be successful.
I suspect he'd had something to drink before he arrived at the party.

Other feelings

I'm pleased to say that my father's quite better now.
I'm thankful we haven't much farther to walk.
I'm surprised how fast my money seems to disappear.
I'm ashamed to say (confess) I've forgotten your name.
I'd like to say how grateful we are to you.
I must say some people seem to have no manners at all. (Indignation)

Making the most of spare time

How do you spend your spare time?
What do you do with your spare time?

A   I'm keen on sport, especially football. I play for the local team as a goalkeeper. We usually have a match once a week and we do a fair amount of training during the week.

B   I don't play myself but I enjoy watching matches or listening to radio commentaries. I support our local team and sometimes travel with them to watch away matches. (Cf. home matches)

C   I like anything on, in or under water: water-skiing, swimming and underwater photography. Living near the sea gives me plenty of opportunities to enjoy water-sports. I'm saving up to buy a speed-boat.

D   I spend the weekend climbing whenever the weather's suitable, staying in mountain huts. I go skiing a lot in winter.

E   I go to the theatre (opera, cinema) as often as I can afford it. I don't much mind what play's on provided the production's of a high standard.

F I'm very keen on dancing and spend a couple of evenings a week in the local discotheque. I also enjoy sitting in cafés talking to my friends.

G I'm usually so tired when I come home that I just watch television — any kind of programme — while I do some knitting. Sometimes I do embroidery. At weekends I do a lot of reading.

H I collect jazz records and often invite friends to bring theirs for a jazz session.

Watching television and going to the cinema

A I'm going to the cinema this evening.

B What's on?

A It's a Western: 'Cowboy Come Home'.

B But there's a Western on television tonight. You're welcome to come round and watch it. Why bother to go out and pay for a cinema seat?

A There's a wide screen and the colour will be better.

B Here you can have a comfortable armchair, a drink at your elbow and no journey to make. Besides there are three other worthwhile programmes on: a documentary on underwater swimming, half an hour's sports review and an episode of a mystery serial play.

A I've seen a few episodes of that on Peter's television. You really enjoy that kind of programme, don't you.

B Yes, I do. Last week the hero had kidnapped the gangster boss and was threatening to blow him up if he didn't release his girl-friend — I mean the hero's girl-friend, of course.

A Do you prefer seeing a story as a T.V. film to reading it in a book?

B Oh yes. You can actually see the characters and how they're dressed and watch their expressions. This story takes place in the mountains of Norway and you can enjoy the scenery, the mountains and glaciers and fiords. At one point some of the characters have to ski through a blizzard. It's all so vivid and believable and far more exciting than a book.

A But a film can make everything more exciting and vivid and the darkness cuts out human surroundings completely.

B But you can't choose your programme and it's a waste of money to walk out if you're bored. It's so easy to turn off the T.V. — not that I do turn it off very often.

A That's just it. You're drugged by it: you've given up all your old interests. That's why I won't have a T.V. I still have time to read, invite friends in for a chat or sometimes go to concerts or to the cinema or theatre.

Reading comprehension

Choice of words

In this exercise you must choose the word or phrase which best completes each sentence.

1 Switzerland is well-known for its impressive mountainous
_____ .

A views   B scenes   C scenery   D Nature

2 When he was questioned about the missing ring, he firmly _____ that he had ever seen it.
   A stated **B** denied **C** claimed **D** refused

3 The bank _____ planned to escape in a stolen car.
   A thieves **B** burglars **C** robbers **D** bandits

4 He has to arrange for the _____ of his furniture before he goes to live abroad.
   A sale **B** store **C** disposition **D** sail

5 As the clouds drifted away, an even higher peak became _____ to the climbers.
   A in sight **B** visible **C** obvious **D** clear

6 Shopkeepers are not always so polite as they might be to their _____.
   A buyers **B** shoppers **C** customers **D** clients

7 Prices continued to rise while wages remained low _____ the Government became increasingly unpopular.
   A even though **B** with the result that **C** providing **D** in order that

8 A historical novel is a form of _____ which may include many facts.
   A legend **B** relation **C** short story **D** fiction

9 He had been exhausted but felt considerably _____ after a meal and a rest.
   A relieved **B** refreshed **C** recreated **D** renewed

10 High in the sky a _____ of birds was flying southward.
   A collection **B** flock **C** swarm **D** company

Multiple choice responses

Read through the passage carefully before dealing with the questions and statements that follow it.

The island of Great Britain being small (compare the size of Australia), the natural place for holiday relaxation and enjoyment is its extensive coastline, above all its southern and eastern coasts, though Blackpool, which is probably the best known and most crowded seaside town, and the
5 favourite resort of the mass-population of industrial Lancashire, is on the north-west coast. Distant and little-inhabited areas like Northern Scotland, are too remote for the development of large seaside resorts.

For most children, going to the seaside suggests a week or fortnight of freedom on the beach, ideally a sandy one providing ample opportunity
10 for the construction of sandcastles, fishing in pools for stranded shrimps, paddling in shallow water or swimming in deep. Children's entertainments may include the traditional knockabout puppet show 'Punch and Judy', donkey rides, paddleboats in artificial ponds, mini-golf and the swings and roundabouts in local fairgrounds. Their parents spend sunny days
15 swimming in the sea and sunbathing on the beach. Not that the British sun can be relied on, and the depressing sight of families wandering round the town in mackintoshes and under umbrellas is only too common. However there are always the shops with their tourist souvenirs, plenty of cafés and, if the worst comes to the worst, the cinema to offer a refuge.
20 The average family is unlikely to seek accommodation in a hotel as they can stay more cheaply in one of the many boarding-houses. These are usually three or four-storeyed Victorian buildings, whose owners spend

230

the summer season letting rooms to a number of couples or families and providing three cooked meals a day at what they describe as a reasonable
25 price, with the hope that in this way they will add enough to their savings to see the winter through. Otherwise there are the caravan and camping sites for those who prefer self-catering.

Nowadays, even when an increasing number of people fly off to Mediterranean resorts where a well-developed suntan can be assured, or explore
30 in comfort Swiss lakes and mountains or romantic Italian or Spanish cities, the British seaside is still the main attraction for families, especially those with younger children. As they queue for boat trips, cups of tea or ice-cream under grey skies and in drizzling rain, the parents are reliving their own childhood when time seemed endless, their own sandcastle the
35 most splendid on the beach, the sea always blue and friendly and the sun always hot.

Here are a number of questions or unfinished statements about the passage, each with four suggested answers or endings. Choose the one you think fits best in each case.

1 A reason suggested in the first paragraph for the appeal of the British seaside is that
   A it is within easy reach.
   B it is an ideal place for children.
   C most holiday resorts are in the warmer south and east.
   D a large number of people enjoy going there.

2 Children enjoy the seaside because
   A they can be sure of a sandy beach to play on.
   B they are allowed to do as they like there.
   C it offers a period of enjoyable escape from school routine.
   D there are a variety of enjoyable ways of spending time there.

3 It is suggested that as a form of holiday entertainment the cinema
   A is visited only if there is nothing better to do.
   B is the only place there is to go to in bad weather.
   C is the best place there is to go to in bad weather.
   D has nothing whatever to recommend it.

4 What reason is suggested for running a boarding-house?
   A The owners earn their living by doing this.
   B This helps to pay for the upkeep of a large house.
   C The money they make will keep them through the winter.
   D The resulting supplementary income will ensure a living for several months.

5 What attraction has the British seaside got for many parents in comparison with European resorts?
   A They can take their families with them in their own country.
   B There are more ways of enjoying themselves there.
   C They can relive happy memories.
   D It takes them less time to get there.

Composition

Subjects for
practice

1 In a strange town you find an old bridge, an ancient tower or a ruined chapel. The guide book provides a thrilling, romantic or tragic story associated with one of these. Write this story in between 120 and 180 words.

2 The duties of either a secretary, a waiter in an expensive restaurant, an air hostess, a nurse or your class teacher. Your explanation should be between 120 and 180 words in length.

Use of English

1 **Fill in the each of the numbered blanks in the following passage with one suitable word.**

'I'm sorry, sir,' said the bank clerk, 'we can't let you have these travellers' _____(1) until we've entered details in your passport.' 'But I've only got five hours,' said Phillip, anxiously. 'My plane is leaving _____(2) evening.' 'We remain open _____(3) three o'clock,' the clerk told him.

So when Phillip was on his way to the airport _____(4) that afternoon, he asked the driver to wait outside the bank _____(5) he collected the cheques.

The plane was to leave at half-past five and there was still a long _____(6) to the air terminal. For a time Phillip merely watched his surroundings, but shortly before _____(7) at his destination, he began checking the things he would need for boarding the plane. Tickets, money, the address of his hotel, travellers' cheques. Yes, _____(8) was there. Just a moment, though. How _____(9) his passport? Horrified, Phillip went through his pockets. He suddenly _____(10) that he must have _____(11) his passport at the bank, though he had no memory of doing so.

Whatever could he do? It was now five past four and so there would be _____(12) little time to return to the bank, which would in _____(13) case be closed now. This was the first time he was representing his firm and he had an important appointment with the manager of an insurance firm in Paris at ten o'clock the following morning. Without a passport he would be _____(14) to board the plane. _____(15) that moment, the taxi drew up outside the air terminal. Not knowing what to do next, Phillip got _____(16), took his suitcase and paid the _____(17). He then became aware of a good deal of confusion in the building. A voice could be heard over the loudspeaker.

'We very much regret that owing to a twenty-four-hour strike of airport staff, all flights for the rest of today have had to be _____(18). Passengers are advised to get into touch with their travel agents or with this terminal for details of tomorrow's flights.' The voice continued to give advice and instructions. Phillip gave a deep _____(19) of relief. He would have to let his firm know about this situation but, thank goodness, he would have the _____(20) of calling at his bank the following morning to recover his passport.

2 **Complete each of the following sentences with an appropriate phrase like the one shown in the examples.**
   Examples: He sat down in the armchair he thought of buying *to see how comfortable it was.*
   The inspector asked the class a lot of questions *to see how much they knew.*

   1 He took the temperature of the bath water _____
   2 We asked when the dog had been born _____
   3 He counted the number of students in the room _____
   4 When the train arrived at last, I looked at my watch _____
   5 She counted the money in her purse _____
   6 She checked the distance to London on a map _____

3 **Column A lists twelve sentence openings, each of which can be completed by one of the endings in Column B. Write twelve sentences, consisting of each of the sentence openings followed by a suitable ending.**

A	B
She wanted	to watch television
She suggested	
She would like	watch television
She thought	
She did not mind	watching television
She made us	
She enjoyed	that we would watch television
She spent a lot of time	
She sat	
She saw us	
She let us	
She has stopped	

4 **Complete each of the sentences below with one of the following six words, changed to the correct form as necessary. A negative form may be needed in some cases.**

   fly flow lie lay need pass

   1 During the past three months, John, who is a salesman, _____ to many countries in the world.
   2 Did you buy any petrol last weekend? No, I had enough so I _____ any.
   3 Thank goodness that restless dog _____ down now and is quiet.
   4 Whenever he _____ the statue of Queen Victoria, he raised his hat respectfully.
   5 Whenever the weather was suitable, the twins _____ their model aeroplanes in a nearby field.
   6 He _____ a bright pink envelope on the manager's table and then hurried away.
   7 On the Duke's wedding-day, everybody danced in the streets and wine _____ freely from the fountains.
   8 You _____ have made so much noise.
   9 After he _____ sleepless for five hours, he got up.

10 I _____ the shop every day this week and have never seen it
open.

5 **Write the exclamations that might be made in the following cases.**
Examples: You think a film is boring.
What a boring film!
You are surprised that someone hasn't written to you.
How strange that he hasn't written!

1 You think a room is very warm.
2 You are admiring a friend's dress.
3 You are shocked by the number of mistakes a fellow-student has
made.
4 You are really tired.
5 You discover it is much later than you had thought.
6 You are expressing your opinion of an acquaintance who always
does as little work as possible.

Interview

Reading aloud

Expressing emphasis

The meaning of a sentence varies in speech according to the emphasis
placed on individual words. The following sentence can be said in a
completely neutral way without any special emphasis:
Sonja has bought a mink cape for her mother.

At least six different meanings can be given to this sentence by means of
varying emphasis. Here are three of them:
Sonja *has* bought a mink cape for her mother — somebody has denied
this.
Sonja has bought a *mink* cape for her mother — not a tweed one.
Sonja has bought a mink cape for her *mother* — not for herself.

Emphasis is expressed by increasing the *force* and the *range* of the voice.

So it was George who said that.

I've never heard such an idea.

A whole sentence can be emphasised.

Wherever have you been?

Compare: Where have you been?

Auxiliaries and modal verbs sometimes express emphasis.

I can't understand it.

I did tell you.

Passages

Read through the following passages silently, underlining any words you
think would be emphasised in speech. Then practise small groups of words
where emphasis would be used. Finally read the whole passage aloud,
using emphasis to convey the meaning intended. Suggest a situation in
which each of the passages might be spoken.

1 It's not that I mind your talking about me behind my back, though that's something I'd never do about you. But to say such mean, untrue, cruel things about me when I've never given you any cause to is just horrible. Well, I used to think you were my friend but not any more. I never again want to have anything at all to do with you.

2 Lovely day for a sail round the bay. Out to the lighthouse and back. Only two pounds and half price for the kids. Leaving in five minutes. No, lady, you won't be seasick: smooth as the palm of your hand. No, sir, you can't take dogs and certainly not a big one like that. Can't you tie him up somewhere for half an hour? Only two places left. Come along and enjoy a nice blow. Any more for the Mary Lee?

3 Mr and Mrs Carter, is it? Well, you're very welcome. I'll show you your room. Sorry there are rather a lot of stairs to climb. Yes, they are a bit narrow. Think of those Victorian ladies going up them in their crinolines! Can you manage that suitcase, Mr Carter? I'd offer to help but I'm not so young as I was. We're nearly there now. There! Isn't that nice? Just look at that wonderful view. Yes, I'm afraid that window's stuck but you'll be nice and warm here. And you can't fall out, can you. Would you like a nice cup of tea? And some nice fruit cake? No dear, you won't have to pay for it. No extras at Cliff View. Come down as soon as you're ready and I hope you're going to have a wonderful time here in Brightpool.

Structured communication

Postcard messages

Suggest messages you might send to a friend that would fill the correspondence half of a picture postcard in these situations.

1 You are in the middle of a very enjoyable holiday.

2 You have just completed your first week in a new job or school.

3 You have unexpectedly got engaged to be married.

4 You are in hospital after a road accident.

5 You have recently changed your address.

Expressing opinions

1 Why do you think that crime stories — in books or on television — are so widely popular?

2 Do you think that as a result of a higher standard of living in many countries, young people tend to be more spoilt and less tough and adventurous than they were two generations ago?

3 In your opinion does climate influence the character of a nation to any great extent?

Topics for a prepared talk

After preparing a few notes, speak for about two minutes about one or more of the following topics.

1 An unusual job: what it consists of and the qualities needed to carry it out satisfactorily.

2 Ghosts and other supernatural manifestations.

3 Some examples of superstition common in your country.

Talking about a timetable

The cruise liner SS Golden Sun leaves Venice on Monday 5th May for a cruise of the Central and Eastern Mediterranean, calling at the ports listed below. Dates and times of arrival and departure are shown together with local excursions that have been arranged at the various ports.

You and possibly another student are calling at a travel office which can book one of these cruises for you. The clerk there has only one brochure so provides all the information you need in answer to questions asked. You want to know about such things as dates and times of arrival and departure, length of time spent at some of the ports and excursions that can be booked. You will also want some information about the boat: kinds of accommodation available (two, three or four berth cabins with or without showers), restaurants, bars, lounges, swimming pools, duty-free shops, cinemas etc. (Here the tourist office clerk may have to use some imagination in answering.)

Three or more students could be involved, with one of them providing the information. Alternatively the teacher can take the role of clerk.

DATES MAY	PORTS	ARRIVAL	DEPARTURE	EXCURSIONS
5	Venice		19.00	
6	Dubrovnik (Yugoslavia)	15.00	19.00	Visit to the city
7	at sea			
8	Heraklion (Crete)	10.00	14.00	Visit to Knossos
9	Alexandria (Egypt)	15.00		Visit to Cairo
10	Alexandria		20.00	Visit to the Pyramids
11	Haifa (Israel)	15.00		Visit to Nazareth
12	Haifa		21.00	Bethlehem and Jerusalem
13	Limassol (Cyprus)	9.00	17.00	Mountain coach tour
14	Rhodes (Greece)	14.00	18.00	Ancient city of Lindos
15	Piraeus (Greece)	11.00	18.00	Visit to Athens
16	at sea			
17	Venice	16.00		

Speech situations

Suggest what you might say in each of the following situations.

1 A very pleasant and likeable person insists on trying to win your support for an organisation or political party you have no interest in.

2 A talkative friend telephones you at a time when you are very busy.

3 A friend isn't certain whether to trust a baby-sitter who has offered his/her services. You yourself have found the person somewhat unsatisfactory though you haven't previously mentioned this to your friend.

Note: A *summit conference* is one between the heads of the world's most powerful states.

The *Commons* is the House of Commons, the elected assembly of the British Parliament.

A *storm* suggests angry scenes.

1 Suggest one possible reason why the actual stories in the above illustration are not presented in English.

2 Arrange the headlines in order of what you would regard as their importance in world affairs.

3 Suggest briefly some stories behind the headlines.

4 What are some of the reasons for workers' strikes?

5 What would the weather forecast have been if this paper had been published last night?

6 Look at the Index. Which page would you turn to first and why?

7 Suggest some subjects of letters to the editor.

8 Comment on the petrol advertisement in the bottom left-hand corner. Would it persuade you as a motorist to buy the petrol? Why or why not?

9 Suggest some subjects for the small ads on page 15.

10 *Role-play:* As an editorial committee you are having a discussion about what items (possibly imaginary ones) of today's news should be included in the edition of the paper that will be put together this evening ready for tomorrow morning. Indicate how much space should be given to each item and how it might be treated.

Talking about a photograph

1 Give a brief description of what you can see in this picture.
2 As a holidaymaker, suggest why you would or would not enjoy sitting here?
3 What is the purpose of the light tower at the end of the quay?
4 What features of the photograph give an impression of inactivity? What movement can you see?

Topics

The attractions of a seaside holiday to (a) adults (b) children.
The pleasures of owning a small boat.
Suggest ways in which people who live a long way from the sea can spend their holidays.
If you can't afford to spend a holiday elsewhere, suggest ways of enjoying one at home.

General guidance and practice

**1 Revision of
should and would**

Notice the principal uses:

(a) Reported speech (with certain exceptions *would* is common to all persons):

I told him I *would* come at once.

(b) Conditions: in the result clause of Conditions 2 and 3. *would* is sometimes used in first person forms, especially in a business letter:

If you left immediately, *you would (you'd) be* in time.

If you had (you'd) left immediately, *you would (you'd) have been* in time.

(c) Forms such as:

I should (I'd) be pleased to come.

We should (we'd) like to thank you.

(d) *should* as an alternative to 'ought to':

You *should* see a doctor. (advice/duty)

The weather *should* be better tomorrow. (probability)

(e) *would* as an alternative to *used to* (see page 72).

(f) *would* in a request:

Would you come at two o'clock, please.

Practice

Use a form of the verb in brackets incorporating *would* or *should* in each of the following sentences. Explain which of the above forms you are making use of.

(a) When I had a free day, I (explore) the surrounding countryside.
(b) If I were you, I (refuse) to carry out his orders.
(c) (Remove) please your shoes from the table.
(d) You (persevere) in your ambition: don't get discouraged.
(e) He said he did not know whether he (join) the association.
(f) The butter (melt) if it had been left near the stove any longer.
(g) People who live in glasshouses (not throw) stones.
(h) The film star received a letter saying that his son (kidnap) if he did not hand over five thousand pounds. (Passive Voice)
(i) The defeated general announced that his army (surrender).
(j) Many years ago countrywomen (spend) much of their time spinning thread and weaving cloth.
(k) (Have) you time to knit me a cardigan for next winter?
(l) That dog (not keep) outside in his kennel in such bitterly cold weather. (Passive Voice)
(m) He (work) all the afternoon if you had not disturbed him.

Notice: (a) The occasional use of the simple past of the verb 'will' followed by the infinitive in the 'if' clause when willingness is indicated. This resembles a conditional form but is not really one:

I *should* be pleased if you *would* help your friend with his pronunciation.

It *would* help me very much if you *would* all be punctual to meals.

(b) In a first condition, *should* can suggest even greater improbability:

If you *should* get lost, you can easily take a taxi.

Take out an insurance in case you *should* be ill.

Otherwise, *would* and *should* are used in result but not in condition clauses.

2 Revision of the use of articles

A noun used in an abstract sense is not accompanied by the definite article unless it is defined in some way:

We all admire *courage*.

The book describes *the courage* of a small group of explorers.

The courage that can endure uncomplainingly a long period of suffering is perhaps the noblest.

A noun which is abstract when used in one sense may be common and therefore accompanied by either a definite or indefinite article in some other sense. Examples are: *truth, power, light, youth, life, authority, character, virtue*.

Is *youth* the best part of life?

The youth was serving as a building apprentice.

He enjoys *life*.

He is interested in *the life* of Cromwell.

He has had *an exciting life*.

Nature has no definite article when the creative force is referred to.

Weather may be accompanied by *the* but not by *a*.

Space without an article refers to outer space and to space in general.

The space refers to the distance between two objects or times.

Gerunds have no article when they refer to the action done, provided they are not limited by a following phrase: '*The writing of books* . . .'. A gerund may be accompanied by an article or demonstrative adjective when referring to the product of the action:

I can't read *this writing*.

We admired *the painting*.

The singing sounded pleasant.

Remember that an uncountable noun (e.g. *bread, money, rain*) is not in normal circumstances preceded by the indefinite article.

Practice

Insert definite or indefinite articles where they are needed in the following sentences.

(a) _____ generosity of the old lady was appreciated by all who knew her.

(b) _____ pride goes before a fall.

(c) She has lived _____ life of self-sacrifice.

(d) _____ life is not always what one makes it.

(e) Mankind is now exploring _____ space.

(f) Why not fill _____ space between the two houses with a garage?

(g) _____ riding is a popular form of exercise.

(h) He rebels against _____ authority.

(i) He has been given _____ authority over the department.

(j) _____ local authority controls the public library.

(k) Do you believe that statesmen always tell _____ truth?

(l) I doubt _____ truth of his statement.

(m) Telling _____ truth is not always a comforting virtue.
(n) What _____ weather! I have never experienced such _____ chilly weather in August.
(o) _____ weather in England is very variable.
(p) He is interested in the study of _____ nature.
(q) _____ age often envies _____ youth.
(r) _____ youth touched his cap politely and offered his help with my bag.
(s) You have _____ power to set matters right.
(t) The development of _____ nuclear power is one of the major tasks of science today.
(u) Representatives of _____ great powers are meeting in Geneva.
(v) _____ power does not always corrupt.
(w) He had no high opinion of _____ singing of the opera but _____ acting was superb.
(x) _____ teaching should be a profession of a high standard.
(y) _____ teaching we had was not of a high standard.
(z) _____ drawing shows imagination and skill.

3 Uses of whose

Interrogative adjective

Whose umbrella is this?
Whose camera are you using?
I don't know *whose* gloves these are.

Interrogative pronoun

Whose is this?
Can you tell me *whose* this is?

Relative pronoun

Subject: We were talking to the woman *whose* husband was arrested yesterday.
Object: This is Mr. Atkins, *whose* book you reviewed last week.
May I introduce you to Mr. Lane, *whose* cousin you used to live with.
Where things are involved, either *whose* or *of which* may be employed:
This is a work of art *whose value* will be even more highly esteemed by future generations. (or: a work of art *the value of which* . . .)

Practice

Complete the following sentences using the word *whose*. A suggestion of the sense of the addition is given at the end of each incomplete sentence.

(a) This valuable sword must have been owned by some great leader. I wonder _____ (be).
(b) I have found some gloves. _____ (be)?
(c) Today's sermon was preached by a missionary, _____ (life; spend; Africa).
(d) At the funeral the chief mourner was the tragic father, _____ had killed. (son; the bandits).
(e) This is the famous ancient olive-tree, _____ (age; unknown).
(f) The film star, _____, has given an interview to the press. (new film; show; London).
(g) We shall have to select one of these three drawings: John's, Geoffrey's or Mildred's. _____? (choose)

(h)   The director of the company was obviously one of those men _____ (life; devoted to business).

4   Adverbs

(a)   The normal rule for forming an adverb is to add *-ly* to the adjective:
> *slow   slowly*
> *beautiful   beautifully*

When an adjective already ends in *-l*, this is doubled:
> *cruel   cruelly*

(b)   Spelling changes include the dropping of a final *-e* when the adjective ends in *-le*. The same change affects the adjective *true*:
> *true   truly   whole   wholly*
> *able   ably   regrettable   regrettably*

(c)   In certain cases *-y* changes to *-i* in polysyllables:
> *merry   merrily*

and also in monosyllables ending in *-ay*:
> *gay   gaily* (or *gayly*)

most monosyllables, however, retain the *-y*:
> *dryly, slyly, shyly, coyly*

(d)   Certain adjectives ending in *-ic* add an *-al* before the *-ly*:
> *pathetic   pathetically*
> *characteristic   characteristically.*

Notice: *accident* (noun), *accidental* (adjective), *accidentally* (adverb).

(e)   Adverbs cannot be formed in the normal way from adjectives ending in *-ly*. An adverbial phrase must be used:
> *friendly   in a friendly way*
> *lively   in a lively manner*

A similar difficulty applies to certain Past Participles including *tired, bored, frightened, annoyed, worried, offended*:
> He spoke sharply, *as if he were annoyed.*
> He turned his back on me, *as though offended.*

There is no adverb from *difficult; with difficulty* is the usual adverbial phrase.

(f)   Some adjectives do not change. These include: *hourly, weekly, monthly, yearly, fast, hard.* Cf. *He works hard* with *He hardly works.*

Other adverbial phrases are: *every minute, every day* (cf. the adjective *everyday*), *once a century*, etc.

(g)   Remember the well-known change: *good   well.*

(h)   Some adjectives change in meaning when transformed into adverbs. These include:

present	*presently*	*direct* (Adj & Adv)	*directly*
scarce	*scarcely*	*hard* (Adj & Adv)	*hardly*
bare	*barely*	*high* (Adj & Adv)	*highly*
mere	*merely*	*short* (Adj & Adv)	*shortly*
large	*largely*	*near* (Adj & Adv)	*nearly*

(i)   *Notice also the adverbs: exceedingly, extremely, immensely,* meaning 'very' in a strong sense, and the two adjective forms *lowly* and *kindly.*

Practice

Complete the following sentences, using an adverbial form of each of the adjectives in brackets.

(a)   He works (hard).
(b)   He was (eager) waiting his turn to answer.
(c)   She greeted me (friendly).
(d)   Dustmen often empty dustbins (noisy).
(e)   She paints (good).
(f)   He climbed the steps (difficult).
(g)   He is paid (weekly).
(h)   He is (whole) sincere.
(i)   He yawned (bored).
(j)   I dropped it (accidental).
(k)   We were entertained (royal).
(l)   She spoke (sympathetic).
(m)   She smiled (coy).
(n)   He commented (dry) on the speech.
(o)   He has promised to come (present). He won't be long.
(p)   I (mere) asked a question.
(q)   They giggled (silly).
(r)   I shall have finished (short).
(s)   Can I go from Waterloo to Southampton (direct)?
(t)   He'll be back (direct).

5   For, since, during, in

These are all prepositions when used in time phrases. *Since* can also be a conjunction with a time meaning.
For is used to indicate a length of time which passed, has passed, is passing or will pass:

> He had travelled *for twenty-four hours*, and he stayed there *for twenty minutes.*
> I have already been in England *for three months.*
> I am staying in England *for three years*; then I shall go to France.
> The acrobats will perform *for a quarter of an hour.*

Since as a preposition also indicates a period of time, but the moment when the period began is indicated. It is normally used only with perfect tenses, and rarely in the future. If the group of words introduced by the conjunction *since* is a subordinate clause, the Past Simple tense may follow, though a Perfect Tense will appear in the main clause.

> The rain had never stopped *since the time they had arrived* at the holiday resort.
> That pipe has been leaking *ever since the plumber installed* a new tank.

During never indicates length of time. You cannot say *I am here during six months.* (Nor can you say *I am here since six months.*)
During indicates 'in the course of', 'within a certain space of time':

> *during the interval, during his childhood, during the epidemic.*
> You must not talk *during his lecture.*
> The barrister has dealt with many unusual cases *during his long career.*

In as a preposition indicating time can be used with three different meanings:

(a)   Before the end of, in the space of:

> If I run, I can get to the station *in five minutes.*

(b)　At the end of:

>　The skirt will be ready for you *in a fortnight*.
>　I shall start work *in a month (in a month's time)*.

(c)　To indicate the year, season, month, period of the day in which something happens:

>　*in 1215, in summer, in March, in the afternoon*.

For and *since* may also be used as conjunctions with other meanings:

For is a co-ordinating conjunction: that is to say, it can link two clauses of equal importance. When used in this way, it can never begin a sentence:

>　He knows no one in the town, *for* he has only recently settled down here.

Since, a subordinating conjunction, has much the same meaning. It may begin a sentence:

>　*Since* you know so much, perhaps you can tell me why you made such a simple mistake.

Practice

Insert *for, since, during,* or *in* where appropriate in the following sentences.

(a)　She must have been wearing that hat _____ Noah came out of the ark.

(b)　_____ the Great Plague of London _____ 1665, hundreds of people were dying every day.

(c)　I wanted the photographs developed _____ not more than five hours.

(d)　_____ he had no ladder, the workman could not erect the television aerial.

(e)　The strikers have agreed to discuss their grievance with the employers _____ two days' time.

(f)　Nobody knows what became of him _____ he never came back.

(g)　The guarantee lasts _____ one year.

(h)　He has been looking poorly ever _____ his serious illness.

(i)　Many great discoveries were made _____ the reign of Queen Elizabeth I.

(j)　_____ you refuse to give me further particulars, I regret that I cannot help you.

(k)　Having dozed _____ half an hour, he was ready to concentrate _____ the next four hours.

(l)　_____ he was released from prison, he has managed to keep out of further trouble.

6　Adverbial expressions with at, on, in

at

at the beginning	at school	at present
at the end	at church	at home
at the top	at eight o'clock	at sea
at the bottom	at night(fall)	at table (eating)
at the side	at dawn	
at the front of the class	at dusk	
at the back of the class	at Christmas	
at the weekend		

He arrived at the Airport.
Meet me at the far corner of the park.

in

in 1837	in time	in the street
in February	in the eleventh century	in the road
in winter	in front (of)	in a car
in the morning	the fish in the sea	in an armchair
in the afternoon	in the sky	in a deck chair
in the evening	in the middle (of)	in my hand
in daylight	in the midst (of)	in prison
in darkness	in the North	in the open air
in the past	in Japan	in a loud voice
in the future	in Surrey	

The bookcase stands in the corner.
He arrived in London.
She has a ribbon in her hair.

on

on Tuesday	on the blackboard
on the 1st April	on the ceiling
on his birthday	on top of the wardrobe
on the wall	on both sides
on a chair	on a horse
on a bicycle	on foot
a hat on his head	on the radio
shoes on his feet	on television
the shop on the corner	a smile on his face

In some of the above examples other prepositions may be used according to meaning. One leans *against* a wall for example.

Practice

Where necessary, replace the blanks in the following sentences with a suitable preposition.

(a) The child has a balloon _____ his hand.

(b) There is a big cobweb _____ the corner of the attic.

(c) She has an emerald ring _____ her third finger.

(d) The liner arrived _____ Liverpool _____ six o'clock _____ the morning.

(e) The beautiful mermaid _____ long golden hair and _____ a silver comb _____ her hand was sitting _____ a rock _____ the sea, singing happily _____ a clear voice.

(f) The distinguished visitors were sitting _____ chairs _____ a platform _____ one end of the hall. There was a loudspeaker _____ the wall _____ the back of the hall.

(g) The unhappy recruit, with boots that were too big for him _____ his feet and a hat that was too small for him _____ his head, was _____ his knees _____ the floor, a scrubbing brush _____ his hand, and a bucket _____ front of him, trying to remove the oil and grease from the surface.

(h) For your homework do the exercise _____ the top of page three, and give it in to me _____ Wednesday.

(i) He arrived _____ home _____ half past two _____ the afternoon and left _____ home _____ a quarter to twelve _____ night.

7 Revision of prepositions

Insert suitable prepositions in the following sentences.

(a) The prisoner of war escaped _____ the fortress.

(b) The class treated the teacher's suggestion of extra homework _____ silent contempt.

(c) She kept fidgeting _____ her watch strap and appeared to be in a highly nervous state.

(d) He was crouching on a bench in the corner aware only _____ his misery and failure.

(e) One _____ one the Members of Parliament filed into the lobbies.

(f) Many foreigners in England have considerable difficulty _____ making themselves understood.

(g) Aren't you ashamed _____ your selfish behaviour?

(h) The millionaire had a passion _____ orchids.

(i) At Christmas English homes are often decorated _____ holly, mistletoe and paper chains.

(j) We must get rid _____ that elm tree: it is damaging the foundations of the house.

(k) The clergyman reproached the youth _____ his thoughtlessness towards his parents.

(l) Some people laugh _____ the creations of many modern sculptors.

(m) A child's life is usually made up _____ many small but absorbing experiences.

(n) He gave me a gold sovereign _____ a present.

(o) Science is still largely ignorant _____ the causes of many kinds of cancer.

(p) The puppy was playing _____ a slipper.

(q) Most boys are keen _____ football.

(r) The majority of the club's supporters were doubtful _____ the team's chances in the coming match.

(s) The clown was so comical that even the circus attendants burst _____ laughing.

(t) The boy had been up to mischief again and again and at last he was sent to bed _____ disgrace.

(u) Are you really impressed _____ the nonsense he talks?

(v) The lorry was travelling _____ a considerable speed when the accident happened.

(w) The Government has embarked _____ a new economy scheme.

(x) He bowed low to the aged leader _____ a sign of respect.

11 Related Talents

I had a curious collection of aunts. They all lived locally and each expected me to visit her at least once a fortnight. I therefore had a frequent opportunity of comparing their individual eccentricities.

Aunt Helen was married to a clergyman, the vicar of a nearby parish. A
5 conscientious but reserved man, the latter preferred the peace of his library to parish affairs and concerned himself mainly with church duties. It was Aunt Helen who ran the parish. With incredible efficiency, she organised charity bazaars and subscriptions, rebuked the erring, bullied committees and entertained a daily gathering of helpers, voluntary and conscripted, to
10 tea, cake and instructions. It was she who gave me a bicycle for a Christmas present: I was in this way better equipped for her numerous errands. She was an admirable woman, whom I take the greatest pains not to resemble.

Aunt Beatrice, her junior, had divorced her thoroughly unsatisfactory
15 husband several years previously. She opened a snack bar in an area of small workshops; she gave good value, and soon had to extend her premises and employ extra staff. Within two years she could afford to put a manager in charge and give all her time to the care of her four children. She prepared meals substantial enough for a Sahara-bound camel and
20 made me eat up every morsel. She was a shrewd judge of character who expressed her opinions bluntly and frankly, sparing no one's feelings. Nevertheless she was well-liked, and got on well with everybody, largely on account of her honesty, courage and warm-hearted generosity.

Widowed Aunt Dorothy lived alone. Having a comfortable income and
25 no children, she had no need to work. Plump, plain and gifted with a vivid imagination, she devoted most of her time to gossip. Her keen eye missed nothing and she specialised in discovering other people's secrets. She would make some carefully-chosen but apparently innocent remark and then watch the effect it had on each of her companions. She noticed a great
30 deal and skilfully guessed many things she could not actually discover. As a result she treated her close friends to some sensational items of information which only later became generally known. Aunt Dorothy could have been a first-class novelist or adviser to women's magazine readers — as a smalltown housewife, she was certainly wasting her unusual abilities.

35 But it was the shy spinster, Aunt Margaret, who provided the really staggering sensation. For years she had nursed her aged and invalid father, who had died when she was fifty. Faded, inconspicuous, dowdy, she had bought a bungalow, adopted four cats and a parrot, and apparently restricted her ambitions to growing chrysanthemums. It was a year after
40 her father's death that the extraordinary secret of her double life leaked out. For the past ten years she had been supplementing her income by the creation of fiction under a pen name. No fragrant romances or even cosy domestic detective mysteries. Tough Dan O'Ryan, whose heroes had square jaws, handy revolvers and straight punches (together with
45 humorous blue eyes), was in real life a single lady dealing with nothing fiercer than four fluffy tabby cats and a parrot whose knowledge of American slang had always bewildered us.

Notes on the passage

Title   *related*   This is an example of a *pun* as the word has two meanings here: the four aunts were relations, and their talents were related (they had some things in common).

1   *curious* has two meanings (a) strange (b) inquisitive, interested in finding out more about things and people. The word can have both meanings in this example: *Cats are curious animals.*
curiosity (Unc): *Curiosity may lead to interesting discoveries.* (C): *He has collected many curiosities, including ancient masks, during his explorations of unknown regions.*

2   *a fortnight*   never **fifteen days.*

2   *an opportunity* = an occasion or chance that one is able to make use of.
a possibility = something that may happen. Note: *possibility* rarely follows the verb 'have', unlike *opportunity: There is a possibility that before the end of the century there will be regular flights to the moon but few people will have the opportunity of going.*
Which? (a) There was no _____ of food supplies running out. (b) He has had no _____ of reading your novel. (c) He seized the _____ of having a short rest. (d) He was worried by the _____ that there might be alcohol in his drink. (e) _____ knocks only once. (f) There are plenty of _____ to gain promotion in this job. (g) Bear in mind the _____ of unexpected illness. (h) Make the most of your _____ (Plural).

3   *eccentricities* (Adj *eccentric*) describes behaviour that is unconventional and a little strange.
An eccentric is a person of odd behaviour.

4   *A vicar* is a clergyman of the Church of England. *A priest* is more usually attached to a Roman Catholic or Greek Orthodox church. In the case of a Nonconformist church, the word *minister* is often used. These are Church of England clergymen, arranged in order of importance: *archbishop, bishop, vicar, curate. A dean* is the clergyman in charge of a cathedral. *A churchwarden* is a layman (not a clergyman) who shares responsibility for church business matters. *A verger* keeps the church tidy and in good order. *The organist* plays the organ and as *choirmaster* he trains the church *choir. A parish* is a division of a county, with its own church and vicar. A *diocese* is controlled by a bishop.

4   *nearby* (Adj): *a nearby house;* (Adv): *He lives nearby.*

5   *prefer* means 'like better than something else'. Do not use it for 'like': *I prefer cats to dogs. I like cats better than dogs.*

5   *a library* = a place in which books are read and from which they are borrowed.
a bookshop = a shop from which books can be bought.

6   *concern* has several meanings. (a) anxiety: *There is some concern about his health. They are concerned about his safety.*
(b) something of interest to or having to do with a person: *That is no concern of yours. This letter concerns you. He is concerned in the discussions.*
(c) a firm: *He has shares in a building concern.*
(d) take an interest in: *As Mary's legal guardian, he has always concerned himself in her welfare.*

8   *charity* (Unc) = giving to those in need. *A charity* (C) = an organisation doing this.

8   *erring*   *to err* is to do something wrong or to make a mistake. *errors* = mistakes: *an error of judgment.*
a fault = a bad point in a person's character or in the construction of something. Notice the common accusation: *It's (all) your fault.*
an errand = a short journey made for shopping, taking a message, etc.

9   *voluntary and conscripted*   *A conscript* is a soldier doing his compulsory military service.

Notice these apparent but not true opposites: *voluntary service; an involuntary start* at a sudden noise.

different people; *indifferent* to criticism (taking no notice of).

valuable pictures; (opp. *valueless*) *invaluable* advice (very valuable)

famous writers; *infamous* criminals.

sensible ideas (opp. *senseless*); lying *insensible* (unconscious).

interested in an idea (opp. *uninterested*); a *disinterested* observer (neutral, not taking sides).

12 *take pains* = take trouble: *take pains with one's work.* If one is hurt, one *feels pain;* a wound can be *painful* (opp. *painless*)

16 Cf. He did *valuable* work for the hospital. He bought an *expensive* car.

18 *charge* has several meanings.
Noun: (a) amount to be paid: *They make an extra charge for delivering goods.*
(b) a criminal accusation: *He was arrested on a murder charge.*
(c) violent forward movement: see Verb.
(d) amount of explosive material or electricity.
Verb: (a) ask a price: *We charge an extra pound for delivery.*
(b) accuse of a crime: *The police charged him with murder.*
(c) move forward violently: *An angry crowd charged through the streets.*
(d) provide equipment with explosive material or electricity: *recharge a battery.*
in charge of = responsible for: *in charge of children/an office.*
take charge of = take/accept responsiblity for: *He took charge of the luggage.*

19 *bound for* = on its way to: *The ship is bound for India. homeward bound* = on one's way home.
The pages of a book are *bound (bind, bound, bound)* in a cover or *binding.*

20 *morsel* = fragment, small piece.

20 *shrewd* = having a keen judgment of people and business matters.
cunning and *crafty* both suggest an unpleasant, calculating and possibly dishonest cleverness: *a cunning fox; a crafty dealer* who tries to cheat customers.

21 *sparing no one's feelings* = speaking plainly even if it hurts the person addressed.

26 *devoted herself to* = gave all her time to. Cf. *a devoted mother* who loves and gives all her time to her family. *a devoted couple.*

31 *treat* and *treatment* have various meanings.
treat (Noun) = a special pleasant experience: *a birthday treat; What a treat to see the sun today!*
treat (Verb) = (a) behave towards someone or something with a certain effect: *An animal-lover treats animals with kindness; well-treated, badly-treated, ill-treated.*
(b) pay for another person's food, drink or entertainment: *As it's your birthday I'll treat you to the cinema.*
(c) deal with a subject, matter, question: *He has treated the subject of his book in an unusual way.*
a treaty = an agreement between countries. *treatment:* medical treatment by a doctor; good or bad treatment by parents or an employer.

33 *a novelist* writes *novels* which are long stories. *Non-fiction* is writing about true facts; *fiction* is largely based on the imagination. A novel is written in *prose,* not *poetry* (a *poem*).

34 *ability* is more often used than *capability: He has the ability to do better.*
Cf. *able to:* After many weeks' teaching, he is now *able to* swim.
And *capable of:* It is so hot, I really don't feel *capable of* walking far.

35 *spinster* = the official title of an unmarried woman, who is usually referred to as a *single woman.* The colloquial term *old maid* suggests that she is plain, narrow-minded, strictly conventional and prim.

36 *invalid* = any sick person who is ill for some time (not a *disabled* soldier).

37 *dowdy* = wearing uninteresting, old-fashioned clothes. *shabby* = wearing clothes that are no longer in a good condition. *smart* could be the opposite to both these words. Notice also *fashionable.*

40 *a leak* = a hole through which a liquid can escape: *The kettle has a leak/is leaking.* Secret information also can *leak out.*

41 *supplement* (V) = add to. Some newspapers have extra sections called *colour supplements.*

42 *A pen name* is another name used by an author. *A stage-name* is used by an actor. A *nickname* is a playful or shortened name given to someone. A *pet name* is given to show special affection, often to small children. A criminal may have *an alias.*

43 *tough* means hard to break or cut: meat may be tough (opp. *tender*). It may also describe a person who can face hardship, pain or danger.

43 A *hero* or a *heroine* is *heroic* and shows *heroism*. A *villain* is the bad character in a book or play. He may not look *villainous* though his *villainy* may soon become clear.

44 Adjectives of shape: *square, oblong/rectangular, round/circular, triangular, oval.*

44 *punch* with a fist; *slap* with the palm of the hand; *kick* with the foot; *poke* with the finger; *scratch* with the nails; *nudge* with the elbow; *shrug* one's shoulders.

45 *deal with* something that has to be done; *cope with* difficulties and problems.

Phrasal verbs

get

The following are among the most common of the many uses of this verb.

get at something normally out of reach.
get away = escape.
get away with = do something without getting the expected punishment.
get back (a) something lent (b) to a point one started a journey from.
get down from a high place.
get hold of = grasp or obtain something.
get into/out of a car, a bus, a train, an aeroplane.
get on/off a bus, a bicycle.
get into trouble by doing something that incurs punishment or unpleasantness of
    some kind.
get up to mischief = do the small naughty things that a child might do.
get on = make progress.
get on with (a) one's work (continue doing it) (b) other people (be on friendly
    terms with them).
get out of a room through a window.
get out of doing some unpleasant duty (avoid doing it).
get over an illness or sorrow (recover).
get ready for = prepare for.
get through a lot of work or pass an examination.
get to = arrive in/at, reach.
get up to a certain point in a book or in learning.
get one's own way = do what one wants in spite of opposition.

Practice

Complete each phrase or sentence using one of the above phrasal verbs.

(a) _____ a purse from a handbag.
(b) He has never _____ the loss of his wife.
(c) The cat could not _____ from the roof.
(d) He always expects to _____ as he is thoroughly spoilt.
(e) _____ apples high on a tree.
(f) _____ a destination.
(g) _____ money owed.
(h) _____ well and hope for promotion.
(i) _____ the end of Chapter 2.
(j) The pilot _____ the aeroplane and then _____ again.
(k) _____ for being late for work.
(l) Our puppy chews slippers and _____ in similar ways.

(m) How are you _____?

(n) _____ for a holiday.

(o) _____ all his homework in an hour.

(p) Somehow the policeman _____ the man's gun.

(q) He always _____ helping with the washing-up.

(r) _____ home after midnight.

(s) He has _____ cheating so far but he will be found out soon.

(t) We were locked in and could not _____.

(u) _____ the wrong bus and then _____ again.

(v) He does not _____ his stepfather.

Pronunciation

These need care: clergyman /klɔ́:dʒɪmən/; efficiency /ɪfíʃənsi/; bazaar /bəzá:/; bullied /bʊ́lɪd/; Sahara /səhá:rə/; chrysanthemum /krɪzǽnθɪməm/; extraordinary /ɪkstrɔ́:dənəri/; wild /waɪld/; bewildered /bɪwɪ́ldəd/.

Stress and sound changes: eccentric /ɪkséntrɪk/; eccentricity /eksentrísɪti/; compare /kəmpéə/; comparative /kəmpǽrətɪv/; conscience /kɒ́nʃəns/; conscientious /kɒnʃiénʃəs/; prefer /prɪfɔ́:/; preferable /préf(ə)rəbl/; preference /préf(ə)rəns/; admire /ædmáɪə/; admirable /ǽdmərəbl/; admiration /ædməréɪʃən/; courage /kʌ́rɪdʒ/; courageous /kəréɪdʒəs/.

ju and juː (as in *u*se): curious /kjʊ́(ə)rɪəs/; rebuke /rɪbjúːk/; numerous /njúːmərəs/; inconspicuous /ɪnkənspíkjʊəs/.

dʒu and dʒuː (as in *jui*ce): indivi*d*ual /ɪndɪvíˈdʒʊəl/; *du*ties /djúːtɪz/; *ju*nior /dʒúːnɪə/.

ə (as in *a*go): lo*ca*lly /lɔ́ʊkəli/; freque*n*t (Adj) /fríːkwənt/; vi*ca*r /víkə/; libr*a*ry /láɪbrəri/; committee /kəmíti/; volu*n*t*a*ry /vɒ́ləntəri/; *su*bstantial /səbstǽnʃəl/; morsel /mɔ́:səl/; charac*te*r /kǽrɪktə/; *o*pinio*n* /əpínjən/; passionately /pǽʃənətli/; inn*o*cent /ínəsənt /; invalid (N) /ínvəlɪd/; inc*o*nspicu*ous* /ɪnkənspíkjʊəs/; parr*o*t /pǽrət/; fragra*n*t /fréɪɡrənt/.

ɪ (as in *ci*ty): *re*tiring /rɪtáɪərɪŋ/; *e*quipped /ɪkwípt/; *re*semble /rɪzémbl/; knowl*e*dge /nɒ́lɪdʒ/; secr*et* /síːkrɪt/.

Others: shrewd /ʃruːd/; analysed /ǽnəlaɪzd/; reactions /rɪǽkʃənz/; romance /rɔ́ʊmæns/; tough /tʌf/; square /skweə/.

Names: Helen /hélɪn/; Beatrice /bíətrɪs/; Dorothy /dɒ́rəθi/; Margaret /má:ɡ(ə)rɪt/.

Grammatical and structural points

therefore and *then*, being adverbs, cannot join word groups:

He is a lawyer *and therefore* he should have a good income.

He finished the letter and signed it, *and then* slipped it into an envelope.

Prepositions

(a) concerned *with* travel arrangements; gifted *with* musical ability.

(b) equipped *for* a long journey.

(c) specialise *in* eighteenth-century literature.

(d) adviser *to* school-leavers; benefits restricted *to* staff members.

(e) Notice: resemble a relative (no preposition).

(f)   *on account of* his illness.

(g)   all his possessions *together with* his friend's dog.

Expressions for use in written work

(a)   My relations all live *locally*.

(b)   He organised everything *with incredible efficiency*.

(c)   She *gives all her time to* her children.

(d)   The magistrate was *a shrewd judge of character*.

(e)   She *expressed her opinions frankly*.

(f)   He *spared no one's feelings* in his criticisms.

(g)   He *got on well with* everybody.

(h)   He was *wasting his ability (his talents)* in this job.

(i)   The secret of his engagement *leaked out*.

(j)   *a good command of* a language.

Spoken English

In a restaurant

Head Waiter   Good afternoon, madam. Would you like to sit here? I'm afraid there are no other places free at the moment.

Margaret   I'd prefer to sit alone but I suppose this will do. Have you a menu, please?

HW   Certainly. One of the waiters will bring it at once.

(A waiter brings a menu and waits while Margaret reads it.)

Margaret   I'll have the fixed menu at £5. Does that include wine?

Waiter   No, madam. Wine is separate.

Margaret   I'll have the clear soup, please, followed by roast pork, apple sauce, mashed potatoes and brussels sprouts.

Waiter   I'm sorry, madam. The pork's off now. There's only the steak pie still available.

Margaret   Anything cold?

Waiter   Yes, madam. There's cold chicken and salad and also ham and tongue with salad.

Margaret   I'll have the chicken. And I'd be most grateful if you'd serve me as quickly as possible as I've got an appointment at two-fifteen.

Waiter   I'll do my best, madam. What would you like to drink with it?

Margaret   Oh, a small beer — some kind of lager will do. I shan't have time for dessert but perhaps you could bring a black coffee before I finish the main course.

In a bookshop

Shopkeeper   Can I help you in any way?

Customer   Well, I'm trying to find two Christmas presents, both books, one for an elderly aunt and one for my young nephew.

Shopkeeper   Could you give me any idea of their tastes in books?

Customer   One of the books could be a crime story, possibly something by Craig Bronx or Rock Cannon. There's a collection of short stories by Bronx that has just come out, I understand, 'Boomerang Bullets'.

Shopkeeper   We haven't got that in stock at the moment, but we could order it for you. Do you know the name of the publisher?

Customer   It's a Thriller Society special — a paperback. How long is it likely to take to come in?

Shopkeeper	About a week.
Customer	All right. Now the other. Crime wouldn't be approved of, oh no. Perhaps something on wild life or antique furniture. A collection of eighteenth-century essays or I see you've got Henry James's 'Golden Bowl' but that's probably been read before. 'Memoirs of an Ambassador', or no, I'm sure this new edition of 'The Climber's Manual' will be most warmly welcomed.
Shopkeeper	But surely your aunt doesn't go climbing, madam?
Customer	My aunt? No, of course not. The crime book's for her.

Daydreams

If I'd had the chance, I'd have been a research chemist who'd have made some great discovery that would have changed the world.

If I'd had the sense to train as a doctor instead of becoming a research chemist, I'd have been able to do something worthwhile and satisfying.

If I had a beautiful figure, I'd be a highly-paid model and perhaps also find a rich husband.

If I hadn't got a husband and family, I'd train as a secretary and get an exciting job abroad.

If I had time, I'd write that novel I've had at the back of my mind for so long.

If I had a car, I'd tour Europe, stopping at all the small interesting places that nobody else has time for.

If I had a long enough holiday, I'd save up for a couple of years and travel round the world.

If I had a house of my own, I'd give up my job as stewardess on a liner and work as a waitress, just to be in one place.

If I weren't so stupid, I'd think of something wonderful that I really could do, though I'm poor, plain, always busy and living in a tenth-floor flat in a suburb of Birmingham.

Reading comprehension

Choice of words

In this exercise you must choose the word or phrase which best completes each sentence.

1 You are _____ me as if I were a criminal.
   A regarding   **B** treating   **C** using   **D** considering

2 Your annual _____ to the Social Club is now due.
   A charge   **B** contribution   **C** subscription
   D payment

3 The invention of the train enabled many more people to travel _____.
   A independently   **B** freely   **C** readily   **D** free

4 His compass and maps proved _____ to him in his walking tours.
   A valuable   **B** worth   **C** profitable   **D** valueless

5   As one of the four _____ of the company he often had to attend important policy meetings.
    A   directors   **B**   bosses   **C**   controllers   **D**   governors

6   A strong westerly _____ flattened the corn though it brought no rain.
    A   gale   **B**   current   **C**   breeze   **D**   storm

7   He does not _____ his fellow-workers and there are often disagreements between them.
    A   get on with   **B**   take to   **C**   put up with
    D   go on with

8   He has impressed his employers considerably and _____ he is soon to be promoted.
    A   nevertheless   **B**   accordingly   **C**   however   **D**   yet

9   During the _____ the audience strolled and chatted in the foyer.
    A   gap   **B**   pause   **C**   break   **D**   interval

10 Groups of tourists visit the national park to see the many _____ animals there.
    A   fierce   **B**   wild   **C**   untamed   **D**   savage

Multiple choice responses

Here are a number of questions or unfinished statements about the reading passage on page 247, each with four suggested answers or endings. Choose the one you think fits best in each case.

1   It is clear from the passage that Aunt Helen's husband was
    A   elderly.
    B   strict.
    C   nervous.
    D   unsociable.

2   Why did the writer visit the four ladies so often?
    A   She was interested in observing their contrasting personalities.
    B   They lived very near her.
    C   They were her closest relatives.
    D   They considered she ought to see them at regular intervals.

3   Aunt Helen gave the writer a bicycle so that she could
    A   do Aunt Helen's shopping.
    B   do a lot of local jobs for her aunt.
    C   visit her aunt regularly.
    D   carry things about for her aunt.

4   One of Aunt Dorothy's methods of gathering information was to
    A   ask questions.
    B   collect the information from close friends.
    C   observe people's behaviour in certain situations.
    D   listen to other people's gossip.

5   Which of the following could have provided a clue to Aunt Margaret's double life?
    A   Her pen name.
    B   Her parrot.
    C   Her additional income.
    D   Her secretive life.

Composition

Write on any of the following subjects, using between 120 and 180 words.

1 You suddenly realise you have forgotten to send birthday greetings to a close friend living at some distance from you. Write a short letter apologising for and explaining your forgetfulness, giving one item of news and promising to write in more detail in a few days' time. You should make the beginning and ending like those of an ordinary English letter but do not include these in the number of words.

2 The following advertisement appears in a newspaper: 'Beautifully-furnished modern flat to let. Lounge, two large bedrooms, kitchen, bathroom. Central heating. Hot and cold water. Excellent decorative condition. Garage. £95 a week. Telephone 91/827364.' You telephone for further details. Write down the telephone conversation.

3 Explain why a certain district of your country or a certain town attracts tourists and holidaymakers.

4 Explain why you would be contented or bored if you lived in the country.

5 Describe the main shopping street of your town on a very hot day and then on a very windy day.

6 Write the list of instructions which might appear in a room in which you normally work or in a classroom, explaining what should be done if fire breaks out.

7 Give advice to someone who is going to do one of the following things:
   (a)   go walking and possibly climbing in mountains
   (b)   buy a second-hand car
   (c)   go on a camping holiday
   (d)   start learning a foreign language.

8 Describe the room in which you are now sitting.

9 You recently had a meal in a restaurant and came out thoroughly dissatisfied. Write an account of what happened.

10 Describe one of the following people, including his or her appearance, interests and behaviour: a very active and sociable person *or* a shy and sensitive person *or* a very lazy and untidy person.

11 Write two letters, each of about 100 words in length. One is from yourself to a readers' adviser of the magazine 'Challenge' in which you ask for advice about going to England to study against your parents' wishes. The other is the reply you receive. Invent names where necessary.

12 Fred was a quiet middle-aged man who lived alone, worked in the local bank and spent his spare time reading or gardening. One day two thieves with guns came to his house and Fred behaved in a quite unexpected way. Tell the story of what happened.

Use of English

1　**Finish each of the following sentences in such a way that it means the same as the sentence before it.**

1　He might not have heard the news.
　It's possible _____

2　'I think it would be a good idea if you saw your solicitor,' he told me.
　He suggested _____

3　He started his training as a long-distance runner three years ago.
　He has _____

4　Could you send me the information as soon as possible?
　I should be _____

5　You won't find such beautiful beaches anywhere else in the world.
　Nowhere _____

6　It was not necessary for you to make quite so many mistakes.
　You _____

2　**Complete each of the following sentences with one of the five words or phrases.**

1　When he heard the bad news, he broke _____ completely.
　A away　**B** in　**C** down　**D** up　**E** out

2　Their walking-tour through Lapland never came _____.
　A on　**B** off　**C** out　**D** round　**E** in

3　He has always gone _____ strange hobbies like collecting bottle-tops and inventing secret codes.
　A into　**B** by　**C** in for　**D** through　**E** for

4　The branch unexpectedly gave _____ and the surprised cat found herself suddenly on the ground.
　A way　**B** in　**C** away　**D** back　**E** up

5　He criticised everything and everybody and even ran _____ his few friends.
　A against　**B** into　**C** down　**D** over
　E away from

6　I cannot understand how you _____ these depressing surroundings.
　A put up with　**B** get on with　**C** make do with
　D get into touch with　**E** carry on with

7　My eldest brother intends to take _____ skating next winter.
　A to　**B** in　**C** away　**D** on　**E** up

8　Can you possibly make _____ what he has written here?
　A for　**B** up　**C** out　**D** up for　**E** do with

3　**Complete each of the sentences below with one of the following conjunctions:**

　　　since, although, in case, even if, while, provided that, unless, as soon as

1　Tom often rides without a light _____ this is not allowed.

2 You can borrow my tape-recorder _____ you return it to me to-morrow.
3 _____ he saw me, he shouted that I had cheated him.
4 This room will never be painted _____ we do it ourselves.
5 He will make little progress in his studies _____ he has little knowledge of the language.
6 _____ I had taken a taxi, I should still have missed the train.
7 He has taken out some insurance _____ he should be taken ill and be unable to work.

4 **Complete each of the following sentences with an appropriate form of the verbs *say, speak, talk* or *tell*.**

1 During the past three years, he has _____ his own language very rarely.
2 Early poems and stories were only _____ as there was no written language.
3 Have you _____ the class where to meet you?
4 He seldom _____ but when he does, he _____ sense.
5 He _____ so softly that we could not hear what he _____.
6 'Be especially careful not to lose your passport,' the guide _____ me.
7 She _____ that she cannot _____ the difference between the twins.
8 He always _____ what he thinks about other people.
9 His suggestion of giving up his job is only _____; he will never do it.
10 Although I _____ to him in a friendly way, he did not answer.
11 They are _____ to have spent many years in Alaska.

5 **Write out the following in dialogue form, making all necessary changes. Begin like this:**
Doctor What's your name and address?
Me I'm Richard Foster and I'm staying just now at the Palmera Hotel.

The doctor asked me my name and address. I told him I was Richard Foster and was staying just then at the Palmera Hotel. I was a sales representative and had arrived two days before. He asked me what the trouble was and I explained that that day and the previous one I had had a violent headache. The tablets I had taken had made no difference. In reply to his question, I said that I very rarely had headaches. He asked me whether I was accustomed to the very hot and humid weather and brilliant sunshine. I told him that this was my first experience of the tropics. When he wanted to know how long I would be staying there, I answered that I would be leaving for England the following week. He told me to spend the next day in a darkened room, to wear sunglasses when I went out and to take some tablets which his assistant would give me. These would relieve the headache. If the headaches continued, I was to get in touch with him again. I thanked him and said goodbye.

6　**A careers adviser at a university has been asked for help in finding a job by four arts graduates. Firms and other organisations often inform her about vacancies to be filled and she then recommends suitable and interested students. Four jobs are available at present.**

A　A suitable person to train as a reporter on a well-known local newspaper. Good promotion opportunities with possibility of later international assignments.

B　An assistant in the university library with excellent promotion possibilities after specialised training.

C　A junior assistant lecturer in literature in an overseas university.

D　A highly-paid secretary to a celebrated author, well-known for his bad temper.

The four students involved may be described as follows:

1　Luke Lock: of average academic ability. Engaged to be married. Has spent two vacations working in his father's office and has shorthand and typing skills. Placid and easy to get on with, lacking imagination but reliable and sensible.

2　Sue Saunders: clever and with wide interests. Very adaptable. Unmarried. Energetic, original, self-confident, ambitious though somewhat impatient and critical.

3　Jane Johnson: excellent examination results. Married but with no children. Extremely capable in research study: has concentration and an orderly mind. A reserved person of somewhat narrow interests.

4　Michael Miggs: capable rather than brilliant. Unmarried. Adaptable, sociable and interested in people and places. Expresses his ideas effectively.

Having considered the matter carefully, the careers adviser makes suitable recommendations in a four-paragraph report. Use about 50 words to complete each of the following paragraphs, expressing your own recommendations with reasons.

Paragraph openings
I can recommend as a journalist _____
I would suggest as a library assistant a certain _____
A suitable student for the junior assistant lectureship would be _____
The best qualified person for the secretarial post should be _____

Interview

Talking about a photograph

1　Do you think this man is a criminal? Suggest reasons for and against this idea.
2　Suggest why he is standing there.
3　Why does the picture appear sinister and even frightening?
4　What is the relationship between the picture and the story about the four aunts?

Topics

Why do some people enjoy reading detective stories?
What forms may crime in a large modern city take?
Suggest some reasons for the present-day increase in violence.

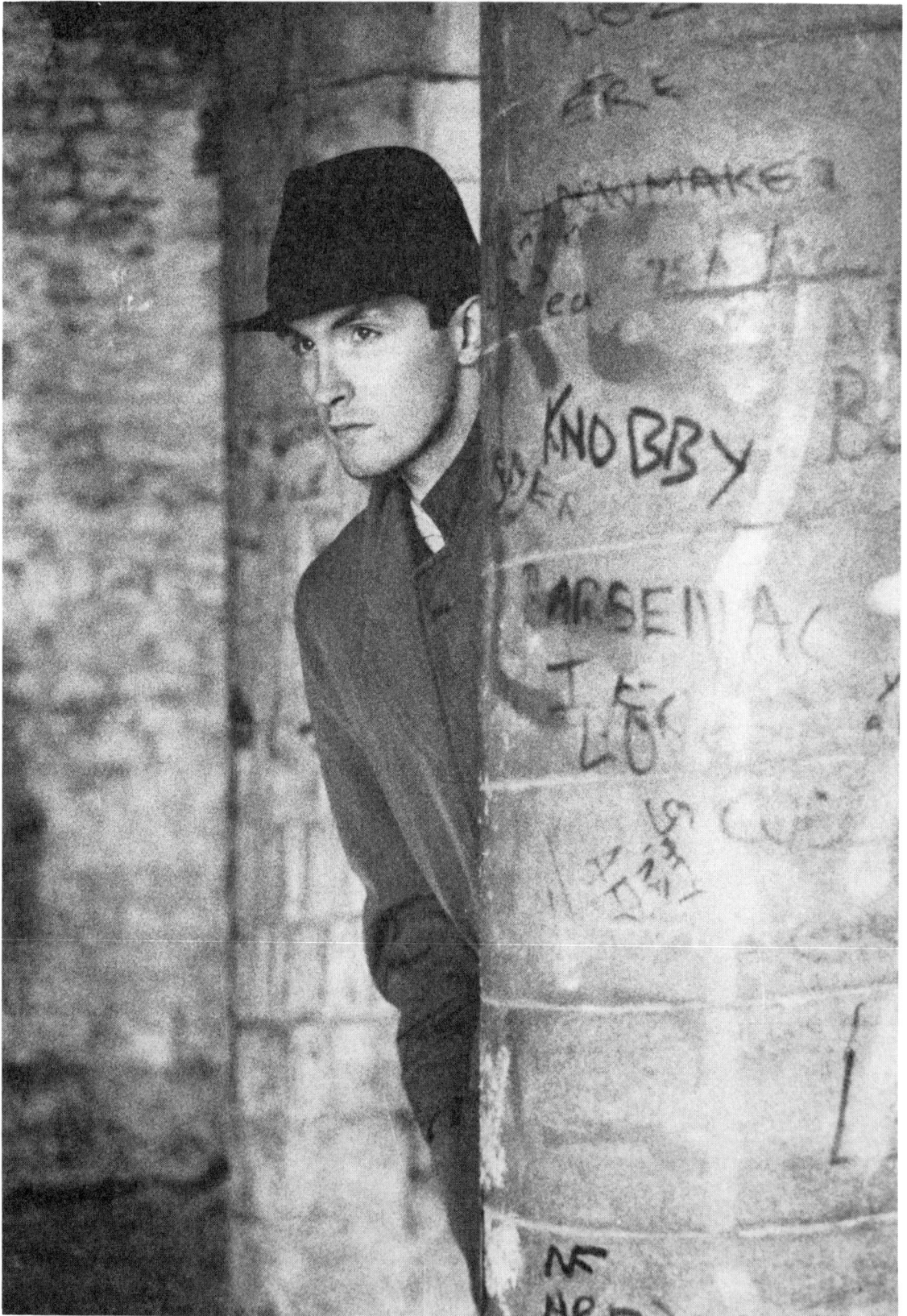

Reading aloud

General advice

Before reading aloud each of the following passages, look through it silently, giving careful attention to the following points:
1 Pronunciation: vowels, diphthongs and consonants
2 Weakenings: syllables and words
3 Word groupings and pauses: for meaning and effect. Notice where final consonants of words within a group will attach themselves to following vowels helping to ensure smooth continuous reading, separated only by pauses.
4 Intonation
5 Emphasis

Suggest a situation in which each of the passages might be heard.

Passages

1 I'd like you to take these things to the post office first. There are two parcels to be weighed and stamped accordingly and a registered letter: make sure it goes express. Then take this prescription to the chemist's. You can call for the medicine when they've made it up on your way back. Then drop in at Mrs Campion's and see if she's feeling better today and if she thinks she'll be able to come to tomorrow's committee meeting. But don't stay there chatting. And then there are two books to be renewed at the library. Now, can you remember all that?

2 Now I'm going to give back last week's compositions. In general I'd say they show considerable improvement though there are still too many careless mistakes. Are you quite sure you always read through slowly and carefully all you've written? With no television or radio on to distract you? I have some doubts about that. And some of you still aren't giving enough thought to planning your compositions. However at least you've stopped thinking in your own language and translating into English: I didn't notice a single mistake that that might have caused. In fact on the whole I was quite pleased with them.

Structured communication

Talking about a street plan

Here is a plan of the old town of Almchester, which attracts a fair number of tourists as many of the buildings and sites, in particular the Cathedral and the Castle Ruin, are several centuries old.

(a) Locate various places and explain to the rest of the class exactly where on the plan to look for them. Places could include:
St Margaret's Cathedral   The General Post Office
The Bus Station   The Railway Station
Truck Road   The various car parks
The Boat Hire Station

(b) Ask in the Information Office your way to the following points and suggest the answer you would get in each case.

the Cathedral   the Castle Ruin   the Railway Station
the General Hospital   the car factory   the golf course

(c) Which do you think might be one-way streets? Why?

(d) Where might the four sets of traffic lights in the town be?

(e) Which street would you choose to live in? Why?

(f) As a tourist interested in history and spending one day in the town, how would you spend your time? Use your imagination to give short descriptions of the places you see.

(g) In what ways can the townspeople spend their free time?

(h) Explain why you would or would not like to live in Almchester.

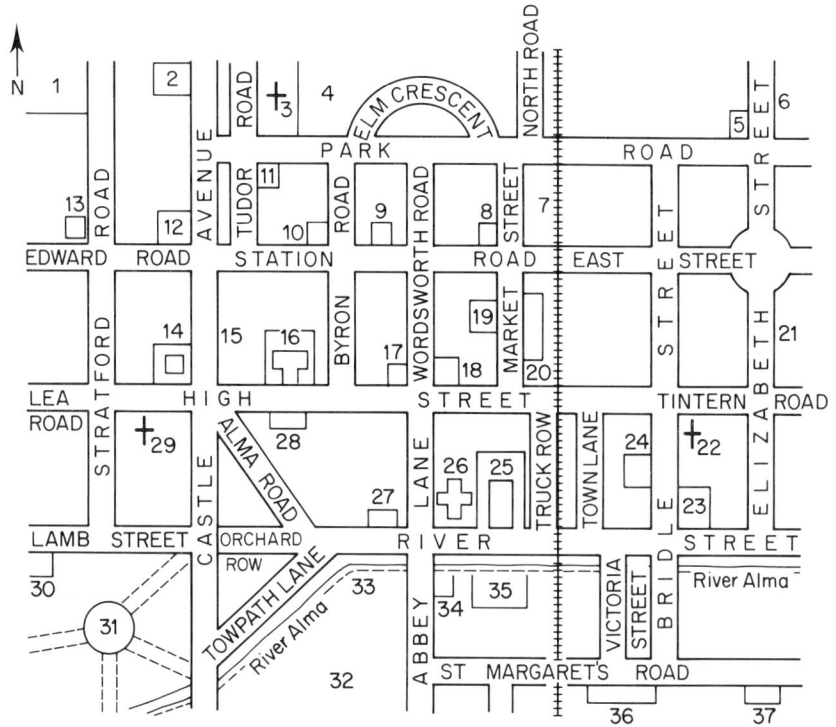

KEY

7	Railway Station
14	Bus Station
12 20 25 30	Car Parks
17	Tourist Information Office
18	General Post Office
16	Town Hall
36	General Hospital
10	Public Library
28	Playhouse Theatre
9	Odeon Cinema
19	Market
6	Car Factory
23	Sweet Factory

HOTELS
| 8 | Station Hotel |
| 27 | Abbey Hotel |

PLACES OF INTEREST
26	St Margaret's Cathedral
31	Castle ruin
34	Museum

SPORTS AND RECREATION
2	Indoor swimming pool
4	Sports field and public tennis courts
35	Open air swimming pool
1	Golf course
24	Children's playground
33	Boat hire station
21 32	Public parks

CHURCHES
26	St Margaret's Cathedral
29	All Saints' Church
3	Holy Cross Church (Roman Catholic)
22	Methodist Chapel

SCHOOLS AND COLLEGES
5 11 37	Primary Schools
13	High School
15	Technical College

Speech situations

1 Imagine you are Aunt Helen in the reading passage. The parents of a young man who has lost his job on account of laziness and drunkenness have asked you to give him some serious advice. What do you say?

2 Aunt Beatrice's neighbour is thoroughly spoiling her two young children and they are almost completely out of hand (uncontrollable). Aunt Beatrice gives blunt, frank but useful advice to this neighbour. What does she say?

Expressing opinions

1 Which of the four sisters in the reading passage do you prefer and why?

2 What is your opinion of efficient independent women who are more interested in a useful career than in running a home?

3 What are some of the reasons why a lot of people enjoy gossip?

4 What is your opinion of detective stories and thrillers.

Topics for a prepared talk

Make a few notes on one or more of the following topics which you should talk about for about two minutes.

1 A short introduction to the work of a well-known author of your country.

2 Some of my relatives.

3 The pleasures and responsibilities of keeping pets.

Horoscopes

1 Yesterday morning you read in the morning paper your horoscope, which was one of the following four. For once the prediction turned out to be completely true. Describe exactly what happened during the day. Then discuss with the other students some of the topics below the horoscopes.

A	B
You will have a day of suprises, not all of them pleasant ones. All will be well if you take things calmly. The evening too will be an unusual one.	A close relative will make things difficult for you in the morning and you will quarrel with a colleague in the afternoon. Both times you will be in the wrong.

C	D
You will go on an unexpected journey in difficult circumstances. Something you say will cause trouble.	During the day you will have a slight accident from which you will learn a useful lesson. You may also overspend.

2 Find someone in the class who was born under the same sign of the Zodiac as yourself and ask the class if there is any similarity between you.

3 What are some other ways in which people try to discover the future?

General guidance and practice

1 Gerund and infinitive constructions

This is an attempt to put some kind of order into an extremely complicated problem. The list is very far from complete but most of the verbs needed by the Intermediate student are included. The classification is not ideal but may serve as an aid in memorising.

A dash indicates that the form in question is never used, a bracket that it is uncommon and an asterisk that a note follows the tables.

Like, dislike, etc.

like	reading	to read
love	reading	to read
want	—	to read
wish	—	to read
long	—	to travel
enjoy	travelling	—
prefer*	staying	to stay
dislike	travelling	(to travel)
hate	travelling	to travel
loathe	travelling	—

Start, continue, finish, etc.

begin	learning	to learn
start	learning	to learn
continue	learning	to learn
keep	learning	—
remain	standing	—
spend time	learning	—
finish	working	—
stop*	speaking	to speak
cease	trying	to try
delay	writing	—
postpone	writing	—

Positive and negative tendencies

agree	to starting	to start
consent	to starting	to start
decide	—	to start
determine	—	to start
resolve	—	to start
try	starting	to start
attempt	—	to start
struggle	—	to reach
hope	—	to win
mean	—	to go
intend	going	to go
consider	going	—
propose	going	to go
arrange	—	to go
plan	—	to go
prepare	—	to go
get ready	—	to go
ask	—	to go
invite	—	to go

suggest	going	—
beg	—	to go
encourage	—	to go
coax	—	to go
urge	—	to go
persuade	—	to go
inspire	—	to go
advise	—	to go
tempt	—	to go
recommend	going	to go
remind	—	to go
remember*	going	to go
forget*	—	to go
allow	—	to go
let	—	go
make	—	go
cause	—	to go
force	—	to go
compel	—	to go
order	—	to go
teach*	—	to walk
train	—	to walk
help	—	to walk
can't help	laughing	—
can't resist	buying	—
dare*	—	to go
need*	mending	to mend
risk	losing	—
manage	—	to pay
afford	—	to pay
deserve	—	to go
enable	—	to go
ought	—	to go
avoid	going	—
omit	going	to go
neglect	going	to go
grudge	going	—
refuse	—	to go
deny	going	—
fail	—	to go
miss	going	—
dread	going	—
escape	going	—
threaten	—	to go
regret	going	—

Miscellaneous verbs

claim	—	to know
conspire	—	to kill
practise	playing	—
happen	—	to remember
pretend	—	to like
seem	—	to grow
appear	—	to grow
excuse*	my forgetting	—

264

forgive*	my spoiling	—
mind	(my) waiting	—
prevent*	my working	—

Other verbs

Positions of the body: *stand* looking, *sit* thinking, *lie* dreaming, *kneel* praying.

The senses: *see, notice, watch, observe, hear, smell, feel.*
These are accompanied by the Present Participle when the action described is continuous, otherwise by the infinitive.

After prepositions

With a very few exceptions the gerund follows a preposition whether it forms part of a phrasal verb or is used independently. Here are some examples of phrasal verbs and verbs followed by a preposition, all of which would require the gerundial form of any verb coming after.

> confess to, object to, look forward to, submit to.
> apologise for, blame for, compensate for, punish for, use for, pay for, reproach for, charge for.
> approve of, boast of, despair of, accuse of, talk of, think of.
> complain about, grumble about, talk about, think about.
> congratulate on, depend on, rely on, insist on, count on, go on, keep on.
> profit from, hinder from, prevent from, save from, protect from.
> succeed in, persevere in, persist in, specialise in.
> warn against; leave off; feel like.

Here are a few other forms:

> used to, accustomed to, afraid of (*also* afraid to do), ashamed of (*also* ashamed to do), aware of, capable of, conscious of, a method of, the necessity of, the problem of, worth doing, proof of, take pride in, interested in, absorbed in, busy doing, How about going?

Many adjectives are followed by an infinitive:
> difficult to understand, eager to hear, necessary to know, etc.

And certain nouns:
> the courage to risk, the liberty to go, etc.

Notes on the above table

Prefer	She prefers to stay at home today.
	She prefers reading to speaking.
Stop	He stopped walking.
	He stopped to pick up a letter.
Dare	I dare to come. I dare not come. Dare you come?
	I don't dare to come. Do you dare to come?
	I dare you to jump.
Need	He needs to work. He need not work. Need he work?
	He doesn't need to work. Does he need to work?
	This shoe needs mending.
Excuse	Please excuse my coming late.
Forgive	Please forgive my coming late.

| *Prevent* | He prevented my studying. He prevented me from studying. |

Forget,	Did you forget to telephone him?
Remember	No, I clearly remember doing it.
	(The same rule applies to both verbs.)

Teach, Show, Explain, Demonstrate, Learn, Know, Understand
    He taught the men to stand to attention when he entered.
    He taught the men how to construct bridges.

Apart from *teach* and *learn, how to* must follow all the other verbs above, not the simple infinitive alone.

The gerund as subject or object of a sentence

Riding is an enjoyable form of exercise.
Riding a camel is probably not so pleasant.
He teaches *riding*.

(The gerund follows *teach* only when a definite subject is taught. One teaches a person *to speak* correctly or *how to speak* correctly, as explained above.)

The perfect infinitive

You ought *to have finished.*
He is said *to have resigned.*
He seems *to have fainted.*
You must *have heard* what I said.
You could *have written.*
They are supposed *to have been studying.*

The infinitive expressing purpose

In most cases it is enough to use the infinitive alone, without *so as/in order*:

He stopped *to open* his umbrella.
She paused *to drink* some water.
He ran *to catch* a bus.
He went out *to get* a newspaper. (Cf. He went out *and got* a newspaper.)

The use of *and* with a following verb is common with such verbs as *go, come, run, hurry up, sit down* and *lie down*:
Come *and* get your dinner.
Hurry up *and* finish.
Notice however such expressions as *to go shopping, to go riding*.

Here is an example of the infinitive following an adjective or an adverb modified by *too*:
It is now *too late to telephone* him.

Here is a slightly different use of the infinitive of purpose:
He was *chosen to/appointed to/bribed to/change* the existing regulations.

so as to, and *in order to* are used where the purpose is emphasised, and essential with a negative form of the infinitive:
Go to bed early *so as to be quite fresh* in the morning.
He put his season ticket in his pocket *in order not to lose it.*

Practice

Replace the verbs in brackets below by their correct form, infinitive or gerund. In some cases, the correct preposition or adverb will also have to be supplied.

(a)   The doctor insisted (give) the patient oxygen immediately.

(b)   Fascinated, we watched the snake (crawl) silently across the grass.

(c)   How do you always manage (escape) (help) (do) the washing-up?

(d)   If you practise (dive) often, you will learn (do) it without (cause) such a splash.

(e)   Would you like (sit) (watch) television? I should prefer (play) tennis. I prefer (move) about to (sit) still.

(f)   Do you mean (risk) (catch) pneumonia by (go) out now that it has started (pour) with rain?

(g)   I cannot forgive her (refuse) (allow) me (use) the telephone. I feel like (write) to the owner of the house (complain).

(h)   The student hopes (specialise) (photograph) wild life. He is looking forward (spend) his holiday (get) (train) in (use) extremely complex cameras.

(i)   I blame you (break) that window, and I intend (make) you (pay) (repair) it. That may teach you (be) more careful not (damage) other people's property and (stop) (throw) stones.

(j)   Your daughter is very anxious (go) to University (study) languages and I should like (suggest) your (encourage) her (do) so. You will not regret (send) her if you can afford (do) it, as she will certainly profit (continue) her education.

(k)   Would you remind the students (remain) (stand) until the distinguished visitors have left the platform. I ought (remember) (tell) them this morning but I was busy (prepare) a speech and I forgot (do) so.

(l)   The sick child missed (play) with his friends and never failed (be) at the window (see) them (run) to school.

(m)   I left her (cook) the dinner while I went (shop) but I cannot rely on her (carry) out anything I ask her (do).

(n)   Do you remember (warn) me not (be) too quick-tempered and (advise) me (learn) (control) any impatience?

2 General revision of tenses

Use the correct form of the verbs in brackets below, inserting the adjacent adverbs, nouns or pronouns in the right position.

Immediately I heard the news about Aunt Margaret, I (go) to see her. She (work) in her garden when I (arrive). One of her cats (watch) her. I (go) up to her.

'(Know) you what I just (hear)?' I (say).

'(Be) it about Mrs. Mills's twins?' she (reply). 'I (wonder — Past Simple) whether you (hear). Dorothy already (telephone).'

'It (be) about you,' I (say), 'What (hide) you from us for so long? Why not (tell) you us?'

'I (know) not what you (talk) about,' (say) Aunt Margaret, (look) guilty.

'What (do) you for the past ten years?' I (ask). 'And what (be) the title of the next one when it (appear)?'

'So you (find) out at last,' (say) Aunt Margaret. 'Oh dear, what (think) Aunt Dorothy when she (hear)?'

I (be) suddenly speechless. For once Aunt Dorothy's piercing eye (fail) her. She not (suspect even) the sensation which (be) right under her nose.

3 Word order: inversion after negative adverbials

In order to emphasise the idea they convey, certain expressions, many of them adverbial and all having some negative force, may precede the verb they are associated with. When this happens, the subject and verb of the following main clause are inverted, that is to say, the verb precedes the subject as in the normal interrogative form.

The main types of expression involved are:

Single words

(These may also introduce phrases or clauses.)
Nowhere, Never, Neither, Nor (as conjunctions and also as pronouns or adjectives except when 'neither' is subject of the following verb. The first two often appear as *Nowhere else* and *Never before*.

Phrases

> *At no time, By no means, In no case, In no way*
> *Not even then, Not until the end* (etc.)
> *Only then, Only after several minutes*
>   (the suggestion is: not before . . .)

Clauses

> *Not until he had finished speaking . . .*
> *Only when he goes to church . . .*
>   etc.

The words *Scarcely, Hardly, Seldom, Rarely* and *Little* all have negative force:

> Never before *had disaster seemed* so close.
> Nowhere else along the coast *is there* such shallow water so far from land.
> Not without considerable difficulty and suffering *was the rebellion eventually crushed.*
> At no time *did the refugees receive* help from their more fortunate fellow-countrymen.
> Seldom *have I seen* such a crowd of people.

Neither, Nor

> They don't like the cold. Neither *do we.*
> Neither of the books is in print. (subject)
> In neither room *was there* a wash-basin.
> Some people can't swim nor *will they ever learn.*

If the opening expression is a subordinate clause, the verb in that clause is not changed; it is the verb in the following main clause that is affected:

> Only when I give special permission, *may you write* in pencil.
> Not until he had removed his shoes, *did he enter.*

After such expressions as these, it is quite incorrect to use the subject and verb in the normal order. Yet this inversion occasionally results in what seems a very unnatural form of speech or writing, as for example:

> Neither of these books *could we obtain.*

In such cases, it would be more usual to keep the normal sentence order:
>   *We could obtain* neither of these books.
or use either the passive or a verb and adjective:

Neither of these books *could be obtained*.
Neither of these books *was obtainable*.

Practice

Rewrite the following sentences so that the adverbial expression in italics comes at the beginning of the sentence. Make any other necessary changes.

(a) The critics have *rarely* been so enthusiastic about a Shakespearian production.
(b) The college tuition fees will *under no circumstances* be refunded.
(c) He will inherit the estate *only if his elder brother has no children*.
(d) The tide had *hardly* started to ebb when a damp mist crept over the estuary.
(e) I have *never in my life* felt so completely paralysed with terror.
(f) You will *not* be allowed to leave the table *until you have eaten your prunes and custard*.
(g) You will find such fine and delicate lace *nowhere else in the world*.
(h) I have *never* met such a devoted and unselfish couple as our old caretaker and his wife.
(i) He appreciated his friend's sacrifice *only when he realised what it had cost him*.
(j) The injured man did *not in any way* blame the driver of the van.
(k) He realised *little* that he had missed his last chance.
(l) She sits out of doors *only when it is exceptionally warm*.

4 Revision of relative and interrogative pronouns and adjectives

What part of speech and what part of the sentence is each of the words italicised below?
Example: The first is an interrogative pronoun and is subject of the verb.

(a) *Who* is there?
(b) Is there anyone *whom* we can trust?
(c) *Whose* coat is this?
(d) He asked me *which* one he could have.
(e) *Whom* have they elected?
(f) Where is the boy *who* looks after the sheep?
(g) *Whom* can one rely on?
(h) *What* can I do?
(i) The chops *that* are being fried are for dinner.
(j) *Which* is best?

What

What can be:
(a) An interrogative pronoun or adjective:
   What are you doing?

(b) An exclamatory adjective:
   What a nuisance!
   What stupid people!

(c) An adjective meaning *the amount that, that* or *those*:
   What money he has is kept in a bank.
   I will provide you with *what tools* you need.

(d) A relative pronoun meaning *the thing which, that which*:
   What I understand least is the grammar.
   What the workers demand is better wages.

Other pronouns and adjectives

Meanings of *whoever:*

(a) 'anyone who': *Whoever says that is a liar.*
(b) the emphatic form of the interrogative *who?: Whoever can that be knocking at this time of night?*

Meanings of *whatever:*

(a) 'anything which': *He will do whatever you ask*
(b) the emphatic form of the interrogative *what?: Whatever can we do now that we have missed the last train?*
(c) 'none at all', 'nothing at all': *Nothing whatever remained to be done.*

Whichever:

'the one that': *Choose whichever you like.*

Adverbs

Meanings of *however*:

(a) 'to whatever degree': *Telephone me, however late it is.*
(b) 'yet, all the same': *He protested violently. He obeyed, however.*

Meanings of *whenever*:

(a) 'at any time that': *He comes whenever he can.*
(b) an emphatic form of *when.*

Meanings of *wherever*:

(a) 'at any place that': *Sit wherever you like.*
(b) an emphatic form of *where.*

Relative 'That'

That may replace the relative pronouns *who, whom* or *which* when the pronoun introduces a defining clause. *That* is commonly used as a relative pronoun replacing a noun qualified by *only* or a superlative adjective, and also to follow the pronouns *all, everyone, everybody, anyone, anybody, anything, someone, somebody, no-one, nobody, nothing, none.* Here again it may be omitted when it is in the accusative case.

The first *that* arrives will win.
The only one *(that)* we saw.
The best thing *that* . . .
All *(that)* they can do . . .
Everybody *(that)* one meets . , .

Practice

Complete the sentences below with suitable relative pronouns, adjectives and adverbs.

(a) I have no money _____.
(b) _____ justice can you hope for from those rogues?
(c) _____ hair ribbon is this on the floor? Is it Betty's?
(d) He adores bananas, _____ ripe they are.
(e) _____ little Irene tumbles down, she laughs.
(f) I could not see _____ it was they were waving to.
(g) _____ that plant needs is sufficient soil.
(h) _____ obstructs the police will be arrested.
(i) All _____ I ask for is peace and quiet.

5 Like, as

Many mistakes are made as a result of confusing these two words.

Like is usually an adjective or adverb, as in these examples:
He is not in the least *like* his father.
It looks *like* leather.
She sings *like* a bird.
What will the weather be *like* tomorrow?

Alike is used for the adjective with no following noun or pronoun:
The twins are exactly *alike*.

Notice the idiomatic expressions:
It looks like rain. (It seems as if it is going to rain.)
Those hooligans *look like* causing trouble.
I *feel like* going for a walk.

As can be:
(a) an adverb:
    as good, *as* much

(b) a relative adverb or pronoun:
    As to your salary, that will be settled later.
    He is not so clever *as you*.
    Is he *as* old *as I* (am)? *(formal)*
    Is he *as* old *as me*? *(colloquial)*

(c) a conjunction, with various meanings:
    (i) 'at the moment that': *He stopped me as I was passing his gate.*
    (ii) 'because': *She cannot come as she is busy.*
    (iii) 'in the way that': *You should speak quietly and slowly as your friend does.*
    (iv) 'giving the impression that': *He behaves as if he owned the street.*
    (v) 'in the position of': *He is employed as a clerk.*

Compare: He is acting *as* legal adviser to the company.
    He is acting *like* a madman.
    It looks *like* thunder.
    It looks *as if* there will be a thunderstorm.
    I feel *like* nothing on earth. (rather ill)
    I feel *as if* I were going to faint.

Practice

Use *like, as, as if* or *as to* to complete the following sentences.

(a) The Town Council has chosen Thompson _____ the next Mayor.
(b) Use the margin _____ your guide.
(c) That tea is _____ sweet _____ syrup.
(d) With a face _____ a pudding she behaves _____ she were a beauty queen.
(e) The weather looks _____ improving at last. I feel _____ I were no longer a solid block of ice.
(f) He works _____ an office boy and spends money _____ a duke.
(g) The tourist is surrounded by pigeons _____ he walks across Trafalgar Square.
(h) The mongrel dog looked _____ a bulldog from the front and a greyhound from the rear. People regarded it _____ a curiosity.
(i) The general insisted on taking hostages _____ he did not trust the defeated leaders.

(j) If only you could type _____ my last secretary!

(k) Why not go to evening classes _____ she did?

(l) Don't dash into the road _____ that.

(m) The Prince Regent acted _____ king when his father was ill.

(n) I should like your advice _____ whether I should sell the property at the price offered.

6 The use of commas

Rules for the use of commas are far less rigid than those in many other languages, and writers vary in the extent to which they employ them. The underlying principle is that the comma indicates a pause of some kind, though many pauses are not indicated by commas.

Subordinate noun clauses are not separated off as in Germanic languages:

What you have told me amazes me.

I do not understand *what they are saying*.

The possession of wealth is *what many people desire*.

Here are a few cases where the comma is normally employed:

(a) To separate phrases in apposition:

Mr. Herbert Smith, *the Mayor of Chelmbury*, is highly respected in the town.

(b) Before opening inverted commas within a sentence and when closing them before the end of the sentence:

He whispered, *'Be careful to keep this hidden,'* before adding in his normal voice, *'and is your father quite better?'*

(c) To separate off non-defining clauses:

The village of Axton, *which dates from Saxon times*, will be flooded by the new reservoir.

(d) To separate the items in a list. A comma is not usual before the final connecting 'and':

During his life he has collected *stamps, butterflies, first editions, antiques, orchids, coins and pepper pots*.

(e) When a noun is qualified by two or more adjectives of more than one syllable, the adjectives themselves may be separated by a comma:

He has an *abrupt, unpleasant* manner of speaking.

(f) After an opening adverbial clause or, often, after an opening participial phrase. When the main clause comes first, the comma is much less usual.

As he speaks four languages fluently, he hopes to become an interpreter.

Meeting him unexpectedly, I forgot to ask him about his new job.

He has difficulty in expressing himself *as he stammers badly*.

(g) After certain introductory phrases which are not essential parts of the sentence:

On the other hand, . . .

In any case, . . .

7 General revision of punctuation

Insert whatever punctuation marks or capital letters are required in the following sentences.

(a) blackbirds sparrows and robins busily looking for crumbs were suddenly scared away by a prowling cat.

(b) professor gregorys new book which was published earlier this week has the title the unfortunate reign of richard II.

(c) why should i have to obey the orders of a boy half my age grumbled the elderly clerk.

(d) the bus to liverpool street station goes along oxford street you can catch it at oxford circus.

(e) next january he is taking an examination in italian and spanish he is at present studying at the european language college in south middle-sex.

(f) we have received messages from mars shouted the small boy isn't it exciting.

(g) if they work for forty two hours a week the workmens wages total £135.

(h) students examinations will be set for all intermediate classes before christmas.

(i) in less than two months time spring will be here we shall be enjoying all the flowers that make early march so enchanting.

(j) shakespeares the merchant of venice one of his comedies which is now being performed at the st jamess theatre contains the well known speech which begins with the words the quality of mercy is not strained.

(k) dr smith mr white b a mrs jones and miss e robinson the last of these has already published several books are collaborating in the preparation of a new dictionary.

(l) the train leaves at 9 12 a m we should be at the station by nine o'clock.

8 Revision of prepositions

Supply the correct prepositions in the following sentences.

(a) The tramp prefers a life _____ the open air _____ a settled existence.

(b) The nuns devoted their lives _____ helping poor families living _____ the slums.

(c) One of our undergraduate guides was specialising _____ science, the other _____ law.

(d) A successful spy needs to be gifted _____ an almost photographic memory.

(e) That resourceful young officer has been promoted and is now _____ command of a tank regiment.

(f) No wonder he is getting fat! He seems to restrict his activities _____ eating and sleeping.

(g) The actress has lost the exquisite diamond brooch which she was given _____ a wedding present.

(h) No one knows why the ex-king's memoirs were published _____ a pen name.

(i) Witches, ghosts and fairies are imaginary creatures that could never exist _____ real life.

(j) She often has reason to regret the fact that she is married _____ a test pilot.

(k) Wearing high-heeled court shoes, she seemed hardly equipped _____ a day's ramble.

(l) The speaker said that he was not concerned _____ people's morals but _____ their education.

12 Bitter Memories

It is just possible that our village Entertainments Society may dare to present a concert this coming winter. I am doubtful about it. We have not had one for five years, the last having been a catastrophe that some unfortunate victims still brood over to this day, and certainly none of these will
5 risk presenting another yet.

It had seemed to have every prospect of success. Most of us had helped to decorate the village Recreational Hall with artificial flowers; the platform had been converted into a stage with thick red velvet curtains and footlights. The performers were all immensely keen on taking part though
10 perhaps not all were brilliantly talented. The Chairman of the Society was going to announce the items and we were pleased to see that, besides our own villagers, the audience was made up of a fair number of people from villages round about.

The early part of the concert went off comparatively satisfactorily. The
15 village blacksmith sang sentimentally, if a little hoarsely, about his passion for the sea, which we knew he had never seen; young Billy Martin recited a poem about a cavalry charge at an appropriate breathless speed; the church choirmaster gave a violin solo; and Jimmy Fowler achieved some remarkable conjuring tricks from a book he had been given as a birthday
20 present.

It was Miss Finch's piano solo which was the first of the disasters. Unfortunately two of the local hooligans, Charlie Brown and Ted Forbes, had somehow been admitted. The former had already been in an approved school, while the latter was on probation. They stood near the exit during
25 the first few items, eyeing Jimmy's tricks contemptuously but silently, merely whistling satirically instead of applauding at the end. As Miss Finch, their former teacher, appeared, they clapped, solemnly and slowly. Nervously and hurriedly she propped her music on the stand and started to play in obvious distress, with more and more mistakes as she became
30 increasingly confused. Suddenly an outer door at the side of the stage blew open with a loud crash. A draught of icy air swept across the stage, lifting Miss Finch's music from the stand and depositing it on the keys with a final impossible chord. As Miss Finch stared, horrified, at the rebellious sheets, Charlie's voice rang out from the back:
35 'Looks as if even her music book couldn't stand it!'

'Last note wasn't so bad though,' came Ted's comment.

While the Secretary's wife went up to console Miss Finch, who had burst into tears (she was having considerable difficulty in comforting her), Frank Bridges, the village constable, was severely reprimanding the two
40 culprits.

'Even you should be ashamed of yourselves,' he growled sternly, 'You thoroughly deserve to be thrown out and if you misbehave yourselves once more, you will be.'

Ted was about to protest insolently, but Charlie knew better. His past
45 experiences with the law had taught him the futility of open defiance so he pretended to be sorry.

'Sorry, sir,' he apologised with false humility. 'We just couldn't help laughing.' His eyes were wide and innocent of evil.

Undeceived Constable Bridges returned to his place. Three ladies begged Miss Finch to start again but she refused and escaped from the hall still sniffing audibly.

Mrs. Dunn, the butcher's wife, a stout soprano, took her place. Soon she was singing to us about the tall, dark, handsome young man who was breaking her heart, though, as Mr. Dunn was neither tall, dark, handsome nor young, we began to wonder who this could be. It was in the middle of her song that the kitten appeared. Sooty black as a witch's cat, she must have taken advantage of the few moments when the door had been open. She emerged from the side of the stage, momentarily investigated the piano, scampered across and patted the cord attached to the curtain and started playing with the tassel. A few quiet giggles came from a section of the audience; Mrs. Dunn continued singing, ignorant of her rival attraction. Suddenly the kitten noticed this special friend of hers, whose scraps of lamb and liver she had often enjoyed. With a swift leap she scrambled up vigorously on Mrs. Dunn's shoulder and started rubbing the lady's cheek, purring noisily and wagging her tail. Mrs. Dunn's top tragic A became a startled shriek before dying away and Charlie's voice came from the back of the hall:

'Heard one of her pals and wanted to make it a duet.'

By the time Constable Bridges had risen from his chair, both the offenders had cleared out, and had taken refuge in their favourite pub. Somewhat flushed and indignant, Mrs. Dunn soon recovered; the kitten was expelled in disgrace, and the lady was persuaded to give an encore, which was loudly applauded.

During the interval, refreshments were served, including sandwiches, sausage rolls, tea and soft drinks. The atmosphere was a little strained but since we had got rid of the unwelcome intruders, everybody was gossiping in a specially friendly way. Surely nothing more could go wrong during the next hour.

For the first half hour everything continued fairly satisfactorily, though there were of course the worrying moments, in particular when little Susan Sykes tripped and fell down during the children's dancing. The final disaster, oddly enough, was apparently the triumph of the whole show.

Little Cecil Timms was the odd-job man of the village. He was short, timid, solemn; he had freckles, thick-lensed spectacles and a pale feeble moustache. Few people ever noticed him, and those that did tended to make fun of him and tease him. To the Secretary's amazement he had volunteered to give some impersonations, and impressed by one or two examples, the Secretary decided that, as no one objected to his taking part, he might be worth seeing.

Blushing, fidgeting nervously with his tie, blinking timidly, he faced us silently for a minute. Then he produced a cigarette which drooped from a corner of his mouth; his hands found his pockets; he sneered insolently. 'What, you're offering me a job? Think you'll ever catch me working? What do you take me for?' Cecil Timms had vanished and Ted Forbes lounged arrogantly before us. Before we had time to applaud, back and arms straightened; a frown creased his forehead; his whole body swelled with self-importance. 'Now then, it may be Saturday night, but we're not having that noise.' Constable Bridges was keeping order at closing time. Everyone had enjoyed these, but as one by one the well-known villagers were imitated, more and more cleverly and more and more maliciously and cruelly, we realised that Cecil Timms, who had suffered neglect and mockery for too long was having his revenge. We chuckled, then roared with laughter with tears in our eyes — at least all but a few of us, whose enjoyment seemed rather lukewarm. As we came away from the hall we all declared that next year Cecil Timms would be our star performer.

And yet ever since that night there has never been another concert, and Cecil Timms has only to join a group of his associates for an immediate hush to follow. They no longer laugh at him but they remember urgent jobs which call them away within a few minutes. He is treated with respect but is a rather lonely man.

There have been several newcomers to the Society since that date, who urge us to revive our annual concerts. They reproach us for our lack of interest. Now they are insisting on having one just after Christmas. But surprisingly few people have volunteered to perform. And Cecil Timms is not among those that will be asked.

Notes on the passage

Vocabulary

Title *bitter* Chocolate, coffee, memories and feelings can be *bitter;* milk or a facial expression may be *sour;* wine is *dry* or *sweet* though it can go sour when opened and unused.

Title *memory* (Unc): I have a very bad *memory.*
a memory (C) = a remembered experience.
a souvenir = an object bought to remind one of a happy experience such as a holiday.

1 *entertain* friends in one's home = provide hospitality for them.
A conjuror, pianist or comedian entertains people by providing *enjoyment.*
divert (turn away) people's attention from something.
a diversion = (a) some kind of relaxation (b) an alternative route when a road is being repaired.

4 *brood* A *broody* hen is one sitting on eggs, often looking sad and thoughtful. A person *broods over* (thinks deeply and sadly about) his sorrows.

6 *a prospect* = something that may happen: *His job offers good prospects.*
a prospectus = a booklet explaining the programme of a school or firm.

7 *artificial* flowers, silk, teeth, limbs. *synthetic* rubber. a *false* beard, identity. *forged* documents. *counterfeit* money. *imitation* jewellery, gold, leather. *fake* pictures (deliberately made to deceive).

9 *footlights* illuminate a stage.
A *spotlight* illuminates one performer.
limelight = general stage lighting. *be in the limelight* = be the centre of public attention.
A building is *floodlit.*
A *searchlight* shows an object such as an aeroplane in darkness.
Cars have *headlights.*

10 *the Chairman:* the *chairman* of a committee; the *principal* of a college; the *headteacher* of a school; the *proprietor* of a hotel; *the managing director* of a firm; the *landlord* of an inn.

12 *an audience* at a concert; *a congregation* in a church.

15 *A blacksmith* hammers on an *anvil* in a *forge.*

19 *A conjuror* performs various tricks, apparently by magic. *A juggler* throws up and catches balls. *An acrobat* balances and leaps. *A clown* amuses.

23 *An approved school* is a place to which young people in trouble with the law are sent for training and reform. If the offence is not a very serious one and is their first,

they may be *put on probation*. They must report for a certain period to a *probation officer*, who tries to help and advise them.

If goods are bought *on approval*, the customer has the opportunity of examining them thoroughly first before buying them.

25 *contemptuous* = feeling contempt. *contemptible* = deserving contempt: *Cruelty to a helpless animal is contemptible.*

28 *the stand* = the music stand on the piano.

29 *Distress* usually suggests unhappiness but *a ship in distress* needs help.

31 *draught* has several different meanings:
   (a) a current of air moving through a room: *catch cold from sitting in a draught.*
   (b) the amount of liquid drunk at one time: *He finished the beer at one draught.*
   (c) a circular counter used in playing *draughts*, a game played on black and white squares.
   (d) *draught beer* is beer drawn straight from the cask or barrel without having been bottled.

   A *draughtsman* is a person who draws detailed sections of such things as machine parts, vehicles, bridges, buildings.

32 *a key* (a) opens a locked door; a *keyhole*; a *key-ring*. (b) a *piano key;* a *typewriter key;* the *keyboard*. (c) The symphony is *in the key of* C major.

33 *a chord* = two or more notes played together. *cord* = thick firm string. *discord* = two or more notes played together without harmony; disagreements and quarrels.

35 Charlie is playing with the two meanings of *stand*: 'remain upright' (the music has fallen) and 'endure without complaining' (suggesting that Miss Finch's playing was so bad that even the copy of music could not bear it). This play on words is known as a *pun*.

37 *burst into tears*   Cf. *burst out laughing/crying.*

39 *reprimand*   A soldier is *reprimanded* for not doing his duty.
   A wife gently *reproaches* her husband for forgetting her birthday.
   Mother *scolds* the children for making too much noise.
   A clergyman *rebukes* a young man for drinking too much.

45 *futility*   He made a *futile* attempt to catch the lizard. His attempts were *unsuccessful/in vain*. (All three of similar meaning.)

   defy (N *defiance*): He *defied* the school rules by refusing to wear uniform.
   deny (N *denial*): The shopkeeper said Gavin had stolen the radio but he *denied* this.

49 He *deceived* me with his lies.
   He *disappointed* me by breaking his promise to take me to the theatre.

51 *audible* = can be heard. *visible* = can be seen.

57 *take advantage of* = make the most of an opportunity. *By taking advantage of my ignorance of local prices he was able to overcharge me.*

58 *momentarily* = for a moment. He must have the treatment *hourly, daily, weekly, monthly, yearly.*

59 *scamper* = run excitedly like a small child.
   scramble = climb as best one can, using hands and feet.

63 *leap* is similar to *spring* (not to be confused with *run*.)
   A *leap* (Adj) *year* has 366 days.
   He drank from a cool *spring* (often at the *source* of a river).
   Rome has many beautiful *fountains*.

64 *vigour* but vigorous. *humour* but humorous. *honour* but also honourable.

65 A *top A* is a high musical note.

66 He was *startled* by the shot. He *started* (jumped) with alarm when the shot was fired.

66 Their voices *died away* in the distance. That fashion has quite *died out* now.

68 *pals* = a colloquial word for 'friends'.

70 *clear out* = a slang expression meaning 'to go away' 'to leave'.

70 *take refuge* = find a place of safety, some kind of shelter. A *refugee* comes from another country to escape danger.
a bus shelter is a construction under which *to shelter* when waiting for a bus.

70 *favourite:* my *favourite* radio programme, not 'preferred'.

71 A person *flushes* when indignant or offended. He *blushes* when shy or embarrassed. He probably looks *flushed* when he has a high temperature.

71 *recover* from an illness (N *recovery*). He is now *convalescent* and should soon be quite better.

72 *expel* an unsatisfactory pupil from school. He is then in *disgrace. disgraceful* opp. *admirable*.

75 *soft drinks* = non-alcoholic drinks, e.g. *lemonade, orange squash, lime juice*.

75 *strain* = weaken by overwork. *eyestrain; a strained muscle; nervous strain. strained relations* between two countries or people.

81 *trip* = fall or almost fall while moving: *trip over the edge of the carpet.*
skip = jump over a turning rope: *a skipping rope.*
stumble = fall or nearly fall through putting one's foot down badly.

83 *An odd-job man* undertakes various small jobs like gardening and repairs without being specially trained for any.

84 *freckles* = brownish spots on the skin sometimes caused by the sun.
wrinkles = folds in the skin, usually of older people.
dimples = small hollows in the cheeks or chin, especially when a person smiles.
spots = small marks on the skin, possibly caused by an illness such as measles.

84 Telescopes and glasses have *lenses* (Sing *lens*).

87 *impersonations* = imitations of people.

90 People *fidget* by constantly moving their fingers or other parts of their bodies; they *wriggle* by twisting their whole body, rather like a snake.

90 *blink* by closing two eyes; *wink* by closing one.

92 *insolent; impertinent; impudent; cheeky* All these adjectives suggest rudeness and offensive behaviour to another person, possibly someone in authority. *insolent* (N *insolence*) is the strongest. Note: *What a cheek!*

94 *What do you take me for?* A colloquial expression for 'What kind of person do you think I am?'

95 *A lounge* is a sitting-room where one can *lounge* or sit in a relaxed position. Public houses are forced by law to close at a certain time, called *closing time*.

100 *malice* (N *malicious*) = spitefulness, the desire to hurt people.

104 *lukewarm* and *tepid* both suggest a lack of real warmth.

Pronunciation

Special difficulties. conjuring /kʌ́ndʒərɪŋ/; draught /drɑ:ft/; chord /kɔ:d/; constable /kʌ́nstəbl/; severely /səvíəli/; defy /dɪfáɪ/; deny /dɪnáɪ/; butcher /bútʃə/; sooty /súti/; shriek /ʃri:k/; encore /ɒ́ŋkɔ:/; sandwiches /sǽn(d)wɪdʒɪz/; sausage /sɒ́sɪdʒ/; welcome /wélkəm/; particular /pətíkjələ/; triumph /tráɪəmf/; fidgeting /fídʒɪtɪŋ/.

ə (as in *a*go): *s*uccess /səksés/; *a*udience /ɔ́:dɪəns/; comparatively /kəmpǽrətɪvli/; contemptuously /kəntémptjʊəsli/; *s*atirically /sətírɪkli/; *a*pplauding /əplɔ́:dɪŋ/; insolently /ínsələntli/;

innocent /ínəsənt/; vigorously /vígərəsli/; persuaded /pəswéɪdɪd/; atmosphere /ǽtməsfɪə/; spectacles /spéktəkəlz/; volunteered /vɒləntíəd/; impersonations /ɪmpɜ:sənéɪʃənz/; arrogantly /ǽrəgəntli/; maliciously /məlíʃəsli/.

ɪ (as in city): remarkable /rɪmá:kəbl/; whistling /wíslɪŋ/; deposit /dɪpɒ́sɪt/; audibly /ɔ́:dɪbli/; revenge /rɪvéndʒ/; recite /rɪsáɪt/.

ju and ju: (as in use): contemptuously /kəntémptjʊəsli/; futility /fju:tílɪti/; duet /dju:ét/.

Sound changes: rebel (N) /réb(ə)l/; (V) /rɪbél/; rebellious /rɪbéljəs/; able /éɪbl/; ability /əbílɪti/.

Others: recreation /rekrɪéɪʃn/; hoarsely /hɔ́:sli/; merely /míəli/; instead /ɪnstéd/; culprits /kʌ́lprɪts/; disgrace /dɪsgréɪs/; lounge /laʊndʒ/; icy /áɪsi/.

Grammatical and structural points

(a) *Nouns used as adjectives*
This is a common construction in English.
Examples from the passage: *Entertainments Society, village blacksmith, church choirmaster, piano solo.* Other examples: *a house door, a dog kennel, a car licence, a clock face, a street lamp, a school playground.*

(b) *the former . . . the latter*
Mr. and Mrs. Long both have jobs: *the former* is a builder while *the latter* is an architect. (Notice: the *former* comes before *the latter*.)
Another use: Miss Finch was their *former teacher*.

(c) *While* may have the meaning 'whereas': Anne likes to spend her free time out of doors *while* Graham prefers to stay at home reading.

(d) Do not confuse *no . . . more* and *no . . . longer*:
Cf. I really cannot eat *any more*. He has *no more* money left. (Amount)
and: I must not stay *any longer*. The old man can *no longer* work. (Time)

(e) Do not confuse *either . . . or* and *neither . . . nor*:
We can *either* play cards *or* watch television.
He will *neither* help us *nor* remain quietly out of our way.

(f) In line 15 *if* means *though*: *His writing is clear, if somewhat untidy.*

(g) More reflexives: ashamed of *yourselves*; misbehave *yourselves*.

(h) *Verbal constructions*
Infinitive: deserve to be; beg to start; volunteer to give.
Gerund: risk embarking; can't help laughing; continue singing; catch me working; insist on having; have difficulty in comforting; keen on taking part; worth seeing.
Clause: We realised that he was having his revenge.

Prepositions

(a) ashamed *of*; take advantage *of*; ignorant *of*; guilty/innocent *of*; lack *of*.
(b) decorate *with;* *with* a loud crash; have difficulty *with* a problem; (but: have difficulty *in* doing something); oblige *with* an encore; fidget *with*; roar *with* laughter; *with* tears in our eyes; treat *with* respect.
(c) *in* disgrace.

(d) burst *into* tears.
(e) doubtful *about*.
(f) brood *over*.
(g) keen *on* (taking); *on* probation; insist *on*.
(h) *at* a certain speed.
(i) escape *from*; emerge *from*.
(j) attached *to; to* his amazement.
(k) impressed *by*; one *by* one (one after the other).
(l) ability *for* observation (ability to observe); reproach *for* (forgetting).

Expressions for use in written work

(a) The audience *was made up of* people of all ages.
(b) There may be a fuel shortage *this coming winter*.
(c) *a fair number of*.
(d) He is *reasonably/comparatively* hard-working.
(e) He *achieved* success.
(f) *take advantage of* our low prices.
(g) *By the time* he had finished it was too late to go out.
(h) Refreshments *were served*.
(i) He dislikes everybody, his own family *in particular*.
(j) *Oddly enough*, we met last in Sydney.
(k) *To my amazement*, the stranger knew my name.
(l) *It might be worth* meeting him.
(m) *One by one* (one after the other).
(n) He was *having his revenge*.
(o) *Surprisingly few* people live in the town centre.

Common mistakes: elementary

This is a summary of some of the words and expressions that are often confused or used wrongly in English. It may be useful to study these carefully, especially those known to cause individual difficulty, a few days before doing the examination.

1 Common words confused because of their sound and spelling

were/where; their/there; no/know; new/knew; to/too; of/off; being/been; than/then; by/buy; quite/quiet; blue/blew; through/threw; red/read; full/careful(ly); till/until; leave/live; beat/bit; seat/sit; feel/fill; thing/think; who's/whose; it's/its; dinner/dining; writing/writer/written; four/fourteen/forty; left/felt; passed/past; weather/whether; cloths/clothes; lose/loose; at last/at least.

2 Common words sometimes spelt wrongly

with; which; goes; tries; another; cannot; except; goodbye; homework; all right.

3 Common verb forms sometimes used wrongly

run ran run; choose chose chosen; hide hid hidden; fall fell fallen; feel felt felt; send sent sent; lay laid; say said; pay paid; play played; stay stayed.

4 Other words or phrases confused	interesting/interested (and other -ing and -ed forms); become/get; high/tall/long; wide/large; thick/fat; while/because; when/if; at first/first; at last/last; look for/look after; bring/take; put on/wear; put off/take off; can/can speak; turn on/open; turn off/close; sea/lake.

5 Singular and plural forms and use of articles

Singular only: (i.e. singular verb, no *a*) information, furniture, luggage, money, hair, news, weather, shopping.

Plural only (i.e. plural verb): people (Sing. *person*), the police, trousers, scissors.
(But *a pair of* trousers/scissors — Sing.)

Compare: travel   a journey;   work   a job.

Article: He is *a* doctor, *a* teacher.   Doctor Morgan; Captain Harris. most houses; both brothers.   go to school, to church, to bed.

6 Adjectives

(a)   It is a very bad mistake to confuse *his* and *her. His* means 'of him'; *her* means 'of her': *his wife, her brother.*

(b)   Another very bad mistake is to add *-e* or *-s* to an adjective. The only adjectives with a plural form are *this/these, that/those.*

(c)   a lot of/a great deal of/plenty of/work (Singular). many/plenty of/a lot of/friends (Plural).

(d)   a little work/a few friends (some);   little work/few friends (not enough);   only a little/only a few.

(e)   he is very tired/he is too tired to work.

(f)   as hard as/not so (as) hard as.

(g)   work hard (a lot)/hardly work (very little).

7 Common mistakes with verbs

(a)   *Wrong forms:*
     *He go. (goes)   *He did not walked. (walk)   *I did not be. (I was not).

(b)   *Wrong question form:*
     *Go you? (Do you go?)   *Where he went? (Where did he go?)
     *When you come tomorrow? (When are you coming tomorrow?)

(c)   *Omission of the subject:*
     *Is a cold day. (It is a cold day.)
     *When he came to the house, (*) knocked at the door.
     (he knocked at the door)

(d)   *Two objects:*
     *He is looking for a paper which he has seen it recently.
     (which he has seen recently)

(e)   *Tenses:*
     (i)   Do not start in the Past and then change to the Present so as to make your writing more exciting.

     (ii)   Do not confuse Present Simple and Present Continuous:
          He *comes* from Italy.   The house *stands* in a park.

     (iii)   Do not confuse Past Simple and Present Perfect:
          You *made* a cup of tea an hour ago.   She *has just made* a cup of tea so it is still hot.

        (iv) Remember the Present in Adverbial time clauses:
            I shall go home as soon as/when/before it *gets* dark.

(f) *Use of verbs:*
    He *is* hungry, thirsty, hot, cold, right, wrong, sleepy.
    He *is* twenty (years old).
    He gave his bag to the porter (Not: to the train — give to a person but not to a thing.)

(g) *Reflexives:*
    She has washed her hands. He has broken his leg. He feels ill/tired/cold. He enjoyed himself at the party. He enjoyed the party.

(h) *Constructions:*
    before/after/by/for (Prepositions) *doing.*
    enjoy doing; stop working.
    make him go away; let him help.
    He *wants his son to be* a doctor.
    He *thinks he is* right/He *is thinking of buying* a car.
    know how to address an envelope.
    see him *fall/see* him *reading.*
    He used my pen to write his name with (Purpose).
    He is *too* ill *to come*/He is not old *enough to read*.

8 Prepositions

On   on the wall, on the blackboard, on the first floor, on Wednesday, on the first of July, on my birthday, be on holiday.

In   in a picture, in the sky, in the street, in January, in autumn, in two hours' time, interested in.

To   go to London, talk/speak to friends, say goodbye to a friend.

Cf.   *in* the morning/*at* night; arrive *in* London/arrive *at* a station.
come *out of*/wait *outside.*
I stayed *for* a week/I met him a week *ago.*
since last Saturday/*for* five days.

9 Word order

Be careful to avoid the following mistakes. The correct forms are given in brackets.

*Then went he home. (he went)
*When I have time, can I finish it. (I can)
*I have it sold. (sold it)
*If I him see. (see him)
*I enjoyed/liked very much that book. (I very much enjoyed that book/I enjoyed that book very much.)
*He read slowly the letter. (He read the letter slowly.)
*In the garden there are flowers. (There are flowers in the garden.)

10 Punctuation

Commas

I know where it is. What I need is a holiday. (no commas)

Apostrophe

the man's leg (a person)   the leg of the table (a thing).

Capital letters

speak Greek   an Italian   (nouns and adjectives of nationality);
Cambridge Street   Waterloo Station   the River Severn;
Uncle George   Aunt Elizabeth.

Common mistakes: intermediate

These need careful study and revision. In some cases you may need to refer back to the course book to make sure what form is correct. Most mistakes in using these words and expressions probably result from carelessness however, so written work should be checked carefully with these points in mind.

1 Words whose meanings are sometimes confused

opportunity/possibility;   meaning/opinion/intention;
library/bookshop;   novel/short story;   teacher/professor;
client/customer;   announcement/advertisement;
prospect/prospectus;   receipt/recipe/prescription;
allowance/permission/leave;   repetition/rehearsal;
invalid/disabled person;   factory/fabric;
warehouse/department store;   oven/stove;   cooking/kitchen.

understand/realise;   realise/recognise;   ignore/not know;
know/get to know;   look at/watch;   notice/remark;   say/tell;
rent/hire;   save/spare;   lend/borrow;   drive/ride;   go/walk;
go with/follow;   bring/take;   forget/leave;
wait for/assist/attend;   like/prefer;   criticise/blame;
claim/pretend;   deny/defy;   inspect/control;
overwork/do overtime;   must not/need not;   lose/loose;
pick/pick up;   grow/grow up;   fall/fall down;
take place/take one's place/take a seat;
take part/take someone's part;   agree to do/agree with/accept;
persuade/convince;   he died/he is dead;
enter for/pass (an exam);   go to a dance/go dancing;   act/play;
affect/effect.

worn/worn out;   hard-working/busy;   careless/carefree;
bored/annoyed;   advanced/superior;   punctual/exact;
older/elder;   deceived/disappointed;   late/too late;
middle-aged/medieval.

2 Verb forms sometimes confused

find, found, found/found, founded, founded;   buy, bought, bought/
bring, brought, brought;   fly, flew, flown/flow, flowed, flowed/
flee, fled, fled;   wind, wound, wound/wound, wounded, wounded;
rise, rose, risen/raise, raised, raised;   lie, lay, lain/lay, laid, laid;
get, got, got/forget, forgot, forgotten;   beat, beat, beaten/hurt, hurt,
hurt.

3 Uncountables, plurals and the use of articles

Uncountables

knowledge   advice   progress   employment   traffic   shopping
sightseeing   dancing   aircraft   machinery.

Plural

contents   cattle   surroundings.

Articles

No article is used with abstract nouns that are not defined.
Cf. quietness/the quietness of the night/a strange quietness.

The following also take no article: man (mankind)   Nature   space   (in
the universe)   youth (the period)   life (in general)   page two.

Note the use of articles in the following:
the Mediterranean (a sea)   the twentieth century   the River Trent   the
5th November   the North   the United States   the Alps.

Compare the following: have a cold, a headache, a pain, a cough;
have toothache, earache, indigestion, influenza;   play the piano, the
violin, football, cards.

4 Adjectives

last (next) week/the last (the next) week;
latest/last, later/latter, next/nearest.
Possessive adjective always before 'own': my/his/our own house.
the actual pen he used/present-day events;
so small/many,   such a small house/such small houses;
everybody (Pronoun) (not: *all people);
a stone wall   a silk dress   paint something green.

5 Adverbs

no more (quantity)/no longer (time);
in a friendly(leisurely) way;
this afternoon (not: *today afternoon or *today in the afternoon).
Adjectives: everyday   indoor   outdoor
Adverbs: everyday   indoors   out-of-doors.
yet/still/always; ago (*Direct Speech*)/before (*Reported Speech*).

6 Verbs

(a) *Constructions with the gerund:*
suggest, avoid, risk, mind, spend time, keep, finish, busy, worth,
used to, accustomed to, prevent from, succeed in, look forward to.

(b) *Constructions with the infinitive:*
It is impossible for him *to do it*. You had better *ask*. He would
rather *stay*.

(c) have something done: He has had his watch *repaired*.

(d) look like an invalid; look as if he is very ill.

(e) He gets up very early. Never *He *uses to* get up very early.

(f) You do not/did not have to stay.

(g) I hope *so*. I want *to*. I *know*.   (in answer to a question)

(h) An accident *happened*. A man *came*. Not **There* happened . . ., **There* came . . .

(i) *Second Condition:*
He would help you if you asked him.

(j) *Reported speech:*
He told me he had first met her a week before. (tense changes)
He asked me where I was living. (word order)

(k) *make* a mistake; *do* homework, an examination, a test, shopping, a course, exercises; *have* a picnic, a dream; *go* for a walk, a drive; *take* a photograph; *ask* a question; *give* a lecture; *pay* a visit.

(l) a lot to *do* (Not *to work).

7 Prepositions

(a) beside/besides; as far as/until; go towards/fight(lean) against.

(b) *at* the same time *at* that moment *at* university *at* (a speed of) ten kilometres an hour *at* my friend's (house) *at* the fishmonger's.

(c) *on* holiday *on* business *on* fire *on* a journey *on* the way to *on* the sea.

(d) *in* my opinion *in* this way *in* the north of *in* German *in* a field the highest mountain *in* the world.

(e) *at* Christmas *on* my birthday a present *for* Christmas *at* the age *of* sixty a man *of* sixty.

(f) pleased, satisfied, angry, disappointed *with*. stay *with*.
proud, sure, afraid *of*.
enter a room. leave a house.
sorry *for* a person. sorry *about* an action.
surprised *by*. a play *by* Shakespeare.
with grey hair/a long beard/blue eyes.
run *past* the house. pass the house.
succeed *in*. insist *on*. depend/rely *on*.
talk/speak *to* someone *about* something.
remind *of*. apologise *for*.
provide a person *with* something. provide something *for* a person.
marry someone. married/engaged *to* someone. divorce someone.
divorced *from* someone. he is divorced.

8 Conjunctions

(a) I shall not go *if* it rains.
I shall go *even if* it rains.
I shall take an umbrella *in case* it rains.

(b) *while* he was walking. Cf. preposition: *during* his walk.

(c) He took a map *so as to* find his way.
He took a map *so that he could find* his way.

9 Expressions

I don't know *what he looks like* (Not: *I don't know *how he looks*).
What was the film *like*? (Not: *How was the film?*)
a fortnight (not: *fifteen days).

Index